Wilt

Larger than Life

Robert Allen Cherry

TRIUMPH
B O O K S
CHICAGO

Library of Congress Cataloging-in-Publication Data

Cherry, Robert Allen, 1943–
    Wilt : larger than life / Robert Allen Cherry.
      p. cm.
    Includes index.
    ISBN 1-57243-672-7
      1. Chamberlain, Wilt, 1936–1999 2. Basketball players—United States—Biography. I. Title.

GV884.C5C44 2004
796.323'092—dc22
[B]

                                     2004051731

This book is available in quantity at special discounts for your group or organization. For further information, contact:

Triumph Books
601 South LaSalle Street
Suite 500
Chicago, Illinois 60605
(312) 939-3330
Fax (312) 663-3557

Printed in USA
ISBN 1-57243-672-7
Design by Patricia Frey

The quotations from Terry Pluto's *Tall Tales*, copyright 1992, on pages 12, 118, and 329, and those from Pluto's *Loose Balls*, copyright 1990, on page 298, are reprinted with the permission of Simon & Schuster Adult Publishing Group.

To My Parents

Joseph and Mary Cherry

CONTENTS

Foreword

The world of professional basketball is as big as the men who play the game, and Wilt Chamberlain was the biggest man in the game. I found him to be one of the most interesting, complex people whom I have ever been around.

There is no doubt that Wilt was one of the greatest players ever to play the game of basketball. Many might say he was the greatest player ever. Why? He was the only player the rules of the game were changed for. His dominance of his sport was overwhelming.

I can remember when he was acquired in the trade that brought him to the Lakers; everyone thought that surely there would finally be a world championship basketball team in Los Angeles. Chamberlain, Baylor, and West: how could they lose? We did lose, and for everyone involved, it made for very trying times.

But things changed in 1971 when Bill Sharman was hired as our coach. Something magical happened, and after a record-breaking season, the Lakers finally won the NBA championship trophy. Wilt was idolized in Los Angeles, and I'm sure that for the first time he felt that the city and Lakers fans were in awe of his incredible talent.

But the complex side of Wilt was always there. Despite his incredible records and accomplishments, for some strange reason he never felt people and the press truly appreciated him and his many contributions to the game. I remember him saying like it was yesterday: "No one roots for Goliath."

None of us on the Lakers team had ever played with someone of Wilt's caliber, and we didn't know what to expect when he arrived. I think that all of his teammates enjoyed him, and I quickly developed a great respect for him. He claimed to be an expert on everything, and there was no subject out of bounds to him.

Most of us, Wilt included, were on the downside of our careers, and adjusting all of our games helped turn us into champions. We were finally a team and not a bunch of talented individuals. Without Wilt I never would have won a world championship. I am forever grateful that I had the opportunity to experience that feeling as a player.

When I would see Wilt after our basketball careers were over, we'd talk about present-day players and how he thought that he would fare against them. I was always struck by how he still felt slighted and under-appreciated and noticed he was often bitter. His legacy is the true testament of his greatness: the records that he set and the rules that were changed to minimize his dominance will probably always remain.

From his bad knees to his bad hip, basketball had taken a toll on Wilt, and in his later years, the pain kept him from being as active as he would have liked. But he bore the pain with dignity and his unique personality never really changed.

The memories that I have of Wilt Chamberlain will never leave me. He was truly one of the most misunderstood men that I will ever know. He was a proud man, a sensitive man, and a very nice person. He made me laugh and he made me think, and he was always entertaining. People expected more from Wilt than any other player in the game, and criticism was very painful to him.

I am proud to have known Wilt and fortunate to have played alongside of one of the most talented athletes ever. He made me a better player and I will always be thankful for that. I am most proud to say that he was my friend, my colleague, and a confidant. We shared incredible highs and lows and always had a special connection.

—Jerry West

Preface

Why Wilt? Why write a book about Wilt Chamberlain?

Why not?

He was one of the most acclaimed and charismatic athletes of the 20th century, and it has been more than 25 years since he was the subject of a new biography. Besides, having sold my business and traveled the world, I was looking for someone to write about.

I asked a friend what he thought of my writing a biography of Albert Schweitzer. "What do you know about Albert Schweitzer?" came his immediate reply. I saw his point. I don't speak German. I know nothing about, and have little interest in, philosophy or theology, and while I did spend two years in Africa (the continent where Schweitzer settled), I'm tone deaf—whereas the German-born doctor was a philosopher, theologian, and authority on Bach. My friend said he always thought the old saw of writing about something you know made sense.

Well, I know basketball. Maybe not as well as some, but I know it in every bone of my body (although this book is about much more than just Wilt as a basketball player). Wilt said that had he grown up elsewhere he might have pursued other sports, but he grew up in Philadelphia, where "basketball was king." Me too. And the throne of that kingdom on the scholastic level, circa the fifties, was located at 59th Street and Lancaster Avenue—Overbrook High School. That's where Wilt and I played on the varsity, although I followed him by six years and had somewhat less of an impact on the school, league, city, and game.

When Wilt died, the story was front-page news across the country. No city mourned or honored Wilt more than Philadelphia, as no city cared or wrote more about him when he was alive. And over the years, no newspaper devoted more space to Wilt than the *Philadelphia Daily News*, whose sports section has been among the finest in the country for decades.

In addition to the many newspaper articles written and television reports aired following Wilt's death, Philadelphia's all-sports radio station devoted an entire day to Wilt. All day and night listeners shared Wilt stories, each one more interesting and amusing than the last.

I thought I knew Wilt: Great athlete. Almost superhuman strength. Lost too many times to Bill Russell and the Boston Celtics. Rich. Opinionated. Arrogant. Big house in Los Angeles. Twenty thousand women. But listening to the callers recount their tales of and enjoyable encounters with Wilt, I began to suspect there was a Wilt the well-versed sports fan, myself included, was unaware of. And then came the clincher late at night on the Friday following Wilt's Philadelphia funeral: I read a wonderful story in the *Daily News* about Wilt and Paul Arizin's granddaughter, Stephanie Arizin. As any fan from my generation knows, Paul Arizin was a teammate of Wilt's on the 1959–1960 Philadelphia Warriors and a man whom Wilt always admired. Reading the story about Wilt befriending Stephanie Arizin moved me to tears. After reading it I said to myself, "I'm going to write a book about Wilt."

Many of us hatch grand schemes at 1:00 in the morning that, in the light of day, don't appear so grand or doable. But when I got up that next day the thought of writing a book about Wilt still seemed like a good idea. Almost five years of research and writing later, it still does.

Prologue

He was blessed with devoted friends, adoring fans, and loving siblings. He was famous for almost 50 years, a millionaire many times over, and the lover of countless women. Yet Wilt Chamberlain died alone in his oversized bed.

He outshone, without trying, most other sports stars and celebrities. He dominated every venue with his magnetic personality and presence. He intimidated by his size and his persona.

Even among fellow professional athletes, his strength and athleticism are legendary. He moved 6'8", 225-pound men like cups of coffee.

"He made the improbable look routine," as an observer wrote.

Hall of Fame coach Alex Hannum considered him not only one of the greatest athletes of his time—but of all time.

His appetites were also the stuff of legend. He consumed enormous quantities of food and drink. Gargantuan, too, was his sex drive.

He had insomnia for most of his adult life, but functioned well on little sleep. He often drove cross-country without stopping or sleeping.

He always carried between $5,000 and $10,000 in cash. "Who is going to rob me?" he asked.

He was a sharp businessman and negotiator, yet easy to take advantage of on matters he didn't care about. Until he was told, he didn't realize his pension was worth a million dollars.

He achieved so much success and independence that he was able to rise each day and decide what he wanted to do—and in what city or country and with whom he wanted to do it.

He was charming. Funny. Loquacious. Loyal. Giving. He was also moody, petty, and obnoxious—a real pain in the ass at times, according to his closest friends. Fondly recalling his idiosyncrasies and overwhelming personality, friends like to imitate his unforgettable, deep voice—when he would begin a thought with, "My man . . ."

He was a contrarian who rarely admitted to being wrong. The best his friends got was, "You *may* be right"—and that was usually days or weeks afterward.

It was not easy being his friend for he rarely returned phone calls. And he demanded the relationship be on his terms.

Yet, in 1984, he flew from Los Angeles to Philadelphia and back—in the same day—just to "approve" the wife-to-be of his longtime friend and physician.

He surrounded himself with the best legal, financial, and medical people; and the best in clothes, cars, and furnishings. He often said no one understood him as well as his lawyer of almost 40 years, Sy Goldberg. "I didn't understand him," Goldberg said. "There were demons in him I never understood."

He had a diverse range of friends throughout the country. Most were not celebrities. One is a female firefighter; another writes screenplays; one runs a resort; another is a volleyball beach bum. One is the first black lieutenant governor in Colorado's history; another a retired liquor salesman. He compartmentalized his friends; he didn't want them comparing notes.

He relished having friends over for dinner—usually steak or turkey, always prepared by him. He was an excellent cook, as friends recall. Despite his wealth, there were no servants. He washed the dishes by hand. His sister Barbara was one of the few people he allowed near his kitchen.

He knew a smattering of words in a dozen languages. He first learned to appreciate different cultures when, as a young man, he traveled through Europe with the Harlem Globetrotters, his favorite team. From then on he never stopped traveling. Italy was his favorite country, although he never settled there. He moved to Los Angeles in 1968 and owned a condo in Hawaii during the seventies. In the mid-eighties he spent a lot of time in Vancouver, Canada, to which he spoke of moving. Late in his life he lived a few months each year in Florida, particularly attracted to the young women of the Miami Beach bar scene.

He loved to show off his extraordinary body and strength, and even as a young man appreciated the value of exercise and diet. He ran five miles almost every day the last 20 years of his life (until a deteriorating hip immobilized him).

He never forgot he was black, but he wasn't obsessed with race. Most of his closest friends and all of his advisers were white, but he had black friends, some going back to childhood, with whom he regularly talked.

He supported a Republican candidate for president, for which the black community tore into him.

He was proud when blacks succeeded and quietly made donations to help aspiring black athletes and causes. His battles were not over color.

One of his professional teammates thought he had the sensitivity and temperament of an artist. Another called him a pussycat. He acknowledged he did not have a killer instinct in sports.

He claimed to have made love to twenty thousand women, for which he was lambasted, ridiculed, and made the butt of jokes. A business wanted to pay him to advertise its product with the line: "It satisfies more women than Wilt Chamberlain." To which he responded, "Who said I satisfied them?"

He was a great supporter of women's athletics (and his involvement had nothing to do with sex). His favorite sister, a fast runner, was denied opportunities to compete in the fifties (like so many woman athletes), and he vowed to help other girls compete. And he did, in word and deed, by spending thousands of dollars to sponsor girls teams in Southern California.

He said that he never married because he liked the freedom to make love to many women, although he also said that it is better to make love to the same woman a thousand times than a thousand women one time. His nomadic lifestyle did not lend itself to being accountable to anyone, least of all a wife. Yet his parents had a successful marriage.

He played—always with gusto—polo, tennis, volleyball, and paddleball; he also water-skied and ran track. He regularly played checkers, dominoes, and backgammon—all of them exceedingly well. He played backgammon with Lucille Ball, one of Hollywood's better players. "I whipped her ass," he later told an interviewer.

He befriended the terminally ill 16-year-old granddaughter of one of his professional teammates and called her almost every Friday night the last 15 months of her life. They'd talk for 45 minutes to an hour.

He built his dream house of redwood and canyon stone on three acres atop California's Santa Monica Mountains, overlooking the San Fernando Valley and the Pacific Ocean. It took five railroad cars' worth of redwood to build the triangular-shaped home. "I wanted the feeling of the house to be like the Baptist church I remember when I was growing up," he said. (Though not many Baptist churches have a pink circular room furnished with a waterbed.)

He enjoyed reading history and biographies. The rooms in his home and the hallway bookcases contained hundreds of well-thumbed books on many subjects.

He loved music and was learning to play the saxophone in the last months of his life.

He was fascinated with the stars—in the sky, not the ersatz ones in Hollywood. His bedroom had a retractable roof through which he gazed into space using an expensive telescope. He usually slept with the roof open, the better to experience the balmy California nights and to gaze upon something even bigger than himself—the universe.

While he loved the company of women (and they were attracted to him in droves), he was also a man's man. But more than anything, he was a loner.

Fans continued to write him letters, even in the final years of his life.

He helped dozens of his friends financially and gave hundreds of thousands of dollars to charity, almost all of it anonymously. He left the bulk of his multimillion-dollar estate to charity.

He got lonesome late at night, especially in the last years of his life when declining health kept him at home. He'd call old friends, sometimes waking up the ones on the East Coast. "Do you know how many people live in Shanghai?" he'd ask. It was his way of starting a conversation. Most of his conversations lasted for an hour or more.

He was a world-class complainer and he loved to argue—about anything.

He cheated at games—but not in the sport that made him famous.

His death in October 1999 at age 63 shocked the sports world, particularly his contemporaries, to whom he was "Superman."

He loved children, although he never had any. More the pity, for friends say he would have been a wonderful father.

And, oh yes, he also played basketball.

Chapter 1

My son and Wilt were together when they were teens. He used to sit on my doorstep. My son was into basketball, and he and Wilt would practice at Haddington. I used to worry that my son thought he was going to get as tall as Wilt. And I thought, "I can't make him grow."

Wilt was about the ugliest child I've ever seen. He grew up to be not so bad looking, but as a preteen, he was ugly. And he had very little to say. He had a brother, who I saw occasionally but didn't have too much contact with. He was a handsome kid—that's why I noticed that Wilt was so ungodly ugly.

—Ruth Butler, mother of one of Wilt's childhood acquaintances

The Ugliest Child
I've Ever Seen

Wilton Norman Chamberlain said he weighed eight pounds, 10 ounces and was slightly over 22" long at birth, which is neither particularly heavy nor particularly large for a newborn. Yet he grew to be a giant, and that biological fact determined his life's course, for he became the most dominant basketball player in history and one of the 20th century's greatest athletes. His birth date was August 21, 1936, his birthplace, Philadelphia, Pennsylvania. With the exception of Benjamin Franklin, he is probably the most famous Philadelphian.

His hardworking, lower-middle-class parents had eleven children, of whom nine survived—three boys and six girls. Wilt was the fourth youngest and was closest to his younger sister Barbara. Wilt almost died from pneumonia as a child and, as a result, lost a year in school. Thus, he and Barbara were in the same grade, often the same class, from the fourth grade through high school.

Wilt's family was close, stable, and loving. "Our parents made us stay connected, especially when we were younger," Barbara recalled.

His parents were of slightly more than average height—his father 5'8½", his mother, 5'9". Besides Wilt, who was over 7', the only tall sibling was the oldest child, Wilbert, who was 6'5", although Wilt claimed that an ancestor was 7'2".

His father, William Chamberlain, was a janitor at Curtis Publishing, the company that published the *Saturday Evening Post*. Handy with tools, he also earned money by fixing things for his neighbors. Wilt's mother, Olivia, was a homemaker and a housekeeper in primarily Jewish households, from whom she, and then her sons and daughters, developed a taste for Jewish-American foods. Sy Goldberg, one of Wilt's closest friends and confidants for almost 40 years, fondly recalled an incident in the eighties when Wilt reached over a swinging kitchen door and snatched a handful of steaming-hot potato *latkes* (pancakes) being readied for their Hanukkah celebration. And at a Passover Seder at the Goldbergs' Los Angeles home, Wilt insisted that those present read every line from the *Haggadah*, which tells the story of the exodus of the Jews from Egypt. Many Jews tend to condense the reading, but Wilt insisted they perform the entire Passover ceremony, which can run to an hour. Hardly devout, and a practitioner of no religion, Wilt was just being Wilt.

———————

"Wilt's father was a nice, but passive guy," Wilt's high school coach, Cecil Mosenson, recalled. "When I was in the house, his mother was in charge of everything. She was formidable in a pleasant way." She was the only person Wilt feared and, according to close friend Zelda Spoelstra, while his mother was still alive, Wilt never would have made the infamous 1992 claim of bedding twenty thousand women.

His sister Barbara acknowledged:

> No doubt about it—our parents were the greatest influence on his life. My parents were not into sports, except for boxing. My dad was a boxing fanatic. My mother could care less about sports. Her thing was to make sure we were polite, kind, and gracious. That's all she cared about. By the time Wilt came along, my parents were older. They didn't put a lot of emphasis on the fact that he ended up being famous. They just wanted him to walk down the street and speak politely to everyone.

The Chamberlain home was the place for kids in the neighborhood to congregate. Marty Hughes, one of Wilt's childhood buddies and, in their teenage years, Barbara's boyfriend and Wilt's high school basketball teammate, remembered: "If we were going to a movie or a game, we met at his house. Mrs. Chamberlain was like another mother to the neighborhood kids. It was a very strong, very together family."

Everyone speaks well of Wilt's mother, praising her sense of humor, her natural elegance, and her warmth. She was also an excellent cook who taught her daughters, as was common in that era, how to cook. Wilt's favorite meal was his mother's chicken and dumplings, with her apple cobbler for dessert. She and Wilt's sisters knitted sweaters for the boys in the family. And once Wilt became too tall to wear store-bought clothes, the uncles on his father's side, most of whom were tailors, made his pants.

At Wilt's behest his parents moved to California in 1963 but, after his father's death in 1968, his mother, whose lifelong friends remained in the Philadelphia area, moved back East to Maple Shade, New Jersey. Wilt arranged through his accountant to pay his mother's rent every month. Thirty years later the accountant still remembers the address to which he sent the checks.

Barbara Lewis, who called her brother by his nickname "Dip" or "Dippy," recalled:

> When my mom was dying [in 1984], she came to California to say good-bye to her children. There were five of us there. She was sicker than we expected. She was fine the first few days but then got very sick. She was lying in my bed, and Dip came over and immediately got into bed with her. He began to feed her because she was too weak to feed herself. He knew she loved fish, so earlier he had gone and bought every kind of fish you could think of to see if he could get her to eat. He was just such a loving person. Mom knew that when he came, he would get into bed with her and hold her. When she was dying, she was waiting for him to come back from Europe. Everyone else had left the hospital. He came in, went straight to the hospital, and stayed until she died. She died in his arms.

While growing up, all the Chamberlain children held at least one job, often two, and besides earning spending money, pooled their resources to help their parents buy furniture or household goods. According to his parents, Wilt was like his brothers and sisters, except, as his mother said, "He always wanted to be the best in everything he did." Eight to ten inches taller than other kids his age by the fourth grade and gawked at from an early age, Wilt was never like anyone else.

Wilt cut lawns, cleaned gutters, scrubbed steps, and ran errands. At age five, he used to get up before sunrise to help a milkman on his route, until his mother told the milkman that Wilt, who because of his height appeared older, was too young to help. He worked in a corner mom-and-pop candy store, one of many that dotted Philadelphia's neighborhoods in the fifties, and he had a newspaper route. Blessed with an exceptional memory and a head for numbers, years later Wilt still remembered the number of customers he had on weekdays and weekends. As Eddie Gottlieb, for whom Wilt played professional basketball, said many times over the years, Wilt always gave his employers their money's worth.

Wilt and his chums also earned money shoveling snow off the walks and driveways of homes in Wynnefield, an area with four- and five-bedroom stone colonial homes about a two-mile walk from Wilt's more modest neighborhood. "He was the organizer," his good buddy Marty Hughes recalled:

> We'd wake up at 5:00 in the morning and his mother would make a big breakfast for us. We'd leave his house at 6:30, and he already had everything mapped out. We'd go through the neighborhood, he'd collect the money, then we'd go back to his house where his mother made us another big meal, and he'd divide the money. To me he was like a big brother, even though we were the same age. He was always the leader.

Wilt told Jack Kiser, a reporter for the *Philadelphia Daily News*, who wrote many insightful articles about him over the years: "It wasn't that I had to work. My family wasn't rich, but it wasn't poor either. I just wanted to have a nickel or dime in my pocket to spend, as I wished to be different from the other kids."

Ernest Butler lived a block from the Chamberlain family and occasionally hung out with Wilt and his buddies. "Wilt was always very serious," Butler remembered. "The guy would give you the shirt off his back. If he knew you didn't have money, and if we were going somewhere, and if he had some, he'd give it to you. The whole family was nice."

Some people thought the young Wilt was mentally "slow," according to one of his oldest and closest friends, Vince Miller, who maintained that Wilt was just "shy and timid." Plus he had a stutter. If one listened carefully to the adult Wilt speaking, traces of the stutter remained to the end—although, as anyone who was on the other end of a one- or two-hour phone conversation with him can attest, it certainly never stopped him from talking. Sonny Hill, a Philadelphian who is another lifelong friend, suggested that Wilt's ability to overcome his speech impediment is even more impressive than his great accomplishments in athletics.

Tom Fitzhugh, a childhood friend who lived a few blocks from Wilt and went through elementary, junior, and senior high school with him, contended that:

> Wilt was not smart in school. Later on in life, because of his exposure and experience, he learned to say the right things. I know—I went to school with him. He had trouble reading and was in a special reading class. In elementary school they called it "OB." It was funny to us; we used to call it "out of brains." And then in junior high school it was called "RR"—remedial reading.

Bob Billings, Wilt's teammate and college roommate, had a different opinion:

> If he had never played athletics, Wilt would have been successful. He was very bright. And he was highly motivated, I think because of his parents. We had other talented athletes at school, but there was just something different about him.

"My brother was fun, crazy, and focused," Wilt's sister Barbara recalled. "I didn't even know what the word [focused] meant when we were younger, but I know now that was what he was."

And he was a protective big brother: Wilt drove Barbara and her high school beau, Marty Hughes, to their high school prom, telling her that winter night, "I don't trust anyone else driving you." Wilt went to the after-prom parties but didn't attend the prom—though it was his, too. Fitzhugh thinks Wilt didn't attend the prom because he couldn't get a date—although he was quick to point out that he didn't have a prom date either until Barbara Chamberlain fixed him up. "Wilt never had a girl in high school," Fitzhugh said. "He was a freak, as far as girls were concerned. He was probably a virgin when he came out of high school."

Al Correll, a West Philadelphian who knew Wilt for 50 years, concurs:

> I don't remember him ever having a date in high school. He wasn't the girls' first choice around Philly when he was growing up. It was

like, "Who wants to go out with this tall, skinny kid." That's why I think he put in his book [so many years later] that he had been with twenty thousand women. Those who know him know he wasn't the women's choice when he was going to Overbrook.

———————

The Chamberlains lived at 401 North Salford Street, in West Philadelphia. The neighborhood had, by that time, become primarily black, partially as a result of the large migration of blacks who, after World War II, had fled the Jim Crow South in pursuit of work in the large factories of industrial Philadelphia. The Chamberlains' was a large corner brick house, with a little side yard, the biggest home on the street and one of the few in that neighborhood with a garage. The Chamberlains, like most Philadelphia families in the early fifties, did not own a car, so Wilt's father rented out the garage. Over the garage was a flat roof, with perpendicular iron bars set around the perimeter as a fence. On muggy August nights, Wilt slept on the roof—even as a boy he seemed to prefer sleeping with only the stars above him.

The other homes on North Salford Street are about 15 feet wide. A five-foot alley, leading to small backyards, runs between every two homes. About 22 feet separates one side of the narrow street from the other—both sides lined with brick homes, their small front porches decorated with iron or wood railings. Many of the homes had cloth awnings in the fifties; now they are aluminum. Salford runs perpendicular to Haverford Avenue, a busy commercial and residential street with an abundance of retail stores. That once-busy street has seen better days. But the street on which Wilt grew up, unlike some of the surrounding areas during the 21st century, is still tree-lined and the homes are well maintained.

———————

Surprisingly, the young Wilt disliked basketball, believing it was a game for sissies. What he loved to do was run: "I'd play kids' games with my brothers and sisters, games like hide-and-go-seek. Most of them were older than me, so I had to learn to run fast or I'd have never won a game."

Wilt attended the George Brooks Elementary School, six blocks from his home, and there, as a member of the track team, he had his first contact with organized sports. Wilt and his sister Barbara were, respectively, the fastest and second-fastest runners in their grade. "I was rather shy," Barbara recalled:

I didn't want to beat the boys. He used to say, "You have to beat them." He'd take my hand and, with both of us running, make me practice. He made me do a lot of things because he was fearless. We would run and run at Haddington [a nearby recreation center] until it came time for the track team.

As a fourth-grader, Wilt was selected to anchor the school's 300-yard shuttle relay team in the renowned Penn Relays, the track competition held annually at Franklin Field on the University of Pennsylvania's campus. He also ran in a track event held in Convention Hall in Philadelphia where, many years later as a professional basketball player, he and Bill Russell would hold their titanic battles. But at this point in the story, he was a skinny fourth-grader running the final 75-yard lap, leading his team to victory. "The applause made me tingle all over," he remembered, vowing then and there to become a track star.

He undoubtedly would have, but for the changes to his body. By age 10 he was already 6' tall. By junior high school he couldn't keep track of his height, so quickly was he growing. "One summer I went down to Virginia for a vacation with some relatives, and when I came back home my sister Barbara met me at the door and said, 'Who are you? I don't know you.' She was probably kidding," concluded Wilt, "but I did look different. I had grown four inches."

Once asked by a high school teammate how he managed to have such a strong upper body while having such skinny legs, Wilt replied, "I used to go down and pick cotton at my uncle's place."

It was during such summers in Virginia that mosquitoes mercilessly attacked him, leaving festering sores that permanently scarred his then-spindly legs. Self-conscious about the scars and his rail-thin legs, and wishing to protect himself from blows to his tender shins, Wilt wore knee pads over his shins and high socks when he realized that his size made him a natural for basketball. To keep the socks up, Wilt, who claimed he couldn't afford tape, used rubber bands. And to make sure he always had a ready supply, he slipped a wad of rubber bands around his wrist during a game. He wore rubber bands on his wrist off the court, as well, until he was about 45 years old—and they became his trademark. In a 1986 interview with *Sports Illustrated*, Frank Deford asked Wilt, "Where are the rubber bands?" Wilt's reply: "I kept wearing them because it reminded me of who I was, where I came from. Then suddenly, about two years ago, I felt that I just didn't need that reminder anymore. So I took off the rubber bands." Another Wilt trademark was the headband, which he popularized as one of the first players to wear one when he played for the Los Angeles Lakers in the latter part of his career.

Wilt was particularly friendly with four neighborhood boys, all of whom attended elementary, junior high, and senior high school with him. Their bond was a love of basketball, and they spent much of their childhood at the nearby Haddington Recreation Center, where they learned to play the sport—indoors in winter, outdoors in summer. All five of these childhood friends (Tommy Fitzhugh, Marty Hughes, Howard "Biddy" Johnson, Vince Miller, and Wilt) eventually played on the same high school team. And of these close childhood friends, all but Fitzhugh were starters on their championship high school team.

The boys were so close that in the summer of 1952, right before entering high school, all five accepted jobs working in the kitchen of Camp Pine Forest, in Pennsylvania's Pocono Mountains, about 95 miles from Philadelphia. Most of these camps were then owned by physical education teachers, coaches in the Philadelphia school system, or ex-Philadelphia professional basketball players. Working 12-hour days, seven days a week in a steamy, hot kitchen, Fitzhugh remembers what he earned that summer: $275—and he was happy to make it. Fitzhugh also vividly recalled the following incident between him and Wilt:

> We were washing dishes and it was very hot. There was no air-conditioning in the kitchen. We had automatic dishwashers, but first we had to scrape the garbage off and prewash the dishes. I'm leaning over the tub. I'm soaking wet from sweating. Wilt threw a cold glass of water on my back. I'm shocked. But to him it's a big joke. I let it pass. Then he's leaning over the tub. I took a pitcher of cold water and dumped it on him. He got upset and came out swinging. I thought I was going to get creamed. He grabbed me and pushed me into the tub. It was a funny fight because the floor was slippery, so we were sliding and couldn't get any leverage. Sparky [the cook] heard the commotion, came in, and broke it up. We made up, but there was always tension after the fight.

There was one other incident that happened not long into their time at camp. "We were sound asleep," Fitzhugh recalled. "Sparky and his assistant came into our quarters and said, 'Chamberlain, get your things. Let's go.' The next day we found out that Wilt and a buddy were fired." What had happened, according to Fitzhugh, was that a counselor on night patrol had spotted two large figures, tall enough that they didn't need a lift of any sort, peeking through the window of one of the girls' bunks. The two ran away, but it was determined to be the towering Wilt and his tall buddy.

––––––––––

The Haddington Recreation Center was conveniently located across the street from the five friends' elementary school and only a 10-minute walk from their homes. There they played, but also watched, some of Philadelphia's finest basketball players: future college stars such as Hal Lear (Temple), Jackie Moore (La Salle), and John Chancy (Bethune-Cookman). As they and their games matured, the boys (especially Wilt) were taken under the wings of these older players. Ultimately, Wilt became the most famous of all the great Philly players who trod on those hallowed Haddington courts. In 2001, that facility, now known as the Sheppard Recreation Center—but still a haven for children—named its gymnasium and a reading and computer room after its most famous neighborhood resident.

"Some of his childhood friends and I always talk about how mature my brother was for his age," Barbara recalled. "Maybe it was because he played on so many teams [with older players] once he decided, at age 13, on basketball. He played for the YMCA, in the Narberth Summer League, the Police Athletic League [PAL], at the Haddington Recreation Center, and for the Vine Memorial and Mt. Carmel Baptist Churches."

Wilt played on an intraschool basketball team at Shoemaker Junior High in 1951. In what might be the first mention of Wilt Chamberlain's name in a box score, the school paper, *The Cobbler*, lists the results of a game between two eighth-grade teams. Wilt's team won—he and his longtime friend Vince Miller led all scorers with seven points each. And in 1953 he led his YMCA team to the national title at High Point, North Carolina. "Even before attending Overbrook, when he was in junior high school, Dippy used to come over and watch us practice," said Mel Brodsky, who played for the school. "Coach Cozen arranged for him to come. Dippy was big enough but didn't know how to dunk the ball. I remember laughing like hell watching Harold Lear, who was 6', teaching him how to dunk the ball."

Wilt said many times that his competitive instinct came from his father, whom he described as an excellent checkers and pinochle player. Wilt also wrote that his father taught him sleight of hand in cards. Wilt loved most games and hated to lose in any of them—whether it was cards, dominoes, checkers, backgammon, tennis, volleyball, even putting, which was the extent of his pursuit of golf, one of the few sports he neither liked nor excelled in. Bob Billings roomed with Wilt for away games in college, and they became—and stayed—good friends. Billings remembers playing hearts with Wilt on college road trips and, although they didn't play for money, Wilt "would either win or throw the cards away. He just had to win. He hated to get beat at anything."

Thirty-five years later, Billings and Wilt were putting for fun at the private golf club that Billings' company had built. Wilt wouldn't let them leave the putting practice area until he had finally won a putting contest. "He was so competitive, but in a nice, friendly way—never an antagonistic way," Billings recalled. "And he loved to laugh about the competition. He'd tell everybody how he beat you: 'I waxed him in tennis. I waxed him in pool. I buried him.'"

Barbara Lewis, on her famous brother:

> He wanted to show that he could do what an average person could do—only better. That's why he participated in many other things besides basketball. He didn't want his size to be a factor. He even wanted to play jacks better than me. (But he couldn't.) He wanted to learn everything.

Wilt's competitiveness led him, once he was older and had money to spare, to gambling, which he liked to do on horses or in Las Vegas, where in the seventies and eighties he was a frequent visitor.

He also had the need, probably born of insecurity, to demonstrate how smart and knowledgeable he was.

Al Attles was one of his NBA teammates and closest basketball friends. In the book *Tall Tales*, Attles recalled the following conversation with Wilt:

> We'd be in a plane, and the pilot would say, "We're flying over Omaha." Wilt would say to me, "How many people live in Omaha?"

I'd say, "How do I know? I'm not a census taker."

Wilt would say, "Take a guess."

I'd say, "I don't know . . . 325,000."

Wilt would say, "377,888."

I'd say, "Come off it, Wilt. You don't know."

Wilt would say, "I'll bet you."

To keep him happy, I'd say, "All right, two bucks says I'm right."

He'd say, "No, the bet is $2,000."

I'd say, "Wilt, I can't bet you $2,000 on how many people live in Omaha."

He'd say, "Then you don't know."

I'd say, "No, I don't want to bet."

He'd say, "Well, if you won't bet, then I must be right."

On and on it would go.

Even as a youngster, Wilt would make outlandish bets. He'd be playing handball, remembers his sister Barbara, and he'd say, "'I bet you $10,000 I can beat you.' We didn't know what $10,000 was when we were kids. But that's typical of him."

Unfortunately, Wilt's well-known gambling habit led to allegations that he bet on basketball games, including those he was playing in. After his death in 1999, files from a three-year FBI investigation during the late sixties were made public under the Freedom of Information Act. The files indicate that unnamed sources claimed that Wilt bet heavily on basketball and engaged in point shaving, but always bet that his team would win. Since sports betting was not a federal offense, the FBI never pursued that aspect of Wilt's alleged behavior. Their concern was whether Wilt cheated—that is, controlled the outcome of a game so those betting on it, possibly including himself, would profit.

Commenting in 2000 on the FBI files, which had recently been made public, an NBA spokesperson asserted that neither the investigation nor any wrongdoing on Wilt's part had ever been brought to their attention during Wilt's career. The spokesperson added that betting by any player, even a wager favoring his team to win, would result in suspension or expulsion under the rules that have been in place since "at least the early fifties."

As Stu Bykofsky reported in a *Philadelphia Daily News* article shortly after Wilt's FBI file was released, "Those who want to believe that Wilt bet on games are supported by the indisputable fact that Goliath loved to gamble." However, the FBI records and investigation failed to produce any evidence that Wilt ever threw a game or was involved in illegal sports gambling.

Friends and family rallied to Wilt's defense, including Barbara, who insisted that Wilt would not have bet on basketball because if he had gotten caught, it would have embarrassed his parents and his sport, and he would not have taken a chance on that happening. Besides, "he was just way too honest" to break the law, she contended. "If he wasn't faithful to what he was doing, he wouldn't do it. That's probably why he remained single all his life."

"What do you expect an informant to say?" railed the late Leonard Koppett, who covered the NBA for the *New York Post* and *The New York Times* during the years Wilt played:

> He was giving the FBI information they wanted! If you want to tell me that such-and-such a person, on such-and-such a date shaved points, OK. Show me the evidence. The fact that an informant said someone did anything is, without evidence, self-serving hearsay. There was never any talk among the basketball community in those days of Wilt gambling. Anyone can spread any kind of rumor they want, but no one took them seriously that I know of.

It is one thing to practice some deception at cards or tennis—which every one of Wilt's friends acknowledged he did—but quite another thing to do so in a professional basketball game. Wilt cherished the legend of Wilt Chamberlain—in his mind (and in that of many others) the greatest basketball player of all time—and cheating in basketball, were he discovered, would destroy that legend. Because there is no evidence that he ever did so, it was, and is, a calumny for the FBI or anyone else to say or speculate otherwise.

———————

While Wilt's desire to win was intense, when he lost, for the most part—at least in basketball—he lost graciously. Unfortunately, in a key college game and in numerous playoff series during his professional career, more often than not, his team lost. And for this he was branded a loser, the bane of his adult existence.

But as David Shaw, of the *Los Angeles Times*, wrote of Wilt:

After his team lost so often to Bill Russell's Boston Celtics, many people called him a loser. They were wrong. He set scoring records and rebounding records that still stand, and in the two seasons that he had the best coaches and teammates, his team won NBA championships—and set records in the process. It bothered Wilt more than he would ever admit to be branded a loser, and perhaps that's why he competed so ferociously in every arena and always wanted so desperately to win, insisted so fervently that he was right in any discussion, no matter how trivial.

Chapter 2

Wilt had three things to overcome: he was tall, he was black, and he had a speech impediment. I remember when we were about 15 and we were in New York to play the Harlem Y. We're walking down Broadway and white people are walking by and saying, "By golly, Martha, look how tall that nigger is." Wilt couldn't hide inside himself. You can't hide when you're 6'11" and 15 years old. That left scars on him.

—Sonny Hill, lifelong friend

In Wilt's sophomore year, his coach, Sam Cozen, said to me, "Do you know any girl who can dance with this guy?"

I told him I'd ask around, so I went to this girl named Dolores Hamilton and said to her, "Mr. Cozen wants to know if you wouldn't mind staying after school and going to the girls gym and dancing with Dippy."

She said she would and then coach Cozen said to me, "I don't want anyone to know this is going on. You stand at the girls gym while they're in there dancing and if anyone hears music and wants to know what is going on, just tell them to move on."

So I stood at the door while they were in there dancing. And that helped him with his coordination.

—Al Pachman, high school classmate

He came into high school very humble. By his junior year he was cocky as hell. He knew he could get anything he wanted and go to any college he wanted.

—Mel Brodsky, high school teammate

Please Don't Call Me Stilt

Wilt often said that had he grown up in Oklahoma, he might have become a football player; or had he grown up in California, he might have become a track star—but he grew up in Philadelphia, where, in his words, "basketball was king."

In the fifties one could field a top professional basketball team comprised *only* of players who had attended Philadelphia high schools, which is what Eddie Gottlieb, owner of the Philadelphia Warriors, did in the 1959–1960 season. That squad featured Tom Gola, Ernie Beck, Paul Arizin, Guy Rodgers, and Wilt Chamberlain, all graduates of Philadelphia high schools (and all, save Wilt, graduates of Philadelphia colleges). Surprisingly, Arizin did not play basketball when he attended La Salle High School, but he became an excellent college player at Villanova and a fabulous professional. Gola played for La Salle High School and, later, La Salle College, where he had one of the greatest collegiate careers; Beck played at West Philadelphia Catholic High School; Rodgers was a standout at Northeast High; and Wilt attended Overbrook High School. Indeed, more people probably know that Wilt attended Overbrook than the total number who know what high schools Michael Jordan, Barry Bonds, Tim Duncan, Mickey Mantle, and Tiger Woods attended.

The number of top-flight NBA and college coaches nurtured by Philadelphia's basketball air is also impressive: Eddie Gottlieb, Harry Litwack, Chuck Daly, Jack Ramsay, John Chaney, Herb Magee, Jimmy Lynam, Paul Westhead, Jack McCloskey, Freddy Carter, Don Casey, and Jim O'Brien.

From the forties to the sixties, no Philadelphia high school produced a larger number of accomplished basketball players than Overbrook, nor won more Public League titles—nine in 13 years. While Wilt is the most famous basketball player from Overbrook, he was neither the first nor the last good one. By the seventies,

12 Overbrook graduates played in the NBA. Only one high school, DeWitt Clinton of New York, has sent more of its graduates (13) to the NBA. A magazine article in 1965 said of Overbrook, "It is the only high school in the country that could enter an alumni team in the National Basketball Association and not finish last." An exhibit at the Naismith Memorial Basketball Hall of Fame, in Springfield, Massachusetts, honors a select group of high schools that hold a special place in the game's scholastic history—among them is Overbrook.

In Wilt's time, the mid-fifties, Overbrook's student population was 60 to 70 percent white, 30 to 40 percent black. Almost all of the white students were lower-, middle-, or upper-middle-class Jews from the Wynnefield, Overbrook Park, and Greenhill Farms sections of Philadelphia; the blacks were lower- to lower-middle-class (with a smattering of middle-class representatives) from the formerly Jewish but, by mid-fifties, almost entirely black, sections of West Philadelphia. The school had a proud academic and athletic tradition, with little, if any, racial tensions. Blacks and whites liked each other; small groups of whites even attended black parties. But so as not to paint too romantic a picture of racial bliss, blacks tended to hang out with blacks and whites with whites. Where young black men and young white men often came into contact outside of school was on the basketball court—in schoolyards, church and synagogue basements, recreation centers, and indoor and outdoor leagues.

Possibly because of the positive experience he had as a young man with whites—both in school, in athletics, and from the white shopkeepers he encountered in West Philadelphia—Wilt did not define his life in racial terms. That's not to say he wasn't aware of, and at times affected by, the racial climate of the country while growing up.

Maybe because it was hard to miss or to forget someone as tall as Wilt, or maybe he is just one of those indelible characters, but many Philadelphians, especially those in and around the geographical area in which he grew up, have vivid memories of Wilt. What follows are four of what could be four thousand such recollections.

George Willner, an Overbrook graduate and Philadelphia attorney, recalled an incident in 1954 when Wilt came to the William B. Mann schoolyard in Wynnefield, which was Willner's elementary school:

> Wilt's with one of the white guys who played for Overbrook, who also
> lived near Mann. Wilt goes into Yassen's, a mom-and-pop grocery store,

and buys a kosher pickle for a nickel. He comes into the schoolyard with a big smile on his face, sucking on the pickle. He didn't bite it; he sucked it. I'm 5'6" now, but at that time I was even shorter; and Wilt was 6'11". And it was me and Wilt against five other guys. He said to me, "Don't worry about it. Nobody's gonna score on us." And nobody did.

Larry Einhorn was nine or ten when, on another occasion, Wilt came to the Mann schoolyard:

In walked Wilt and Allan Weinberg, who played on the varsity with Wilt. What Wilt did, I'll never forget: to show his athletic prowess, he took a football and lifted his right leg and threw the football under his leg the length of the schoolyard.

Steve McGill, an Overbrook grad now in his early sixties, used to see Wilt at Beeber Junior High School, site of a nighttime basketball league:

I'm going to guess he was 17, though I'm not sure, but he was still at Overbrook. He had in his duffel bag a beautiful, carved wooden box, with little slots where you could fit things, and he had knives in there. When I asked him why, he said, "I carry them for my protection." And the interesting thing is, he would never admit to being Wilt. I would say, "You're Wilt, aren't you?" And he would say, "No, that's my brother."

Steve Kane, a graduate of the class of 1956, also remembered Wilt:

When we used to have lunch at Overbrook, Wilt had this thing about making money, because he wanted to eat three or four lunches. One of the ways he used to make money was to arm wrestle white kids. He'd challenge two or three of us at a time. We'd pile schoolbooks up to get our elbows high enough so we could match his hand. We'd all put up a buck. Nobody ever beat him and, believe me, he had a lot of takers. He'd clean up.

Wilt's sister Barbara recalled, "Overbrook's students were extremely close. Your friends were like family." Jimmy Sadler, a teammate of Wilt's, reminisced:

After the championship games, the Jewish students used to have fabulous parties in their big houses in Wynnefield. Black kids went, too. It was a great feeling, the closeness the students had with each other. Wilt loved Overbrook. When I visited him at his house in L.A. in the nineties, he said, "Let's talk about old times. I don't want to talk about what I'm doing now."

In his later years Wilt wore an Overbrook letter jacket for interviews, for appearances on television sports shows, and to basketball games. The black-and-orange jacket with the orange *O* was specially made for him prior to his induction into the school's Hall of Fame in 1991. On more than one occasion, Wilt said that his years at Overbrook were the happiest of his life.

It was while covering Wilt at Overbrook that Jack Ryan, a sportswriter for *The Evening Bulletin*, tagged the 6'11", 200-pound sophomore with the nickname "Wilt the Stilt," a name Wilt hated until the day he died. "It makes me think of a big crane standing in a pond of water or some freak in a sideshow," he declared.

Hal Freeman, a reporter for *The Philadelphia Inquirer*, recalled the first time he was alone with Wilt. "I walked him about halfway home from school," Freeman recalled, "and he said, 'Please don't call me Stilt.' I said that was fine with me, but a few days later, there it was again, in one of Ryan's stories. Pretty soon everybody was using it. I gave in, too."

So did all the reporters for Philadelphia's three daily newspapers, particularly headline writers, for whom the name was a boon: "The Stilt Gets 44 as Overbrook Wins"; or "Stilt's 48 Outscores Bok."

Larry Mann remembered a scrimmage arranged between his school, Cheltenham High, and Overbrook. "During the warm-ups, I talked to Wilt. My coach had warned me, 'Don't call him anything except Wilt or Dipper. Don't call him 'Stilt.'" But for the most part, Wilt was stuck with "Wilt the Stilt"; even today it is listed as one of his nicknames in *The Official NBA Encyclopedia* (the other is "the Big Dipper").

Wilt's siblings, childhood Philadelphia friends, and Overbrook classmates tended—and still tend—to call him by the nicknames he preferred: "Dippy," "Dip," or "Dipper." Mel Brodsky, one of those teammates, maintained, "I never called him 'Wilt' in my life. He was 'Dippy.'"

Wilt explained in newspaper interviews the origin of his nickname:

> When I was about 10, I was kind of big for my age, and I was always
> bumping my head in doorways and places where the ceilings were low.
> I was playing in an empty house one day with some boyfriends, and I ran
> smack into a low-hanging pipe and gave myself a beautiful black eye. My
> pals got a good laugh and told me next time I ought to dip under when
> I came to something like that. They started calling me "the Dipper"
> after that, and it became "Dipper" and then just "Dip" or "Dippy."

In fact, "Dipper" was painted in large, red letters on the rear bumper of the
Oldsmobile he drove while in high school. And "Dipper" was stitched on the
cuff of the custom shirts he wore many years later.

Those nicknames evolved into "the Big Dipper," which evokes his intimidating presence, as well as some of his offensive moves on the basketball
court—specifically his signature "finger roll," where he funneled the ball
toward the basket. The "Big Dipper" is also the term used to refer to part of
our galaxy's most famous constellation (called *Ursa Major* in Latin). Wilt liked
the majesty of the nickname as opposed to the freakishness of Stilt. He liked it
so well that Ursa Major is what Wilt called, and posted on the door of, the
unique house he built in the early seventies on a mountaintop in Bel Air, high
above Los Angeles; and *Ursa Major* was also the logo on his stationery.

His postbasketball friends and acquaintances, many of whom he met in
California through volleyball or track, called him Wilt or Wiltie; or the name
he often used to refer to himself, Uncle Wiltie. Zelda Spoelstra, one of his
closest friends during the last years of his life, called him Norman. Bill
Russell—friend, foe, and for many years, enemy—called him Wilton Norman
Chamberlain; while Wilt, when they were on speaking terms (and they were not
for two decades), called him William Felton Russell.

—————

Speaking at the ceremony in 2000 at which the Golden State Warriors retired
Wilt's number, Barbara Lewis shared this anecdote:

> As everybody knows, Wilt was known for breaking rules. And one of
> the first rules he broke was that No. 13. He insisted on wearing No.

13, because they didn't use that number in the forties and fifties, when he came up playing basketball.

Well, knowing Wilt, he had to challenge that. He insisted on wearing 13 when he played church leagues and for the YMCA. But when he got to Overbrook, they didn't have a 13, so he came to my parents and said, "I want to be No. 13. Who came up with this idea that you can't be No. 13? Who the heck said No. 13 was a bad-luck number? I'm going to make it a good-luck number. I want to wear it."

In those days, children did what their parents said, and Overbrook didn't have a No. 13, so our parents said, "No, you have to pick another number."

And since he was humble in those days, he picked No. 5.

But 13, of course, is the number Wilt wore in college and in the pros.

———————

Wilt's first scholastic basketball outing was a preseason game in December 1952. Tony Catanio, now a New Jersey resident, played in it and remembers jumping center against him:

I had been playing for three years. [The Catholic high schools began in ninth grade while the Public League schools began in tenth grade.] I got in the pivot. I used to take a jump shot. Of course, against him the first thing I did was "eat it." I was a little peeved. I tried again and I "ate it" again. So I said to myself, "I'll fix him." I used to play around with an underhanded scoop shot. So I pulled it off. I threw the underhand scoop and it went in. He patted me on the rear end, and said, "Nice shot, kid." And I'm thinking, "What is this guy saying? I've been playing high school for three years. He has never been on a high school court before."

Wilt scored 24 points in the Overbrook victory.

Doug Leaman, an Overbrook teammate, remembers the first time he saw the young giant:

I felt sorry for him. His legs were so long and skinny, and he had a good, muscular upper body. And I thought, "He's gonna break one of those twigs some day." . . . We knew he was good, but we didn't know he'd be the best basketball player in the world. We knew he'd get scholarships at every college in the country. But I always thought he would break his legs or something, and he'd be incapacitated. I really did.

During that first year, the 1953 season, Wilt averaged 31 points per game, slightly more than his career average as a professional (30.1). Overbrook lost once during the 12-game regular season; that was to Benjamin Franklin High School. Claude Gross, selected to the All–Public League team the previous year, led Franklin with 32 points. (Wilt was to see more of Claude Gross, for he married Wilt's sister Selena.)

Overbrook played Lincoln High in the semifinals of the Public League championship, defeating them 72–56. "After the game I walked into the Overbrook locker room and congratulated the players," recalled Allan Kessler, a Lincoln player. "And standing naked in the corner was Wilt. I walked over to him. He said, 'What do you want?' And I said, 'I just wanted to see the size of your dick because you're 7', and it ain't so big.' He didn't say anything and I walked away. It was big enough, but I wouldn't give him that satisfaction." More than big enough, as those who saw Wilt naked in locker rooms attest. Not for nothing did his Harlem Globetrotter teammates call him "Whip," among other nicknames.

Overbrook won the Public League championship in Wilt's first season—the school's fourth league title in six years, defeating Northeast High School, 71–62. Wilt tallied 34 points, making 10 of 15 free throws, while Guy Rodgers led Northeast with 26. Like most of the Philly basketball players of that era, Rodgers attended a local college, in his case, Temple University, where he was an All-American.

Beginning in 1939 and running until 1980, the winners of the Philadelphia public and Catholic high school championships met for the city title. Having won the Public League championship in 1953, Overbrook faced West Philadelphia Catholic High School, the defending city champion. Bob Devine, who played college basketball at Notre Dame and was a member of the West Catholic team that year, remembers the event:

> We closed practice that week. We put Joe McGinn, a junior varsity player, on a table in front of the basket. When we would shoot, he

would knock all the shots. And there was also a Christian Brother [the men who teach at West Catholic] named Brother Anthony, who ran around with a window pole. Every time we'd shoot, he would knock down the ball. We had to shoot higher so "Wilt" could not block our shots. We just practiced all week doing that.

The night of the game, nobody knew what we were going to do. The element here was to surprise Wilt. We put four guys on Chamberlain: myself and Moose Gardler in front of him, and Jack Rowan and Charles Eltringham behind him. And Billy Lindsay ran the floor.

Wilt played well, scoring 29 of Overbrook's 42 points. His teammates played poorly. It also helped West Catholic's cause that Billy Lindsay had the game of his young life. He made 12 of 13 shots from the field (and 8 from the foul line), ending up with 32 points. To everyone's amazement, the West Catholic Burrs defeated the Overbrook Panthers for the city championship, 54–42. It was the first, but not the last, time that a Wilt Chamberlain–led team failed to win a championship game that people assumed was theirs to win because of Wilt's presence.

In 1997, Billy Lindsay—the West Catholic player who starred in that championship game 44 years earlier—was dying of cancer. Boyhood friends held a fund-raiser to defray some of his rapidly rising medical expenses. One of those neighborhood guys was Ernie Beck, graduate of West Catholic High, All-American at the University of Pennsylvania and, for a season, Wilt's teammate on the professional level. They had not been in touch for many years, nor were they particularly close during their basketball careers, but Ernie decided to write Wilt about the forthcoming fund-raiser. "Bill is dying from terminal cancer," Beck wrote Wilt, "and his time is short. His fondest memories are of the great game he had against Overbrook in that title game when he played against you and they won."

On the night of the fund-raiser, which occurred only two weeks before Lindsay succumbed to the disease, the following letter was read aloud to Billy and his friends:

> Hey Billy,
> Heard from an old friend things could be better; so I wanted you to know that you have, as I'm sure you have many, a friend out on the West Coast hoping all the best will come your way.

Our paths have not crossed very much, but it always seemed to me that it was not close to 45 years ago but only a couple of yesterdays that you *almost* single handed, cool as a cucumber, shot that jumper on us to give West Catholic that victory.

Did you know I almost went to West Catholic? We could have been a good pair, that's if you would have given me the ball. Keep the faith and my prayers go out to you and yours.

Love and Peace,

Wilt

P.S. Excuse my writing. I went to a *public* school.

———————

Playing for Overbrook or in a local summer league wasn't Wilt's only basketball outlet that year. He played at least one game (and probably others) under an assumed name—the most publicized case taking place in Cumberland, Maryland, against a team of former college players for which he reportedly received $10. Many other talented basketball players from that era, usually college-age, played games under fake names because, as Wilt suggested, "It was a way for us good young guys . . . who weren't really getting much competition . . . to develop our skills." Besides not wanting their coaches to know they were playing in games where they could possibly get hurt, the players wanted to avoid any potential issues concerning payment because accepting money as an amateur could be a violation of NCAA rules.

When a local reporter broke the story, Wilt denied it, but years later he confirmed the truth of it and said the money had been for expenses. Wilt explained that players used fake names "because we knew what the NCAA would say if they found out who we were. I've always been ashamed of having done that—not of having played, but ashamed of having given in to the hypocrisy of the NCAA, rather than fighting it."

After the basketball season, there was track—Wilt's first, and most enduring, love. He won the Public League high-jump championship in 1953. His high school track coach, Ben Ogden, said that Wilt's stride could have made him one of the best runners ever. Had there been the kind of money available to world-class track stars when Wilt was at his athletic peak in the sixties, as there is nowadays, and if professional athletes were permitted to participate in the Olympics, as they now can, Wilt would have competed in the decathlon, he said many times.

Irv Goodman wrote a story about Wilt for *Sport* magazine in 1955. Titled "The High School Kid Who Could Play Pro Ball Now," Goodman wrote: "Probably as amazing as anything about this amazing athlete is his stamina. While other big men are usually the first to sit down for a rest, he would be the last, if his coach would let him." Besides his incredible endurance, Wilt had almost superhuman strength and great speed.

But his teammates also remember a lighter side of Wilt. Allan Goldberg remembers a bus trip to Olney High School for a track meet during his last year at Overbrook, which was Wilt's first:

> Wilt sat at the back of the bus because his feet couldn't fit under the seats. I sat next to him because I was pretty big, too. There was a cop on Broad Street directing traffic, and as the bus passed him, Wilt put his hand out of the window and lifted the cap off the traffic cop's head. We drove another block or so, along Broad Street, and there was another cop in the middle of the street, directing traffic. Wilt took the cap he had taken off the first cop's head and placed it on the head of the second cop, who was also wearing a cap. But now [the cop] had two caps. When the bus stopped at Olney High School, there were two or three police cars. They asked, "Who did it?" But nothing happened.

Donald Presser, of Philadelphia, recalled:

> Wilt and I went through geometry and algebra together. He was a decent student. He was a nice, quiet kid, kind of laid-back. We were in 11th grade, with a class full of 10th-graders. I guess they had read about him—he was already a celebrity. I suppose the other kids figured they'd bump into him somewhere along the way, but I don't think they expected to see him in one of their classes the first week of school. So they were gawking at him. They were in awe of him—he was so big. The teacher tried to start the class, and she noticed everybody was distracted, so she said, "Wilt, are they embarrassing you?" And he said, "Not at all."

That jibes with the memory of another Overbrook classmate, Harry Powers, who said that Wilt carried his celebrity with incredible dignity.

In the 1954 basketball season, his junior year at Overbrook, Wilt had a new coach, an Overbrook and Temple University alumnus, Cecil Mosenson. At 23, Mosenson was just five years older than Wilt, yet found himself charged with handling the most famous young athlete in the world. "We had played against each other in a lot of independent leagues," remembered Mosenson. "We knew each other. He was terrific with me. As he got older, he became somewhat of an egotist. I don't blame him; I would be an egotist, too, if I were Wilt Chamberlain. The players surrounding Wilt were not in awe of him. Ira Davis was his own man and would tell Wilt off in a minute. And the Sadler brothers would tell Wilt to go to hell. Nor did I sense the other players resented Wilt's scoring."

Still, there were the times when Wilt would intercept one of his teammates' shots and guide it into the basket, there being no offensive (or defensive) goaltending in those years. "Jimmy Sadler used to get mad as hell at Wilt," teammate Vince Miller recalled. "A shot could be almost in the rim, but the last guy to touch it would get credit. Jimmy would shoot; Wilt would tip it in on the way down."

Mel Brodsky, who became an excellent player for Temple University and was drafted by the Minneapolis Lakers, remembered how the team practiced foul shooting, where Wilt would take off from the foul line and dunk the ball. Overbrook never employed the tactic in a game, even though it was a legal move in 1954.

While Wilt had a good relationship—at every level of his basketball life—with his teammates, there were times when the young man was moody and contrary. Before one game, against Frankford High, Wilt was horsing around at practice, not putting out much effort. Coach Mosenson got fed up. He and Wilt exchanged words, and Wilt left practice in a huff. There are various versions of what happened next. Ira Davis, who was the cocaptain of Overbrook's 1954 squad and a future Olympian in the triple jump, maintained that the players, who didn't like Wilt's attitude at that practice, decided to teach him a lesson by not giving him the ball during the Frankford game, which was played the following day.

Mel Brodsky remembers what happened differently: Brodsky, who had the use of his older brother's car, usually drove his teammates to the game—on a first-come, first-served basis. On the day in question, the car filled up, and there was no room for Wilt, who had to take public transportation to the game. Angry at being left out—though it was not intentional on the part of his teammates—Wilt refused to shoot when he got the ball during the game. Seeing what Wilt was up to, Mosenson benched him for much of the game. Overbrook still won, but, whatever the reason, Wilt ended up scoring only 12 points, his lowest game total as a high school player.

Davis said the next day the team discussed matters at practice and made up—pity for Roxborough High, Overbrook's next opponent. More than making up for his 12 points against Frankford, Wilt scored 71 against Roxborough, setting a new Public League scoring record and tying the state mark.

Doug Leaman said, "Most of our games, with Wilt in there, were romps. Me and the other players were trying to score double figures so we could get scholarships, but Wilt's scoring 30 and 40 points. So we ended up only playing a half. It wasn't fun." As Leaman once wrote about the other starting Overbrook players, they were considered excess baggage, although they were excellent basketball players.

Once again Overbrook defeated Northeast High for the Public League basketball title. Wilt scored 40, while Jimmy "T" Parham and William "Sonny" Hill, two Philadelphia high school legends, led Northeast in scoring. Hill was another longtime friend of Wilt's. (His Philadelphia summer league, at which local high schoolers have honed their skills since 1960, was the recipient of $50,000 from Wilt's estate.)

In the city title game, March 5, 1954, Overbrook routed South Catholic, 74–50. Wilt had 32 points, leading Overbrook to a 19–0 season and the city title.

————————

During Wilt's high school years, Eddie Gottlieb owned the Philadelphia Warriors, then the name of the city's professional basketball team. Gottlieb was an important figure in Wilt's life, as well as a founding father of, and a giant in, the National Basketball Association. Haskell Cohen wrote publicity for the financially struggling NBA; he also performed public-relations functions during the summer for a resort. Gottlieb (who dreamed of the Philadelphia high school star one day playing for his Warriors) and Cohen secured a job in the summer of 1954 for the young Wilt at a resort owned and operated by Milton and Helen Kutsher in the Catskill Mountains. That was fine with Wilt, who was always willing to work hard to earn money. Thus it was that Kutsher's Country Club, for $13 a week plus tips, acquired the world's tallest and, in his own words, "the world's hardest-working bellhop." And Wilt acquired a second family.

"My husband came to me when he was going to hire him," Mrs. Helen Kutsher remembered:

> Of course, at that time we were a rather small hotel. He said, "Helen, I want to tell you we're going to hire a young man, he's close to 7'. He's coming out of Philadelphia. He's young and he's going to be working here as a bellhop. We're going to have to get a bed for him. And I'm going to have to get a uniform made to order."
>
> And I said to my husband, "Why are we doing this? It's not exactly the most important job in the hotel."
>
> He said, "The young man is a very special young man. You just watch. He's growing and he's going to be very, very important. He's just at the start." He also said to me, "He requires a lot of milk. So when he goes to eat, make it possible for him to have his own quart of milk. Tell the staff that is what we are doing."

"At Kutsher's they had several two-story units," Haskell Cohen recalled:

> Wilt worked with another bellhop, a small kid. Wilt would pile all the bags on his back. Then he'd send the small kid up to the second floor. The kid would open the window and Wilt would put the bags above his head and hand them to the kid. Bellhops worked for tips and no one ever saw a guy carry more bags than Wilt, so he cleaned up.

"Wilt worked here for two summers [1954 and 1955]," recalled Mark Kutsher, one of Helen and Milton's three children, who now runs the resort. "They were enjoyable years for him, and he became very close to our family. And stayed that way for the rest of his life. He was always a great friend. He loved my parents, especially my father, who, in some ways, was a father figure for him."

In the forties and fifties, college basketball was more popular than professional basketball. Many of the top college players worked as busboys and waiters at the Catskills resorts. Each resort fielded its own team, and the play was of the highest caliber. One summer three members of Kentucky's national championship team worked at Kutsher's: Frank Ramsey, Cliff Hagan, and Lou Tsioropoulos. The coach of Kutsher's team was a young man whose parents, frequent guests at the hotel, had asked the Kutshers to give their son a summer job. That young coach was Arnold "Red" Auerbach, later, of course, the legendary coach of the Boston Celtics.

By the summer of 1954, B. H. Born had finished his career at Kansas University, where he was an All-American basketball player and was MVP of the 1953 NCAA championship. And Auerbach was by then the Celtics coach. Born was debating whether to accept an offer to play with the Fort Wayne (now the Detroit) Pistons in the NBA. He and Wilt played against each other that summer in 1954. As Born recalled:

> Red Auerbach told Chamberlain that I was an All-American, the NCAA MVP, and I'd probably eat him up, so he was to just do the best he could against me. Until after the game, I couldn't understand why Wilt was so mad and trying so hard. Red had sicced him on me.

Wilt, *a high school junior*, had 25 points; Born, the college All-American, 10. "He just chewed me up," Born recalled. "I decided that if there were high school kids in that part of the country that good, I wasn't going to make it in the pros for very long." Forgoing the NBA, Born remained an amateur, accepting a job with, and playing industrial league basketball for, the Caterpillar Tractor Company.

Red Auerbach tried to convince Wilt to attend college in New England so that Red, under the NBA's territorial draft rules, would have the right to draft him. Wilt chose to attend college elsewhere, and Wilt and Red were never again on the same team (except NBA All-Star Games). No one ever got under Wilt's skin, or into his head, like the master psychologist Auerbach. Imagine if Wilt had Auerbach's talents and psychology working with, instead of against, him during his professional career.

Even after he became one of the most famous and sought-after athletes in the world, Wilt enjoyed returning to Kutsher's Country Club, gossiping and kibitzing with the Kutshers, 40 years later, and reminiscing about the days when he set up the mah-jongg tables for the hotel's guests. In 1994 Milton Kutsher suffered a stroke. Helen Kutsher recalled how Wilt would sit by her husband, holding Milton's limp hand in his own massive one. Wilt even returned to

Kutsher's in the last summer of *his* life, in August 1999, sick, hobbled by pain, and with only two and a half months left to live. Years before, Wilt wrote the following inscription in the copy of his autobiography that he gave to the Kutshers:

> To Milton and Helen,
> I love you both. Words cannot express my feelings that 40 years of having a second mom and dad has meant to me. Most people have not been lucky enough to have had one set of great parents.
> Love, Wilt

———————

Summer over, Wilt returned to Philadelphia for his senior year in high school, the most famous scholastic athlete in the country. With the money he had earned at Kutsher's, he paid approximately $700 for a 1947 Oldsmobile, the first in a long line of cars he would own. Buying cars, driving them too fast, and then spending lots of money maintaining them were constants in Wilt's life that brought him great pleasure.

Jack Ryan, who tagged Wilt with the nickname "Stilt," covered high school basketball in Philadelphia for 40 years for the old *Evening Bulletin*. He reported in a preseason exhibition game that Wilt had grown an inch during the past year and was 7' tall at the beginning of the 1954–1955 season.

Irv Goodman's *Sport* magazine article described Wilt in his senior year in high school:

> Wilt does so many things well that he would have been a good ballplayer if he had been a mere 6'. He runs like a little man . . . he has basic court savvy, he can hit with a one-hander from the corner, thrown off the ear, or with a two-handed set shot from outside. He passes well out of the pivot, learns and develops quickly, and thinks in sound basketball terms. It is when all this is packaged in a 7' frame of bone and muscle that the total talent becomes awesome—and most desirable.

Awesome he was, but coach Mosenson still believes he could have had a better attitude:

I don't think Wilt worked hard enough to improve his basketball skills. I think he could have had better offensive moves. Everything he had was because of his natural physical ability, except that fadeaway jump shot. He worked on that fadeaway shot, which I hated and tried to stop him from using, but he wouldn't stop taking it. He was stubborn. I told him, "If I were guarding you, I'd hope you'd take that shot." He never really worked on turning into the basket until later when he decided to dunk.

Overbrook lost only once during the 1954–1955 basketball year, a controversial one-point season-opening holiday tournament loss to Farrell High School of western Pennsylvania, which had won 73 straight home games and was the host of the tournament. The officiating was so bad that even the fans in attendance, most of whom were rooting for Farrell, apologized to Wilt and the Overbrook coach and players after the game.

Wilt set the state scoring record in January 1955, scoring 74 points against Roxborough. A month later, his record fell to Stoughton "Stodie" Watts, who poured in 78 points in a suburban Philadelphia league game. Not to be outdone, Wilt scored 90 points the next week to recapture the record. Undefeated in league play, Overbrook easily won the Public League championship for the third consecutive year, beating its rival, West Philadelphia, 78–60.

The 1955 city championship game pitted Overbrook against West Catholic, the school that had upset Overbrook two years prior. The game was held at the Palestra, located on the University of Pennsylvania's campus, and not 15 minutes from Wilt's parents' home. It was 7:00 on the night of the game and Wilt was nowhere to be found. Coach Mosenson recalled the scene: "The team manager comes rushing down to me saying, 'They won't let Wilt into the Palestra.' I said, 'What do you mean they won't let Wilt into the Palestra?' 'He doesn't have a ticket,' the manager answered. 'Nobody gets into the game unless you have a ticket.'" A Public League official went and got him admitted, to coach Mosenson's relief. Ever the entrepreneur, Wilt didn't have his allotted tickets because he had sold them.

In Wilt's final scholastic game, Overbrook crushed West Catholic for the city title, 83–42. Wilt scored 35 points, while his buddy, Vince Miller, had 31.

During Wilt's three years at Overbrook—the 1953, 1954, and 1955 seasons—Overbrook posted a record of 56–3. Wilt led the school to two city and three Public League championships, averaging 37 points for his high school career and 47 points during his senior year alone. (He's off by a few points in his autobiography, when he says he averaged 50 per game.)

But his high school athletic career wasn't quite over; after an absence of a year, he again participated in the Public League track championship. In May 1955, wearing a checkered cap, he won the Public League high-jump championship for the second time, jumping 6'1". He failed in three attempts at 6'2½", which would have been a meet record. And then for dessert, he won the shot-put title with a throw of 46'10½". Wilt claims in his autobiography that in the championship he jumped about 6'6"; and while he did jump that high in college, he never did in high school, at least not in competition.

In its early years, the National Basketball Association had both a regular and a territorial draft, the latter of which allowed a team to draft a college player from its geographical area in exchange for a first-round draft pick. The thinking among the NBA owners was that local college stars would attract fans and alumni to the professional game—and the struggling league needed all the fan support it could muster. The draft radius extended 50 miles from the city in which the professional team was located.

With Wilt due to graduate from high school, Eddie Gottlieb lobbied to change the territorial draft to include high school players. Ned Irish, the equally strong-willed owner of the New York Knickerbockers, was against such a modification, but Gottlieb prevailed and the league owners voted seven to one for the new rule in April 1955. Soon thereafter, Gottlieb became the first person to invoke the territorial draft to secure the rights to a high school athlete, picking Wilt four years in advance of the 1959 draft. Luckily for Gottlieb—though some would say luck had nothing to do with it—Wilt did not attend a college in a city located within 50 miles of an NBA team, for in that case Gottlieb's Warriors would have lost the rights to Wilt in the 1959 draft. (The territorial draft, which was a relic of the old NBA, remained in effect through 1965. Paul Arizin, Tom Heinsohn, Jerry Lucas, and Bill Bradley are among the well-known players selected by their respective teams under the territorial draft.)

No athlete before, and not many since, has been pursued by as many colleges as was Wilt. In this, as in so many areas, he was the "first." "He got 120 offers," recalled Cecil Mosenson. "UCLA told him they'd make him a movie star. Other colleges told him they'd send him to dental or medical school. An alumnus from the University of Pennsylvania came over in a big limousine and said, 'Wilt, why don't we take a ride to New York tomorrow and take a look at what Harry Winston, the big jeweler, has.'" Coach Mosenson was even offered a coaching position—if he could deliver Wilt.

Where will Wilt go? The sporting public—and more than a few college coaches and boosters—wondered in the winter and spring of 1955. How big a story was it? After Wilt selected a college, *Life*, then the most popular magazine in the country, featured a five-page story on the effort to recruit and land him.

Wilt wanted to attend college outside Philadelphia, great as the Philly tradition in college basketball was—and is. "He didn't want another big city," recalled George L. Brown, a friend and adviser. Southern schools did not want blacks at that time, so that eliminated the great basketball power Kentucky. When people thought of college basketball in 1955, no one thought of the far West or Pacific Northwest. John Wooden's UCLA dynasty would not begin until 1964, when the team led by Gail Goodrich and an All-American guard named Walter Hazzard (Overbrook High School class of 1960) won the school's first NCAA basketball title.

Wilt wasn't interested in New England and passed on New York because he didn't want to be that close to Philadelphia. So that left the Midwest, whose colleges produced some of the country's finest basketball and where Wilt visited the universities of Cincinnati, Illinois, Indiana, Michigan, Michigan State, Iowa, Northwestern, and Kansas.

Don Pierce, then sports information director at Kansas University, saw a photo of Wilt in 1952 and has been credited with bringing Wilt to the attention of the school's basketball coach, the legendary Forrest "Phog" Allen, whose voice supposedly sounded like a fog horn, thus the memorable nickname. And surely B. H. Born, the Kansas All-American almost run off the court by Wilt in the summer of 1954 in the Catskills, had told Phog about the young Philly phenom.

But it wasn't until the winter of 1955 that Allen began to recruit Wilt and actually saw him play. Allen flew to Philadelphia in January 1955 and attended the Overbrook-Germantown game. That evening Wilt received a local award as "the outstanding scholastic athlete in Philadelphia." Coach Cecil Mosenson recaptured the event: "Phog Allen came to the Cliveden Award Banquet and introduced himself to me. Then he sat down with Wilt's mother and he *schmoozed* her. And she loved him."

When Mosenson and Mrs. Chamberlain talked to Wilt about attending Kansas University, Wilt was not enthused, but because the school sent plane tickets, Wilt and Mosenson took a trip to Lawrence, Kansas, a lovely university town located 40 miles from Kansas City. Mosenson recalled that "before taking off, it was snowing, and they had to deice the plane. When we arrived in Lawrence at about 3:00 in the morning, there must have been 50 people waiting for us."

Phog Allen assembled a lineup of distinguished Kansas citizens, black and white, to win Wilt's heart for the university. The prominent blacks in the group included Lloyd Kerford, a successful businessman from Atchison, Kansas, whose son and daughter had graduated from Kansas; Etta Moten, a concert singer and KU grad, class of 1931; Dowdal Davis, who had visited Wilt in Philadelphia and was the publisher of the *Kansas City Call*, a newspaper with a black readership; and George L. Brown, class of 1950, who was a journalist at the *Denver Post* and a Colorado state senator—the first black ever elected to that body. The white members of the group were Calvin Vanderwerf, then head of the KU chemistry department, who, on a trip to Philadelphia, had convinced Wilt and his parents of KU's academic worth; and Roy Edwards, KU class of 1942, a wealthy businessman who, along with his wife, Joan, were devoted to the university.

"It was common knowledge that Eddie Gottlieb also encouraged Wilt to go to college in Kansas in order to keep him away from an NBA city," alleged the late Alex Hannum, who had been an NBA coach. Even if true, there were other Midwestern schools that would have enabled Gottlieb to select Wilt under the territorial draft because there was not a professional basketball team within 50 miles of them.

What Kansas most had in its favor was Phog Allen, one of college basketball's greatest coaches. Allen won or shared 24 conference championships in his 39 years at Kansas. He helped to found the National Basketball Coaches Association, was the driving force behind the decision to include basketball as an Olympic event in 1936, and had helped to coach the United States Olympic team to a gold medal in 1952. For many years he was the winningest coach in college basketball history. His record was surpassed by Adolph Rupp, Kentucky's coach, who had played for Allen at Kansas. And Rupp's record was surpassed by the current holder, Dean Smith of North Carolina fame. He, too, played basketball at Kansas for Allen in the early fifties. All of them are part of Kansas' rich basketball tradition. Furthermore, James Naismith, the game's *inventor*, coached Allen at Kansas. (And for those who like irony, Naismith is the *only* losing coach in the school's fabled basketball history.)

There was one more element in Wilt's decision, although it was not likely the deciding factor: "There were incentives," Wilt's high school coach, Cecil Mosenson, recalled. "I'm not going to say there weren't incentives." And unless you believe in the tooth fairy, one has to assume that many other schools pursuing Wilt also offered "incentives," by which coach Mosenson means money. Wilt told reporters for several New York newspapers in 1985 that he received approximately $4,000 from "two or three godfathers" when he played at Kansas. This was in addition to the standard college scholarship of the time, which in 1955 included free room and board, tuition and books, plus $135 a year for selling football programs and helping with other athletic jobs, which was worth about $1,100 per year in 2002 dollars.

Told that Wilt Chamberlain had selected Kansas from the hundred-plus schools that had pursued him, Phog Allen is reported to have said, "I hope he comes out for basketball."

Three hundred and fifty-two young men and women graduated from Overbrook in 1955. One of them, Barbara Chamberlain Lewis, recaptured the ceremony:

> What comes to mind the most for me is when we were walking down the aisle at our high school graduation in June 1955 at Overbrook High School. He was on the left side of the aisle and I was on the right. As we reached the door to walk, we gave each other the OK sign with our thumbs. Luckily, my name was called first and my family cheered, because when they called Wilt's name the audience cheered and gave him a standing ovation. I was so proud of him and pretended they were cheering for me as I cried with sad tears of joy, realizing that my brother Dippy was on his way to becoming a very special and unique person, not only in my eyes, but the whole world's.

After the graduation ceremony, there was a party at the home of one of Wilt's classmates, Carole Cherry. Her younger brother, then age 11, stayed up late, for how often did the most famous basketball player in the city, soon to be the most famous in the world, come to his parents' house? Add the author to the long list of people who remember when and where they were when they first saw "the Big Dipper."

Chapter 3

Growing up in small-town Kansas, Wilt Chamberlain was the first black man in public life whose name I knew. He was a hero to us small-town sports fans, and still is a hero today.

—A letter in the *Kansas City Star* following Wilt's death

I remember the first time we met each other. Wilt had driven his car and parked it against the fieldhouse. We were there for the freshman orientation for the basketball team. It had rained, so it was muddy, and when we came out from our meeting, we got into his car, and it was stuck in the mud. There were four of us in the car. Two or three of us got out, and we tried to push the car away from the building. Finally, Wilt said, "Billings, get behind the wheel." He got out of the car. He went to the front and lifted that sucker up and pushed it out.

—Bob Billings, college friend and teammate

Wilt never wanted to be thought of as a goon. He was so big and so strong, but he wanted to be known as a well-rounded person. And he loved Kansas University. The man kept his KU letter jacket in perfect condition for 40 years. That should tell you something right there.

—Al Correll, Philadelphia friend and Kansas basketball player

Flippin' with the Dipper

Wilt Chamberlain picked up Doug Leaman at the Leaman house to begin their 1,100-mile drive to Kansas University, to which both had been given athletic scholarships. Leaman, a white guard from Overbrook, was a good, but not fantastic, player. Wilt resented that none of his black teammates, particularly his close friends, gifted guard Marty Hughes or 6'5" forward Vince Miller, were offered scholarships—both, in Wilt's opinion, far more legitimate big-time college prospects than Leaman. Years later Wilt told Hughes he should have done more to help him and Miller receive scholarships to Kansas. But did Miller and Hughes have the academic credentials to attend Kansas? Not according to longtime classmate and teammate Tom Fitzhugh. "None of us were academically prepared, including me," Fitzhugh said. "It has nothing to do with intelligence." But whatever rancor Wilt felt about this racially tinged recruiting faux pas (real or perceived) was smoothed over by the charm of Phog Allen and the excitement of going away to college.

Because Leaman admitted he had a tendency to fall asleep at the wheel, Wilt drove the entire way. They brought sandwiches for lunch, and after hours of driving through the flat prairie land, they stopped for dinner somewhere in Kansas. What happened next, Leaman recalled, is as vivid to him today as it was 50 years ago: "This big guy behind the counter said to us, 'We don't serve Negroes, but you can eat in the back room.' Wilt went nuts. He had a BB gun and started shooting it all over outside."

Wilt's reaction was due to frustration and surprise as much as plain anger. It was the first time he had seen racism in Kansas, much less been its target. On his two recruiting trips there, he had been chaperoned and insulated like a Miss America contestant, apparently never realizing that Kansas was, in

43

some respects, still a segregated state. That diner was a different Kansas than the one Wilt had been shown, and he was still seething over the incident when he and Leaman arrived at Phog Allen's house late that night. Leaman later remarked that Wilt intended to turn around and head back to Philly, but Allen sat him down, sent out for hamburgers, and calmed his anger with sweet phrases.

Ironically, it was Leaman who left Kansas—and that after only two days—homesick and in "puppy love," as he recalled. Leaman never spoke to Wilt again, feeling that he had somehow let the big guy down by his withdrawal. Leaman, who became a high school teacher and basketball coach in the Philadelphia area, followed Wilt's career, even writing about his high school teammate in suburban Philadelphia newspapers many years after the fact.

Many American cities were segregated in 1955—officially and unofficially. Lawrence, Kansas, with a population then of about twenty-five thousand, was one such community, although black people were probably treated better in Lawrence than in the South.

Wilt wouldn't have remained in a segregated Lawrence. Nor did he have to. Coach Allen's son, Mitt, was a county attorney, and he let it be known around the otherwise friendly small college town that the days of segregation were over. The influential and well-liked businessman and KU booster Roy Edwards did likewise through friends who owned the Dine-A-Mite Restaurant, the in-place for students to go after KU basketball games. As Maurice King, Wilt's only black teammate, recalled: "Every business in Lawrence wanted to identify with Wilt. After our games or anytime, if Wilt walked into a place with five or six blacks, nobody dared to bother him."

The then-chancellor of the university, Franklin Murphy, told Al Correll, a Philadelphian who had followed Wilt to Kansas to play basketball, that Wilt would come to him and complain about a segregated situation, and the chancellor would follow through to change things. But, as Correll pointed out, Wilt was never one to lead a march or demonstration publicly protesting segregated facilities. "He would go to Chancellor Murphy and say, 'If you don't straighten this out, I'm leaving,'" Correll suggested. "But Wilt wasn't thinking in terms of all African Americans; he was saying, '*I'm* not going to be treated like that. *I'm* not going to sit up there' [in then-segregated movie theaters]. Of course it had an impact on the rest of us African Americans. But what he did, he did largely for himself."

The pattern of successful and fairly well-off people befriending and advising Wilt that began with the Kutshers in New York State continued at Kansas, as it would throughout his life. In college, Wilt relied on businessman Roy Edwards, one of the KU alumni who recruited Wilt. Roy and Joan (pronounced *Joanne*) Edwards' Kansas City, Kansas, home became a sanctuary where Wilt could escape the fishbowl in which, like it or not, he lived.

The Edwards family, which included three young children, saw the most of Wilt during his freshman year, when, as Joan said, Wilt was a little homesick. He may have acted differently with his peers, but around her family Mrs. Edwards stated:

> He was always pretty shy and didn't talk a lot. And he was one of the most polite people I've ever been around. I loved that young man.
>
> He was great with the neighborhood children. Usually he didn't appear until 7:00 at night. He'd devour my fried shrimp and fried potatoes. We had a basketball court out back, and he would start to shoot. Pretty soon the neighborhood kids would come around, and their parents, too—he was like a magnet. He would lift those little kids so they could put the ball in the basket. And he used to kid even me. He'd say, "You want a boost?"

The Edwards' Dutch colonial home had a narrow sunroom where Wilt used to sit in front of the fireplace on a sofa. "He would slouch down, making it harder to get by," Joan remembered. "You couldn't get past him because his feet were just about in the fireplace. It was the darndest thing I've ever seen. The children just loved that. They would say, 'Wilt, come sit on the sofa.' He used to tell my daughter Susan, then age five, to run around the room and see if she could get by before he got his legs down."

"I was 11 at the time," recalled R. A. Edwards, Roy and Joan's son, who is now in his fifties and the president of a bank. "Wilt used to sell programs at the football games. He wore a brimless cap, like a Scottish tam. People would line up 25 to 50 deep; they just wanted to buy a football program from him. I'm sure he signed autographs some of the time, too. He just went out of his way to be nice to people. Here I was, a young and impressionable boy, and he was as warm and as considerate as anybody I've ever been around."

Wilt's first day on campus was September 7, 1955. In his freshman year, he lived in Carruth-O'Leary dormitory and slept in a specially constructed bed. His roommate was Charlie Tidwell, a track-and-field star from Independence, Kansas. Wilt and Tidwell roomed together for three years—a case of opposites attracting, as Wilt was extroverted, confident, and assertive, while Tidwell was quiet, shy, and unassuming.

Of his basketball teammates, Wilt was closest to Bob Billings, another son of Kansas, this one from Russell, a community in the center of the state. During a tour of the lovely KU campus, part of which is on a hill referred to as Mt. Oread, Billings recalled that he and Wilt clicked from the first time they met. "We studied together, we practiced basketball together, we just related well," commented Billings, who roomed with Wilt when the basketball team went on the road. A Phi Beta Kappa at KU, Billings became a successful developer of luxury homes in Lawrence and always remained in touch with Wilt.

A description of Wilt as he was about to burst onto the national collegiate scene appeared in a *Philadelphia Inquirer* profile of him:

> Remarkably agile, graceful, and swift for his size, he wears No. 13 for luck, size 14 shoes for comfort, tailor-made clothes by necessity. . . . He looks lighter than his 240 pounds, most of which are centered in well-developed chest and wide shoulders. He has unusually long, extremely thin legs. His waist is a mere 31 inches. Flatfooted, he can reach 9'6" into the air. With a leap he can easily reach 12'6" or better. From fingertip to fingertip with arms outstretched, he measures 7'2".

On the night of November 18, 1955, Wilt lived up to every rave clipping when he led the Kansas University freshmen to an 81–71 victory over the varsity—the first time the freshmen had ever beaten the varsity. The Dipper scored 42 points and swept 29 rebounds, making believers of the entire state. They saw he was no height-bound goon or freak, but an exceptional athlete at the beginning of his prime. He soared and glided, dunked and finger-rolled, banked his signature fadeaway jumper shot, blocked shots, ran the court, passed the ball adeptly, and hustled on defense. For the varsity, it was scary. For the fans, it was ecstasy tempered with regret that freshmen weren't eligible for varsity play back then. The way most of the KU rooters saw matters, the only thing standing between Kansas and three national championships was Wilt's freshman year.

"When we were freshmen, there were small towns that would ask the university to send some KU players out to put on a clinic," recalled Monte Johnson, a walk-on member of the squad (and many years later the KU athletic director). "Four of us went to Emporia [Kansas]: Bob Billings, Lynn Kindred (who was from Emporia), myself, and Wilt. We put on an exhibition for the kids. One young man, in a question session, asked Wilt how high he could jump, taking only one step for a start. Wilt went back one step, kind of a long stretch back, and jumped up and put his finger over the top of the backboard and slid it back down. It was the most graceful move I've ever seen." John Parker, the cocaptain of the Kansas squad, confirmed that he, too, saw Wilt touch the top of the backboard. (So, years later, would Al Domenico, the trainer of the Philadelphia 76ers.)

Wilt's Kansas world was jolted when the university announced that Phog Allen, one of the reasons Wilt had selected the school, must, like every KU employee, retire after the academic year during which he turned 70. Try as the popular and wily Allen did to have the rules changed, the university wouldn't bend, which meant that the great Phog Allen wouldn't coach Wilt after all. Coincidentally, Allen turned 70 the night the Kansas freshmen, with Wilt at center, defeated the varsity. One wonders if Wilt would have attended Kansas had he known that Allen was never to coach him.

Dick Harp, Allen's assistant coach, was now at the helm. Harp was a fine *X*'s and *O*'s coach, all agree, but it is never easy to replace a legend. Resentful that Allen wouldn't be there to guide him and the team, Wilt never had a good relationship with Harp, "and Dick Harp could never live up to Wilt's 'memory' of Phog Allen, who never coached him," observed Jerry Waugh, Harp's assistant. Allen didn't help Harp when, in a moment of pique, he said you could take Wilt, two coeds, and two Phi Beta Kappas and win the national championship.

In addition to not getting along with Harp, Wilt resisted Harp's efforts to coach him. "The thing about Wilt," said Waugh, the Kansas assistant, "is that he'd look at you and say, 'Yes, sir. Yes, sir.' And go ahead and do what he was going to do anyway. It was kind of polite disobedience."

———————

With Wilt's freshman year over, Kansas fans salivated at the prospects for Wilt's sophomore season. A widely read story by an up-and-coming sportswriter named Jimmy Breslin appeared in the December 15, 1956, issue of *The Saturday Evening Post* under the melodramatic title, "Can Basketball Survive Wilt Chamberlain?" It did survive, but not without some changes.

Throughout his life, Wilt wasn't bashful about claiming his place as basketball's greatest player. He used to point out how many rules were modified solely with him in mind. Effective as of the 1956–1957 season, Wilt's first year on the varsity, offensive goaltending—by which a player could reach above the cylinder and guide an attempted shot into the basket—was no longer permitted. Also, on a foul shot, the shooter's foot could no longer pass the imaginary vertical plane of the free throw line until the ball hit the rim or backboard—no taking off from the foul line for Wilt and "dunking" his foul shot. At a later time, that move was made famous by Julius Erving in the NBA All-Star dunk competition, and then later by Michael Jordan. The rules for inbounding a pass under your own basket were also altered because of Wilt. His team, prior to the rule change, could take the ball out of bounds behind their basket and throw it over the backboard into play. It was a sure two points with Wilt on the court to grab it and put it in the hoop. And the lanes around the basket were widened, then widened some more, even in the professional league—always to contain Wilt's advantages over mere mortals. "How many rules did they ever change for Michael Jordan?" Wilt used to ask in the nineties, part of his case that he, not Jordan, should be considered the greatest player of all time.

There have been few varsity debuts in collegiate sports as widely anticipated as the night in December 1956 when Kansas played Northwestern—Wilt's first varsity game. He didn't disappoint: "Those fabulous stories about Wilt 'the Stilt' Chamberlain are true. He proved it last night," an Associated Press article about the game began:

> The 7' sophomore from Philadelphia scored 52 points and grabbed 31 rebounds, shattering the Big Seven and Kansas scoring marks and the school rebound record, leading Kansas to an 87–69 victory over a good Northwestern basketball team.

To this day, Wilt's 52 points remain the KU record for scoring in a single game and that record is believed to be the single-game scoring record in a varsity debut in NCAA history. (Northwestern's center that night was Joe Ruklick, no slouch of a player, who had 22 points. Six years later Wilt and Ruklick would be teammates in the NBA, and Ruklick had *the* assist in the most amazing basketball game Wilt—or anyone else—ever played.)

KU had a strong squad in 1956–1957, and it was ranked No. 1 in the preseason polls. The starting five were cocaptains Gene Elstun and John Parker, Lew Johnson (replaced at the semester break by Ron Loneski after his broken foot had healed), the senior Maurice King (an all-conference player who held school records that Wilt would obliterate), and the big fella from Philly at center—the main reason for the team's top ranking.

Kansas won its first 12 games, but then lost, 39–37, in the final moments of an away game in which Iowa State assigned a man to guard Wilt; the other four defenders played a zone. KU then won its next five games. "Wilt led by example," Bob Billings said. "He wasn't someone who was going to be running up and down waving a flag." Kansas then lost 56–54 to an Oklahoma State team coached by the legendary Henry "Hank" Iba when Oklahoma State held the ball the last three minutes and 30 seconds, then made a last-second shot—this being long before the 45-second shot was adopted by college basketball in 1986.

Run with Kansas, you lose—and lose big. Hold the ball, keep the score low, and you have a chance. Collapse men around Wilt, hold and grab and hit him. The referees won't—or more realistically, can't—call a foul every time down the floor. "After some of our games, Wilt would have marks all over his back," teammate John Parker recalled. "The opposing players practically had to tackle him to get a foul called."

Nevertheless, these were heady days for KU basketball fans. Either Kansas or North Carolina was ranked No. 1 or No. 2 throughout the 1956–1957 season. Fans flocked to home games at the new Allen Fieldhouse, which was named after the team's longtime coach and was then the second-largest basketball arena in the country. (The largest in 1956 was at the University of Minnesota.) Attendance increased by eighty-five thousand during Wilt's first season. Wherever Wilt played, at whatever level of the game, fans wanted to see him. And more fans wanted to see Wilt in action than anyone else who has ever played the sport, with the possible exception, years later, of Michael Jordan.

Wilt couldn't wear the No. 13 in high school, but he could in college. Looking at grainy black-and-white 16-millimeter films of Wilt's Kansas years, one sees the moves associated with him: his graceful finger roll where he funnels or dips the ball toward the basket, and his fadeaway jump shot. He threw crisp and effective passes to his teammates cutting to the basket, blocked countless shots, and hustled back on defense.

In later years, Wilt lamented that younger sports fans and younger sportswriters had never seen him play, for few films exist of him at his peak—his college to early and midprofessional career (1956 to 1967). Many fans remember or have seen television video of him from the latter part of his professional career (1971 to 1973), by which time he was heavier and slowed by a knee injury—but even then was formidable.

In the eighties, Wilt used to chide television commentators who marveled at the way big men such as David Robinson and Hakeem Olajuwon ran the court. "Did you ever see a 7' center like David Robinson end up at the end of a fast break?" Wilt would ask rhetorically, imitating the commentator. "Yeah," Wilt would say, providing his own answer, "I saw someone do it in 1955." And so he had.

Max Falkenstien is a Kansas fixture who has broadcast state athletic events on radio and television for five decades. In 1957, while working for WREN-AM in Topeka, Kansas, he invited Wilt to cohost a weekly 30-minute music show called "Flippin' with the Dipper."

Wilt would drive to Topeka on Saturday mornings and play recordings of popular songs. During one show, Wilt, who was a communication major at KU, was about to play the record "Don't Let Go" when he quipped, "Every time I play basketball I think the opposite of this title. I look down at some of those guys and think, 'Man, let go.'"

Coach Harp feared the radio show might violate NCAA rules, so "Flippin' with the Dipper" lasted only six weeks. "Dick Harp was one of those guys who lived in eternal fear that he would be the cause of the school going on probation," said Jerry Waugh, the assistant coach. "I'm sure Wilt had additional inducements to be at the University of Kansas. I didn't know them, nor did Dick. But Dick had to live with the arrangements that were agreed upon. That put him in a tough situation."

Besides his part-time stint as a disc jockey, Wilt had other things to do with his limited time. He was already receiving huge amounts of fan mail and, according to Billings, tried to answer each letter personally. He liked to bowl and even won a campus bowling tournament. Ever competitive, Wilt also enjoyed playing cards and games, which pursuits brought the following comments from Bill Mayer, then the managing editor of the *Lawrence Journal-World* who also helped his small staff cover the basketball team. "He loved to cheat at cards. Wilt sat at a bridge table and loomed clear up in the air. He always knew what everybody else had. And if it was checkers, he'd figured out a way to sneak a couple of checkers on the board." But it never seemed to bother the people against whom he was playing, Mayer said. "They figured, 'That's just Wilt.'"

Wilt also had to contend with his celebrity status. Falkenstien, recalling the time three thousand people showed up for a KU practice before a game against Washington in Seattle, remarked that it was difficult for Wilt to maintain any degree of privacy because he attracted so much attention. The result was that Wilt "built a shell around himself," according to Falkenstien.

In his book, *Max and the Jayhawks*, Falkenstien mentions that when KU played Colorado, Wilt visited his friend George Brown, who was a state senator there. One time, Wilt spent the night with Brown and did not return until the bus was ready to leave with the rest of the team around 7:30 A.M. As Falkenstien observed, "Coach Harp was faced with a tough dilemma handling Wilt, because Wilt sort of did what he wanted to and went where he wanted to go."

Monte Johnson has a different perspective:

When we traveled, he wasn't separate from anybody. He'd play hearts with the guys; he'd listen to music. I had a brother who got me a tape recorder that I took on team trips. Wilt just loved to play tapes on this recorder and, eventually, he bought it from me.

He was one of your friends, one of your teammates. Until he passed away, every time I'd see him, it was the same way: he treated you like one time you were an important part of his life. And I never treated him any differently. I wasn't in awe of him. But there was one thing I always told him: "If you only knew what you did to influence the identity of your teammates over their lifetimes, you wouldn't believe it."

I can't tell you the thousands of times people would say to me, "You were actually a teammate of Wilt Chamberlain's?" And I would jokingly say to Wilt, "I bet no one ever said to you, 'You were a teammate of Monte Johnson's?'"

On trains, the mode by which the team traveled to many away games, Wilt tried to stuff his 7' frame into a Pullman compartment, his teammate John Parker recalled. Once in the hotel, he slept catty-corner on a normal-sized bed.

"He liked to play cards and dominoes," teammate Maurice King recollected. "That's what we'd do when we were in hotels. He didn't like to go out too much because of the crowds he attracted. People would follow him and come up and bother him. He also liked to play games like, name the capital of Yugoslavia or the world's tallest mountain ranges. He'd come up with the damndest answers. And if I didn't know, I'd say, 'Wait a minute, Wilt, where you get that from?' He would kind of intimidate us with his answers."

Monte Johnson was backup center in their sophomore year and because of Wilt's strength took tremendous punishment. "The one thing we learned in practice with him, you never wanted to be under the basket when he was getting ready to dunk. The chances of getting your fingers jammed were about 99 percent because the ball came through so fast. We were accustomed to that, but in a game, the opposing players would get their fingers jammed a lot"—or worse. In an NBA game Wilt dunked the ball so hard it broke Johnny Kerr's toe. (And being too embarrassed to let anyone know he had a broken toe from Wilt's dunk, Kerr ran down the floor, acted as if he tripped, then grabbed his foot and left the game.)

Wilt's stamina was legendary and was especially impressive after a tough practice when the players would have to run quarter- or half-miles as a conditioning exercise. Johnson recalled that:

> Wilt had such unbelievable endurance and speed that, if he took off running, there wasn't any chance that anybody would keep up with him. He glided around the track and had the grace of a deer. I said to the coach, "It might look like it helps us to chase him, but it may kill us because you can't catch someone who runs that fast." After practice, he was the only one who wasn't tired. I never saw him tired.

In that ancient year of 1957, before anyone ever used the term "March Madness," 23 teams played for the NCAA title. Today, 65 teams compete. Kansas won the Big Seven title (as the conference was then known) with an 11–1 record, securing a bid to the Big Dance. Their next hurdle before the national championship was the Midwest regional, held that year in Dallas. "I remembered my experience there and I told Wilt, 'We're going to have trouble,'" recalled Maurice King, his black teammate.

And trouble they had, starting with official notification that the tournament hotel would not accommodate Kansas' black players. Coach Harp refused to separate his team. "If we can't all stay together, none of us will be staying here. We're not going to put Maurice and Wilt in private homes," Harp declared, so the whole team stayed in Grand Prairie, Texas, midway between Dallas and Fort Worth. "We had to be escorted around with police cars, ate in the hotel where we stayed, and couldn't eat with anyone but ourselves," recalled John Parker, cocaptain of the team. (Whatever one thinks of Harp as a coach—and Dean Smith thought well enough of his abilities to hire him as an assistant coach for North Carolina after Harp left Kansas—let the world remember him as a decent man.)

The first game of the Midwest regional pitted Kansas against an all-white Southern Methodist University team. The game was on SMU's court, where the home team had not lost in 35 consecutive games. John Parker wrote about the experience for *American Heritage*: "The crowd was brutal. We were spat upon, pelted with debris, and subjected to the vilest racial epithets imaginable." Nevertheless, Kansas prevailed in overtime, 73–65. An angry crowd surrounded the bus that was to transport the KU team back to Grand Prairie, and a motorcycle caravan had to accompany them back to the hotel.

Matters were not much better the next night at the regional championship— KU against another Southern favorite, Oklahoma City. The contest was also marred by racial comments from fans and Oklahoma players alike. King said he and Wilt didn't respond to racial slurs with fists, "We just beat their rear ends." Kansas demolished Oklahoma City, 81–61. King recalled that a few Oklahoma City players apologized to him and Wilt after the game, but police still had to escort the KU team off the court and to the airport.

There remained four teams vying for the 1957 national collegiate championship: Kansas; San Francisco, whose great center, Bill Russell, since graduated, had led them to the title the previous two years; Michigan State, with one of the great leapers in basketball, Jumpin' Johnny Green; and North Carolina, the nation's only undefeated major college team. But most everyone knew who the winner was going to be—the Jayhawks of Kansas. Even the site of the final favored Kansas. It would be held in Municipal Auditorium in Kansas City that year.

Kansas crushed San Francisco, 80–56, in its semifinal game. North Carolina needed three overtimes to defeat Michigan State, 74–70, in its semifinal game. "We should have lost to Michigan State," recalled Tommy Kearns, a starting member of the North Carolina team. "Johnny Green's sitting on the foul line with 11 seconds left. We're down two points, and he's got a one-and-one. If he makes one, the game is over. [This was before the three-point shot.] He misses. We go down, with seconds left, and tie the game." And then North Carolina wins in overtime.

The NCAA championship was March 23, 1957. It was Kansas against North Carolina, the two best teams in the nation. Though North Carolina, with a 31–0 record, was ranked No. 1 at the end of the regular season, it was the underdog against No. 2 Kansas with its 24–2 record.

The Kansas starting five consisted of Maurice King (6'2"), Ron Loneski (6'5"), John Parker (6'), Gene Elstun (6'3"), and Wilt (7'-plus)—each one of whom, except Wilt, would play as a guard in today's game.

Frank McGuire, who had taken St. John's to the NCAA finals in 1952, coached North Carolina. Although McGuire had left New York, he continued to recruit from the playgrounds and, particularly Catholic, high schools of that city. His five starters were point guard Tommy Kearns (5'11"); Bob Cunningham, who at 6'3" was tall for a guard in the fifties; Pete Brennan (6'6"); center Joe Quigg (6'8"); and Lennie Rosenbluth (6'5"). As McGuire was wont to say, his starting lineup that year "was made up of four Irish Catholics and a Jew, all from New York, and playing in Baptist country in North Carolina."

Before the final, Jeremiah Tax, covering the game for *Sports Illustrated*, approached North Carolina's Kearns and said, "You know, you guys don't have a chance." Kearns replied, "Jerry, we're gonna win."

"They used to scare Frank to death by saying throughout the season, 'We're not going to lose,'" Jane McGuire, Frank's widow, recalled.

No one remembers with certainty who suggested it or why, but McGuire, looking for an edge, chose the 5'11" Kearns to jump center against Wilt. It was an interesting move, a touch of New York moxie, for North Carolina wasn't going to win the jump even if Quigg jumped center against Wilt. Why not make Kansas wonder what else McGuire had up his sleeve?

Kansas started in a four-man zone with Maurice King guarding Rosenbluth, Carolina's leading scorer. North Carolina raced to a 19–7 lead, making its first six shots—not a bad start in a national championship. Behind, Kansas was forced to abandon its zone defense, and Quigg, North Carolina's center, immediately moved to the outside, from where he could score. Wilt had no choice but to come out from the basket and guard him, and that set the stage for the rest of Carolina's team to outrebound their Kansas counterparts.

On defense, Carolina, employing variations of a 2-3 zone defense, collapsed around Wilt, as opponents had done all season. Other than Wilt, the rest of the Kansas squad couldn't find the basket. North Carolina made 64 percent of its shots during the first half, Kansas an abysmal 27 percent. North Carolina led at the half, 29–22.

Was history repeating itself? In Wilt's first year at Overbrook, the team had been favored to defeat West Catholic for the city title, but the gods of basketball intervened and Overbrook lost.

In the second half of the NCAA championship, with nine minutes gone, Kansas took the lead for the first time, thanks to Wilt's scoring. And then, leading 40–37 with 10 minutes left in the game, Kansas went into a stall. Bob Billings:

> For a lot of years they said it was the greatest final in the history of the NCAA. But it was a terribly boring game because you were just standing around a lot. It might have been exciting for the fans because it was close, but it was boring for the players, at least for our team, because we wanted to run.

The All-American Lennie Rosenbluth fouled out with 1:45 remaining in the game, having scored 20 points. Wilt single-handedly kept KU's hopes alive and, with 1:15 left in the game, KU still held the lead. Then Kearns made two clutch foul shots to tie the game at 46, and that's where it ended in regulation play.

For the second time in the tournament's history, there was to be an overtime for the national championship.

Each team scored two points in the first overtime.

Both teams tightened up in the second overtime, which was scoreless. Kansas chose to hold the ball, which meant that Wilt did not attempt a field goal in the second overtime.

In the third overtime, North Carolina took the lead at 52–48. Then, getting the ball down low, Wilt scooped in a basket, was fouled, and converted the foul shot. The score was 52–51, North Carolina. Maurice King tied the game by converting a foul shot. Gene Elstun then made one of two foul shots, putting Kansas up 53–52 with 10 seconds to play. Joe Quigg drove toward the basket on Wilt, and King, reaching in for the steal, fouled him. Timeout was called by coach McGuire, who went against the conventional wisdom—in that situation the *opposing* coach usually calls a timeout, hoping the opposition player, in this case, Quigg, who had missed his only free throw that game, would think about what was at stake and, maybe, he'd choke. So much for conventional wisdom: Quigg made both shots, and North Carolina was up 54–53 with five seconds remaining in the game.

Kansas called a timeout in an attempt to come up with a play to win the national championship. Everyone in the building knew Kansas would try to get the ball to Wilt, preferably down low. McGuire instructed his players to foul Wilt if he got the ball.

Taking the ball in at half court, John Parker threw it to Ron Loneski, who was near the key. Loneski, 6'5", turned and lofted a soft and low pass to Wilt. Joe Quigg jumped from behind Wilt and deflected the poorly thrown pass into the hands of Tommy Kearns, who threw the ball skyward. "By the time the ball came down," to quote sportswriter Frank Deford, "North Carolina was the national champion." Kansas, shocked and bitter, was the runner-up in one of the most memorable games in NCAA championship history.

"I've never seen a locker room in my life where people were so devastated," recalled Bill Mayer, who covered the game for the *Lawrence Journal-World*. "There's Wilt, there's Parker and King, and Dick Harp breaks down in tears. The guys who were on that team will tell you that they have never gotten over the pain of that moment." As Kearns observed 44 years after the game:

> Dick Harp, in retrospect, made a strategic error [by slowing the game down when Kansas finally went ahead]. We had played three overtimes the night before, and here we're playing in another. He should have come after us. We were willing to let them run out the clock in the overtimes. Once they got the lead, they should have been more aggressive.

Wilt was named the tournament's MVP, only the second time a member of the losing team was so honored. Yet Wilt thought he had let down the entire state of Kansas when the team failed to win the championship in that fateful contest. He was hardly at fault—he had scored 23 of Kansas' 53 points and had 14 rebounds, half his team's total rebounds. He had shot 46 percent from the field, while the rest of the Kansas team managed to convert a sorrowful 26 percent of their shots. And North Carolina outrebounded Kansas 40–28. Those facts—and poor coaching—are why Kansas lost a game it ought to have won.

"If we had won that title, it might have changed Wilt's life," said Bob Billings, his best friend on the team. "He wouldn't have had to go 10 years being labeled a loser. Wilt was named MVP of the tournament. The rest of us didn't play worth a damn. It wasn't his fault. He was never a loser in anything he did in his life." Recalled Tommy Kearns:

> Destiny said that Wilt was going to win three national championships, and it did not happen. How could it not happen? Because Wilt didn't deliver? Well, actually, Wilt delivered very well. It just so happened he played against a team that was blessed. It was a freak. I love my teammates, and I love Frank McGuire, but we were very, very lucky.

Kearns contended that the game was a defining moment for him: "It's extraordinary what one point can do to one's life. That event changed my life."

Twenty-some years after the memorable clash, Kearns, the 5'11" guard who had jumped center, and Wilt ran into each other in New York, got together for dinner, and ended up becoming good friends. "I've never heard of any friendship like ours," Wilt told Frank Deford of *Sports Illustrated*. "I mean, starting off meeting in that game, like *that*, and then ending up friends, which is more important than any game, *ever*."

Kearns often stayed in Wilt's Bel Air home in the eighties, the two men drinking expensive wine, which they both enjoyed, and watching a game on television. Invariably, Wilt and Kearns talked, among other things, about The Game, which had taken place during their college careers. Kearns says both agreed that if the two teams had played ten times, Kansas would have won nine of them.

Little consolation, that. Wilt considered it the bitterest defeat of his basketball life.

Chapter 4

Wilt has always been a very private person, especially in terms of his relationships with women. He didn't talk about his dates, and women weren't trophies to him. And the people he befriended at KU were few and far between—myself, Charlie Tidwell, Bob Billings, and Shannon Bennett. And in certain areas of his life, he kept us at arm's length.

—Maurice King, college teammate and fraternity brother

Once you got to know Wilt, he was very personable. He could keep you in stitches. He was not really a loner, as many people believed. But if he thought you were going to exploit him, he would clam up and not say a word.

—Shannon Bennett, fraternity brother

It was hard for Wilt to put his faith in many people. Being in his position, many little people tried to exploit him. I say little in reference to character, not size. There were always those who enjoyed hanging around to pick up the crumbs that might fall off their 7' cake. No matter where we went to play ball, it seemed that he had a thousand cousins who needed tickets to the game—free tickets, that is. One of Wilt's weaknesses was being too big-hearted. He never turned down any of these requests, and very often he was left holding the bag. You'd expect a 7' person to have an extra big heart, but his was even out of proportion to his size.

—Bob Billings, in a college English paper that profiled his friend

Brother Wilt

There were rumors Wilt would leave Kansas after his sophomore year, but in May 1957, he announced that he would return to school. He was named to the *Look* magazine All-America team in 1957 with, among others, Elgin Baylor of Seattle, later a teammate on the Los Angeles Lakers; Chet Forte, Columbia's fine little guard who gambled himself to destruction as a senior producer for ABC's *Monday Night Football* years later; and Guy Rodgers, Temple University's even finer guard, who would become an NBA teammate of Wilt's and a lifelong friend. Also selected were Frank Howard, who before bashing home runs for the Washington Senators played basketball at Ohio State; Jim Krebs, against whom Wilt battled in the Midwest regional; and Lennie Rosenbluth of North Carolina, who was to have a short and mediocre professional career before moving to Miami, where he became a high school teacher.

Basketball made Wilt rich and famous, but track remained his first love. He had chosen to attend Kansas because, in addition to playing for Phog Allen and the monetary inducements, which other schools allegedly matched or topped, KU had a long tradition of producing excellent track-and-field performers and teams.

Wilt competed as a member of the Kansas track team in the high jump, triple jump (called the hop-step-and-jump at that time), and the shot put. While he did not officially run sprints or distances, throughout his professional career he was usually the fastest man on the basketball team. Add to this his legendary endurance and it is apparent why he was disappointed that the rules of the day, after he became a professional basketball player, prohibited him from pursuing his dream of competing in the decathlon. He certainly had the requisite speed, stamina, and strength to become an Olympian, maybe even a medalist.

Because one can't speculate on what he might have accomplished in track and field, let us examine what he actually did with hardly any time to practice the sport. As a freshman, he jumped 6'4¾", setting a Big Seven Conference freshman indoor record. He placed third in the Big Seven freshman shot-put events, indoor and outdoor. In April 1956—wearing a blue-and-red-plaid cap (which he never removed, even when jumping), a green shirt, and black trunks with an orange stripe (Overbrook's colors)—he competed as an unattached contestant in the prestigious Kansas Relays, tying for second in the high jump (the winner of the event was Charley Dumas, then the world record holder) and placing fourth in the triple jump. In May 1956, he jumped 6'3½" to tie for first in the high jump in the Big Seven outdoor track championship—even though earlier in the month he had missed training, suffering from the effects of inflamed tonsils, trouble with his teeth, and a sore wrist.

In 1957, his sophomore year, Wilt won the conference outdoor high-jump championship by jumping 6'5"; tied for first in the Drake Relays, jumping 6'6½"; and, in the Kansas Relays, again placed second in the high jump, at 6'6", and third in the triple jump.

Bill Mayer, then the managing editor of the *Lawrence Journal-World*, recounted one of Wilt's impressive athletic feats:

> We played Oklahoma in basketball on a Friday night, here in Lawrence, when Oklahoma had one helluva team. And they pounded the living daylights out of Wilt, just beat him to a pulp. I think he got 32 points. This was on a Friday, and the finals of the Big Seven indoor track championship were the next night in Kansas City in the Municipal Auditorium. Wilt goes in, and with a minimum of practice during the week—he had been just fiddling around—he sets a school record and ties for the Big Seven championship, jumping 6'6¾". [The Big Seven Conference became the Big Eight in 1959, and is now the Big Twelve.]

Attending Kansas at the same time as Wilt were Bill Nieder, the silver medalist in the shot put in the 1956 Melbourne Olympics, and Al Oerter, who would become one of only two track contestants to win a gold medal in four consecutive Olympics. (Carl Lewis is the other.) Oerter accomplished his historic feat in the discus, but he was no slouch with the shot put.

One fall night in 1956, John Novotny, later a real estate agent in Lawrence, Kansas, but then a student at KU, observed Wilt Chamberlain, Al Oerter, and Bill Nieder—three of the strongest human beings on the planet—behind Carruth-O'Leary Hall. They were there to determine who could throw a 16-pound shot the farthest, backing their words with their money.

Novotny told the tale to Chuck Woodling, the sports editor of the *Lawrence Journal-World*. Wilt loved to bet, said Novotny, who lived two doors from Wilt in the dormitory:

> There we were on that grassy knoll. Oerter threw first, then Nieder threw one past his. Then it was Wilt's turn. He turned his back, bent over and intertwined his fingers with the shot in his hands and sling-shotted it over his head. It went about two feet farther than Nieder's throw.

No matter that throwing a shot like that in a track-and-field meet is illegal: Wilt won the bet. "I lost my dollar," Novotny said. "I think Wilt must have made about nine bucks that night."

In addition to his basketball teammates, the people at KU with whom Wilt probably spent the most time were the brothers of Kappa Alpha Psi, one of two black fraternities on campus. (The other was Alpha Phi Alpha.) Though not every member of the fraternity was an athlete, just about every accomplished black athlete at KU during the fifties and sixties pledged Kappa Alpha Psi—Maurice King, Wilt, and Bill Bridges (basketball); Charlie Tidwell and Ernie Shelby (track); Curtis McClinton, Homer Floyd, and, in the sixties, the great Gale Sayers (football). This was also a national pattern: Oscar Robertson and Bill Russell, among many other great black athletes, were Kappas at, respectively, the University of Cincinnati and the University of San Francisco.

Though Wilt pledged and was inducted into the fraternity during his sophomore year, he remained in the Carruth-O'Leary dormitory and did not move into the fraternity house until his junior year, 1957–1958. About 22 young black men were Kappa brothers, but only about 15 lived in the fraternity house, which was located right across from the football stadium and was demolished years later when its foundation began to sink. Wilt slept in a specially constructed twin bed, 7'6" long. As in the dormitory, his roommate in the Kappa house was Charlie Tidwell, the gifted athlete who became a five-time national collegiate champion in the 100-yard and 220-yard hurdle competitions, as well as, at one point, the coholder of the world-record in the 100 meters and the world-record holder in the 200-yard and 200-meter outdoor low hurdles. (In later years, Wilt ranked Tidwell, who also played baseball and football, with Bill Sharman and Jim Brown as the three greatest all-around athletes he'd ever seen.) Tragically, the quiet and well-liked Tidwell committed suicide in 1969. He was 32.

There were only 300 to 400 blacks scattered among KU's 8,500 students in the mid-fifties. Even famous black athletes were not invited to join white fraternities or attend white fraternity parties—and, circa 1957, there were none more famous on any campus than Wilt Chamberlain. Though Wilt never restricted himself to being with any one group or kind of person—just the opposite—at that stage in his life he had more in common with some of the black brothers of Kappa Alpha Psi than with anyone else on campus. Bob Billings, his white teammate and friend, was an exception.

"Because of the social situation [for blacks] at Kansas at that time, it was much better for us to get involved in social activities on the campus through the fraternity," said Maurice King, a teammate of Wilt's who was also a fraternity brother.

"He was among guys who could relate well to him. He felt part of the fraternity house and wanted to be part of it," recalled Shannon Bennett, another Kappa to whom Wilt became close.

Bennett was from St. Louis, had graduated from KU, and was attending its law school when Wilt moved into the Kappa house. Wilt was always described by childhood and college friends as mature for his age, and though Bennett was three years older than Wilt, they were more like peers. Bennett believes that he and Wilt also bonded because both of them hailed from big cities. As with any friends, they enjoyed each other's company. "You weren't talking to a dummy when you were talking to Wilt," said Bennett, who retired as a lawyer for the Justice Department in 1993. "He enjoyed his college experience. He'd really let his hair down when he was around the guys in the fraternity house."

Bennett and Wilt, as is the wont of college students away from home and in the process of discovering themselves, talked for hours, often late into the night—in Wilt's case that was easy, for even then Wilt required little sleep, maybe three or fours hours a night. And though they were both aware of the less-than-perfect state of racial relations on the campus—and in the country—they didn't allow race to poison or blight their college experience. Said Bennett:

> I don't think [the racial climate] affected Wilt's attitude toward people or his basketball. He liked other athletes, like Bob Billings. Wilt was not obsessed with race. He had his life, and lived it, with all kinds of people.

There was one theme on which the young Wilt was adamant—finding the right woman to marry. Bennett remembered:

> He told me many, many times he did not want to make the mistake of marrying someone who was only interested in what he could do for her financially. He wanted someone who was in love with him, for being himself.

Sometimes Wilt and Bennett, with or without Dave Harris, another Kappa with whom they were friendly, got in Wilt's car on the spur of the moment and went to Kansas City for barbecue at Gates or to Arthur Bryant's, both considered by connoisseurs, then as now, among the country's best barbecue establishments.

"We had the best of both worlds," Bennett observed. "We were in a lovely college town but only a half hour's drive from Kansas City." And though neither Bennett nor Wilt was much of a drinker, Kansas City had numerous jazz and blues clubs. Bennett, like many others, recalled that Wilt always loved music, and their clubs of choice in Kansas City were two places patronized by a black clientele, the Orchid and the Blue Room, the originals of both long since victims of urban renewal. In his first book, Wilt claimed that the club owners paid him to stop by, figuring his celebrity would bring cachet and fans to the clubs. Although Bennett could not confirm this, he recalled from his home in suburban Maryland that "when the club owners saw Wilt, they'd open the doors wide to welcome him in for free. And because I was with him, I got in free as well."

Most of the black students at KU in the fifties were from Kansas City, which meant that on weekends many of them returned home to party with their friends. That was another reason Wilt and his fraternity buddies ventured to Kansas City (or Topeka).

"We'd get on the Kansas turnpike in Wilt's Oldsmobile," Maurice King remembered. "The speed limit was 80 miles per hour, and we might be doing 100. On a couple of occasions, the highway patrol got behind us. They'd recognize the car and jump off at the next exit. They never stopped us." King also recalled another car incident with Wilt the summer after Wilt's freshman year, when he stayed in Kansas City to work for General Tire Company:

> We were playing basketball around Kansas City. We're driving down the road in that Oldsmobile and, about 60 miles outside of Chicago, it seemed like the bottom fell out of the car. We're sitting on the side of the road trying to figure out what to do when an old gentleman and his wife stopped. They were driving a Hudson, I believe. When Wilt got out of the car, the two old people looked up at him, quickly identified who he was, and said, "We're going to help you." They pushed us all the way into Chicago, 60 miles. When we got to Chicago, that Hudson was smoking worse than Wilt's car.

King, who was president of KU's Kappa chapter in 1956–1957, revealed the circumstances surrounding the first time Wilt ever fouled out of a high school or college basketball game:

> It was the Oklahoma game, at Kansas. Part of the reason Wilt wasn't himself that night was he was going through the fraternity initiation. He had been kept up late for several nights prior to the game. Back in those days, along with pranks, we actually put a paddle on these guys. . . . Wilt was feeling the pain and was not himself. He fouled out the night after going through the final initiation into the fraternity.

Even so, he managed 11 points and Kansas won the game.

King, an all-conference player at Kansas, played one season with Wilt, 1956–1957, his senior and Wilt's sophomore year. King had a brief career in the NBA and afterward became an executive with Hallmark Cards in Kansas City, from which he is now retired. A Kansas native, King introduced his childhood friend Elzie Lewis to Wilt. And Lewis, while visiting Wilt in Philadelphia, met

Wilt's sister Barbara. As much as he liked Wilt, Elzie liked Barbara even more—he married her, and they have been married for more than 40 years.

As for Wilt's dating while at Kansas, King observed:

> You hardly ever saw Wilt with a woman *and* a bunch of guys. If Wilt was pursuing a woman or dating somebody, he would do that alone. He was very private in terms of his relationships with women. He didn't talk about his dates, and women weren't trophies to him.

Friends would make the same observation 20, 30, and even 40 years later: Wilt was a very private person—in spite of one fatuous public boast concerning his love life that made national news. (That infamous remark will be addressed later.)

Another person with memories of the young Wilt is Jesse Milan, the fraternity's adviser and "godfather." Milan, then 29, taught school in the Lawrence public school system—indeed, he was the first black to teach in a desegregated Lawrence school system. He recalled:

> The most outstanding thing to me about Wilt is that whenever we had a function at the fraternity house, Wilt always made sure he was not the focus of attention. He was a member of the group. His mother and father had imparted humility in him. That doesn't just happen. He came to Lawrence as a celebrity, but he didn't use his celebrity to try to get some advantage for himself, including his dealings with women. He used his celebrity to see what he could do to help somebody else.

———

During Wilt's junior year, in December 1957, Kansas (and Wilt) went to Philadelphia for a game with St. Joseph's College. Normally the two teams would not have played each other, being in different conferences and located so far from one another, but this was an opportunity for the hometown fans to see the Philly-born phenom. The game was held at the Palestra, the fabled home of Big Five basketball and the forum in which Wilt, as a scholastic athlete, had led Overbrook to two city titles. Reporting on the game, in which KU defeated St. Joseph's, 66–54, *The Evening Bulletin*'s Jack Ryan wrote that the Kansas coaching staff wasn't helping Wilt to improve his game. And no less a basketball person than Eddie Gottlieb observed of Wilt's game that night, "He doesn't look any better than he did when he played in high school or on the playgrounds."

Also watching the game were two local high school basketball players: Wayne Hightower, who led Overbrook to three city championships, and Al Correll, a 12-letter man in four sports from West Philadelphia High School. Both eventually accepted basketball scholarships to Kansas, where they roomed together. "The reason we went to Kansas was because of Dip," recalled Correll, retired from his executive position with the Tacoma (Washington) Parks Department. "He sent me a letter and said I ought to come out [with Wayne]."

Correll shared his memories of the unforgettable recruiting trip he and Hightower made to Kansas:

> We visited Wilt's room. He had a thesaurus and said that every day he tried to learn a new word. He did that so people wouldn't think of him as a dumb jock. We were there for four days and he took us every-where. We'd go to the Blue Room or the Orchid Room in Kansas City. They used to say he spent more time on the Kansas Turnpike than anyone else.
>
> One night he took us to a club in Topeka, Kansas. He was doing about 110 miles per hour in that Oldsmobile he had. We were scared as hell. He had the top down, and he was flying. It was me and Wayne Hightower. We didn't make a sound. He was flying so fast it was scary. But that's the way he did things. Everything was to the extreme.
>
> There was a big change in Wilt from the gawky, awkward person of 1955 to the man-about-town in 1958. In Philly he was reluctant to do and say too much because he felt ill at ease. It was his hometown— Philly people knew him "when"; people in Kansas knew him "then." All of a sudden he was on a big stage, and he was a quick study. If you talked to him for a minute, he'd watch what you were doing, how you acted, and have it down pat the next day.

The 1957–1958 basketball season was disappointing for Kansas—opponents held the ball and packed the defense in against Wilt. The team had lost three of the starters from the 1956–1957 club—a club that had come within two points of the national championship. Wilt also missed some games because of epididymitis, a urinary infection that had inflamed his testicles. Wilt said in his book that he got the injury after being kneed in the groin during a game. Others on campus thought he had contracted the "clap," which Wilt vehemently denied, but that didn't stop campus wags from referring to him, during his illness, as "the Big Dripper."

He was ill and out of the lineup for the KU–Oklahoma State game, which KU lost in overtime. With Wilt still out, KU lost its second game in a row, this one to Oklahoma, 64–62. Wilt returned, and Kansas resumed its winning ways. In one of those victories, after scoring 35 points against Missouri, he fouled out—only the second time in his high school or collegiate career. (Of course, one of Wilt's oft-mentioned accomplishments as a professional is never having fouled out of a game.)

With Wilt still under the weather, KU lost to intrastate rival Kansas State in double overtime. A month later with a healthy Wilt, KU slaughtered Kansas State, 61–44. Against Colorado, coach Harp tried a slowdown game in which Wilt took only six shots, scoring but six points—the lowest total in his high school or college careers. Kansas won the game, but the coaching tactic was symptomatic of a season that was going wrong.

"It was not fun basketball," Billings recounted. "We were just out there chasing people throwing the basketball back and forth. It was exciting because Wilt was there, but it was not something that would have challenged someone like Wilt."

Teammate Monte Johnson said, "I always wondered—and still wonder—what would have happened if we had employed a full-court press. That's what negates a delaying game. Usually you don't pressure full court because your center can't cover, but Wilt could have covered anyplace. I also wonder how good he would have been had he had a highly motivational coach, like Phog Allen. Dick Harp was a good teacher, but to bring the most out of someone, you have to be a motivator."

Of Harp, Wilt said, "I liked Dick Harp as a person, as a man, and that's more important than anything else. But I don't think he was the coach for us at that particular time. I think Phog Allen could have done the job for us, and we would have won two or three national championships if he had remained coach."

Disappointed and increasingly frustrated with his college basketball experience, at least Wilt kept his sense of humor. After the KU-Missouri game, he displayed his forearm with the clearly visible imprint of two rows of teeth, and joked, "Tell 'em that if they're short of food over here, we'll get them some."

In spite of the difficulties, Wilt averaged 30.1 points, still a KU record for a single-season average. Kansas posted an 18–5 record and ended up second in its conference. (Kansas State was first.) Because, in those years, only the conference champion was invited to the NCAA tournament, Wilt and Kansas were unable to avenge the heartbreaking triple-overtime loss to North Carolina the year before. The man who was supposed to bring three national championships to Kansas was 0 for 2 and counting.

Wilt was again named to the All-America team, whose lineup in 1958 also included Elgin Baylor and Guy Rodgers (both making the team for the second year), and Oscar Robertson (then beginning his fabulous career at Cincinnati). Were there ever four greater players named to a college All-America team? (No disrespect intended to Don Hennon, a 5'8½" guard out of Pittsburgh, who was also on the team that year.)

But Wilt had had his fill of college. He wanted to earn money for himself and his family, so he had decided to leave Kansas. He sold the exclusive rights of his announcement to *Look* magazine for $10,000—this at a time when professional basketball players earned about $9,000 for a season. In the article "Why I Am Quitting College," under his own byline but cowritten by Tim Cohane and I. R. McVay, Wilt criticized the tactics employed against him by opponents—holding the ball and holding him: "The game I was forced to play at KU wasn't basketball." He also wrote that his father, then 57, still worked as a handyman for $60 a week, and his mother, then 56, worked as a domestic. "I want to fix it so they can stop working and enjoy life more." (It would have taken Wilt's hardworking father more than three years to earn what his son did for that one article!)

Wilt had led Kansas to 24–3 and 18–5 records, while averaging 29.3 and 30.1 points per game in the 1957 and 1958 seasons. Decades after his last college game, he was still the holder of a slew of Kansas basketball records: the single-game record for points (52), rebounds (36), field goals (20), and free throws (18); the highest scoring average in a season (30.1); the highest average in a career (29.9); and the highest rebounding averages in a season (18.9) and a career (18.3).

The young Wilt had witnessed and experienced the ugly, violent racism of Dallas in the 1957 NCAA regionals, had been disappointed and heartbroken by the defeat in the NCAA championship, and mistakenly believed he had let the entire state of Kansas down. But he had also expanded his intellectual horizons through exposure to new places and people. Many times over the years he reiterated that he had no regrets about spending three years at Kansas University.

On May 24, 1958, Wilt left Lawrence in his flame-red 1958 Oldsmobile convertible. That car—and Wilt—were later the subject of an NCAA investigation, the result of which, in 1960, was to ban Kansas from participating in NCAA basketball tournaments for two years because a "known representative of the athletic interest of the University put [out] $1,564 for the purchase of the year-old car" for a player. Although the report never named the player, the Associated Press verified that Wilt was the one involved.

Over the next 40 years, Wilt rarely returned to Lawrence. On the few occasions that he did—to visit Bob Billings, or once to have breakfast with Al Correll as a stop on a cross-country drive, or to attend a football homecoming in 1975—he kept a low profile, at least as low as Wilt Chamberlain could. When, at last, he made a very public final return in January 1998, it turned out to be one of the most emotional and satisfying days of his life. But that episode comes later in Wilt's story. Now begins his life as a professional basketball player.

Chapter 5

When you're a kid, a black kid, the Harlem Globetrotters were like heaven. I watched guys like Andy Johnson, Goose Tatum, and Marques Haynes. To play with those guys? Are you kidding? I grew to love those guys and to love playing with them. If it wasn't for the challenge of playing with the best players in the world, I'd probably have never left the Globetrotters.

—Wilt Chamberlain

On the trip to Russia with the Harlem Globetrotters, we were in Lenin Stadium, and they assigned a dressing room to the team. The players were getting dressed for one of their games. They were in rather close quarters. Remember, these were young kids—Wilt was 23. The others were his age. They were like kittens. You bump me, I'll bump you back. And before you know it, two of the guys set on Wilt. They started playfully pushing and shoving him. And finally one of his teammates hit Wilt a little too hard. He took these two guys, twisted each of their shirts, and lifted both of them off the ground. Each of these guys weighed over 200 pounds. It looked like he had two little crackers in his hands. I thought he was going to hit their heads together. It was an amazing demonstration of strength.

—Dr. Stan Lorber, team doctor on the Globetrotters' Russian trip

We were staying in Milan, in the Cavalieri Hotel. The sidewalk was blocked [with fans wanting to see Wilt] and I couldn't get in. Then, Wilt stuck his head out the window and the mob yelled, "Viva Weelt." He loved it.

—Dave Zinkoff, announcer for the Globetrotters' European tour

Viva Weelt, Viva Weelt

In Wilt's day, the National Basketball Association forbade a young man from entering the league until his high school class graduated college—that was spring 1959 in Wilt's case. So after his departure from Kansas University at the end of his junior year, Wilt signed a contract to play with the Harlem Globetrotters. Thus began his most satisfying basketball experience, bar none, and one that he returned to many other summers, even after he entered the NBA.

Since the first decades of the 20th century, there had been local and regional professional basketball leagues, most of them short-lived—the Hudson River League, Interstate League, Metropolitan Basketball League, New England League, Western Pennsylvania Basketball League, Midwest League, to name a half dozen. Teams traveled near and far for games (and a paycheck), with the top players often playing for more than one team (depending on who came up with the money or offered them the most for their services on a particular night). Among the most successful barnstorming troupes of the twenties were the Original Celtics, the Philadelphia SPHAs (pronounced spas) , the New York Renaissance, and the Savoy Big Five—the last two composed entirely of African Americans.

Many basketball games in that era were held in dance halls, and spectators attended the games as much for the opportunity to dance afterward as to see a basketball game. The SPHAs, whose name is an acronym of its former sponsor, the South Philadelphia Hebrew Association, played in the Broadwood, whose floor was, on some occasions, waxed and slippery—ideal for dancing but not for basketball. The New York Renaissance—or "Rens" as the team was called— took its name from Harlem's famous Renaissance Ballroom, while the Savoy Big Five got *its* name from the ballroom in Chicago that sponsored the team.

Abe Saperstein was a young Chicago promoter who bought the Savoy Big Five club and, wishing to associate the all-black team with the most famous black community in the United States, renamed them the Harlem Globetrotters—never mind that they were based in Chicago and the only trotting they did for their first 20 years was throughout the United States. Saperstein, all 5'5" of him, turned out to have a remarkable flair for promotion as well as inexhaustible energy. "He made the bookings, handled the promotion, took care of the travel arrangements, pushed the tickets, counted receipts," the syndicated columnist Red Smith would write years later. For lack of money, Saperstein dressed his players in uniforms that had been made in his father's tailor shop. Not until some time in the thirties did the Globetrotters wear the uniforms with which they are so well identified— white-and-red-striped shorts, blue jerseys with stars on them, and horizontally striped red-white-and-blue high socks. Their first game as Harlem Globetrotters was on January 7, 1927, 48 miles from Chicago in that famous basketball haven of Hinckley, Illinois. They earned a total of $75 for their effort: $20 to Saperstein, $10 to each of the five players, and $5 for expenses. Twenty thousand games, 100 million spectators, and 115 countries later, the Globetrotters probably rank as the best-known and most-loved sports team ever.

While the public associates the Globetrotters with their comic routines—or reams, as the players call them—in their original incarnation, before spicing up the games with comedic antics, the Globetrotters were among the finest basketball players in the world. They were good enough to win the *Chicago Herald American*'s World Professional Tournament in 1940 (the winner of which was generally recognized as the best professional team in the world), and talented enough to defeat the future NBA champions in an exhibition game in 1948. (That championship Minneapolis Lakers team, incidentally, was led by George Mikan, at 6'10" basketball's first overpowering big man who, before Wilt, was considered the greatest center to play the game.) As if the aforementioned doesn't establish the Globetrotters' basketball pedigree, the reader should know that each spring, from 1950 to 1962, the Globetrotters also played a series of coast-to-coast games against a college All-America team. Future professionals like Guy Rodgers, Tom Heinsohn, and Tom Gola, who weren't on the court to play the role of hapless foils, played against the Globetrotters before joining the NBA. These games were legitimate, hard-fought athletic competitions, and most of them were won by the Globetrotters. So the men who wore the Globetrotters uniform were never just basketball clowns—anything but.

Black Americans in the forties and early fifties had few nationally known sporting heroes of their own color to root for. Joe Louis and Sugar Ray Robinson were the most prominent, and, once he broke the color line in baseball, Jackie Robinson made the list. Blacks were barred from the NBA until 1950, and even then it was almost a decade before black players made their presence known. When it came to basketball heroes in the forties and early fifties, blacks had the Globetrotters, who represented, in the words of author Blake Eskin, "a bastion of black athletic excellence." And none of this cultural history was lost on the subject of our story—or his childhood friends: "The Globetrotters were our favorite team," recalled Wilt's boyhood buddy, Marty Hughes, "and we did lots of things like them. That's where we learned how to handle the ball."

When blacks finally were permitted in the NBA—which they have since dominated for many decades—the Globetrotters lost their talent pool. Indeed, the first black to *sign* an NBA contract, Nat "Sweetwater" Clifton, was a Globetrotter alumnus who played for the New York Knickerbockers in the 1950–1951 season. Chuck Cooper was the first black *drafted* by an NBA team—in this case, the Boston Celtics, always in the vanguard in showcasing black talent, to the Celtics' ultimate benefit. To complete the historic trinity of black pioneers in the NBA, Earl Lloyd became the first black to play in an NBA game; that was with the Washington Capitols on October 31, 1950.

Saperstein had known about Wilt for years—who in the basketball community did not? He was also a good friend of Eddie Gottlieb's, as well as a minor shareholder in Gottlieb's team, the Philadelphia Warriors. They were so close that Gottlieb accompanied the Globetrotters after they began traveling to Europe every summer (so did the Warriors announcer, Dave Zinkoff).

As with most of Wilt's athletic milestones, his signing with the Globetrotters in 1958 was a big deal and was duly noted by all the newspapers of the day. There had been reports in the newspapers that Wilt was contemplating an alternative offer to lead a team of college all-stars on a tour of South America, but Wilt opted for the sure money offered by the Globetrotters. Abe Saperstein, businessman par excellence, paid Wilt the then-astronomical figure of $65,000 to sign—five times (or more) the average NBA salary and much more money than anyone had ever dreamed of earning to play professional basketball. (The highest-paid Globetrotter before then had been Goose Tatum at $35,000, but by 1958–1959, he had left the Globetrotters to form his own club. His replacement, by Wilt's time, was Meadowlark Lemon, who said he earned about $14,000 that year.)

Wilt's widely publicized signing ceremony took place at Toots Shor's, the famous bar-restaurant in New York that was a hangout for sporting and entertainment celebrities. Wilt received a $10,000 signing bonus, recalled Vince Miller, Wilt's closest childhood friend, who had driven up from Philadelphia with him for the ballyhooed event. After Wilt changed into the Globetrotter uniform for the publicity photographs, which ran in newspapers around the country, he asked his Philly buddy, Miller, to hold on to his $10,000 in cash because he did not want to leave it in the dressing room. Miller recalled years later that on the ride back to Philadelphia they'd look at the money "just to make sure it was real."

Then Wilt began spending it, buying a car for his dad and a house for his family. That 13-room, semidetached brick home in West Philadelphia at 6205 Cobbs Creek Parkway still stands, if a little worse for wear, and cost Wilt about $15,000. Only his parents, two sisters, and one brother moved in because, by 1958, the older Chamberlain children were living on their own. Wilt occasionally stayed there in subsequent years.

Each summer, beginning in 1950, the Globetrotters toured Western Europe. They usually played one-night stands throughout Germany, Austria, Spain, Portugal, and Belgium; London, Paris, and Italy were worthy of one-week engagements. Fans lapped them up, finding the tall, black Globetrotters exotic and treating them as athletic royalty. Many of the post–World War II Europeans lacked money to travel, and those were the days before television had shrunk the globe. It was among their first exposures to American sports and entertainment, and a reason why the Globetrotters continually were referred to as "Goodwill Ambassadors." But more than anything, the team put on a great show, and fans thronged to see them play.

In the summer of 1958, the Globetrotters were in the midst of a three-and-a-half-month, 15-country tour when they were joined in Milan, Italy, by Wilt. He promptly fell in love with European food, its architecture and historic cities, and the continent's women. Indeed, to read his first book, one might think that all he and the other Globetrotters did on their European tour that summer was chase women. But, of course, they also played basketball, usually against a group of American all-stars who traveled with them, with a few local "all-stars" sometimes thrown into the mix.

Wilt's usual position was center, but not on the Globies, because they had Meadowlark Lemon, "the clown prince of basketball," in the pivot. It was from this position that Lemon, for more than 20 years and more than five thousand games, orchestrated the comedy routines, and it was around him that most of the reams revolved. Wilt played guard and, fancying himself an all-around player, he enjoyed it and took advantage of the opportunity to improve his dribbling and ball-handling skills. Wilt loped down the floor, took part in the Globetrotters' signature "weave" at the foul line, and, at a prearranged signal, broke for the basket, there to receive the ball from a behind-the-back or other razzmatazz pass from Meadowlark Lemon. Wilt then slammed it through the basket to the delight of the crowd.

When he wasn't throwing the ball through the hoop, Wilt sometimes engaged in Globetrotter antics. One particular crowd-pleaser involved Lemon falling to the floor, pretending to be hurt. Wilt would come over, ostensibly to help, but instead, as Lemon gleefully recalled, "Wilt would pick me up like I was a rag doll—I weighed about 210 pounds then—and throw me eight to ten feet in the air and then catch me. People don't realize how strong he was. He was probably the strongest athlete who ever lived."

Wilt, who had never been out of the United States, enjoyed the new experiences and the camaraderie of the Globetrotters. He could, for the first (and last) time in many years, enjoy playing basketball. No one expected him to lead his team to a championship—the goal was to entertain, not to win titles. He wasn't "the show"; he was part of the show, and this appealed to him.

———————

After the European tour was over in mid-September of 1958, the Globetrotters returned home. On October 17, they defeated the Philadelphia SPHAs before 19,137 spectators in Chicago Stadium (at a time when NBA clubs were happy to draw 8,000 to a game). Then on October 18, 1958, Wilt Chamberlain had his debut in the most famous sports arena in the United States—New York's Madison Square Garden. In a benefit for a local charity, the Globetrotters played the Philadelphia SPHAs, and the New York Knickerbockers played a team of college all-stars. In mid-November, Wilt appeared in his hometown, only the second time since high school that the local hero had played in Philadelphia. (The other time was in 1957, when Kansas played St. Joseph's University.) On Christmas Eve in 1958, the Globetrotters returned to

Philadelphia to defeat the Hawaii 50th Staters, the nightcap of a doubleheader that also featured the Philadelphia Warriors against the defending Western Division champions, the St. Louis Hawks. A Philadelphia writer observed that St. Louis' Bob Pettit was only 26 years old, and that Pettit's 23-points-per-game career average was the highest in NBA history. (That it was, but not for very long.) The Globies also came back to Philly in March 1959, a month before Wilt's first contract with Saperstein ended.

If there was a negative to the Globetrotter experience, it was the constant travel, according to Jerry Saperstein, Abe's son, who as a young man joined the team's European tours during school vacations and, once old enough, functioned as a traveling secretary for the club. The Globetrotters played seven nights a week (and an occasional Saturday matinee), about 250 times a year. At that time, more people watched them than watched any other sports team. More popular in the early fifties than any NBA club, they often were scheduled as the first game of a doubleheader, with two NBA teams playing in the nightcap. (All the more reason Abe Saperstein was angry when the new Los Angeles NBA franchise was awarded to Bob Short, the Minneapolis Lakers' owner, rather than to him, as he thought had been promised by the league's owners for services rendered.)

On a typical day the Globetrotters rose before sunrise for a 7:00 A.M. departure, either by plane or, more often, by bus. The guys stumbled onto the bus and slept, kibitzed, or played whist or poker—or a combination thereof—until they arrived at the next destination, some five to six hours later. They usually checked into their hotel around 1:00 or 2:00 in the afternoon. As they had to be at the arena or armory by 5:00 to practice routines for an 8:00 game, they usually had only a few hours in the afternoon to relax, sightsee, play more cards, or seek out a woman for an after-game tryst. But not Wilt. "Every time we showed up in a town in the United States, the media was waiting for him, or the local promoter had lined up commitments at a local college, high school, or hospital—anything that could generate last-minute publicity," Jerry Saperstein recalled. "And Wilt never complained and never failed to be there."

Through his father's ownership of the club and his traveling with them on school vacations and summers, Jerry Saperstein got to know Wilt well. Only three years separated the two young men. They'd sit on the Globetrotters' bus for hours and talk about music, sports, and women. "You couldn't help but be in awe of Wilt as an athlete and a human being," Saperstein recalled from Boca

Raton, Florida, where, after a lifetime in the sports industry, he has retired. "As good as he was on the floor, he was that good off it. I never met an athlete who had those qualities." Forty-two years after first meeting Wilt and his family, Saperstein recalled that "when Wilt died [in October 1999], his sister Barbara called to console me. I told her, 'I'm supposed to be calling you.'"

Wilt was particularly friendly with Globie teammates Bob "Showboat" Hall and Meadowlark Lemon. In one of the last interviews of his life, Wilt said that while others might cite Dr. J or Michael Jordan, *he* considered Lemon the most "sensational, awesome, incredible basketball player" he'd ever seen. Factoring in Wilt's inclination to be contrary, he no doubt appreciated Lemon's considerable basketball talents, most of which, by necessity, were reined in by the nature of his role on the team. Even Globetrotter alumni, who played with the club before or after him, were dear to Wilt, among them Andy Johnson, Woody Sauldsberry, Carl Green, and Connie Hawkins. "I always wondered why the Globetrotter experience was so important to him," Jerry Saperstein said. "Even when he finished an NBA season, and was getting the highest salary in the NBA, he'd hop on a plane and come to Europe and play with the Globetrotters. He loved it—the kibitzing, traveling on the bus. He wasn't treated like a superstar on the bus. He was treated like one of the guys. He could give as well as he took. Showboat [Bob Hall] would always call him 'Whip' or 'Whipper.' They also called him 'the Big Dipper' or 'Dip.' The one thing I never heard the players call him on the bus or in the dressing room was 'Wilt.'"

———————

Wilt's Globetrotter contract ended April 15, 1959. A month later he signed to play with Eddie Gottlieb's Philadelphia Warriors in the NBA. But before beginning his NBA career, he spent part of that July in Moscow, where for the first time the 'Trotters had been approved by the Soviet authorities to play nine basketball games.

This was the height of the Cold War, when there was little contact between Americans and Russians. To the Russians, the tall, black American basketball players were about as familiar as men coming from Mars. It was while strolling outside the Kremlin during the Moscow tour that a car approached some of the Globetrotters, who were sightseeing before that night's game. The car stopped and out stepped the Soviet Union's premier, Nikita Khrushchev, who said, "Ah, basketball." The Associated Press reporter who witnessed the encounter described the scene this way: "The 7' Chamberlain and others nearly as tall made a startling contrast to the chubby, pink premier." The 5'5" Abe Saperstein, whom the reporter characterized as also pink and chubby like the premier, was quoted as saying, "I'm not short. I'm Khrushchev's height."

Meadowlark Lemon recalled there was not much to do at night after their games. There were no restaurants open at that hour, as anyone who visited Moscow in the fifties (and well into the eighties) can attest. If the players weren't playing cards in their hotel rooms, they were sitting around talking. But the young, mischievous Wilt entertained them in a way only he could: when they were walking about in the wee hours of the morning, Wilt would pick up the front end of a small automobile, move it, then do the same to the back end. "He'd 'walk' the car around the corner, and do this with 10 or 15 cars," Lemon recalled from his home in Phoenix, Arizona, where he leads a ministry.

In spite of these pranks, the Russians were so taken with their visitors that after the games they would encircle the court and the 'Trotters would walk around it shaking the well-wishers' hands. The nine-game trip was a great success, except the Russians paid Saperstein in rubles, which couldn't be taken out of the country or converted to dollars or any other worthwhile currency. Saperstein ended up buying lots of caviar and furs with the money. That didn't stop him, however, from adding the countries in Eastern Europe to the Globetrotters' annual summer tour.

It was not just in foreign countries that Wilt, whether with his team or alone, attracted attention. Wherever Wilt went in the United States, he was usually approached by someone with a Philadelphia connection or by people who just wanted to engage him in conversation, if only to tell friends and relatives they had met Wilt. If he were in a good mood, he welcomed the advance. But if, particularly later in his career or life, he had been badgered for his autograph or interrupted at an inappropriate time, he could look right through the person with a chilling indifference—the Philly or Overbrook connection be damned.

George Clayton, a Philadelphia native, is one who experienced the friendlier Wilt. When he was stationed at McConnell Air Force Base in Wichita, Kansas, Clayton ran into Wilt at a bar in early 1959:

It was early in the afternoon. The Globetrotters were in town touring. He was sitting there alone, eating two Cornish hens. Maybe there were two other people in the bar. I told him that I had run track at Bartram [a Philadelphia high school]. He was glad to see someone from home. He was just a helluva nice guy.

Even more memorable was the experience of Carmen Cavalli who, in 1958, was a student at the University of Richmond but had grown up near Wilt in West Philadelphia and had graduated from St. Thomas More High School. One day the Globetrotters and Wilt arrived in Richmond, Virginia, for a game that night. Cavalli used to tell his teammates on the university's basketball and football teams about playing against the great Wilt Chamberlain in scrimmages between the Public and Catholic leagues, and in organized and schoolyard games. "I used to tell the guys I held him to 48 points," Cavalli recalled.

Cavalli's young teammates asked him to see if he could get Wilt to give them free tickets to that night's Globetrotters game. Cavalli told them he'd call Wilt:

Now I'm holding my breath, thinking that Wilt had been to Kansas, was an All-American; I hadn't seen him in a few years. I didn't even know if he'd remember me. I called the city desk of the local newspaper and asked where the Globetrotters were staying. Turned out they were staying at a segregated hotel. This was 1958, so the Civil Rights Movement hadn't started. I called the hotel, and the person at the desk said Mr. Chamberlain wasn't in, "Would I like to leave a message?"

"Yeah," I replied, "Tell him that Carmen from St. Tommy More called. I'm at the University of Richmond if he can call me back."

About an hour and a half later, when I'm in the dormitory, someone calls from downstairs and says, "Carmen, you're wanted on the phone." I thought it was my mom, but it was Wilt. I said, "Dip, how you doing? This is Carmen from St. Tommy More."

"I know who you are," said Wilt. "It's good to hear from you."

"Hey Dippy, I was wondering if you could do me a favor? I'm on the football team here. I have a couple of guys who'd like to come down to the game tonight. Any chance of getting some tickets?"

He said, "How many do you need?"

"Seventeen," I said.

"Seventeen!" Wilt shouted back. Then there was a pause and Wilt said, "You be down there. I'll get you the tickets."

I go down to the box office and 17 tickets are at the Will Call. There's also a note that said, "Please wait after the game. I want to meet your friends."

Sure enough, after the game he comes out, and I introduced him to everybody. Needless to say, I was the king of the campus. To this day, when we have a reunion, that story comes up.

As a footnote, when I left Richmond, I played a couple of years for the Oakland Raiders in the American Football League. Wilt sent a congratulatory note to my old address in West Philadelphia, at 1425 North Peach Street. Eventually my mother got the note, at 45th and Lancaster, where we had moved.

Just as such encounters with Wilt left pleasant and lasting impressions in the minds of those who experienced them, the Globetrotter years always glowed in Wilt's memory. Forty years later, two of his California friends would recall—using almost the exact same words—how "Wilt's eyes [or face] would light up whenever he spoke of his time with the Globetrotters." Wilt never wavered in his assessment of the 'Trotters: "It was my favorite team," he declared time and time again.

Chapter 6

Wilt was not a mean person. You are what you are. He played hard, he played tough. I saw him get into a few confrontations. He was never in the same league as George Mikan. I think George could be very mean. Maybe it would have helped Wilt, but it's hard to see how he could have been better than he was. He was not a vicious person on the floor. He didn't want to hurt anybody.

—Paul Arizin, teammate, named one of the
50 greatest players in the game's history

The best thing that ever happened to the NBA is that God made Wilt a nice man. He could have killed us all with his left hand.

—Jack McMahon, NBA player and coach

Nobody—not Wilt, not Bill Russell, not Michael Jordan, not Babe Ruth— nobody alone ever wins a team game. Only the team can win. You can only win as a team, you can only lose as a team.

—Leonard Koppett, sportswriter and author

Never Before, Never Again

Compared to big league baseball and football, the National Basketball Association that Wilt joined in 1959 was a small-time operation with eight teams—Boston, Philadelphia, Syracuse, and New York in the Eastern Division; St. Louis, Detroit, Minneapolis, and Cincinnati in the West. Eight guys with cigars in a phone booth, one wag dubbed it.

"In the fifties, a lot of guys were military veterans like myself," recalled Alex Hannum. "And to be honest, we drank beer—a lot of beer. If it wasn't for a hot shower and a cold beer, we never would have played pro ball." Roland Lazenby captured the feel of the league's early years when he dedicated his book on the NBA Finals "to all the guys who played when the lights weren't so bright and the money wasn't so good."

Whereas today's NBA teams, with few exceptions, are owned by multimillion-dollar publicly traded corporations (or individual multimillionaires), the teams in the early days of the league were privately owned and barely profitable. Many failed, but all were run by basketball men: Ben Kerner in St. Louis, Walter Brown in Boston, Ned Irish in New York, Fred Zollner in Detroit (whose team took its name from the automobile pistons his company manufactured), Danny Biasone in Syracuse (immortalized in basketball history when, at his suggestion in 1954, the league introduced the 24-second clock), and, in Philadelphia, Eddie Gottlieb. Unlike Brown—who owned Boston Garden, the Celtics, and a professional hockey team—Gottlieb's income was derived solely from his basketball team, which is why he counted the sweat socks as well as the tickets.

Gottlieb grew up in South Philadelphia, the son of Jewish immigrants from Kiev, Ukraine. He attended South Philadelphia High School and had brief careers as a junior high physical education teacher and part owner of a sporting-goods store. Then he helped organize, played for, coached, and, eventually, owned a team that played under the auspices, at one time, of the South Philadelphia Hebrew Association—and was better known to the world of basketball in the twenties and thirties by its acronym, the SPHAs. Originally an amateur team, the SPHAs barnstormed the country and were one of the premier professional basketball teams of their era, winning seven American Basketball League championships (and finishing as runners-up twice) between 1933 and 1946.

Gottlieb eventually bought the controlling ownership of the Philadelphia Warriors in 1952 and, in doing so, became one of the most powerful and imaginative forces in the fledgling National Basketball Association. He was aptly nicknamed "the Mogul" and "Mr. Basketball." Harry Litwack, Temple University's longtime coach and a member of the Naismith Memorial Basketball Hall of Fame, said of his dear friend and fellow Hall enshrinee: "Eddie Gottlieb was about as important to the game of basketball as the basketball." Leonard Koppett, who covered the NBA for the *New York Post* and *The New York Times* and is the author of the basketball history *24 Seconds to Shoot*, wrote: "Gottlieb was the brains of the league. Maurice Podoloff was the first commissioner, but to his dying days, Podoloff never understood basketball. . . . When anyone inside the league or outside had a question, they went to Gotty."

"Eddie was a fabulous guy," recalled Alan Levitt, who became the Warriors' accountant in 1952:

> He was honest and his word was his bond. He was faster with numbers than I was—and I was fast with numbers. When Eddie owned the Warriors, our entire staff was Mike Iannarella, the ticket man; Dave Zinkoff, the announcer, who was part-time; Harvey Pollack [who kept stats and did publicity]; and myself. Can you imagine running a professional basketball team with five people? But we did it and we did it well.

If one approached Gottlieb and asked him how he was doing, his likely response would be, "What's it to you how I'm doin'?" He was a gruff but good-hearted guy, recalled Hank Greenwald, then an NBA announcer but better known for his career with the San Francisco Giants.

Paul Arizin, one of his star players, remembers Gotty's negotiating style:

> You walked into Eddie's office, and he would say, "This is what you did good [last season], this is how many people we drew, and this is what I can afford to pay you. If you don't want it, good luck in getting a job."

Neil Johnston, then one of the league's stars, once asked Eddie for a raise from $6,000 to $15,000. Eddie reached into his pocket and handed Johnston the keys to his office and said, "Here, if I give you that kind of money, you'll own the team."

"When the players came in to negotiate with Gotty, they trembled because he was tough as nails," the accountant Levitt recalled. "However, when it came to Wilt, the sad-eyed 5'7" Gottlieb would say, 'OK, Wilt, what do you want?' Wilt's reply was, 'I'm listening, Gotty.' Wilt was different—he knew his value."

When Wilt was in high school Gottlieb had begun to lay the groundwork that would lead to Wilt playing for the Philadelphia Warriors. That effort paid off when, in May 1959, Wilt signed a one-year contract with the Warriors for a reported $30,000—though with incentives, it was more likely between $40,000 and $50,000. That would make Wilt's salary more than the amount Gottlieb had paid for the Warriors *franchise* seven years earlier ($25,000). Whatever the actual figure, Wilt's salary made him the highest-paid player in the NBA at that time. Bob Cousy, the star guard for the Boston Celtics, had been the highest paid at $25,000, but that's just chump change for today's NBA players, who average approximately $2 million per year; superstars haul in $10 million to $15 million per season. (Even at that, many feel underpaid and underappreciated.) There was one thing his teammates certainly appreciated about Wilt, however: "He helped us all get raises," Arizin recalled, a fact confirmed many times by Gottlieb.

Gottlieb's philosophy was to draft, when possible, Philadelphia-area college stars, whose fans, presumably, would want to see them play as professionals. The 1959–1960 Philadelphia Warriors had one of the league's best scorers in Paul Arizin of Villanova, and one of its top passers in Temple's Guy Rodgers. The other Philadelphians on the 1959–1960 Warriors were Tom Gola, who had a solid professional career but never achieved the greatness of his college years at La Salle College, and Ernie Beck, he of the distinctive white streak in his black hair, who still holds nine records at the University of Pennsylvania—highest points and most rebounds per season among them. Those five men—Paul

Arizin, Guy Rodgers, Tom Gola, Ernie Beck, and Wilt Chamberlain—had all attended local high schools, had all been named to major-media college All-America teams, and had all played for the professional team in the city in which they were born is unique in professional sports.

The remaining squad members of the 1959–1960 Warriors were Woody Sauldsberry and Andy Johnson, both alumni of the Harlem Globetrotters; Joe Ruklick, the opposing center for Northwestern in Wilt's first collegiate game; and Joe Graboski, Vern Hatton, and Guy Sparrow, the only three of whom it could be said Wilt had no prior connection. The coach was Neil Johnston, a former NBA scoring champion and star pivotman, as the center was then called. Johnston and Arizin had led the Warriors to the NBA title in 1956, but Johnston's knees were shot. Feeling sorry for Johnston, who was about to lose his job to Wilt, Gottlieb appointed him coach—another inexperienced rookie coach for Wilt's first year in the NBA, just like his first varsity season at Kansas.

Ernie Beck recalled Wilt's initial season in the league:

> We used to go up to Hershey [Pennsylvania] for training camp, which was always a bitch: two-a-day workouts—morning and afternoon. You ran and ran and ran. We'd always do laps before every practice in the morning and the afternoon. We'd do 10 to 20 laps around the gym, and Wilt used to lap everybody because he had such tremendous stamina. He was a strong, strong man, yet he was a gentle guy. One of the few guys I ever saw him mad at was Clyde Lovellette.
>
> Wilt used to needle me. He'd say, "Well, Ernie, I even considered going to Penn, becoming an Ivy Leaguer." I'd respond, "Thank heaven you never went to Penn, because I would never have had the records I still have."
>
> Wilt went his own way. He was about 10 levels above the rest of us in terms of fame and personality. One thing I admired in Wilt was he never had an ounce of prejudice. I remember Bill Russell was very bitter, but I never saw any of that with Wilt. Wilt had a lot of friends, black and white.

Paul Arizin observed that Wilt wasn't really a rookie in the sense of having the usual uncertainties about making it as a professional. "Wilt had always been—and rightfully so—very conscious of his own ability. He fit in just like a veteran," Arizin maintained. Wilt was always especially fond of, and had great respect for, Arizin, whom he considered one of the greatest players he ever played with. "Wilt was always a very private person," Arizin recalled. "He went his own way: we saw him at practice and we saw him at games. Guy Rodgers, Woody Sauldsberry, and Andy Johnson were his closest friends on the team. We were all friendly with Wilt, but not a close friendship. He had Vince Miller [an Overbrook buddy] and other people from Philly, who were his close friends, just like I had my friends from the neighborhood, and Tommy Gola and Ernie Beck had friends from theirs."

Teammate Beck recollected that:

> Woody Sauldsberry and Andy Johnson used to tease Wilt, telling him he didn't have all the records and he didn't do all the things [he said he had], that he was just making it up. Wilt brought his scrapbook into the locker room—the one showing that he had scored 90 points in a high school game. All the guys were laughing—they knew he had done it.

In the fall of 1959, as a publicity measure, there appeared in *The Evening Bulletin* a picture of Tom Gola and Paul Arizin measuring Wilt, at 7'1⅟₁₆". (The photograph is distressing to behold: from the passive, though pained, expression on Wilt's face, he seems to feel humiliated and violated. It's as if he were a freak to be measured and marveled at, like a rendition of a prehistoric animal one views behind glass-enclosed exhibits in a natural history museum.)

Though Wilt said he was 7'⅟₁₆", the 7'1⅟₁₆" became Wilt's "official height" in club and league publications, although it was often rounded off to 7'1". To this day, friends and teammates swear that he was taller. "He was 7'3½"," his accountant and business adviser, Alan Levitt, said. "I'm convinced he was taller than the listed figure," asserted Norm Drucker, who refereed hundreds of games in which Wilt participated. "When he came out against players who were 6'10", he looked a foot taller than they did." Maurice King, who had played with Wilt at Kansas, concurred: "I imagine Wilt was 7'2" or 7'4" because I've seen him next to other seven-footers." Jack Ramsay, who at one point was Wilt's general manager, told the *Philadelphia Daily News'* Jack Kiser that Wilt was 7'4". And Kiser, who has probably written more articles about Wilt than any writer, used various heights to describe him—from 7'1" to 7'4".

According to no less an authority than Stan Lorber, Wilt's doctor and one of his closest friends for more than 40 years:

> Wilt was exactly 7'1⅟₁₆". We had a special apparatus built by a scientific team at Temple University Hospital to measure him and all subsequent players. He looked so much bigger than he was because his shoulders were so huge [and his waist was narrow]. Luke Jackson was 6'9" and weighed 270 pounds. Wilt made Luke look like nothing.

The writer Arnold Hano recalled that when he spoke to other tall athletes, some 6'9", he thought of them as big, but he classified Wilt in another realm. "You don't raise your eyes to him; you tilt back your head," Hano wrote.

Following the method employed by his one-time coach Alex Hannum, Wilt always said that when it came to measuring a basketball player, the important point to consider is the length of the arms, for, as he pointed out, his friend and competitor, 6'11" Nate Thurmond, was actually "taller" when they stood face-to-face and raised their arms. More to the point, no one filled a space like Wilt: partly due to his height, partly to his massive upper body, and partly to his magnetism. "He was a guy who dominated every arena he was in," wrote George Kiseda, who covered Wilt for many years, beginning at the now defunct *Evening Bulletin*. "By *arena* I mean room, restaurant, conversation, dressing room, hall, or lobby."

Beginning when he was in his teens, Wilt was proud of and took care of his magnificent body, and he loved to show it off. In his later years, when he rarely donned a jacket or tie, he often wore slacks or shorts and a black tank top—the better to flaunt his massive shoulders (and, as often as not, without anything on his feet; if he wore footwear at all, it was usually sandals).

Wilt always had interests outside of basketball. In August 1959, right before the beginning of his first NBA season, he bought a harness racing horse. He claimed that, because of an ulcer, his doctor advised him to find a hobby. Wilt loved horse racing—watching horses, gambling on horses, and owning horses. Alone or with partners, he purchased a number of harness racers, some of them champions. His first was a three-year-old gelding named Spooky Cadet; its colors were black and orange, just the same as Overbrook's. Forty years later, whenever Overbrook alumnus Herb Rogers ran into Wilt, Rogers used to "demand" Wilt give him back all the money he had lost on Spooky Cadet.

In January 1960, Wilt also cut a record, "By the River," which, more than 40 years later, the Kansas University band played at halftime during KU basketball games. Wilt always preferred the other side, "That's Easy to Say." In this, as in so much, Wilt was ahead of his time: today's black basketball superstars—Shaquille O'Neal and Allen Iverson, for example—make the obligatory rap recording.

Taking advantage of the interest generated by Wilt's entrance, the board of governors of the NBA voted to extend the season from 72 to 75 games. And, for the first time, NBC decided to broadcast games on television on both Saturdays and Sundays.

On October 24, 1959, in his debut as an NBA professional in storied Madison Square Garden, Wilt led the Warriors to a 118–109 victory over the New York Knickerbockers. He scored 43 points and had 28 rebounds, was 17 for 27 from the field and 9 for 15 from the foul line, and blocked, according to the news accounts of the game, about a dozen shots. (Blocked shots did not become an official NBA stat until the 1973–1974 season.)

"The fellow's astounding," exclaimed Carl Braun, the Knicks' captain. The Associated Press story of the game said, "All of the fifteen thousand–plus Madison Square Garden viewers were talking about this young man whose nimbleness and agility belie his nickname of 'Stilt.'"

Years later Jumpin' Johnny Green, a 6'5" forward, related this incident to a reporter:

> Early in the first half, Wilt took one of those soft fades, and I skyed and pinned it against the backboard. The crowd went crazy, and Wilt just stared at me. A few minutes later, he took another shot, and I blocked him again and, this time, with the crowd screaming as we ran back up court, he looked down at me and said, "Don't do that again, son."
>
> What did I know? So the next time down, he gets the ball, he jumps about 10 feet in the air and starts to slam dunk it *and* me. Well, being stupid, I didn't listen to him, and I go up with him and get my hand on the underneath part of the ball. Suddenly Wilt just let go. I slapped it away and now I'm really full of myself. That's when he looked down at me and said, "If I had put down that shot, you would have lost your hand at the wrist on the rim. Don't mess with me again."
>
> And I didn't, man. I never did it again.

Fred Mannis, then 22 and a resident of Philadelphia, borrowed his father's new car and drove from Philadelphia to New York with some friends to see Wilt's first game. He, too, remembers Johnny Green blocking Wilt's shot, but he remembered it as happening late in the game, and he recalled it being two finger rolls, not two jump shots. "The place went wild. They think, 'This is how we're gonna guard this guy. We'll have a great jumper [Johnny Green] block his shots.'"

That's not exactly the way things turned out. Later in the season, when the Knicks came to Philadelphia, Mannis was again at the game:

> The game had just started. The Warriors have the ball; it goes in to Wilt. He starts toward the basket and goes up. Johnny Green jumps up and gets his hand on the ball and the ball starts toward the basket. It was all Johnny Green could do to get his hand out of the way or else he would have gone into the basket with the ball.

The Warriors' home opener on October 31, 1959, against the Detroit Pistons, attracted the largest crowd in the teams' history: 9,112 were present to see Wilt lead their Warriors to a 120–112 victory. Wilt had 36 points, 34 rebounds, and nine blocked shots.

In Wilt's third NBA game, against the Syracuse Nationals, he set a club record for rebounds with 40; he also scored 41 points and, as a newspaper account had it, "blocked so many shots the official statistician lost count."

Then came his biggest challenge—the Boston Celtics, reigning NBA champions. Boston had been a strong scoring team in the early fifties but lacked a great rebounder. That changed in 1956, when a young man from Oakland, California, fresh from helping the U.S. Olympic team win a gold medal in the Melbourne Olympics, joined the Celtics. His name was Bill Russell. He signed for $17,000, averaged 19.6 rebounds in his rookie year, and was a demon on defense. He might have led the Celtics to the championship in 1957–1958 but for spraining his ankle in the Finals. (He did lead them to the title for the 1958–1959 season.) Lucky for Russell, his job on the Celtics wasn't to score points: "As a kid," teammate Bob Cousy said, "Bill couldn't hit a bull in the ass."

The sports world was excited about the first meeting of Wilt Chamberlain and Bill Russell. Would the Warriors, now that they had added Wilt, be able to compete with the Celtics? And could Russell stop Wilt? Playing at home, Boston won the initial match between the two teams. Wilt had 30 points and 28 rebounds; Russell, 22 points but 36 rebounds. Jerry Tax, who had been assigned by *Sports Illustrated* to cover the game, believed Russell outplayed Wilt and wrote, "What the duel proved, chiefly, is that against Russell, Chamberlain cannot get away with the few simple offensive moves he has found so effective against lesser men."

Jim Heffernan, the beat writer for *The Evening Bulletin*, called that first meeting a "standoff," but recognized that it was the beginning of a classic duel. Likewise, *The Philadelphia Inquirer* stated in a story that carried no byline that the "historic first meeting between Bill Russell and Wilt Chamberlain was a standoff." Wilt said of Russell, "The guy's terrific." Russell said of Wilt, "He's amazing."

In the second encounter between the two teams and the two great centers, the Warriors prevailed, 123–113. Sportswriter Tax, who thought Russell got the best in the first meeting, had to eat some crow: Wilt had 45 points and 35 rebounds to Russell's 15 points and 13 rebounds. "He owned Russell," declared Heffernan in *The Evening Bulletin*.

Wilt and Russell would play each other 13 times that season. (Not counting the playoffs, today's teams play each other two or three times a season.) The Russell-Chamberlain battles were to become the greatest individual rivalry in basketball history and among the greatest in all of sports.

Sandy Grady, then a columnist for *The Bulletin*, wrote as early as seven games into Wilt's career about opponents banging on Wilt. Eddie Gottlieb fumed: "He's being physically abused by the rest of the league." His coach, Neil Johnston, said: "I've yelled my head off at the officials, and it does no good. They're beating Wilt to pieces, and he's not being protected by the refs."

Teammates wanted him to strike back, but Wilt's response was, "Everybody says to knock the other guy off the court. That's not my way; I just want to play my normal game. But if it keeps going like this, I guess I'll have to punch somebody in the mouth."

Actually, it was Wilt who received the blow to the mouth—from Clyde Lovellette of the St. Louis Hawks, in February 1960. Not incidental to his relationship with Wilt, Lovellette was an All-American at Kansas (as, of course, was Wilt) and had been the school's greatest player *until Wilt came along*. But Lovellette owned something Wilt longed for—Lovellette was a member of a

Kansas team that had won the NCAA title (in 1952). On the night in question, Lovellette had picked up three fouls in the first five minutes of the game, one of them from hitting Wilt in the mouth with an elbow. Wilt's two front teeth were loosened by the blow, and his upper lip was badly cut on the inside.

"I was there when it happened," said Ernie Beck, a Warrior teammate. "Clyde had a dirty streak in him, and hit Wilt with an elbow. It was no accident. Wilt's face was blown up; it was pathetic. Clyde did something that was mean and wrong to do."

The Warriors' next game was in Detroit, and coach Johnston didn't want Wilt to play. Yet, with two hours' sleep, having consumed only liquids the previous 24 hours, and despite the considerable pain from two loosened front teeth (which became infected and soon after had to be pulled), Wilt scored 41 points in the Detroit victory. In only his 56th game, he had set the NBA record for points in a season. Bob Pettit, who held the previous record, needed 72 games to set the record.

Less than two weeks later, in a doubleheader at Madison Square Garden, Philadelphia played Boston. Wilt scored 53 against Russell, prompting Jack Kiser to write in the *Philadelphia Daily News*:

> The great center, charged up as never before, proved conclusively here last night that the NBA top perch is big enough for only one man. Namely Wilt Chamberlain. . . . Some of the record-tying crowd of 18,469 came to boo him. They all stayed to cheer him.

In the middle of the season, legendary player and coach Joe Lapchick said Wilt would be the greatest player ever in a year or two. Many thought he already was. League attendance jumped by five hundred thousand in his first year, and the Philadelphia Warriors enjoyed a 37 percent increase.

On a note of lesser importance, Wilt even tapped in a jump ball—from his foul line, at his team's basket. Eddie Gottlieb said it was the first time he had ever seen anyone tap a ball into the basket on a jump ball.

———

In those years, with the eight-team league, the division leader got a bye and the second- and third-place teams competed in the first round of the playoffs. The winner of that game then played the division leader for the title.

In the 1959–1960 season, Boston was once again the Eastern Division leader. Second-place Philadelphia defeated third-place Syracuse in the semifinals. Then the Warriors met the Celtics for the Eastern Division title and the right to meet the Western titleholder for the NBA championship. Boston won the first game, Philly the second, in which Wilt badly hurt the knuckles on his right hand in an altercation with Boston's Tommy Heinsohn. Boston's coach, Red Auerbach, had ordered Heinsohn to play close to Wilt when Philadelphia shot fouls. Heinsohn said, "We have a play to delay Wilt long enough to allow Russell to get down court for an easy shot."

Fed up with being bumped repeatedly and on purpose by Heinsohn after made foul shots at Philadelphia's end of the court, Wilt pushed Heinsohn. Heinsohn then pushed Wilt in retaliation and quickly started backpedaling to avoid being hit. During the altercation Wilt hurt his shooting hand, whether from a body blow to Heinsohn or when other players jumped in to break up the scuffle, no one was sure. With injured knuckles, Wilt scored only 12 points in the Game 3 loss to Boston.

He had 24 points in Game 4, another Philadelphia defeat. By Game 5, with his hand back to normal, Wilt scored 50 and led Philadelphia to its second victory in the series. But the Warriors still trailed in the series, three to two. In Game 6, at Philadelphia, Boston won in the final seconds on a tip-in by Heinsohn. Boston had won the series and the Eastern Division title and went on to defeat St. Louis for the NBA title, its second in a row. (Then, the NBA Finals were over by the second week of April; today they run well into June.)

Wilt broke eight NBA records his first season, averaging 37.6 points per game. He became the first NBA player to average more than 30 points per game, and his 2,707 points demolished Bob Pettit's record of 2,105, set the previous season. Wilt averaged 27 rebounds per game, still another record, and was named the League's Rookie of the Year *and* the Most Valuable Player. Only one other person, Baltimore's Wes Unseld, has ever duplicated that feat. Not since Babe Ruth had a person so dominated a sport. "The greatest season ever accomplished by a rookie in any professional sport," wrote *The Bulletin*'s Heffernan. "Never before and never again" is how the *Official NBA Encyclopedia* describes Wilt's impact on the league.

Yet in the midst of his stupendous debut season, Wilt told the *Philadelphia Daily News*' Jack Kiser that he might quit after his first year. "I'm grateful for what basketball has done for me," Wilt said in February 1960, "but track is my first love. I'm convinced I can break the world decathlon record, and I want to give it a try. If things work out and I'm given that chance, I may not have time for basketball next season."

Stan Lorber, Wilt's doctor and confidant, confirmed that a track promoter had promised Wilt a great deal of money to tour Europe challenging well-known competitors. Doc Lorber told Wilt he should stick to basketball.

Kiser, who enjoyed Wilt's confidence, speculated about why young Wilt would consider quitting with the basketball world at his feet—this three months before Wilt and the Warriors lost to Boston in his first division final. Kiser wrote: "Wilt is a very proud, intelligent person. He is driven by an intense desire to prove himself a gifted athlete and not just a 7'1" freak who can only push basketballs through the nets." The day after losing to Boston in the Eastern finals, Wilt said, "I quit. I'll never play basketball in the NBA again."

A stunned Eddie Gottlieb, who had been negotiating a new three-year contract with Wilt, said that he wouldn't accept Wilt's announcement as final until "we open next season and he's not playing." Adding substance to reports that the Harlem Globetrotters had offered him $125,000 to play for them the next season, in early April Wilt drove his Cadillac El Dorado convertible to Chicago. After arriving, he played a game with the Harlem Globetrotters and met with their owner, Abe Saperstein, who promptly announced that Wilt would join the Globetrotters six weeks hence in Paris to complete their tour of Europe. Ironically, Saperstein and Gottlieb were close friends and business partners at the time, and Saperstein even owned a small percentage of the Warriors. Inevitably, when Wilt had decided in 1959 to leave the Globetrotters after one year for the Warriors and the NBA, it had strained the Saperstein-Gottlieb relationship. Indeed, that summer of 1960 was the first time in five years Gottlieb did not join the Globetrotters on their European tour.

After his meeting with Saperstein, Wilt continued his drive west for a visit with George L. Brown, then a journalist at the *Denver Post*, a Colorado state senator, and a man who acted as a sounding board for Wilt during that period of time. An old friend from Wilt's Kansas years, Brown had been a member of the famed Tuskegee Airmen fighter pilots in World War II and was the first black state senator and the first black lieutenant governor in Colorado's history. "He was a very sensitive young man," Brown recalled years later. "Wilt had a strong desire to be the world's greatest athlete."

Wilt first gained national attention at Philadelphia's Overbrook High School, where he led his team to the city championships in 1954 and 1955. *Photo courtesy of Temple University Libraries/Urban Archives.*

After the basketball season, there was track—Wilt's first, and most enduring, love. Here he is shown as an 18-year-old Overbrook senior, demonstrating the stride that his track coach said could have made him one of the best runners ever. *Photo courtesy of Temple University Libraries/Urban Archives.*

Wilt loved children and encouraged them to participate in sports, as he's doing with this group in the mid-fifties. The "Kutsher's" T-shirt refers to the resort in the Catskill Mountains where Wilt worked during the summers of 1954 and 1955; his relationship with the Kutsher family would last until his death. *Photo courtesy of Temple University Libraries/Urban Archives.*

Wilt warmed to the easygoing personality of legendary Kansas University basketball coach Phog Allen, who would be forced into retirement at age 70 before Wilt could join the varsity. *Photo courtesy of Temple University Libraries/Urban Archives.*

As a Kansas freshman in the fall of 1955, Wilt's dorm room was outfitted with a specially constructed bed to accommodate his size. *Photo courtesy of Kansas University/Spencer Library Archives.*

Wilt's collegiate interests went well beyond basketball—for a short time, he cohosted Flippin' with the Dipper, a weekly music show broadcast from Topeka, Kansas. *Photo courtesy of Kansas University/Spencer Library Archives.*

The biggest man on campus occasionally walked the halls of KU in his Overbrook High School letter jacket. Wilt never outgrew his attachment to his high school and frequently wore a similar jacket for public appearances later in his life. *Photo courtesy of Kansas University/Spencer Library Archives.*

Wilt's varsity debut in December 1956 was one for the ages: 52 points and 31 rebounds against Northwestern. *Photo courtesy of Kansas University/Spencer Library Archives.*

Wilt pulls down a rebound during a Big Seven Conference game against Kansas State in 1957. Decades after his last college game, he was still the holder of a slew of KU basketball records. *Photo courtesy of AP/Wide World Photos.*

Coach Dick Harp and some members of the 1957 Kansas squad, which would lose to North Carolina in one of the most memorable NCAA championship games. Although Wilt was named the tournament's MVP, he considered the defeat the bitterest of his basketball life. *Photo courtesy of Kansas University/Spencer Library Archives.*

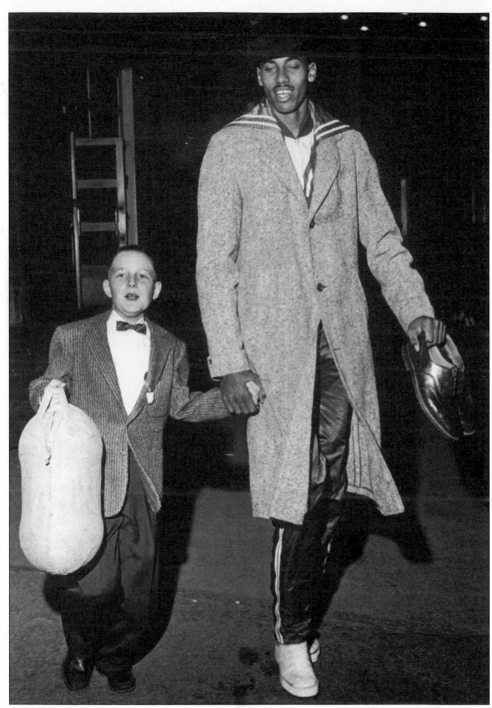

Wilt was friendly with the Edwards family during his three years at Kansas. Here he is with R. A. Edwards after a Christmas tournament game in 1956. *Photo courtesy of Kansas University/Spencer Library Archives.*

By June there were newspaper accounts that Eddie Gottlieb had persuaded Wilt to unretire, but the formal announcement would be delayed until later that summer after Wilt returned from Europe, where he was touring with the Globetrotters. Sure enough, in August 1960, newspapers reported that Wilt had signed a three-year deal with the Warriors for about $65,000 each year, making him, at age 24, one of the highest-paid athletes in professional sports at that time. Actually, Wilt signed three one-year contracts, only the first one of which had his salary written in. "The other two [contracts] were blank," according to Wilt's and Eddie Gottlieb's accountant, Alan Levitt, who also remarked, "That's how much Wilt trusted Ike Richman" (who was both Wilt's and Eddie Gottlieb's lawyer).

Philly fans got used to Dave Zinkoff, the incomparable Warriors' announcer, introducing, "Wilt CHAM-ber-lain" and hearing, during the game, "Dipper Dunk!" In the 1960–1961 season, Wilt's second in the NBA, they heard it often, for Wilt averaged 38.4 points, breaking his own record while setting nine others. He had almost 32 percent of the team's points and grabbed an amazing 36.2 percent of the team's rebounds. By contrast, Bill Russell scored 13.9 percent of the Celtics' points and accounted for 30.4 percent of their rebounds. If Wilt had scored 13.9 percent of *his* team's points, the Warriors would not have been competitive. That, in a nutshell, illustrates the different roles Wilt and Russell fulfilled on their respective teams. And Russell appreciated Wilt's enormous contributions, if some less-informed fans did not. "I can't understand how some people get off criticizing Wilt," Russell said. "What more can they ask him to do?"

Wilt never liked to come out of a game, for he found it difficult to warm up after he had cooled off. "As long as he played 48 minutes at or near full strength, he felt that he was better than any substitute," Gottlieb recalled. It wasn't bad for business, either: "Keep him out there, and give the fans their money's worth" was Gotty's mantra. That the fans got, particularly on the night of November 24, 1960, when, playing against Boston's Russell—the second greatest rebounder who ever played basketball—Wilt grabbed 55 rebounds. Many believe that is the greatest of all Wilt's records.

Yet with all the records and superlative statistics, Wilt and the Warriors failed to make it to the Eastern Division finals that season, having been swept in three games by a strong Syracuse club in the semifinals. The Warriors blew the final game, as they did the series, at the foul line. Boston defeated Syracuse and then St. Louis, the Western champs, for the NBA title. That was three in a row for Boston—and counting.

When Wilt did not respect a coach's ability, he was difficult. And Wilt did not respect Neil Johnston, a once-great player who struggled as a head coach. "My mistake at the time," Gottlieb said years later, "was not getting a strong-handed coach. I tried but I couldn't, so I got Neil Johnston, who had a bad knee and couldn't play anymore. . . . He wasn't ready for the big time."

After the team failed to advance in the 1961 playoffs, Eddie Gottlieb fired Neil Johnston and hired Frank McGuire—the same Frank McGuire whose North Carolina team had upset Kansas in that memorable triple-overtime game of 1957. (And the same Frank McGuire who coached two different college teams to the NCAA finals.) Wilt's state of mind at the time of McGuire's hiring was: "I didn't know the man other than he was the coach who beat me in the most traumatic game I've ever played. And I wasn't so sure I wanted to play for him."

Wilt's doubts must have been laid to rest, as Frank McGuire's widow remembered her husband telling her about the first time, as his coach, he met Wilt:

> Frank had this big, thick book on his desk, and he threw it at Wilt and said, "This is your life."
>
> Wilt took the book, pushed it aside and said, "Coach, only half of this is true."
>
> Frank replied, "Well, if half of that is true, that still makes you a pretty notorious guy."
>
> "Coach," responded Wilt, "I'll never give you any trouble. Don't worry about it."
>
> And, Frank often said, "He never did."

———————

During the summer of 1961, Wilt toured with the Globetrotters again and then spent some time with his parents in the 13-room home he had bought for them in West Philadelphia. He lifted weights in the rec room, the floor of which had been lowered seven inches to accommodate his height, and he often ran in Cobbs Creek Park, which was, literally, across the street from his parents' home.

Wilt and friends also found their way to Atlantic City, only an hour's drive from Philadelphia. There they often visited Club Harlem, a famous nightspot in Atlantic City where Frank Sinatra, Dean Martin, and Sammy Davis Jr., among others, performed. Al Correll, whom Wilt recruited to Kansas, recalled those summer trips:

> Wilt was always a night man. We'd be at the clubs until 4:00 A.M. He'd drive us to our place and we'd say, "See you tomorrow afternoon." And then he might knock on the door, and it's 8:00 in the morning, and say, "Let's play a little bit." So we'd play some basketball. There was something about him with the kind of strength he had that he didn't sleep very much.

Another Philadelphia pastime for Wilt that year was playing in a nighttime summer league with fine local talent. Myron Rosenbaum recalled one such game:

> I normally assigned officials for the games, but this particular night I was reffing the game. I called Wilt for three fouls in the first half. He didn't say a word. I got him for one in the third quarter and one in the fourth. He had five fouls and, still, he didn't say a word to me. After the game he came up to me and said, "What were you trying to Foul me out of the game?"
>
> I said, "I wasn't trying to do anything, Wilt. You committed the fouls, I called them."
>
> He got a big smile on his face, and he put his arm around me and said, "You got a lotta guts, young man."

———————

Summer over, Wilt prepared for his third year in the NBA—and what a memorable season that would turn out to be: talk about "never before and never again."

Chapter 7

The most impressive feat I've ever seen in sports is the season Wilt averaged 50 points a game. When you're averaging 50 points a game and you have a 35-point night, you're 15 points off your average—and 35 points isn't bad. So for Wilt to get 35 points would have been a terrible night for him. I can't believe his feat will ever be equaled by anybody.

—Paul Arizin, teammate during the record-breaking season

A Record for the Ages

I n spite of Wilt's heroics, Boston ran away with the Eastern Division title in 1961–1962. In one game, Wilt scored 62 points, Bill Russell fouled out, and still Boston found a way to prevail. Indeed, the Warriors lost six straight and eight of twelve games to the Celtics that year. With Wilt *averaging* 50 points a game, how could the Warriors lose—to Boston or anyone else? "It isn't a one-man game," said Frank McGuire, the Warriors coach, who was asked the question many times during that season. "We've got our weaknesses. Wilt has simply been superhuman." Those weaknesses, according to McGuire, were the lack of a consistent playmaker and scorer, and a big man to relieve Wilt.

Wilt had his best season at the foul line, shooting 61 percent. "His first year or two, he wasn't that bad [a foul shooter]," Arizin recalled. "He seemed to get worse the longer he played." True, indeed. If one views the few existing films of Wilt shooting foul shots in high school, he had a softer foul shot, with a better arc, than in his pro years. Wilt claimed that his foul shooting deteriorated after he hurt his knees and couldn't bend as easily while shooting free throws. He also wondered if his hands were too big to shoot fouls, but his hands were the same size in high school as in his professional years. By the middle of his career, as even Wilt acknowledged, he was a "psycho case" when it came to shooting fouls. He shot them from the side of the foul line, underhanded, and even several feet behind the line—all to no avail. He was a lousy foul shooter, with a career average of 51 percent. Poking fun at himself, Wilt told the probably apocryphal story of visiting a psychologist to discuss his difficulties on the foul line. By the end of his visits, Wilt said straight-faced, the psychologist could make eight out of ten free throws.

Averaging 10 or more points, rebounds, assists, steals, or blocked shots in any three of those five categories is called a "triple double," and it is an infrequent achievement in basketball. Rare is the game when even one player pulls off a triple double, in Wilt's era or today. Harvey Pollack, first Philadelphia's and then the NBA's maven on statistics, is convinced that Wilt *averaged* a triple double in the 1961–1962 season—for points (50.4), rebounds (25.7), and blocked shots. The problem is that the league did not recognize blocked shots as an official statistic until 1973. "The record book says Elmore Smith holds the record of 17 blocked shots in a single game. I know I kept stats at a game in which Wilt had 25 blocked shots," Pollack recalled. Oscar Robertson remains the only player to ever *officially* average a triple double in a season, one of the more remarkable accomplishments in the game's history. The Big O did it in the 1961–1962 season, in points (30.8), rebounds (12.5), and assists (11.4).

The 1961–1962 season was also the one during which Wilt set the records for most minutes and most complete games played. The NBA season was then 80 games, and Wilt played in *every minute of 79 games* (a record) and missed only the last eight minutes and 33 seconds of one game. Wilt averaged 48.5 minutes per game, even though an NBA game has 48 minutes. The Warriors played seven overtime games that season—five single, one double, and one triple—which explains how Wilt could average more than 48 minutes per game. No one has ever come close to that average and, as most basketball people agree, no one ever will. It is one of the most impressive records for stamina in the history of sports. No fluke that, for eight other seasons Wilt led the league in number of minutes played.

Why did Wilt miss eight minutes and 33 seconds of one game that year? Because he was automatically ejected in the fourth quarter of one game after receiving *two* consecutive technical fouls—the first time he had been ejected from a game in his high school, college, or professional career. The telegram that the referee who ejected him, Norm Drucker, sent to league president Maurice Podoloff tells the story:

> Earl Strom called a technical foul on Wilt Chamberlain for excessive talking. At this point Mr. Strom informed me that Chamberlain made reference to Earl Strom's old mother. Before the foul shot, Chamberlain yelled at Strom that he must be gambling on the game. This was in earshot of all the front-row spectators. I immediately applied another technical and ejected him from the game. He refused to leave immediately, and after a delay of approximately two minutes

and several additional sequences of profane words I applied another technical. He had come back on the court to continue his harangue. At this point he retired to the locker room [three technical fouls were called]. Earl Strom and I recommend a fine of $300.

Given that he was continually grabbed, kneed, held, or otherwise mauled by the opposition, Wilt rarely complained. Longtime NBA referee Mendy Rudolph told a fellow referee, "If Wilt complained about a call, chances are you blew it." (That's ironic because Wilt claimed that a blown call by Rudolph may have cost him and his team a championship.) Those old enough to have seen Wilt play remember his bending down to question a call by Rudolph—Wilt's arms out, his palms up, and, on his face, the exasperated look of a misunderstood man.

"Wilt was never one to complain," recalled Sid Borgia, a top referee from the fifties and sixties. "Only once did he get on me. It was during a timeout, and Wilt yelled, 'If I wasn't black already, I'd be nothing but black and blue.'" Pollack commented that, on more than one occasion, Wilt saved ref Earl Strom from angry fans. Strom said, "When you worked his games, he demanded perfection. If you performed [fairly], he left you alone. If you didn't, he'd let you know."

Norm Drucker was an NBA and ABA ref for 27 years. Now retired, living in southeast Florida, and still trim and natty, Drucker acknowledged:

> Many times, if I made a call, Wilt would say, "Good call," even if it was against him. Playing in the pivot was tough. He got pushed pretty good but never complained, and he never retaliated. He just played basketball. I've seen pro basketball since the inception of the NBA in 1946. Wilt was the greatest center I've seen in professional basketball. The one who is closest is Jabbar.

Drucker made his observations in 2000, before the emergence of Shaquille O'Neal, whom many now consider the center most worthy of comparison to Wilt.

"Wilt liked it most when you had an inside remark," Drucker recalled. "If he tried something [on the court] and it didn't work out, I'd say, 'Why don't you ask Russell? He'll help you out.' Wilt liked that." Asked for his opinion on the relative merits of the two great centers, Drucker replied, "I don't think Russell compared to Wilt if you evaluate them one on one."

When Drucker says that, despite the treatment from opposing centers, Wilt never retaliated, he really means *rarely* retaliated. Drucker should know, for he was a referee in one game when it happened. And, no surprise, it involved Clyde Lovellette, who had busted up Wilt's mouth in 1960 and whom Wilt claimed was the dirtiest player he ever played against. "It was a playoff game in Boston, during the 1963–1964 Finals," Drucker recalled:

> Clyde Lovellette, who was Russell's backup, came in and was pushing Wilt around. Suddenly, they both turned to each other, and Wilt said, "Cut it out," or words to that effect. With that, Clyde put his hands up in a fighting pose. I think Wilt thought Clyde was going to throw a punch, so Wilt hit him right on the jaw. Clyde crumpled to the floor. George Lee, a substitute on the bench, shouted, "Clyde, take the full count. Don't get up."

Tom Meschery, Wilt's teammate, also remembered the fight: "I can tell you, the punch didn't travel more than 10 inches. Clyde fell like a bull in a bullfight."

People mistakenly believe the Lovellette incident occurred during the 1961–1962 season. They assume that Wilt was thrown out of the game and that is why he missed eight minutes and 33 seconds of one game in that season. Not so: the Lovellette "fight" was in 1964.

And then came the game played on March 2, 1962, in Hershey, Pennsylvania. The first, and most lasting, impression of Hershey is the sweet smell of chocolate. The pleasant fragrance permeates the small town in Pennsylvania Dutch country, home of the famous (and still delicious) Hershey Bar. In that unlikely setting, Wilt accomplished one of the greatest individual feats in sports history.

Five games remained in the season. Boston was in first place, familiar territory for them; the Warriors were firmly ensconced in second place—9½ games behind the Celtics. The playoff lineup was not going to be affected by any of the season's remaining games so, in a sense, that night's game between Philadelphia and New York was meaningless. As such, *The Philadelphia Inquirer* didn't bother to send its beat writer to cover it, although *The Evening Bulletin* and the *Philadelphia Daily News* did. Pollack, the Warriors publicity man at the time, filed the story for *The Inquirer*, as he did for the Associated Press and United Press International, as well.

Why would a team from Philadelphia play a "home" game 85 miles from home? Because, in those years, it was common for NBA teams, looking to expand their fan base, to play a few games in other arenas. The Warriors played three home games in Hershey that season, and one game each in Syracuse and Utica, New York.

The game wasn't televised, and there is no film or videotape of it. A fan made an audiotape of the game and, afterward, gave it to Bill Campbell, who called the game for a local Philadelphia radio station. However, the tape did not even record Campbell calling the entire game.

Neither team had played in two days, so each was well rested. One wouldn't have said the Warriors center was well rested, however: he said he had been out all night entertaining a female. Never a good sleeper, Wilt recalled that having been out so late, he decided not to try to grab a couple of hours' sleep because he had to catch an early morning train to Philadelphia. (In some accounts of the day, Wilt says he took an 8:00 A.M. train; in others, it was a 9:00 A.M. train.) Why would he need to catch a train to Philly? Because he lived in New York and *commuted* to Philadelphia for games and practice. "I couldn't sleep on the train because I was scared I'd wake up somewhere in Virginia," Wilt recalled. When he got to Philly, a bus took him and his teammates to Hershey, where they arrived at the Hershey Sports Arena around 5:00—three hours before tip-off. Was it an omen that Wilt had cleaned up on the team card game during the bus trip to Hershey?

With several hours to kill, Wilt visited the pinball and game arcade then located in the Hershey Arena. When he started knocking down clay pigeons and setting records on the pinball machines—in the process winning money from Ike Richman, his and the team's attorney, Wilt later said he "felt" something coming on.

Doubleheaders were common in the NBA in those days. In the preliminary game, the Harlem Globetrotters played against a team composed of football players from the Philadelphia Eagles and the Baltimore Colts. There followed, around 9:30 P.M., the main event—the Warriors versus the lowly New York Knickerbockers, the perennial basement dweller of the Eastern Division. The

Warriors burst out to a 19–3 lead, but the Knicks climbed back into it. Commenting, after the fact, on his 22 first-quarter points, Wilt maintained, "I wasn't thinking about getting a lot of points, but after I made nine straight free throws, I was thinking about a foul-shooting record." Wilt made 10 in a row that night before missing.

At the half, the Warriors led 79–68 and Wilt had 41 points. But no one was taking notice, for there had been many games, particularly that season, when the Big Fella had nearly that many at the half. Indeed, Wilt had scored 67, 65, and 61 points, respectively, in his three previous games.

Paul Arizin, who played in the game, speculated on why Wilt might have wanted to score so many points that one particular night:

> Wilt always liked to wear rubber bands on his wrist. Earlier in the year, when we were playing in the Garden, New York came out with all their players wearing rubber bands on their wrists. That may have annoyed Wilt, being an attempt to embarrass him. Another thing was Darrall Imhoff, the Knicks center, had been an All-American the previous year for California [and had led them to the NCAA title]. Darrall's reputation was as a defensive player, and Wilt especially liked to show defensive players what he could do.

The most likely explanation, however, is that Wilt was hot that night, especially from the free throw line.

Wilt scored 28 in the third quarter, bringing his total to 69. "By then, we all knew I had a great shot at 73 or 78," he said years later, referring to his own single-game records—73 points in regulation, set two months earlier against Chicago, and the 78 points he had scored only three months before, in December 1961, in a triple-overtime loss to the Los Angeles Lakers. It was after the 78-point record output that Frank McGuire predicted Wilt would score 100 points some night. "Actually, I said that in a moment of anger," McGuire said. "The Lakers had been playing three and four men on Wilt that night, and I was mad at the refs for not getting them off his back."

With 10:25 left in the game, Wilt tied his personal mark, and the league mark, of 73 points in regulation time. With 10 minutes left to play, he had 75, after which listeners heard Bill Campbell observe that Wilt's teammates on the Warriors bench were jumping for joy with each field goal he scored.

Wilt took a pass from Guy Rodgers and made a fadeaway jump shot from the foul line for his 79th point—and the new record for points in an NBA game. Almost eight minutes still remained to be played.

After Wilt scored his 84th point, Bill Campbell said to his radio audience, "If you know anybody not listening, call them up. A little history you're sitting in on tonight." Campbell also observed that the fans, hooting and shouting encouragement every time Wilt touched the ball, were thinking about the magic number—100.

Six minutes to play, and Campbell told his radio audience the Knicks were fouling the Warriors in the backcourt to try to prevent the Philadelphians from getting the ball in to Wilt. The Knicks were determined to avoid the embarrassment of giving up 100 points and also began to hold the ball, passing up good shots until the 24-second clock wound down to almost zero.

On a three-on-one break, Al Attles fed Wilt, who stuffed it in for or his 89th point. "Three and a half minutes to go," Bill Campbell reported, "and the kids are hollering, 'We want a hundred.'"

Imhoff, who was trying to guard Wilt, fouled out, to be replaced by Johnny Green. At this point in the game, the Warriors substituted Ted Luckenbill for Tom Meschery, Joe Ruklick for Ed Conlin, and York Larese for Al Attles. Their job was to foul the Knicks so the Warriors could gain possession.

With 2:28 remaining, Wilt scored his 91st and 92nd points on a fadeaway jumper. At the 2:12 mark he had 94 points; the 96th was another of his signature fadeaway jump shots, usually taken 15 to 18 feet from the basket. Larese set up Wilt for a dunk for his 98th point; 1:19 remained. Luckenbill fouled the Knicks' Richie Guerin, who made his free throws.

"The fans were on their feet and screaming," according to *The Bulletin*'s Jim Heffernan, who also wrote an account of the game published 12 days later in *The Sporting News*:

> The players on the Warriors bench squirmed. The tension was at its peak. Wilt intercepted the ensuing throw-in by the Knicks and missed a shot from the foul line. And after the Knicks missed, the Warriors came down court and Wilt moved into the pivot, surrounded by New Yorkers. Ruklick fed the Big Dipper a pass. Wilt missed. He grabbed the rebound and missed again. Luckenbill snared the ball and passed the ball to Ruklick. Joe spotted Wilt under the basket, and lobbed the

ball toward the hoop. Chamberlain grabbed it with both hands and stuffed it through.

One hundred points.

"He made it!" announcer Campbell shouted:

> A Dipper dunk! He made it. The fans are all over the floor. They stop the game. People are running out on the court. One hundred points for Wilt Chamberlain. They stop the game. People are crowding him, pounding him, pounding him. The Warrior players are all over him. Fans are coming out of the stands. Forty-six seconds are left. The most amazing scoring performance of all time. One hundred points by the Big Dipper.

The ball with which Wilt scored the 100 points was given to the Warriors equipment manager, Jeff Millman, who put it in a duffel bag in Wilt's locker, and a different ball was used for the final 46 seconds of play.

For years afterward, many people believed the game never resumed after Wilt scored his 100th point, given the commotion on the floor. Wilt was one of those who mistakenly believed that, saying in many interviews that the game had ended with 46 seconds left to play.

"Wilt sat in my office in 1990, and I played part of the radiocast of the 100-point game for him," Todd Caso, a producer for NBA Entertainment, recalled:

> He had been telling people for decades that it was the only game in NBA history that was never completed. He and I sat there, and he listened to the remaining 46 seconds of the game. He was incredulous that it actually happened. He turned to me and said, "I don't remember a single thing about this." He had been full of the moment and himself, which is understandable, because it is just about the greatest feat in the history of sports. People have told me that after he made the 100th point and, once the crowd was cleared from the floor and the game resumed, he stood at center court. He didn't follow the ball either way. He didn't want to make 101 or 102 points.

The Knicks scored a few more points on foul shots before the game ended, with the Warriors winning, 169–147. Those 316 combined points set an NBA record, since broken. The 169 points the Warriors scored did not break the then single-game mark reached by the Boston Celtics in a 173–139 victory over the Minneapolis Lakers in 1959. Both records were broken in 1986, when the Detroit Pistons beat the Denver Nuggets, 186–184.

By quarters Wilt had 23, 18, 28, and 31 points. Amazingly, he was 36 for 63 from the field and 28 for 32 from the foul line. The rest of the Warriors combined took 52 shots.

He set nine records that night and tied another, among them:

- most points in a game (100)
- most field goals in a game (36)
- most points in a half (59)
- most shots taken (63)
- most points in a quarter (31)
- and, proving God has a sense of humor, most foul shots made (28)

All of the above, save most points in a quarter, still stand.

In the Associated Press story filed after the game, and in dozens of interviews in the ensuing 35 years, Wilt made a point of crediting his teammates for their part in the record. "It would have been impossible to score that many if they hadn't kept feeding me," he said. Wilt acknowledged it was an amazing feat, but he did not consider it his greatest individual record—that was reserved either for the 55 rebounds he grabbed against Russell or for averaging 50.4 points during that 1961–1962 season.

In the locker room after the game, Harvey Pollack snatched a piece of paper and scribbled the number "100" on it. That became the most famous picture from the game and, ironically, it was taken by Paul Vathis of the Associated Press, who was not on assignment but just happened to be there as a spectator with his son. After seeing the famous picture—Wilt holding a piece of paper with the number 100 on it—which has been reproduced thousands of times, Pollack's wife joked that she had never seen him write so clearly.

The Warriors' Al Attles, a tenacious defender never known for his offensive ability, was eight for eight from the field and one for one from the foul line. "Big Fella," he said to Wilt, "I'll have a mental block for the rest of my life. I don't miss a shot and nobody even talks to me."

Guy Rodgers, who had 20 assists in the game, remarked, "There wasn't an easier way in the world to get assists tonight. All I had to do was give the ball to the Dipper."

Not everyone was thrilled that Wilt had hit the century mark. Richie Guerin, an All-Star for the Knicks in those years, while acknowledging Wilt's greatness, remained forever critical of the Warriors for fouling the Knicks so they could get the ball back into Wilt's hands. And Eddie Donovan, the Knicks coach, suggested, "The game became a farce. They would foul us and we would foul them."

Jim Heffernan, who covered the game for *The Bulletin*, eloquently wrote: "Thus, was fulfilled a prophesy made the first time the magnificent 7'1" scoring star of the Warriors played a game in the National Basketball Association three years ago."

The Philadelphia Inquirer and *The Bulletin* acknowledged the phenomenal event with little fanfare. Each had a box announcing Wilt's achievement on its front page (as well as a story in the sports section), while Wilt's 100-point explosion didn't even rank a mention on the front page of the tabloid *Daily News* the next day—there were photos of the actress Tuesday Weld and the astronaut John Glenn and the headline "Girl Nurse, Youth Die in Fiery Crash." Nothing on the cover about the Big Dipper's 100 points.

The Warriors were scheduled to play the Knicks in New York on the Sunday following the Friday night game. Wilt asked for and received permission from Frank McGuire to ride back to New York with Willie Naulls, Johnny Green, and another member of the Knicks, rather than take the bus back to Philadelphia. Wilt said he fell in and out of sleep during much of the ride. When he was awake, however, he said that he heard the Knick players muttering over and over, "Can you believe that SOB scored a hundred points against us?" When they dropped Wilt off at his apartment at 97th Street and Central Park West, he claims to have said to them, "You guys are sure nice to this SOB—letting me score a hundred points, then giving me a ride all the way back to my apartment. Thanks, fellows."

Without question, The Game is historic. Today, many teams in the NBA do not *average* 100 points per game. And no two players on the same team have ever scored 100 points between them.

No film of The Game exists, which Wilt rather liked because that adds to the aura and mystique of the moment. And 100 has a nice ring, much better than 97 or 103.

The Hershey Arena holds approximately 7,200 people. A total of 4,124 attended the game, even though many more thousands claim they were there that eventful night, some of them even telling Wilt they saw him do it at Madison Square Garden. "When people tell me they were at the game," Wilt liked to recall, "I never correct them. I always let them feel like they saw it. I just say, 'So you saw it? Hey, well good. I was there, too.'"

Two days later, the Warriors played the Knicks and, after the game, Darrall Imhoff quipped that he "held" Wilt to 58. The last three games of the season, Wilt had "only" 30, 44, and 34 points. As an Associated Press article stated: "The Warriors' incomparable Wilt Chamberlain has wound up the regular National Basketball Association season with a record 4,029 points [which is still the record], but Wilt said, 'It doesn't mean a thing if we don't win the title.'"

The Warriors met the Celtics, defending world champions, for the Eastern Division title. Bob Cousy, the team leader, believed this was the best of many great Boston clubs.

In the midst of the seven-game series, Frank McGuire was quoted as saying that he could not understand how Wilt could take such a physical beating and not lose his temper. "Wilt has to be the best-natured guy in the world to stand that punishment and not let loose and clout a couple of those guys," McGuire said. "It's an admirable trait. But I couldn't be that way." Wilt's response was, "I don't like it, but I can't let [the harassment from other teams] bother me." Wilt knew teams goaded him, trying to get him to retaliate, which could lead to his being ejected, and that wouldn't help his team. It was a lesson that he said a coach had drummed into his head when he first began playing church-league basketball as a teenager. "You are what you are," to quote his teammate, Paul Arizin. And Wilt wasn't mean.

This was a closely contested Eastern final. Wilt had 33 in the first game, and Russell "held" him to 41 in the second. Each team won three games on its home court. In the fifth game, a fight broke out between the Warriors' Guy Rodgers and the Celtics' Carl Braun. At one point, Wilt started to go after Boston's Sam Jones, who picked up a courtside chair and, like a lion tamer, fended Wilt off for a few seconds, but then Jones dropped the chair and ran away.

The final game, the most contested of all, was held in Boston. Wilt and Russell played one another to a standoff. A controversial moment ensued when referee Mendy Rudolph called Wilt for goaltending on a hook shot by Tom Heinsohn. Coach McGuire and Wilt were certain Wilt had made a legal block, but the call stood, giving Boston a 107–102 lead with 1:24 left in the game. But later Wilt dunked a teammate's missed shot and was fouled by Heinsohn in the process. He sank the foul shot, an example of how he usually made the critical ones. He had tied the score with 16 seconds remaining. Then, with only three seconds to play, Sam Jones, one of the NBA's all-time clutch performers, hit a jump shot, giving Boston a 109–107 victory and the division title.

In the dressing room after the game, McGuire said, "I don't mind getting beaten, but I hate to lose on a lousy decision like that," referring to Rudolph's goaltending call against Wilt. In a 1997 interview with Bob Costas, Wilt said it was his toughest loss as a pro: "We took them to the limit. They were a great basketball team. We were becoming a great basketball team."

During his basketball career, and as long as he lived, some sportswriters and sports fans continued to ask why Wilt's teams could not beat Bill Russell's Boston Celtics. There are at least nine reasons: Bob Cousy, Bill Sharman, Tom Heinsohn, Frank Ramsey, Sam Jones, K. C. Jones, and John Havlicek, all of whom are in the Basketball Hall of Fame—as, of course, is Bill Russell and their coach, Red Auerbach, one of the greatest professional coaches in the history of the game. The Boston teams had everything—excellent defense and rebounding, an outstanding coach, and many great offensive players. The breakdown on points for the 1961–1962 club shows how well distributed the scoring averages were: Heinsohn, 22.1; Russell, 18.9; Sam Jones, 18.4; Ramsey, 15.3; Cousy, 15.7; Sanders, 11.2; K. C. Jones, 9.2; and Jungle Jim Loscutoff, 5.3. (John Havlicek didn't join the Celtics until the 1962–1963 season.) At one point the team had (if one doesn't count Wilt) the best defensive center (Russell), the best defensive forward (Satch Sanders), the best defensive guard (K. C. Jones), and the best sixth man, first Frank Ramsey and then Havlicek, before he became a starter.

The Warrior *team*, while good, was not as good as Boston's *team*. And no one, least of all the Philadelphia media, ever said they were. *The Bulletin*'s Jim Heffernan pointed out in his story before the seventh game that the Warriors had been underdogs in every game of the series and remained so for the final game. That the Warriors came as close as they did to defeating the Celtics is a testament to Wilt. The rest of the team included Paul Arizin, nearing the end of his great career, and Tom Meschery, at the beginning of his solid career; but, as Meschery is the first to admit, one can't compare him to his Boston counterpart, Heinsohn. At the other forward position was Tom Gola, an excellent rebounder and defensive player but never an offensive powerhouse in the pros. The guards were Al Attles, who was a fine defensive player but not much of an offensive threat, and Guy Rodgers, the superb playmaker who could not shoot. The substitutes were Ed Conlin, Ted Luckenbill, York Larese, and Joe Ruklick—not highly esteemed professional basketball players.

Meschery, who had a game-high 32 points in that fateful seventh game in 1962, contended: "The Boston players, man for man, were better players than the Warriors. To go as far as we did was Wilt's doing. We came within two points of the championship."

Boston partisans—whether fans, media, or players—opt for the view that states that Russell had more intensity and desire to win than Wilt. Ergo, Russell's psychological edge was the difference between the clubs. Begging to differ was Leonard Koppett, a longtime reporter of the NBA for, among others, the *New York Post* and *The New York Times*, and the author of 12 books on sports. Not long before his death in 2003, Koppett said, "Nobody ever wins a team game. Only the team can win. Except for one year in Philadelphia and one in Los Angeles, Wilt was never on a team the rest of which was as good as the Boston Celtics. It's that simple."

Newspaper accounts of Wilt's years in the league bear out the sentiment. The beat reporters covering the Eastern Division Finals between the Celtics and the Warriors were not shocked that the Celtics prevailed—they had been favored to win. People in the league, from players to coaches to beat writers to owners, knew why Boston beat Philadelphia. Being called a loser or a selfish player incensed Wilt, as well it should have, because it is just plain false. Bill Russell wasn't better than, *or even as good as*, Wilt Chamberlain. His *team* was better than Wilt's *team*.

Thus, the 1961–1962 season, his third in the league, was bittersweet for Wilt and his teammates, coming so close to dethroning a fabulous Celtics team, three of whose members—Cousy, Russell, and Heinsohn—were selected to the All-Pro team. So, of course, was Wilt; he was named to the first team, Russell to the second. Wilt had one of the greatest years of any athlete in any sport. He established 10 records during the season. Five of them—average points per game (50.4), most points in a season (4,029), most points in a game (100), most games scoring 50 or more points (45), and most minutes played (3,882)—have never been approached (except by Wilt), and probably never will be, much less ever be broken.

Wilt called Frank McGuire "the finest man and the best coach I've ever played for, before or since." (In later years he added Alex Hannum to his short list of favorite coaches.) As to what McGuire thought of Wilt, he liked to tell the following story, which comes from Terry Pluto's *Tall Tales*:

> One night we were on the road. We had lost. It was about two in the morning. I had gotten a terrible hotel room, and I was standing in the hall. Wilt saw me and asked what was wrong. I said, "Look at this room, it's like a shoebox." Wilt grabbed my key, then gave me his key. "I've got a room twice that size at the end of the hall, Coach. It's all yours." Then he shut the door to my old room in my face, the point being that he didn't want any arguments. He wanted me to take his room.

The Philadelphia Warriors were one of the original teams in the Basketball Association of America, from whence evolved the National Basketball Association in 1946–1947. Under Eddie Gottlieb, the Philadelphia franchise had won the NBA championship in 1946–1947 and 1955–1956, and had produced more NBA scoring champions between 1947 and 1962 (nine) than all the other teams in the league combined. (Scoring honors were as follows: three each for Wilt and Neil Johnston, two for Paul Arizin, and one for Jumpin' Joe Fulks.) All the more reason why the world of Philadelphia basketball was shaken in May 1962, when Gottlieb, despite previous denials, sold the Warriors to a group of New York and San Francisco businessmen for $850,000, by far the largest amount ever paid for a professional basketball franchise. (He had paid about $25,000 for the club in 1952, only 10 years earlier.) Gottlieb told Harvey Pollack that had the Warriors won the 1962 championship, he wouldn't have sold. Maybe, but sell he did.

Why would Gottlieb sell a team that had the most dominant player in the game and that had come within a whisker of winning the Eastern title? Because after years of hard work, having all his assets tied to the team, it was an opportunity of a lifetime, at age 62, to cash in. The highest price ever previously paid for an NBA franchise was $250,000 when the Rochester Royals were transferred to Cincinnati in 1957. And here was an offer for $850,000. Besides, attendance was declining in Philadelphia and throughout the league: in Wilt's first season, 1959–1960, the Warriors drew a record 226,412 fans (or 8,086 per game); in 1960–1961, the next year, they drew 196,223 (6,766 per game); and in 1961–1962, when Gotty claimed the team lost money, they finished with a home attendance of 161,795 (5,579 fans per game).

"Unfortunately, the novelty of seeing Wilt stuff the ball in the basket is wearing off," Herb Good wrote in *The Evening Bulletin*. With the Warriors leaving, who moved in? No one. Thus the city with "the richest pro basketball tradition of all," in the words of Leonard Koppett, had no team in the NBA in the 1962–1963 season.

And what of Wilt? Let's take stock. He owned a lavender Bentley, purchased while he was abroad in the summer of 1962, for which he had paid $27,000 and which became one of his favorite cars. (He kept it the rest of his life, some 37 years.) He was a partner in Big Wilt's Small's Paradise, the landmark jazz club and bar in Harlem he had purchased a year earlier. He had bought his parents a 13-room home in West Philadelphia. He owned an apartment house in New York with Carl Green, a Globetrotter teammate, and land in Los Angeles, on which he would build a 42-unit apartment complex, Villa Chamberlain. He had money in mutual funds. He owned a racehorse. He had cut a phonograph record, though no record promoters were suggesting he quit his day job. He owned more basketball records than anyone ever had or will. And now he was leaving Philadelphia for San Francisco—not the worst place in the world for a rich and famous bachelor to find himself at age 25.

Chapter 8

I got very friendly with Wilt during the year I owned the team. What brought us together, even more than my owning the team, was horses. He loved horses and loved to gamble on horses. I owned harness horses at the time, and he kept saying to me, "I've got to own a piece of a horse." I said to him, "I'm buying a horse next week, Pace-A-Breeze. You can own a piece of the horse." And the horse was terrific, winning from off the bat.

A short time later I said, "I'm buying a yearling." He said, "I've got to come in with you." So we bought this yearling. His name was Rivaltime, and Rivaltime turned out to be the second-best harness horse in the world. There was one problem: the greatest harness horse that ever lived, up to that time, came out that year. His name was Bret Hanover.

—Matty Simmons, former owner of the San Francisco Warriors

The Big Fella's Comin'

The principal stockholder of the group to whom Eddie Gottlieb sold the Philadelphia Warriors was Matty Simmons, then an executive with the Diners Club. Eddie Gottlieb, who took a note for the balance of the money owed him, agreed to move to San Francisco for a short time to advise the new owners, who had no experience in owning or running a professional sports team. Wanting some local ownership on the board of directors, Simmons took in a group of San Francisco businessmen as minority stockholders. One of them was Franklin Mieuli, a radio and television producer for games involving the San Francisco Giants and 49ers.

The New York and San Francisco investors, primarily Simmons and his partner Len Mogul, reasoned that moving the Philadelphia franchise to San Francisco was a can't-miss proposition—after all, Bob Short had recently moved the Minneapolis team to Los Angeles and *his* franchise was thriving. And Gottlieb assured the new owners that, with Wilt on the team, the playoffs were just about guaranteed. Everyone would make money, and Gottlieb, after nursing the newborn franchise to health and receiving the balance of his note, would return to Philadelphia—where, rumor had it, his fellow owners on the NBA board would award him a new franchise.

Besides an ownership that knew nothing about owning a professional basketball team, another problem for the new franchise was the arena in which the team played its home games—the Cow Palace. "We had to sandwich our games between the Grand National [Rodeo] events, and the place smelled like a barn," recalled Mieuli.

San Francisco never had a tradition of professional basketball, nor was it then—and some might argue not even now—a basketball city. Its most significant connection to basketball history probably was the University of San

Francisco's Dons, winners of two collegiate titles in the mid-fifties. The stars on that team were native sons K. C. Jones and Bill Russell, who, by the sixties, were plying their considerable talents for the Boston Celtics. If the hearts of the small number of local basketball fans belonged to any basketball player or team, it was probably to Russell and the Celtics. Into this basketball Sahara stepped Wilt Chamberlain, identified almost solely with Philadelphia at that point in his professional basketball career.

There was a parallel in baseball, a sport in which San Francisco had a rich tradition. San Francisco never really gave its heart to Willie Mays, who had risen to baseball stardom in New York. In contrast, San Franciscans embraced Orlando Cepeda and Willie McCovey, who began their great careers there. Joe DiMaggio, revered in San Francisco, is the exception to the rule. But he was born there, started his fabled career on its baseball fields, and, when he retired after a legendary career with the New York Yankees, returned there to live. San Francisco's basketball fans remained indifferent to Wilt, although they would eventually shower their affection on two other basketball players: Nate Thurmond and Rick Barry.

Though the city didn't take to him, Wilt loved San Francisco for all the reasons so many have fallen under the city's spell—its beauty and charm; its nonconformist, live-and-let-live Bohemian traditions; its sunny days, magnificent views, and great restaurants. With the possible exception of New York, no city in the sixties was more accepting of interracial dating, an important selling point to Wilt. Such relative tolerance for a black man dating white women is one of the reasons Wilt chose to live in New York while playing in Philadelphia. Likewise, it's why he eventually settled on the West Coast, according to one of his dearest friends, as well as his personal physician, Dr. Stan Lorber.

As liberal as San Francisco might have been, Wilt soon learned that, in the early sixties, not everyone in the city was broad-minded. When he decided he enjoyed living in San Francisco so much that he wanted to buy a home rather than to continue renting an apartment, Harry Cox, an African-American real estate agent, assisted him. Cox found a split-level home with an ocean view selling for $39,950. (Today that home would sell for $1 million.) "We put an offer on a house at the full asking price," Cox recalled, "but the offer was rejected when the seller found out Wilt was the buyer. They didn't want to sell to an African American." The owner of the property was quoted in *The San Francisco Chronicle* as saying, "I feel interracial mixing of property devalues property." The ensuing bad publicity forced the owner to change his mind and, eventually, he said Wilt could buy the house. But by that time, through Cox's efforts, Wilt had found a lovely home in the Twin Peaks section of San Francisco.

Other than inexperienced owners, indifferent fans, and an inadequate arena, how was the new San Francisco team? Not without its problems. The team had its third coach in as many years: Bob Feerick, a former NBA player who had been the athletic director at Santa Barbara College. He had never coached in the NBA, nor would he again after his maiden effort. Paul Arizin, a key member of the Philadelphia team, had no desire to leave his family, friends, and hometown, so he remained in the East, where he accepted a job with IBM and, on weekends, played basketball, still at an exceptionally high level, in the Eastern League. Tom Gola, another native Philadelphian, reluctantly made the move out West, but not long into the season, as requested, he was traded back East to the lowly New York Knickerbockers. After his professional career, Gola returned to Philadelphia, where he has enjoyed a successful career in politics and business.

If one ever needed proof that basketball is a team game, look to the 1962–1963 San Francisco Warriors. They had the world's best player but were still dismal, losing 49 out of 80 games. In their division, only the new expansion club, the hapless Chicago Zephyrs (in their second season), who were as bad as their name, played more ineptly. San Francisco failed to make the playoffs and lost money to boot—so much for sure things.

For the first and *only* time, Wilt played on a team with a losing record; it was, as well, the only time that a Wilt Chamberlain–led professional team failed to make the playoffs. One could not fault Wilt for the team's pathetic record: he led the league in scoring once again, averaging 44.8, while making 53 percent of his shots. His teammates made 40 percent of theirs. (If an NBA player averaged 44 points a game today, there would be a movement to put his face on the dollar bill.) Attendance at the Cow Palace was atrocious, with one game drawing only 1,669 dedicated fans.

After just one season, Simmons and the other New York investors wanted out. They sold their shares to Mieuli, who became the team's principal owner. Mieuli knew little about running a basketball team, so Gottlieb agreed to stay on as general manager. Gottlieb wisely hired Alex Hannum to coach the team for the 1963–1964 season, and the two of them—no better basketball minds in the land—drafted a talented center from Bowling Green by the name of Nate Thurmond.

Thurmond was intimidating at 6'11". He averaged 17 points and 17 rebounds in college, earning All-America honors as a senior in 1963. He well recalled the first time he met Wilt:

> We were at a hotel in San Jose, where we stayed for training camp. [Wilt] was like a day late. We were sitting in Al Attles' room and Al kept on saying, "The Big Fella's comin'." Through my college career, everybody had called *me* the Big Fella.
>
> Late one night we heard this big thud on the door, and Al said, "That's the Big Fella." That particular year, which was 1963, Wilt came into camp at 290 pounds. When he opened the door, he just filled the space. I said to myself, "*This* is the Big Fella."

Thurmond reminisced about Wilt at Big Nate's, the barbecue restaurant he owns in San Francisco: "Wilt was very nice to me in my rookie year. He took me down to the Monterey Jazz Festival in his purple Bentley, just the two of us. And he introduced me to Kim Novak. He wasn't into class structure. If he liked you, he liked you."

Unfortunately, even when he liked you, Wilt could hurt your feelings because he considered his willingness to tell the truth—as he perceived it—one of his better traits. For instance, Wilt's best friends on the team were Guy Rodgers and Al Attles. Yet one time Wilt publicly described Rodgers, his Philadelphia buddy, as "a light-skinned guy who wished he were white."

Al Attles, who, after his playing career became a coach and general manager with the Warriors franchise, recalled going to all-night movies with Wilt and Rodgers and getting room service in their hotels after away games. Most nights they ate in Wilt's room because he had a suite, but they would take turns paying for the food.

Also on the team, and a man with whom Wilt occasionally hung out, was Wayne Hightower, who followed in Wilt's basketball footsteps. Not only was Hightower an Overbrook alumnus, but he also attended Kansas, where he had a successful, albeit abbreviated, college career. During his senior year, when he was prohibited by the rules of the day from playing in the NBA, Hightower played for the Real Madrid professional team in Spain, following which he was chosen fifth overall in the 1962 draft by the Philadelphia Warriors and made the move to the West Coast. Unfortunately, comparisons between Hightower, who was a thin 6'8", and Wilt were inevitable. And, equally unfortunate, Hightower always came out on the short end. After all, who could be compared to Wilt Chamberlain?

There were many nights when Wilt went out, more often alone but sometimes with a teammate. He also had friends and associates in every NBA city and usually spent more time with them than with his teammates. In addition, as Thurmond pointed out, "It's no secret that Wilt liked girls, and I was a bachelor, too. If he and I were hanging out, we'd get something to eat and then go to a club. Now, I wouldn't hang out with Wilt every night, because Wilt had his private side." He also had his share of hookers, according to Simmons.

Wilt had prodigious appetites—in all areas.

"I saw him eat a whole apple pie and drink two gallons of milk once," teammate Tom Meschery recalled. He'd drink a half gallon of milk or 7 Up (his favorite soft drink) at halftime and probably a gallon after the game, teammate Matty Guokas remarked. Wilt said that his caloric intake was 6,000 a day, and that he lost 8 to 12 pounds during a game.

Unlike today's teams, which travel on charter planes, the teams of Wilt's era traveled on commercial airlines. Tall as they were, the players then *did not* sit in first class because the teams didn't generate enough money in those years to support such extravagance. (Back then players carried their bags from the airport to a taxi or team bus and were responsible for cleaning their own uniforms, right down to washing and hanging their athletic supporters in the bathroom to dry. Suffice it to say, today's NBA players don't schlep their bags around airports or wash their jockstraps.) Wilt and some of the veterans did have one perk on plane flights—they were allowed to take the bulkhead seats, where there is more leg room.

During the San Francisco period of his life, Wilt enjoyed the friendship of many different types of people. One of these diverse relationships was with the Iranian Jim Bryant, a good friend with whom Wilt liked to play Persian checkers. "Jim followed Wilt around like a puppy," recalled Nancy King, the wife of

Bill King, who announced the Warriors games (and later became the voice of Oakland's Athletics and Raiders).

After Harry Cox helped Wilt buy a house, their business relationship developed into friendship, and Wilt sometimes visited him in Lake Tahoe, where the Cox family and four other black professional families shared ownership of a vacation home. At the time, the Cox family included three boys, the oldest of whom was around fourteen, the second, nine. "Wilt enjoyed playing H-O-R-S-E with them," Cox recollected. "He didn't like to lose at anything, even against my sons. We'd play multiple solitaire, and Wilt would cheat. We used to say, 'Wilt, you can't do that.' He did not like to lose. That was the basic characteristic of Wilt."

These were also the years when Wilt was seeing Kim Novak, who lived in picturesque Carmel, south of San Francisco, and was one of the most beautiful women in the world. Recently, Tiger Woods (now engaged), part African American and part Asian, dated and lived with beautiful blondes and it was a nonstory; it is the same for other black celebrities, which speaks well for the progress in racial matters. But interracial dating, particularly among basketball stars and other celebrities, was not to be flaunted in the sixties—even in as accepting a place as San Francisco. Wilt and Novak kept their relationship low-key, though everyone associated with the team, and many sportswriters as well, were aware of it. Wilt told Cox and others that Novak was the love of his life, but, over the years, he told a number of other friends that other women were the loves of his life.

———

The Warriors' new coach for the 1963–1964 season was Alex Hannum, a 6'7", 225-pound journeyman NBA player. Hannum was a former army sergeant, earning the affectionate and respectful title of "Sarge" among his players. He was tough but fair, and he knew how to coach. He emphasized defense and convinced Wilt that he should shoot less, pass more, and play harder on the defensive end to offset his lower point production. "Alex had a strong personality," Thurmond recalled of his and Wilt's coach: "He was able to stand up to Wilt and make that work for everybody. We all knew Wilt was the man. Alex treated him like 'You're the man, but . . .'"

Hank Greenwald was then the color commentator for the team on radio and TV and one of Hannum's closest friends. (Their relationship went back to the fifties when both worked in Syracuse.) Greenwald said, "I think Alex understood what worked with players. And in Wilt's case, he knew how to relate to him. He knew Wilt wasn't a guy to whom you said, 'Look, this is what you're going to do.' He had to work around Wilt. Alex knew that the comparisons with Russell, where Wilt often didn't come out the best, bugged Wilt. So if Alex was trying to make a point with Wilt to improve an aspect of his game, he'd say, 'You know, as good as Russell is, he'd be a lot better if he'd just do this or that.' And that would get Wilt thinking, and he would start to think it was his idea how to improve his game."

Tom Meschery was a teammate of Wilt's under three coaches: Frank McGuire (in 1961–1962), Feerick (in 1962–1963), and Hannum (1963–1964). "Wilt could tell when a coach really knew the game or was just so-so at it," suggested Meschery. "I'm not saying Bob Feerick or Butch van Breda Kolff [one of Wilt's later coaches] were bad coaches, but they were not great coaches. Frank McGuire was a great motivator, and Alex Hannum was the same way—these were people who had the instincts of a good teacher." And, along with Bill Sharman (who coached him later), Hannum got the most out of Wilt, to the team's, Wilt's, and the coach's benefit.

With essentially the same starters, and the addition of Thurmond, the 1963–1964 San Francisco Warriors, a team that had failed to reach the playoffs the season before, won the Western Division title. They lost in five games in the best-of-seven championship series to a better team—the Boston Celtics. Much of the credit for their success must go to Hannum, who was one of the game's greatest coaches, leading three different teams to titles (though not the San Francisco Warriors) and ultimately being enshrined in the Hall of Fame.

In what was almost an annual ritual, come the summer, after his team lost to Boston one more time, Wilt mulled retiring from basketball. He had thought about it after the 1960 season, when he contemplated touring Europe as a professional decathlete. He would consider it again in the summer of 1964 at Kutsher's Country Club in the Catskills, where he pondered a career in professional football. Also at Kutsher's for the annual clinic for basketball and football coaches was Hank Stram, then coach of the Kansas City team in the American Football League (later to be merged with the NFL). Wilt worked out and caught passes as Stram watched. Duly impressed, Stram said of Wilt, "He would be the greatest flanker in football." Wilt told Tom Gray, the president of the Warriors, he was seriously attracted to a football career. But however serious he was, Wilt decided to stick with basketball.

In the summer of 1964, Wilt also spent some time in New York City with Tom Hoover, an NBA player; Carl Green, an ex-Globetrotter with whom he owned an apartment building in New York; and Cal Ramsey, a New York City ballplayer who played for three NBA teams. Wilt had his Harlem nightclub, Big Wilt's Small's Paradise, where the gang spent many a night, and in front of which Wilt parked his Bentley—no mistaking when "the man" was in. He also sponsored a team in New York's famed Rucker Tournament, which had been in existence since 1946 and served as a catalyst to raise funds for athletic scholarships for disadvantaged Harlem youngsters. Because of contract prohibitions, most current professional basketball players can no longer actively participate in the tournament, now known as the Entertainers Basketball Classic. Back in the sixties, Big Wilt's Small's Paradise team featured (in addition to Wilt) Cal Ramsey, Tom "Satch" Sanders, Russ Cunningham, Al Barden (who had played with Ramsey at NYU), and Freddie Crawford. Their toughest opponent was a team from Brooklyn featuring Walt Bellamy, Connie Hawkins (whose game Wilt always admired and with whom Wilt developed a friendship), Eddie Simmons, and Jackie Jackson, a legendary schoolyard leaper. A very tall, skinny, talented 17-year-old schoolboy from New York's Power Memorial Academy watched these games, waiting for the day when he would be permitted to play in the Rucker Tournament (high schoolers were prohibited). The young man had lots of basketball talent and would become the most written-about high school player since Wilt. That young man was Lew Alcindor, later to change his name to Kareem Abdul-Jabbar.

After the games, Ramsey recalled that members of the group went to Wilt's Harlem nightclub. There they would talk and party until it closed, sometime around 4:00 A.M. From the nightclub, Wilt and his buddies often ended up in Wilt's luxurious two-bedroom apartment that overlooked Central Park West. There, with Wilt providing the food (usually cold cuts), they joked, listened to Wilt's extensive jazz collection, and played cards the remainder of the night.

On some occasions Wilt and his buddies allowed the young Alcindor to tag along. Wilt liked the teenager, even giving Alcindor some of his custom-made clothes. The youth idolized the older star, his flashy cars, and his great bachelor pad complete with a Danish maid, on whom the teenager developed a crush. Of Wilt and those times, Jabbar later wrote, "I stood in awe of him." Years later

Wilt and Jabbar took to publicly criticizing one another, but in the sixties they were mentor and student.

"One night in Wilt's apartment we were playing hearts," Cal Ramsey recalled. "It was me, Wilt, Tom Hoover, Carl Green, Bootsie Dunn, and Kareem. The loser had to drink a quart of water. Kareem lost three straight games and drank three quarts of water. He couldn't drink any more. The rules were 'drink it or wear it.' So we held Kareem down and poured the quart on him."

———

Wilt always took very good care of his body, long before athletes and the general public discovered it was the fashionable and sensible thing to do. In later years he fasted one day a month to clean out his system, and he always kept in great aerobic shape. Stan Lorber, his doctor of more than 30 years, recalled that the first time they met, Wilt—who was 18 years old—analyzed what they had just eaten for lunch and pointed out the nutritional components of the meal.

Wilt also enjoyed drinking, though usually in moderation. But one time in San Francisco, he went on, in the words of Dr. Lorber, a "toot" that left him hospitalized for chronic stomach pains right before the start of the basketball season in 1964. Three weeks of tests failed to establish what ailed him. Based on what looked to them like abnormal electrocardiograms, his San Francisco doctors concluded that Wilt had had a heart attack. Wilt is quoted in a newspaper account at the time as acknowledging that he did have a "heart irregularity," but that it had never given him any trouble.

Perplexed about Wilt's health, the San Francisco doctors turned to Lorber, Wilt's long-standing Philadelphia physician. "Wilt's electrocardiogram in perfect health looked like he had a coronary occlusion," Dr. Lorber, now retired, explained in his lovely southeast Florida home. "He had a very slow pulse rate, usually well below 60, closer to 50. The only way you could make his electrocardiogram look normal was with significant exercise. When he had his first study done, we had him run up and down a [eight-story] building six times to get his pulse above 60 because he was in such good shape. When his pulse got up to around 80, his electrocardiogram looked perfectly normal. We wired Wilt's old electrocardiograms to his doctor in San Francisco, and he wired back the one they had [recently] taken. They were identical."

Dr. Lorber told Wilt to get on a plane and come to Philadelphia for further examination, saying, "I think I know what you have." "What if I should die on the way?" Wilt asked his Philly doctor. "You'll ruin my reputation," Dr. Lorber replied.

Wilt checked into Philadelphia's Temple University Hospital and Dr. Lorber diagnosed Wilt's ailment—as the doctor had suspected—as pancreatitis, not a heart attack. "But that was the last time Wilt ever drank hard whiskey," Dr. Lorber said. "He would drink champagne and wine, but rarely to excess. He'd have it with his meals."

Wilt lost weight during the ordeal, though Dr. Lorber says it was nothing like the 50 pounds reported by newspapers at the time—more like 10 to 15. But Wilt missed the beginning of the 1964–1965 season. Not surprisingly, the Warriors got off to a poor start without their star, losing 16 of their first 21 games. When Wilt rejoined the club, he was out of shape.

"We heard rumors that he had a bad heart, a bad pancreas," Hannum said. "When he rejoined us, we were losing games, and we lost one at home, and he was down in the dumps. The next day I was going to go out on my boat, which I used for waterskiing. I was going with another guy, and I called Wilt and asked him to join us. I picked him up, and we had the best day you could imagine out on the water. We had lunch, water-skied—had a nice, relaxed day. That cemented our relationship. About a month later, Wilt said he was taking us to dinner. He took us to the best restaurant in town, to the best club. He said he was paying us back for picking him up when he was down. That tells you about the man. Up until then I had really only known the player."

Even though they had gone to the NBA championship the previous year, the Warriors had lost money, according to Mieuli, the owner. Of even more importance, the Warriors could not afford to keep Wilt, whose salary was more than that of the rest of the team combined. Besides, Wilt's return forced Thurmond, a natural center, to play forward, retarding his development. In addition, in spite of Dr. Lorber's diagnosis of pancreatitis, the San Francisco doctors stuck by their opinion—Wilt had heart trouble. Years later Mieuli recalled that the team doctor insisted that no insurance company would cover Wilt because of his bad heart. The doctor said, "I'll bet my job on it—he won't last a year."

The Philadelphia coach, Dolph Schayes, remembered what happened next:

> I didn't go to the All-Star Game. I was sleeping at my home in Syracuse. It was 3:00 A.M., and I got a phone call. It was Larry Merchant from the *Philadelphia Daily News*. "What the hell are you

waking me up for?" I yelled. He said, "How would you like to know you have the greatest center in the world to coach?"

So it happened that during the All-Star break, in January 1965, Franklin Mieuli traded Wilt for three unaccomplished players and a reported $150,000. It's the only time in NBA history that the league's leading scorer was traded during the season. The players San Francisco got for Wilt were Lee Shaffer (who because of an illness never showed up), Paul Neumann, and Connie Dierking.

"I was young and dumb. I didn't get enough for him," Mieuli admitted years later in an interview with the author.

As for the doctor who told Mieuli that Wilt wouldn't last a year—he was off by 35 years.

And where was Wilt headed? He was going home.

Chapter 9

A week after the Boston loss, Wilt was at Liberty Bell Park, right outside Philadelphia, where his horse, Rivaltime, was running. I was at the racetrack that Saturday night. One of those big, white limos pulled up and Wilt got out. He was alone. I was approaching the limo just as he got out. As he left the car, I walked up to him and said, "Wilt, my name is Jerry." He started talking to me like I was one of the guys from the neighborhood. We chatted primarily about basketball. We must have talked for 10 minutes. At that moment I adopted him as my idol, because he was such a nice man, such a terrific guy. It was no big thing. But it was a big thing in my life.

—Jerry Malkin, Philadelphia resident

I'm Tired of Being a Villain

In the spring of 1963, after a year's absence, professional basketball returned to Philadelphia with the purchase of the struggling Syracuse franchise by Isaac "Ike" Richman, who was Eddie Gottlieb's lawyer, and Irv Kosloff, their mutual friend and a successful Philadelphia businessman. The price: $500,000—or $350,000 less than what Eddie Gottlieb received when he sold the Warriors. Richman, who assumed primary responsibility for running the team and was the public face for the new ownership, was now Wilt's employer as well as his lawyer and confidant. (Talk about potential conflict of interest. But no such problem ever arose, given their respect and love for each other in what could be termed a father-son relationship.)

There were rumors the new owners were "fronts" for Gottlieb, who still owned part of the San Francisco franchise (because his note had not been paid off) and was barred by league rules from owning part of two clubs at one time. Once free of his ownership of the San Francisco club, so the rumors went, Gottlieb would resume ownership of the Philadelphia franchise. All parties involved denied the rumors, though Dr. Stan Lorber, the man who was both a close friend and the personal physician to all three men, acknowledged in an interview in 2002 that the rumors had been true. Nevertheless, after Gottlieb returned to Philadelphia, he was never the owner, part or otherwise, of the team.

Because the name "Warriors" had been sold along with the franchise, a contest was held to select a new name for the Philadelphia basketball team. Choosing from four thousand entries, a panel of judges decided the team would be known as the "76ers" to commemorate the city's role in the founding of our country on July 4, 1776.

Initially, local fans were cool to the 76ers, a team that had been a rival as the Syracuse Nationals but now was playing as a Philadelphia team in red, white, and blue uniforms. Matters weren't helped when the 76ers finished next to last in their division in 1963–1964, their first season in Philadelphia. Adding insult to injury, Wilt led the old Philadelphia franchise, which had become the San Francisco Warriors, to the Western Division title.

This first 76ers team was largely undistinguished, with the exception of Hal Greer, a 6'2" guard with a deadly medium-range jump shot, and Chet Walker, a 6'7" forward in his second season of what would become an exceptional career. Joining them were Larry Costello and Johnny "Red" Kerr, both fine players who were nearing the ends of their careers. Paul Neumann, Ben Warley, Al Bianchi, Lee Shaffer, Connie Dierking, Dave Gambee, Jerry Greenspan, and Hubie White made up the remainder of this team.

The Sixers player-coach (he played 24 games during the 1963–1964 season) was Adolph "Dolph" Schayes, a perennial NBA All-Star from Syracuse, who was also nearing the end of a fabulous playing career. This would be his first stint as a coach.

The Sixers' prospects for the 1964–1965 campaign improved when they drafted Lucious "Luke" Jackson, a 270-pounder from Pan American University. Even with the 6'9" Jackson providing plenty of muscle as the starting center, this remained a team that had yet to be accepted by the hometown fans and had yet to find a winning style. But all that would change when, in January 1965, in the middle of the season, Wilt Chamberlain brought his dominating basketball skills back home to Philadelphia.

"As far as I was concerned, the 76ers were the old Syracuse Nationals, which was a team I hated," Wilt observed many years later. "Going back home [to Philadelphia] was nice, but I had fallen in love with San Francisco, and I was rather sad to leave. But Ike Richman, my lawyer and my closest friend, talked me into returning, saying, 'This is where you belong.'"

In other interviews, years after the fact, Wilt explained further about his reluctance to return to Philadelphia. "They had a coach, Dolph Schayes," he said, "who had made some disparaging remarks about my ineptness at the foul line. . . ."

Wilt advised Richman not to make the trade, warning his friend (and potential employer) that he might retire at season's end, making the trade a risky financial decision. Even so, and although never publicly acknowledged, Richman accepted an arrangement whereby Wilt, who preferred the freedom and relative anonymity of New York, commuted from his rented apartment near

Central Park to Philadelphia for practice and home games. It was the same thing that Wilt had done during Gottlieb's reign in the 1961–1962 season.

Greer had been "the man" on the Syracuse-Philadelphia club. That changed with the addition of Wilt, as did Jackson's role—literally—because he was forced to move from center to forward. Greer and Jackson wouldn't be human if they hadn't felt some resentment toward Wilt. "There was a little friction in the beginning," Walker recalled. "Before Wilt came it was Hal's team. And he didn't want to give up all his authority. But it all worked out, and we became a great team." No one denied the tensions, least of all Wilt, who years later said, "I learned to fall into the good graces [of] my teammates—the Chet Walkers and Hal Greers. We all became one, but it took a while. I wasn't the easiest guy in the world to wrap your arms around. Also, I'm coming back a superstar. Your teammates know you're going to take some of their stuff away—whether it's scoring or attention. I knew that was going to happen. I had to be prepared for it."

The day after the trade that brought Wilt back home, George Kiseda, the talented beat reporter for *The Evening Bulletin*, wrote: "There has never been a more devastating basketball player anywhere, but Chamberlain has been the target for all sorts of slings and arrows, most of them unjustified. He has the image of a sulker and a crybaby; but he is neither. It's just that he is honest enough not to give namby-pamby answers when he is asked leading questions."

In the Kiseda article, an unnamed person (probably Kiseda himself) asked Wilt if he felt sportswriters had misrepresented him over the years. Wilt's reply is revealing:

> Definitely. There have been several things. First, the business of being a selfish ballplayer. Second, "He plays only one end of the court." Third, "He doesn't play with a winner." All of them are ridiculous statements.
>
> What's a winner? Because we lost by one point in three overtimes to North Carolina in the NCAA, does that mean we weren't winners? [In the pros] we won a division championship; does that mean we weren't winners?
>
> They should look back in the book and see how we lost. Do they attribute that to me?
>
> Why do I have to keep proving a fact? I've been in this league six years. I've led six years in scoring, five years in rebounding, four years

in shooting percentage—yet all you ever hear is, "Wilt Chamberlain is a dunker."

_____

Alan Levitt had become Wilt's accountant in 1959, at first only filing his tax returns. But as the two got closer, Levitt functioned, along with Richman, as Wilt's brain trust. Levitt had power of attorney and handled everything for Wilt, including paying all his bills; the only checks Wilt wrote were those for Levitt's services. (Years later, when Wilt lived on the West Coast, Sy Goldberg assumed Levitt's financial responsibilities while also filling other roles in Wilt's life.)

Levitt recalled Wilt's first game in a 76ers uniform:

> Ike [Richman] had a fantastic imagination and was a great promoter. Wilt was not thrilled to be back in Philadelphia. He came here because of Ike's persuasion. Ike arranged, through Wilt's friend Vince Miller, to have a large group of school kids, maybe 1,500, show up for the game, all with placards saying, "We love Wilt," "Wilt for mayor." I was in the dressing room with Wilt. You could hear the clamor for Wilt. The noise was deafening. He entered the arena and the place went wild. The kids were stomping on the benches, and all the fans were yelling like God had arrived. The cheering went on for 15 minutes. Wilt started to cry, right out on the floor.

Wilt loved the reception, calling it "the greatest thing that has ever happened to me in sports."

Near the end of the 1964–1965 season, Wilt's pancreatitis flared up. The unheard of occurred: he took himself out of the game with 24 seconds remaining—in this case, grimacing in pain. The team and Wilt's personal doctor, Stanley Lorber, explained to the media that Wilt's pancreatitis "causes a burning sensation in Wilt's stomach, and sometimes the pain is so severe he is afraid to take a breath." The cure: medicine and proper diet, the latter not easy to adhere to during the NBA season.

_____

By 1965 the league had nine teams: four in the Eastern Division and five in the West. At season's end, Boston had the best record in the East (so what else was new?), followed by Cincinnati, whose stars included the incomparable Oscar Robertson and Jerry Lucas. The 76ers finished third in their division. By playoff time, the team was adjusting to Wilt and Wilt to his teammates, and the Sixers defeated this strong Cincinnati team, earning another shot at Boston in the Eastern Finals.

Philadelphia and Boston had played each other ten times that season, with each team winning five on its home court. The press considered it an even matchup, with many giving the center position to the 76ers. As Kiseda noted: "Russell almost never outplays Chamberlain; and when he does, it's by a small margin. There are times when Chamberlain completely dominates Russell. (Wilt once averaged 45 points a game against Boston for an entire season.)"

The Celtics won the first game, the 76ers the second, with Wilt prevailing over Russell by scoring 30 points, grabbing 39 rebounds, and blocking eight shots.

The Celtics won the third game, outplaying the 76ers at forward. Jackson was producing only half of the points and rebounds he had averaged during the season, and the Boston press was preventing Philly's guards from getting the ball to the forwards. With Boston up three games to two, Jackson finally broke out of his slump, and he and Wilt, who played fierce defense even though he had five fouls down the stretch, led the way to victory.

Coach Schayes praised Wilt effusively, pointing out that the Celtics challenged Wilt immediately after he got his fifth foul. "And in one sequence," Schayes recounted, "Wilt blocked shots on Russell and Heinsohn back to back." So much for those who claimed that Wilt dogged it when he had five fouls, more concerned with protecting his record of never fouling out of a professional game than he was with winning.

Because Boston compiled a better record during the season, the final game was in the Boston Garden, which, according to Kiseda, would end up being the deciding factor. "Odds are they [the 76ers] will fail," he wrote. The difference between the two teams, he opined, was that at home, "Boston clamps [its] full-court press on the 76ers as if it were a vise. . . . It's a gambling defense that relies heavily on overplaying (conceding the alley to the basket but shutting off the passing lanes between the ball and potential receivers). It's effective because under the basket is the world's best defensive center, Bill Russell, and the Celtics have the world's best defensive forward, Satch Sanders, and the world's best defensive guard, K. C. Jones. They have the most explosive fast break anywhere, but they win with their defense. It creates the enemy errors that make the fast break possible."

In that seventh game of the 1965 Eastern Finals, both centers were fabulous: Wilt made 12 for 15 from the field and 6 for 13 from the foul line for 30 points, and grabbed 32 rebounds. (The rest of the 76ers had 24 rebounds combined.) Russell was 7 for 16 from the field, 1 for 2 from the line, for 16 points, and had 29 rebounds (while the remainder of the Celtics had 37 rebounds, giving them a 10-rebound edge). Russell had eight assists to one for Wilt. Sam Jones scored 37 for the Celtics while John Havlicek had 26—15 of them coming in the third quarter.

Wilt scored 8 of his team's final 10 points, including two critical free throws with 36 seconds left. He dunked on Russell to bring the Sixers a point behind with five seconds remaining. Russell, throwing the ball in bounds for Boston, hit the guide wire on the backboard, a violation that gave the ball back to Philadelphia. Coach Schayes called timeout. He didn't want the ball to go to Wilt for fear the Celtics would foul him, and the game would depend on Wilt making his foul shots. Schayes instructed Greer to throw the ball in to Walker, Kerr to set a pick on Greer's man, and Walker to pass the ball back to Greer, who'd come off Kerr's pick and take the final shot. Wilt would be under the basket for a tip-in, should Greer's shot miss.

Greer, following the coach's plan, lobbed a soft pass to Walker, who was about 18 feet from the basket. But, in the immortal words of Johnny Most, Boston's announcer, "Havlicek steals it! . . . Havlicek stole the ball!"

The Celtics prevailed, 110–109. They had won the Eastern title for the ninth straight year. A distraught Schayes conceded after the game, "I didn't call the right play. The play I called was stupid."

Once again, the dream of a championship had eluded Wilt—as it had in the waning seconds of the 1957 NCAA championship at Kansas; as it had in 1960 and 1962 with the Philadelphia Warriors; and as it had in 1964 with the San Francisco Warriors. And now, back in Philadelphia once again, he was faced with the same disappointment, compounded by the fact that all of the losses had been to the same team—Boston! Russell wins again. Wilt loses again. Losses like this one added to the perception that Wilt couldn't beat Russell and couldn't win a title. Never mind how well Wilt had played. Never mind that but for Havlicek's defensive gem, *Russell* might have been the scapegoat for his last-second gaffe of throwing the ball into the guide wire.

Asked years later if the game was a bitter memory, Walker, for whom the pass was intended, responded, "It's not a bitter memory—but it is a nightmare. I awaken a lot of nights thinking about that game, because the ball was coming to me."

ABC-TV hired Wilt to do the color commentary for the broadcast of the Boston–Los Angeles Finals. Boston won the series in five games. Over the years, Jerry West's Los Angeles Lakers lost to Boston six times in the Finals. No one has ever written or suggested he was a loser because people realized Boston's teams were better than Jerry West's (and Elgin Baylor's) Lakers. Wilt was rarely accorded that understanding. Why?

Perhaps everyone thought because of his size and skills his teams should never lose.

Not long after the season, in June 1965, NBA president Walter Kennedy fined Wilt $750 for behavior "detrimental to the best interest of the league." That fine was the largest in league history at the time, a distinction since broken more than once. And what had Wilton done to deserve the fine? He had dropped a bomb. He had coauthored a two-part series in *Sports Illustrated*, "My Life in the Bush Leagues," which caused all sorts of hell when it was published as the cover story in April, smack dab in the middle of the Eastern Finals.

The two articles are extraordinary, if at times painful, for the insights they provide into the psyche of Wilt Chamberlain at age 29, and how he saw himself and thought others viewed him. Alternating between being temperate and intemperate, rational and irrational, Wilt unleashed one long *kvetch*:

> This is more than life inside a giant. This is the story of my life inside professional basketball—the greatest game ever played, a game that suffers from being bush when it doesn't want to be bush, a game that may always be bush unless some basic changes are made. And when we get to the end of this chapter, the part where they say, "Tune in next week," or the end of the story, where they say, "Can this poor monster from Philadelphia really find happiness?" you'll know how it

143

feels to be Goliath. How it feels to be seven feet and one-sixteenth inches tall with no place to hide. . . .

He went on to complain about his status as a villain, and how he could never really satisfy his critics, who always seemed to find some facet of his game to reprove.

Did newspaper and magazine accounts of the time portray Wilt as a selfish, one-dimensional villain? Overwhelmingly they did not. Wilt's outburst reflected his frustration over the failure of his teams to win championships—first at Kansas, then with San Francisco and Philadelphia. Some of it probably was Wilt projecting—particularly the part about being a villain.

He also criticized Schayes, his coach, which—valid or not—should not have been done in public, especially not in the middle of the championship series with Boston. In fairness to Wilt, he claimed that he had been told the articles would run after the playoffs. He also said in the article that Schayes was probably too nice to coach professional basketball players, but the comment came right after Wilt ridiculed Schayes for the manner in which he conducted practice—punishing professional basketball players by asking them to run laps after one or the other side committed a mistake. Then Wilt lambasted Franklin Mieuli, his former employer in San Francisco, for failing to inform him of the negotiations—either beforehand or during—that led to his being traded back to Philadelphia.

This was absurd. Of course Wilt was aware the 76ers were in trade talks with Mieuli: it was Richman, *Wilt's* lawyer and closest friend, who was negotiating the trade.

And while he was at it, Wilt criticized all the NBA owners for failing to hire good college coaches and for otherwise failing to improve, in his words, "a bush league." Among the grievances, he had one positive suggestion: the league should cut the number of games by 20 percent. (Fat chance of that ever happening.) Wilt did, however, counter his complaints by including the following observation: "Sorry if I've sounded like a know-it-all. But this comes from a guy who loves the game, despite his gripes."

In the second of the two-part series, Wilt wrote, "Sometimes I feel like a guy not exactly living—but being *chased* through life, you know?" He went on to talk about how insensitive the public was toward him, especially about his height (a theme he would repeat many years later in his next-to-last book, *A View from*

Above). He took exception to the way people gawked at him because of his height, asked for autographs, or generally bothered him at inappropriate times. Equally disturbing was having people just stand nearby and watch him, for instance when he was eating, apparently regarding him as "some sort of public property," to use his own words.

In the article, he recounts his experiences for the readers:

> "Hey, boy," they say in that condescending way, "what are you? A basketball player or something like that?" Or, what is worse, they say, "Hey, you. Stand right over here for a minute. I want to have my picture taken with you. Man, the folks back home won't believe *this*." And I'm supposed to stand there and smile like I'm some big, wooly pet. In the old days when I was younger, it was sort of fun. Now it's too much, man.
>
> There are days when it all makes me pretty sad and lonely. I stand on the balcony of my New York apartment and look down at all the normal cats and their girlfriends, maybe just walking hand in hand along the edge of Central Park and, you know, just sort of living. I wonder how it would be for me.

It was a sad portrait of how the young man viewed himself and his relationship to society in general, his sport in particular. Today, strangers probably don't ask tall people, as was common in the fifties or sixties, "How's the weather up there?" (To which Wilt once "answered"—in a possibly apocryphal account—by spitting on his interrogator and saying, "It's raining.")

Wilt became more comfortable with his celebrity as he aged. He tended to get along well with most sports reporters, who found him charming (when he wanted to be) and good copy. The late Dick Schaap, a well-respected sportswriter, observed that the Wilt of the eighties and nineties was very comfortable being Wilt—more comfortable in his skin, Schaap believed, than Bill Russell or Kareem Abdul-Jabbar (the two other giant African-American basketball players often compared to Wilt) were in theirs.

Wilt's comfort was relative, however. Time and time again, in his books and in countless interviews, even during the mid- to late nineties, Wilt returned to the issue of his height. It is evident that the wound remained deep and fresh. Jessica Burstein, a photographer who was also a friend of Wilt's, recalled, "Back in the nineties, I had a photography show—a series of photographs of people at different ages. I wanted someone who was sort of ageless, and I told Wilt I really wanted to do a photograph of him. He came to New York just for the photo. It was really interesting because he said, 'I want you to make me look normal.' He meant normal in size. In some ways, he perceived himself as a freak because of his height, as if he was just some giant."

As Wilt himself declared in his most-often-quoted statement: "The world is made up of Davids. I am a Goliath. And nobody roots for Goliath."

Chapter 10

I know he used to drive cross-country to L.A. after the NBA season was over. Once, he told me, he stopped someplace in the Southwest and a mountain lion jumped on him. He said that he killed the mountain lion with his bare hands. Now I don't know how true that is, but he showed me a scar on his arm that he said was from the claw marks.

—Cal Ramsey, longtime friend who first met Wilt in 1955 when the two were *Parade* magazine high school All-Americans

In the Lion's Den

When his basketball season was over, Wilt often would join the Globetrotters—his favorite of all basketball teams and experiences—for part of their European tour, usually catching up with them in Italy. And either before or after the Globetrotter tour, he liked to drive across the United States, usually alone. "You don't have time to be listening to your stereo; all you listen to is the tires on the road," he once remarked.

Wilt and cars, Wilt and speed—a lifelong love affair. He claimed to have driven cross-country 35 to 40 times, reaching speeds, he said, of 140 miles per hour. He also maintained that he once drove from Los Angeles to New York in 36 hours and 10 minutes, which he claimed was a record until Dan Gurney, a professional race car driver, broke it. And, as Wilt was quick to point out, Gurney had a codriver. Though he talked about competing in an officially sanctioned racing event, that was one of the few sports Wilt never tried.

Wilt did embellish sometimes. Were the long distances he drove with little rest or the speeds at which he says he drove an exaggeration? Stories about his driving habits are legion. According to Dr. Stan Lorber, "Wilt could function well on very little sleep. He'd drive east to west or west to east without stopping at a motel. He drove at 110 or 115 miles per hour."

As for the speeds at which Wilt drove, Al Domenico, Wilt's friend and the Philadelphia 76ers trainer, recalled the ride he took with Wilt in the basketball star's custom-made Maserati. "If that thing had wings, it would have taken off," Domenico declared. "I never got in it again."

Alan Levitt, Wilt's accountant, remembers his experience in the Maserati: "We went for a ride. He took the car up to 150 miles per hour, and we were pulled over by a cop. The cop recognized him and said, 'Go ahead, Wilt.'"

The police, however, didn't always let Wilt go. According to *The Philadelphia Inquirer*, he was cited "for driving through an intersection too fast for conditions, in December 1958, and for passing a red light in Philadelphia, in July 1959." And Pennsylvania once suspended his license for a month for speeding.

Playing basketball with the Globetrotters and driving too fast for comfort were not Wilt's only postseason pastimes. Summertime also meant getting away from the hot city and venturing to Kutsher's Country Club in the Catskill Mountains, where the air was clear and refreshing, and the creamed herring alone was worth the trip, some might say. Wilt, Eddie Gottlieb, Ike Richman, and many other members of the basketball community gathered at Kutsher's to relax, talk basketball, reminisce, and plan for the future.

It was also at this resort that, in the summer of 1954, Gottlieb, with the help of Haskell Cohen, then the NBA publicity director, had landed Wilt, a budding scholastic star, a job as a bellhop. Cohen, a font of Wilt stories, recalled this episode:

> One day up here [at Kutsher's], I had a flat tire and no jack to change the tire. Wilt was only 17 then, but he started to lift the back of my car off the ground with his bare hands when I stopped him. I was afraid he would give himself a hernia.

Over the years, Wilt developed a very special relationship with the Kutshers—Milton and Helen and their children, Mark, Mady, and Karen. "We thought of Wilt as an extended part of this family," Helen Kutsher maintained. "I used to kid him, 'You're like my fourth child.' He always stayed in touch, and we'd talk during the year. He never really left us."

The Kutshers also had a special relationship with the world of basketball, as the sponsors for and site of the Maurice Stokes Annual All-Star Game. To today's young basketball fans, the facts of Maurice Stokes' life, and the annual game that honored him, must seem as remote and hazy as the Battle of Verdun.

Stokes attended high school in Pittsburgh and went on to study at tiny St. Francis College, in Loretto, Pennsylvania. Drafted in 1955 by the Rochester (later the Cincinnati) Royals, he was Rookie of the Year in the 1955–1956 season. He was the nicest of men, as everyone associated with him attests. At

6'7" and 240 pounds, he also was becoming one of the greatest of basketball players. It was Stokes who presented a trophy to Wilt in the winter of 1954, when the Overbrook High School team traveled to western Pennsylvania for a Christmas tournament. Wilt never forgot the moment or the person. "Wilt liked and respected Maurice," Mark Kutsher recalled. "People don't realize what a great ballplayer Maurice was. He was Elgin Baylor before Elgin Baylor. Red Auerbach believed that Maurice would have been one of the greatest ballplayers of all time."

On the last day of his third season, in March 1958, Stokes was knocked unconscious late in a game. He was out for a few minutes but, ever the competitor, finished the game. Two days later, on the plane ride back to Cincinnati, after a playoff game in Detroit, he became unconscious again and fell into a coma for several months. When he finally regained consciousness, he was paralyzed and unable to speak from what was diagnosed as encephalitis. He remained paralyzed and, even after long periods of therapy, was unable to talk clearly for the remaining 12 years of his life. He died April 6, 1970.

Jack Twyman, a teammate, became Stokes' legal guardian and oversaw his care. Ironically, Stokes and Twyman were never particularly close before the illness. As fine a basketball player (and later successful business executive) as Twyman was, his devotion to Stokes marks him as an exceptional person. He lived Rousseau's observation: "What wisdom can you find that is greater than kindness?"

To help defray Stokes' enormous medical expenses, the Maurice Stokes Foundation was created and an All-Star Game was played each summer at Kutsher's. Wilt played in the inaugural game in 1959, even before appearing in his first NBA game. In that summer game, he was selected as the Most Valuable Player, leading his team to victory with 20 points and 20 rebounds—a precursor of the thousands of points and rebounds to come.

Over the years, the best players in the NBA participated in the Stokes game. The top New York sportswriters of the era—Leonard Lewin, Milton Gross, Leonard Koppett—and their counterparts from Philadelphia—Jack Kiser, Sandy Grady, Larry Merchant, Stan Hochman, and George Kiseda—visited Kutsher's, too. In addition to covering the annual Stokes game, they could always get a column out of or about Wilt: his latest contract negotiations or his Paul Bunyan–like exploits, present and past. (But unlike Paul Bunyan's, Wilt's were real.) Gross, of the *New York Post*, recalled in one such column that Wilt was the only Kutsher's bellhop who had carried six full suitcases at once up three flights of stairs.

Wherever he was in the world, Wilt always went back for the Maurice Stokes All-Star event, first as a participant, and later, after he retired, as a spectator—and he was always the main attraction for the fans, regardless of which other NBA players were present. He even chartered a plane to make it to one of the games on time. The presence of Wilt and the other NBA stars drew fans to Kutsher's, and that meant more money in the Stokes Foundation's coffers, which eventually contributed more than $750,000 for Stokes' care.

Although the Stokes summer basketball game is no longer held because current players have lost interest in keeping up the tradition, the Stokes Foundation still raises funds by holding an annual golf outing that is attended by some ex-NBA players. Since Maurice Stokes' death in 1970, the Foundation has continued to raise funds, which it uses to help former NBA players—for example, paying for a brain operation for Tim Bassett and donating $26,000 toward the medical bills of All-Star and Hall of Fame finalist Gus Johnson.

Mady Prowler, one of the Kutsher children, shared her recollections of those long-ago summer games:

> I just remember the excitement of Wilt coming. He always made a big fuss over us kids. He was always happy to see us—me, Mark, and my sister, Karen, who is about three years younger than me. It was great just sitting with him in the office and him talking to Pop, and listening to his stories and following him around, like when I was about eight or nine. We would just hang with him.
>
> At that time [the early- to mid-sixties] all the top players came up for the Stokes game, and Maurice was alive. These fellows remembered playing with him. Wilt was always the biggest attraction. He'd always arrive in a fancy car, the plushest thing in the world. And sometimes he'd bring his Great Danes. They were like ponies.

———

In between his trip to Europe with the Globetrotters and time in the Catskill Mountains, Wilt spent part of the summer of 1965 visiting his parents, who lived in the apartment house he had built in West Los Angeles (and which his father helped manage). Wilt was considering, for at least the third time, retiring from basketball—on this occasion to become a professional boxer.

He had to have realized that his decision would have an effect on others in the basketball world who were important to him both professionally and personally, and no one more than Ike Richman. A wonderfully evocative photograph of Wilt taken at Kutsher's in 1957 shows the giant Wilt with Eddie Gottlieb, Ike Richman, and Milton Kutsher—three short, hardworking, decent, strong-willed, self-made, successful men—all of whom were role models for Wilt and made lasting impressions on him as well. They also loved Wilt; each of them, in some respects, treated him like a son. And Wilt reciprocated with affection and love and, not to be too naïve about these matters, also enhanced the careers of each of these men. "My father was a good and successful lawyer," Richman's son, Mike, recalled. "But when Wilt entered his life, it was a boost to his life and career."

With Wilt's love and affection came a dollop of aggravation, especially for Richman in the spring and summer of 1965 when he was trying to sign Wilt to a multiyear contract and Wilt was thinking about a boxing career. Wilt decided to forgo a boxing career (for the moment) and sell his services to the Philadelphia 76ers instead. The contract was signed in Wilt's room at Kutsher's in August and headlined in the *Inquirer*: "Wilt to Get $100,000 a Year." He reportedly had signed a three-season contract, making him the highest-paid team athlete at the time. Wilt's purported $100,000 contract prompted Boston's Russell to ask Auerbach for $101,000 to make *him* the highest-paid player. That's a nice story for the Bill Russell documentaries and biographies, but even at $101,000 he would have been making less than Wilt. Russell never made more money from his basketball contracts than Wilt Chamberlain did.

Neither Gottlieb nor Richman ever revealed to the media the true worth of Wilt's contracts, if only to keep the other players on the team from demanding more. "Wilt was unquestionably the highest-paid player of his time," Levitt said. In fact, he probably earned more in the 1965–1966 season than the other four starters on the 76ers combined.

No one knew Wilt Chamberlain better than Ike Richman. In an interview with the *Philadelphia Daily News'* Bill Conlin, Richman, the Sixers owner, addressed

Wilt's ambivalence about remaining in the NBA, even though he was the game's brightest star:

> We have in him a great athlete, who because of his height doesn't get the credit he is entitled to. He can bowl with anyone, arm wrestle with any man. . . . He can high jump, jump hurdles, and run with the best. But only in basketball do people say, "It's only because he's big."
>
> What Wilt has is a clash of emotions. He would like to minimize the advantage his height has given to him in order to prove his excellence. I challenge any professional athlete to meet him in any sport other than the one they each participate in for money, with the exception of golf and tennis.

One can't imagine any professional athlete in any sport—not Michael Jordan nor Tiger Woods, Babe Ruth nor Barry Bonds, John Elway nor Shaquille O'Neal—contemplating, much less actually minimizing, his God-given advantage. Why would Wilt even consider doing it?

Because Wilt knew he was so much stronger and more dominant than anyone then playing professional basketball, he must have felt, at times, like a man playing with boys. Then factor in this proud, intelligent man's desire to prove that he was an *athlete*, not just a tall goon. But, in the final analysis, part of his reaction to his dominance defies explanation: it was what made Wilt the man he was—unique in many respects, not just in size.

Chapter 11

I remember training camp at the Jewish Community Center. Wilt and Luke Jackson were arm wrestling after practice. Luke was probably the second strongest player in the NBA at the time. He was close to 275 or 280 pounds, 6'9", a massive man. Wilt would let Luke get him halfway down. Then Wilt would say, "Are you ready?" And he put Luke's arm right down. I said to myself, "You've got to be kidding me."

—Billy Cunningham, 76ers teammate

A bunch of us eighth-grade kids used to watch the 76ers practice in preseason. One day, three or four of us were at the beach near their hotel. Wilt happened to be outside, and we got his and some other autographs. Then we went to the beach and sat there talking to Wilt. Someone had a football and we started throwing it around. We got to talking about bowling, and he said to us, "Come on back and we'll go bowling." Two days later two of my buddies and me went to the team hotel, parked our bikes, and after practice we all hopped into his Bentley and he drove us to Gable's Bowling Alley in Margate. That's when I first saw the record player he had built into the Bentley. We bowled three games. We were all good bowlers, as we played in a league. We were thrilled to sit there for an hour and a half and bowl with him. There were only a few people in the alley, and it was very relaxing for him. He had his own bowling ball. The last game was funny. He had a little lead on me. He took the last shot and bowled it between his legs. He let me win. That was the beginning of my friendship with him.

—Bob Kashey, who, from hanging out at preseason practice, eventually became a 76ers ball boy

All the Bleeping Practice in the World

During the years Ike Richman co-owned the team, the 76ers held their preseason training camp in South Jersey. The team stayed in the Canterbury Hotel (now a condominium) in Longport, New Jersey, but trained five minutes away in the Greater Atlantic City Jewish Community Center in Margate, not far from Richman's summer home.

Wilt arrived a day or so late for training camp. Nevertheless, that was a happy training camp, for the 76ers were confident the upcoming campaign would be the one in which they finally defeated the Boston Celtics. Wilt would be with them the entire season, unlike the year before when he had been traded to the club midseason—when they still managed to take Boston to seven games. To enhance the strong nucleus of Wilt Chamberlain, Hal Greer, Chet Walker, and Luke Jackson, they had drafted Billy Cunningham, a talented rookie from New York by way of the University of North Carolina. They also traded for Wali Jones (who, in those days, spelled his name Wally). Jones, an exciting player, was familiar to Philadelphia fans from his days at Overbrook High School and Villanova University. The team had also picked up Gerry Ward, a 6'4" defensive specialist, who had played one season with St. Louis and one with Boston.

Cunningham and Ward, native New Yorkers, roomed together in an apartment above a delicatessen in Center City Philadelphia. The two of them spent a lot of time that season with Wilt. "I think Wilt embraced me because Frank McGuire was one of his favorite coaches," Cunningham recalled. "I was recruited by Frank McGuire to play at North Carolina. So Wilt took me under his wing." It also helped that Ward and Cunningham, who remained close friends after their basketball careers, are easygoing, likeable people. The three young bachelors just clicked, and it didn't hurt that Ward and Cunningham had not been members of the Syracuse Nationals, as were so many of the 76ers.

After a great playing career, Cunningham coached the 76ers to a world championship in 1982–1983. He reminisced about Wilt at Billy Cunningham's Court, the restaurant and pub he owns in suburban Philadelphia, where the walls are decorated with blown-up photographs of famous 76ers, most prominent among them Wilt and Julius Erving, the latter of whom Cunningham coached. "I think Wilt was ahead of his time," Cunningham said. "He was the first player over 7' who was athletic. Not only was he the fastest guy on our team, there wasn't anyone close. I dare you to name anyone that size as athletic as him. He was ahead of his time as far as lifting weights. It was a no-no in sports. I was told I'd lose my touch if I lifted weights. Wilt was also very outspoken. He would fit in well today. He was also ahead of his time in preparing for life after basketball."

Ward remarked that even during Wilt's second season as a Sixer there was still some resentment toward him from Greer, who had been the star of the team, and from Jackson, who had been forced to move from center to power forward.

"Very seldom did Wilt, Billy, or I go out because people bothered Wilt, always asking for autographs," recalled Ward, who became a successful businessman after his short professional basketball career. "But one night, after a home game, we're walking in Center City Philadelphia. It's about 11:00 P.M. We're playing 'Can you match me?' We're doing stupid things, like three young, single guys. We finally come to a pole, and it's Wilt's turn. He wraps his arms around the pole and lifts himself up and places his body at a 45-degree angle to the pole. He holds himself vertically for about a minute, then he comes down. Billy and I try it. We throw our legs up and come right down. There's no way we can do it for a second."

Another member of that 76ers team with whom Wilt became particularly close was Al Domenico, the first full-time trainer in the NBA. Before 1965, trainers were part time, with competing teams using the home-team trainer, which shows how small-time the league was. "I have nothing but great things to say about Wilt," Domenico said. "There is no perspective with this man until you stood next to him. He was literally a giant. The big guys in the league looked small next to Wilt. If someone were going to make a sculpture of the human body, they would use Wilt's body to make it. Someone bet Wilt he couldn't bowl a game without using the holes in the bowling ball. He did it. I saw it. Then he picked up two bowling balls and palmed them [held them with his hands on top and without putting his fingers in the holes]. One of the 76ers bet Wilt $5 he couldn't put a quarter on the top of the backboard. He jumped up, put it there, and came back down. Went up and got it. And gave the quarter to the guy. I saw it."

Before the Spectrum was built, the 76ers played in Convention Hall, and after games some of the players would go to Pagano's, an Italian restaurant on the outskirts of the University of Pennsylvania's campus in West Philadelphia. According to Domenico, Wilt would stop in occasionally, have a glass of wine, then leave, not being one to linger and drink too much. Whenever Wilt returned to Philadelphia during the eighties and nineties, which was not that often, he made a point of getting together with Domenico, who recalled the following incident:

> Our relationship started as two professionals doing something, and we became really good friends from it. I was pretty sick in 1997. I was in the hospital, and before the surgery I got a call from Wilt. He said, "You're gonna be all right."
>
> The doctors fixed me. Sometime after my stay in the hospital, my nephew, who collects autographs, found out Wilt would be at a signing event. He went to the event and told Wilt that I was his uncle. Wilt stood up and said, "Give him this for me," and Wilt kissed my nephew on the lips. My nephew came to my house the next day, gave me a kiss on the lips, and said, "That's from your buddy Wilt."

———————

Dolph Schayes was selected as one of the 50 greatest players in NBA history (as was Billy Cunningham and, of course, Wilt). Schayes is a prince of a guy—a funny, self-deprecating, caring human being. There is no better ambassador for the sport than Schayes, who was probably too nice, as Wilt once wrote, to be a professional basketball coach. Schayes is the first to tell you he was not much of a coach: "I was a poor communicator," he said during an interview. "I don't think Wilt had too much faith in my coaching."

Schayes was between the proverbial rock and a hard place:

> I got in trouble with the team because Wilt lived in New York. One of the conditions, I think, for Wilt to come back to Philadelphia from

San Francisco was that he could live in New York. Wilt was a night person. I think Wilt felt he wasn't as noticeable at night. He didn't like to practice in the morning. The guys wanted to practice early, to get it over with, so they had the rest of the afternoon off. But because of Wilt, we'd practice late in the day, at 4:00. The guys held it against me. But Ike [the team's owner] said, "There's no other way."

On Friday, December 3, 1965, the 76ers played in Boston, where they had never beaten the Celtics. Ike Richman, as was his wont, was on the 76ers bench cheering his boys on. Six minutes and 42 seconds into the game, Richman—the popular and ebullient owner who had brought Wilt back to Philly—clutched his chest: he was suffering a massive coronary. (For those into eerie coincidences, the score was 13–13, and 13 was also Wilt's number.) Richman's wife, Clare, watching the game back in Philadelphia, saw her husband collapse. Richman was rushed to Massachusetts General Hospital, where he was pronounced dead on arrival. When Domenico confirmed Clare's worst fears, she said in a soft voice, "Tell the boys if they ever won a game, to win this one."

That message, as well as the confirmation that their well-liked owner had died, was conveyed to the players at halftime. The 76ers went out and clobbered the Celtics, 119–103. At one point, Wilt blocked four straight shots, and he had 30 rebounds to Bill Russell's 10 that night. Schayes remembers that Wilt had tears in his eyes throughout the evening. After the game, still visibly shaken by Richman's sudden death, Wilt said, "I owe that man all I have today."

Many times Wilt said that Richman—his lawyer, his most trusted business adviser, the confidant who helped him with his problems, his dearest friend, *and* a father-figure—was, other than his family, the most important person in his life. And now Richman was gone at age 52. Dr. Stan Lorber and Alan Levitt, who were close to both Wilt and Ike, believe that had Richman lived, the remainder of Wilt's life might have taken another direction—Wilt might not have moved to the West Coast, for instance.

Absent their fallen leader, the 76ers still had a half-season to play. They ended it better than Boston—one game better, at 55–25; they wound up 22–3 in games played at home. For the first time in nine years, a team other than Boston finished at the top of the division. And for the first time, Wilt had teammates on a par with what Russell had had for all those years in Boston. Because of it, Wilt didn't need to score as often. He still led the league in scoring, but his points per game declined to 33.5, the lowest of his career. His assist total, however, almost doubled from previous years, proving to everyone that Wilt could tailor his game to the skills of his teammates.

Wilt also had become, in the course of the 1965–1966 season, the greatest scorer in NBA history, surpassing Bob Pettit's record in mid-February. At that time, few NBA records did not belong to Wilt. And in a runaway vote, the players named Wilt the MVP for the 1965–1966 season, the second time he had won it. (In four of the previous five seasons, the MVP had gone to Russell.)

The closer people were to Wilt or the more they understood the game, the more they appreciated his talents and extraordinary strength. Al Domenico, the 76ers trainer for 25 years, related one memorable moment:

I'll never forget the incident with Gus Johnson. Gus Johnson was a monster. You didn't mess around with him. He was a bad dude. Wilt was down at our end of the basket, which was really unusual because Wilt never basket-hung. He always came up with the team. He had gotten the rebound and made the outlet pass. We were on a fast break, and Gus intercepted a pass.

Eight guys were on one side of the court. Wilt and Gus were on the other. And Gus comes down the right side and is dribbling, and Wilt is coming from the left side. And Wilt's like a step ahead of him, and Gus takes off near the foul line for one of those Michael Jordan–like, one-handed, windmill dunks. He's way above the rim. And Wilt's hand went right up—and the ball and Gus' arm hit Wilt right dead in the palm. And boom—that's as far as the ball got.

You'd figure that Wilt's hand would have been pushed back. But it wasn't; it stood up like a pole. His arm didn't move, you could see it. Gus' shoulder popped right out. The force of Gus going into Wilt's hand dislocated Gus' shoulder. Gus just bent down and grabbed his shoulder, sat on the bench. And the next thing you know he was in the hospital. That was the most impressive thing I ever saw on a basketball court.

If Domenico appreciated Wilt, apparently some of the fans still did not, at least according to Wilt. In February 1966, he said, "There are some people—I won't call them fans, because they don't know the first thing about the game—who shout that I'm selfish if I take 30 shots. It's nothing new. I've been hearing it for years. If I scored 40, I shot too much; if I scored 20, I was dogging it."

The 76ers finished the season by winning their last 11 games (and 18 out of their last 21). In the season finale, a must-win away game in Baltimore, they roared from behind to defeat the Bullets, scoring 24 straight points—and winning the Eastern crown by one game. The NBA didn't keep records on that category in 1966, but *The Evening Bulletin*'s account said the 24 points were probably a record for consecutive points. Could Wilt and his teammates stop Boston's incredible run of seven straight NBA crowns? (Winning the Eastern crown from 1960 to 1968 was tantamount to winning the NBA title because the two best teams in the league, with few exceptions, were Russell's Celtics and Wilt's Warriors and 76ers—and both were in the Eastern Division.) This was a talented Sixers team ready to chew up Boston, boldly proclaimed Irv Kosloff, who had stepped to the fore as the team's owner after Richman's death.

Having finished an unaccustomed second, it was Boston that played in the first round of the playoffs, defeating Cincinnati in five games, while Philly had a bye.

In the opening game of the Eastern Finals, the Celtics battered a 76ers team that looked rusty and out of sync, 115–96—in Philadelphia, no less, to the shock of the Philly fans, who thought this was finally the team's year to win. Wilt had his usual solid game: 9 for 19 with 32 rebounds. His teammates shot poorly: Jackson was 3 for 10, Walker 4 for 10, and Cunningham 2 for 9.

"We were a great team," Schayes recalled. "We had a bye in the first round. We had two weeks off. Sometimes a layoff is good, sometimes it is bad. I wasn't hard on the guys in practice. Wilt dominated and he didn't like to practice. Russell never practiced. A lot of great players hated to practice. So when we lost that first game [to Boston], we weren't ready. And Boston was sharp, since they had just defeated Cincinnati. That put us in a hole."

Philly partisans excused the first-game blowout as an aberration. The 76ers were stale, but fans were confident they'd rebound. But Boston whipped Philly, 114–93, in game two. After that shellacking, Joe McGinniss, who was the beat reporter for *The Evening Bulletin* before becoming a best-selling nonfiction author, wrote: "The 76ers could excuse Sunday's 21-point home court humiliation by saying it was due to the two-week layoff between their last season game and the playoffs. Last night, there were no excuses. It was not the layoff that beat them, it was the Celtics. Boston played like champions and the 76ers just played."

While fans and writers fixated on the Chamberlain-Russell duel, there were other battles going on between the two teams, each of which affected the outcome of the series between the league's two dominant franchises. In his book *Long Time Coming*, Chet Walker described them this way:

> Every big game had little games within it. Sanders and I dueled for years, scrapping for position at both ends of the court. . . . Luke Jackson could just bowl over Bailey Howell. We had a huge advantage there. K. C. Jones tried to slow Greer down and make him give up the ball. . . . Two wild cards were Wali Jones and Sam Jones. If either shot the lights out, the other team was in trouble. . . .

The 76ers won the third game, 111–105. Walker and Jackson had solid games, as did Dave Gambee, who started in place of the slumping Cunningham. Wilt was Wilt, which is to say terrific: he had 31 points (on 12 for 22 from the floor and 7 for 17 from the foul line), with 27 rebounds in 48 minutes. And he held Russell to 11 points (with 23 rebounds).

With two days off before Game 4, Schayes announced in the locker room after the game that there would be a team practice the following day. McGinniss wrote about a conversation in which Wilt told Schayes in the dressing room that he was too tired to attend the following day's practice. And Schayes, in effect, pleaded with Wilt to attend, if only to come out and shoot a few fouls. "No, Dolph, I'm not coming. I'm sorry. I just don't want to practice," Wilt was quoted as saying.

Boston won the fourth game in overtime, 114–108. The 76ers were one loss from extinction.

The fifth game was to be held on Tuesday in Philadelphia. For the Monday practice before the game, Wilt remained in New York—or at least he never showed up for the practice in Philadelphia. No one knew for certain where he was, other than that he was not at practice. Making the best of a bad situation, Schayes defended Wilt before the media: "Wilt killed himself yesterday," said Schayes, quoted in Gordon Forbes' article in *The Philadelphia Inquirer*. "He played a great game. So I excused him from practice. . . . Before Tuesday night's game we're going to hold a strategy session. And Wilt will be there."

An unnamed teammate of Wilt's was not quite so understanding. The newspaper account quoted him as saying: "Sure, he should have been here [at the practice]. Isn't Wilt just like you and me? Today was the same as it's been all year long. Wilt misses a practice and it sort of aggravates the guys."

After taking over as the 76ers owner, Kosloff had tried to convince Wilt to move to Philadelphia during the season "for the good of the team"—to no avail. "Wilt refused," wrote Forbes, "claiming it wouldn't have mattered."

The 76ers lost the fifth game, 120–112, ending their short-lived reign as Eastern Division champs. They lost in Philadelphia, no less. The wayward Wilt, however, was magnificent, scoring 46. But his 8 for 25 from the foul line was not so impressive.

"Everyone was asking Russell how the Boston Celtics beat the 76ers in five games when they weren't even supposed to do it in seven," McGinniss wrote after the game. The answer, according to no less an authority than Russell, was that the 76ers had taken Boston too lightly. "Then—and this may sound trite, but it's very true," Russell added, "I think this is a team game. I'm not saying anything bad about Wilt Chamberlain. He had a great season and I voted for him for Most Valuable Player. But any time you take this game out of the team realm, you foul up your team. . . . As for winning this game tonight, we really wanted to wind it up here. We've heard for so many years that we just managed to win because that seventh game was in Boston—I mean we've been getting letters about it. So we wanted to win it here."

John Havlicek said: "I think our defense is what made it so easy. Defense is the hardest thing to play. You get tired of playing it. But that Cincinnati series sharpened us defensively."

In a postgame interview, a writer questioned Wilt about skipping practice. Wilt turned and, pointing to *Bulletin* writer McGinniss, said, "Ask him about it." To which McGinniss replied, "Wilt, you missed 17 foul shots tonight. Don't you think you could have used some practice on the line Monday?"

"All the [bleeping] practice in the world ain't gonna help me at the line," Wilt replied. Wilt and McGinniss exchanged more heated words until a couple of writers and Wilt's friend Vince Miller intervened.

Wilt had an extraordinary fifth game (and series). If not for his 46 points and 34 rebounds (almost equal to the rebounds gathered by all the other Philadelphia players combined), the 76ers wouldn't have been competitive in the final game. He was hardly the reason the 76ers lost to the Celtics. His teammates had a lousy series. But he shouldn't have lived in New York during the season and commuted to Philly for most home games. And he shouldn't have missed practice during the playoffs when he wasn't injured. For that lapse of judgment, he deserves to be criticized.

Even before the end of the series, McGinniss captured the difference between the two teams when he wrote: "Basically, it is a matter of mental toughness. The Celtics, following Auerbach's example, ooze it all over the floor. The 76ers, starting with Schayes, just don't think like winners." You win as a team. You lose as a team. It's that simple.

Wilt and his team lost to Boston in either the conference or league championship five out of his first seven years in the NBA, some of those games decided in the last minute of play. If that doesn't cause a man's stomach to ache, nothing will. It galled this proud, fine athlete—undoubtedly the sport's most dominant player—that he and his team couldn't reach the summit.

Boston defeated Los Angeles in seven games—for its eighth straight NBA title—probably the greatest team accomplishment in professional sports. Auerbach announced in the middle of the series that he was retiring; his replacement was Bill Russell, who would be a player-coach.

For failing to beat Boston two years in a row, Schayes was fired. He would, after a brief coaching stint in Buffalo, become the supervisor of the NBA referees and, eventually, a successful developer in Syracuse.

The 76ers found in their next coach a man who had once defeated Boston for the title (with St. Louis in 1957–1958) and who, unlike Schayes, enjoyed Wilt's confidence. That man was Alex Hannum.

Chapter 12

I was a senior in high school in 1967. Me and my buddies wanted 16 tickets for the Celtics series. So we jumped in a fellow's car. We go downtown where they're selling the tickets—I think it was the Sheraton Hotel.

We jump out of the car and we have the money in our hands. We want 16 tickets. As we're going in, we see Wilt, in a corner, dressed all in black, with a big silver belt buckle. I say to the guy at the counter, "I'd like 16 tickets." The guy says, "You can only buy four at a time."

I say, "Oh, no." So I turn around to my friend and say, "You get your four tickets." He gets his four and I get my four. And we're looking awfully forlorn walking out, wondering how we'll get the other eight tickets for our friends.

As we walk by Wilt, he looks at us and says, "My man," in that deep voice of his. And I'm thinking, "He can't be talking to me, I'm a 17-year-old kid." And Wilt said, "My man, come over here." So we walk over, and he said, "What's the matter?"

I said, "They'll only allow us to buy four tickets each and we want sixteen." He said, "Here's what you do. Go out, part your hair on the other side. Come back in and you can get the other eight." Boy, we're all excited. Here's Wilt Chamberlain telling us how to con the guy at the ticket counter. Butch and I say to the guy in the car, "Give us a comb, give us something," not thinking that we could have just walked back in line. They would never have known who we were. So we go back in line, and get the four each and we have our sixteen tickets. As we're walking out, Wilt gave us a big thumbs-up.

—Ed Gallagher, Philadelphia resident

The Greatest Team

Despite their ignominious exit in five games at the hands of Boston in the playoffs the prior season, the 76ers knew they were every bit as talented as, if not better than, the Boston Celtics. But could they forget past defeats and end the cliquishness that had riven the team? Would they be able to play together and demonstrate, come the playoffs, that they were the best team in the league?

Wilt was reunited with Alex Hannum, under whose firm hand he and the San Francisco Warriors had won the Western Conference in 1964 (but had lost to Boston in the Finals). Wilt agreed to move from New York—where he should never have been—to Philadelphia. He rented a penthouse in the Plaza, then a Center City apartment (now the Embassy Suites hotel). The 76ers hired Vince Miller, one of Wilt's closest friends, as a scout and statistician.

Another friend from the past was Mark Kutsher, whose father, Milton, owned the resort that was so much a part of Wilt's life. Kutsher and Wilt had arrived back in Philly at the same time—Wilt to play basketball, Kutsher to pursue a degree at the University of Pennsylvania. "Wilt and I just hung out. I was a kid," Kutsher recalled from his office at the Kutsher's Country Club, which he now runs. "We were just friends. Throughout Wilt's career and life, he managed to retain a bunch of friends with whom he tried to have a normal relationship. But we'd walk outside to do something and the world would fall in on him. No matter where you went. We'd go to a party at my old fraternity house at Penn. I thought these were intelligent people who would leave him alone. We walked in—and everyone stopped what they were doing. We did that once, turned around, and walked out."

The 76ers starting lineup was the same as the previous season: Wilt, Chet Walker, and Luke Jackson (forming one of the greatest front courts in basketball history). At the guard positions were Hal Greer and Wali Jones. Billy Cunningham, who would have been a starter on most other clubs, was the sixth man. Dave Gambee returned, and Larry Costello, the last of the great two-handed set-shot artists, came out of retirement, but he got hurt and missed almost half the season. The newcomers were Billy Melchionni and Matty Guokas, two local Philly stars from, respectively, Villanova and St. Joseph's, and Bobby Weiss from Penn State. The new general manager was Jack Ramsay, a Philadelphia legend who had been a successful coach at St. Joseph's College (now university) in Philadelphia and who would go on to become a Hall of Fame coach in the NBA.

One of the more important moments for this club occurred in October, even before the season had begun: Wilt and Hannum had a locker-room donnybrook in which they aired some issues that had been simmering. "Everybody was sitting there, and they started," said Cunningham, who was quoted in a newspaper account of the incident. "Alex never backed down. I think the way the coach handled it showed us who was going to be the boss."

Walker said that on more than one occasion the players had to pull Wilt and Hannum apart, so close were they to fighting. Even as they had some differences (and which players and coaches do not?), Wilt respected Hannum, and that was the key word—*respect*. (In their postbasketball careers they became very close, even celebrating Wilt's birthday together at Hannum's Southern California home.)

Players respected Hannum, according to Walker, because he treated them like men and expected them to act accordingly. Hannum, at the right moment, pointed out to Wilt that he had received every plaudit in basketball. If he never played another game, Wilt's fame in the history of the game was assured; but there was one thing missing from Wilt's impressive résumé—an NBA championship. Hannum convinced Wilt that he would help lead him and the 76ers to that elusive title.

With teammates who could score, Wilt shot less and passed more, and thus was able to concentrate more on defense. Wilt wasn't the only Sixer making adjustments. As Billy Cunningham observed, "Luke Jackson could play center. He could play power forward. He could rebound. And probably would have been an All-Star if he played center. But he was willing to sacrifice for the team."

And of All-Star guard Greer, Cunningham said, "He epitomized what a pro was supposed to be. Harold wore thigh pads. He wore a knee brace. He had both ankles taped. He wore bandages on his arm. He had as good a 15- to 17-foot jump shot as anyone who has ever played the game."

"Each guy knew his job," Wilt recalled in a series of interviews with NBA Entertainment. He called Jackson "the ultimate power forward," and Walker "the greatest one-on-one player" he had played with. Wilt pointed out that Greer's jump shot was so good that he used it to shoot foul shots. And Jones played excellent defense and kept everyone loose, according to Wilt.

Never one to avoid speaking his mind, even—or especially—on the most controversial subjects, Wilt said that black and white athletes, in his experience, were not always as friendly or cohesive as one might hope. But the black and white athletes on that 1966–1967 Philadelphia team got along well, mostly due to the influence of Cunningham, whom Wilt credited with bringing them together: "I always think of Billy when the game was over. He'd run his hands through my hair and say, 'Nice game, Big Fella.' We [the members of the team] stopped looking at colors and looked at people."

Always generous and, most of the time, considerate, Wilt quietly picked up the tab in restaurants for his teammates because, as Guokas observed, "He knew he was making 10 times what we were." On the road he'd invite teammates to his room, where he had a big spread of food for them. "Off the floor, Wilt was very gregarious, a caring, generous guy," Ramsay, the team's general manager, remembered. "I think his teammates all liked him. But he was also stubborn and headstrong. I think he had something of a complex that fans didn't regard him as being as good as he wanted [to be regarded]. They only thought he was big."

Years later, many of the players commented about the remarkable team chemistry of the 1966–1967 Sixers, including Hal Greer, who had often butted heads with Wilt. Looking back with the perspective of time, Cunningham said of the 1966–1967 team, "You could walk on the court and you knew in a minute the Big Fella was ready to go. And when he was ready to go, everyone would follow."

By late January, the Sixers had a 45–4 record and a lead of nine and a half games over second-place Boston in the Eastern Division. In one game Wilt shot 15 consecutive times without a miss. That was also the season Wilt shot fouls underhanded. He'd put his left foot approximately 10 inches in front of the right and proceed to clunk his shots off the rim. Over the years Wilt had tried everything to cure his foul-shooting woes. For a time he had even stepped back a few feet from the foul line, prompting referee Norm Drucker to point out that if he couldn't make them from 15 feet, what made Wilt think he'd make them from 18 feet? And instead of facing the basket, Wilt shot some foul shots a few feet left of center—all to no avail.

The 1966–1967 Philadelphia 76ers ended the regular season at 68–13—a winning percentage of .840, then the best won-lost record in basketball history. Philly lost only twice at home, significantly, however, to its nemesis, Boston. In fact, despite finishing eight games out of first place, the Celtics beat the Sixers five times.

In the 1961–1962 season, Wilt took 35.3 percent of his team's shots; in 1966–1967, he took 14 percent. Leonard Koppett, who wrote for *The New York Times*, had this reaction:

> Countless stories blossomed about the new "Wilt"—naturally. They were unfair in their implication, as well as inaccurate historically. Yes, Wilt was playing the best basketball of his career, by far—but not because of any innate deficiency in the past. It was only because he had the right team situation at last—the kind of situation Russell had stepped into from the first when he joined a team that had Cousy, Sharman, Heinsohn, and Auerbach to coach it.

For the first time since entering the league eight years before, Wilt was not the scoring champ. The honor went to Rick Barry, of the San Francisco Warriors, who scored 35.6 points per game. The great Oscar Robertson was second, at 30.5 points per game. And Wilt was third, with an average of 24 points—15 points per game under his then-career average. (However, on average, Wilt only took 14 shots per game that year.) Just to show he could do it if he wanted to, he threw down 58 points against Cincinnati one night.

Wilt still led the league in rebounding (as he did in 11 of the 14 years he played in the NBA) and in field-goal percentage. He was third in assists, with 7.8 per game, almost three better than his previous season, and, no doubt, first in shots blocked had they been officially tallied by the league. Oh yes, he also set an NBA record by making 35 consecutive field goals, another of his records that stands unchallenged to this day. And he shot 44 percent from the foul line. Wilt's league-leading 1,957 rebounds (Russell was second with 1,700) were only

16 less than the combined total for the next three players on that great Sixers team: Jackson, a powerful and superb rebounder, had 724; Walker had 660; and Cunningham had 589. Wilt was voted MVP for the second straight year.

Six players on the 76ers averaged double figures: Wilt (24.1 points), Greer (22.1), Walker (19.3), Cunningham (18.5), Jones (13.2), and Jackson (12.0).

———————

Boston defeated the New York Knicks in four games in the Eastern Division semifinals. Philadelphia, meanwhile, lost its first playoff game to Cincinnati but won the next three to advance. Hannum said of the 1966–1967 Sixers, "We're bigger and stronger and, if we keep on pounding, it will tell on the other team." The Eastern Finals were set—Philly versus Boston. "Déjà vu all over again," to quote the New Jersey philosopher Lawrence Berra.

Or was it?

The circus was in town, allowing the more pessimistic of the Philadelphia fans to take that as a bad omen for the upcoming championship with Boston. Instead of being held at Convention Hall, Philadelphia's home court, the first game of the Eastern Conference Final was played at the venerable Palestra. For one member of the 76ers, the Palestra was a cozy site: Wali Jones played well at the Palestra, first as a scholastic star at Overbrook High School, where he won the MVP in a city championship game in 1959, and later in Big Five games while a college star at Villanova for three years.

The 76ers won the first game of the best-of-seven Eastern Final, 127–113, thanks in large part to Greer's 39 points. Also playing well in the first game was Wally Wonder, as Jones was sometimes called by the Philadelphia media. He had 24 points and 7 assists. All Wilt could accomplish was a quadruple double— 24 points, 32 rebounds, 13 assists, and 12 blocked shots.

The second game was in Boston, and Boston had to win or else it would find itself in a deep hole against a talented opponent. In a tug-of-war, the 76ers won, 107–102. Player-coach Russell criticized himself for the loss. He said that he had stood around at a crucial point in the game and so had his teammates. In the closing minutes Wilt intimidated Boston's players, making them reluctant to shoot, fearful he'd block their shots. Greer, Cunningham, Chamberlain, Jones, and Walker were all in double figures. The victory was especially sweet, and symbolic, for Greer, who had never played on a team that won a playoff game in Boston. After the game, Hannum said, "Wilt is proving he's the greatest player that ever lived. And that's one reason I want the title so much—to prove that he is."

Game 3 was back in Philadelphia, where the Sixers took an overwhelming three-game lead. A record crowd of 13,077 witnessed 41 rebounds by Wilt (breaking his and Russell's playoff record) and lustily cheered their 76ers to victory, 115–104.

Wilt and Hannum praised Russell after the game for his fine play, which included 29 rebounds and nine assists. The stronger and younger 76ers dominated the Celtics late in the game, as they had been doing to opponents all year. They outscored Boston 13–3 in the final three and a half minutes of the game, many of those points coming on clutch jump shots by Jones, who ended the night with 21, and Greer, who was having a great series and scored 30. Once again all the 76ers' guns fired with effect.

Down three games to zip, Boston was expiring. Would the 76ers sweep their arch enemies, who also happened to be the defending world champions, winner of the NBA crown eight straight years?

The fourth game was in Boston, and the pride of the Celtics came forth, as they won the game—but just barely—121–117.

If anyone could come back from a three-games-to-one deficit, it was the Celtics. And Wilt, Hannum, and the 76ers knew it.

The fifth game was back in Philadelphia. Down by 16 late in the second quarter, Wilt and Walker brought the 76ers back. In the third period Jones caught fire, hitting for eight baskets in six minutes. And then the 76ers' speed and strength kicked in and the combination was too much for the aging champions. This powerful Philadelphia team, which many basketball experts rank as the greatest ever, scored 75 points in the second half, winning the game, 140–116.

Finally, the 76ers were the Eastern Division champions.

Wilt, as usual, dominated, with 29 points, 36 rebounds, and 13 assists—a triple double. Greer led in scoring with 32; Walker had 26; Jones, 23; and Cunningham, 21. With three minutes left in the game, the 76ers comfortably ahead, a fan stood on a chair, stuck a cigar in his mouth, and lit it—mocking all those years when coach Red Auerbach used to light cigars to celebrate Boston victories. Now it was Philly's turn to gloat a little.

The Celtics had won with class and now lost with class. They made no excuses for falling to a clearly superior team. Their leader, Russell, said, "A better team beat us; they just beat us when they had to. They retained their poise. We pressured them and got them down, but they came back like champions."

K. C. Jones acknowledged that Wilt was the difference. Koppett noted that Russell had played superbly, which underscored just how exceptional Wilt had been in the series. Wilt, during a postgame interview, summed up his feelings: "I've been chasing them a long time. It's hard to explain how I feel now. But I'll really feel it in July or August. That's when people used to look at me as somebody 7'1" who couldn't be a winner."

For once the champagne was uncorked and flowed in the dressing room of Wilt's team. Some of these 76ers, such as Greer, Gambee, Walker, and Costello, had been chasing the white—or in this case, the green—whale of the Celtics their entire career, which for many of them had begun in Syracuse. In the midst of the whooping and hollering, Wilt Chamberlain, who had been pursuing a title since Kansas unexpectedly lost in the NCAA finals 10 years before and who was no stranger to NBA playoff defeats, reminded his team that their celebrating was premature. "We've got to get four more wins before the season is over," he said. "Let's not lose sight of that."

Who was the 76ers' opponent in the 1967 NBA Finals? None other than the San Francisco Warriors. Hannum would face a team he had coached and helped build into a winner. After all, Hannum had drafted Rick Barry, who was establishing himself as one of the premier scorers (and crybabies) in the league. He also had drafted Nate Thurmond, who had become one of the NBA's top centers; only Wilt and Russell were better. Wilt often said that Thurmond—not Russell—played the best one-on-one defense against him. Thurmond, a low-key and modest man, pointed out that he had the advantage over other NBA centers of covering Wilt during practice when they were teammates in San Francisco for 1964 and part of 1965. Two key San Francisco veterans, Tom Meschery and Al Attles, began their careers as Philadelphia Warriors. The 76ers' Guokas and San Francisco's Barry had roomed together at the University of Miami. And, of course, Wilt had been traded by the San Francisco club to Philadelphia, and, whether deserved or not, he harbored ill feelings toward the club's owner, Franklin Mieuli. So there were more than the usual connections between the two clubs.

Before the contest, Hannum said, "Wilt and Greer and Costy [Larry Costello] all have been part of this strong Eastern Division a long time, getting their heads bashed in by the Celtics. This series is a great thrill for me, of course, but I'm happier for them." He was being too modest; Hannum had to derive satisfaction coaching against the franchise that had fired him a year before. And even though Philadelphia was favored to win the series, Wilt warned his teammates against overconfidence.

Philadelphia won Game 1 at home, 141–135, in overtime. But for a controversial call, the 76ers might have dropped the opener. With five seconds remaining in regulation play and the score tied, Thurmond drove to the basket. Wilt blocked the ball. San Francisco's players thought he had fouled Thurmond in the process, but no foul was called, to the chagrin of the San Francisco partisans.

Cunningham continued to fill the role of sixth man on the potent 76ers team. After a lousy series against Boston in the 1966 division finals (his rookie season), Cunningham had played respectably against them in the recently completed series. In the 1967 NBA Finals, beginning with Game 1, he was terrific: he grabbed key rebounds and had baskets in the overtime of that critical first game.

After the first-game scare, no one on the 76ers was taking the Warriors lightly, if ever they had. Philadelphia showed its grit in Game 2, winning at home, 126–95. Defense was the key. Wilt had 38 rebounds, was 4 for 10 from the field, but shot a horrendous 2 for 17 from the foul line. His 10 points were his low for the year. Despite Wilt's paltry offensive numbers, Thurmond felt Wilt had played a great game: "Wilt just scared us on a lot of shots. He's always a big factor on their defense and when the others play defense like they did, they're an even tougher team than usual."

Greer led the offense with 30 points. In seven out of his last eleven playoff games, Greer had scored 30 or more. Cunningham, referred to as the Kangaroo Kid because of his jumping ability—especially for a white guy, but no one phrased it so indelicately—had become a classic sixth man. Whenever he entered the game, he made things happen. He scored 28 points in 19 minutes in Game 2, and by the series' end had scored a point for every minute he played.

"It was our best defense of the season," Hannum said. In fairness to San Francisco, they were handicapped with their injuries: Rick Barry's ankle was sore and Fred Hetzel had knee and ankle problems.

Bill Sharman, San Francisco's coach, had played with the Boston Celtics from 1951 to 1961. He and Bob Cousy formed one of the sport's greatest backcourt duos, and both are in the Hall of Fame. His playing days over, Sharman became one of the game's finest coaches. After Game 2 in the 1967 Finals, he observed of the 76ers: "If this isn't the best team that ever played this game, it's got to be among the top two or three. They just do everything well, and when their defense is like it was today, what can you do?"

Down two games to none, San Francisco was back on its home court for Game 3, which it won, 130–124. Afterward, San Francisco's Barry said, "I think I played halfway decent in stretches," unbecoming false modesty in a man who had just pumped in 55 points.

The series remained in San Francisco, where in Game 4 the 76ers, with fine all-around performances on offense and defense, prevailed by a 122–108 score. Barry again led all scorers, this time with 43 points (on 41 shots). During the game Wilt fell to the floor. Team doctor Stan Lorber ran out to see if the Big Fella was injured. "Are you all right?" Dr. Lorber asked Wilt. "What happened?"

Wilt's answer: "Nothing happened. Do you realize how many people are watching you on television right now?" Wilt was just resting, a big smile on his face, while his friend got some unasked-for television exposure.

With the 76ers up three to one, the Finals moved back to Philly for what everyone assumed would be the final game. But no one consulted the Warriors, who defeated the turgid 76ers, 117–109. The 76ers were entitled to an off night in shooting, and Game 5 was it. They shot 41 percent from the floor. Their center suffered through a 2-for-12 night at the foul line, although he was 9 for 15 from the floor and gathered 24 rebounds.

Game 5 took place in Philadelphia on a Sunday. In bizarre scheduling, Game 6 was in San Francisco the next day, so everyone schlepped across the country. Leading the series three games to two, the 76ers did not want a seventh game in Philadelphia. Anything, as Wilt knew all too well, can happen in the seventh game of a championship series. (The ghosts of playoff losses past—the last-second goaltending calls in 1962 and "Havlicek steals the ball!"—were no doubt on his mind.)

The Warriors knew theirs was a daunting, though hardly impossible, task. Said coach Bill Sharman, "Against every team in this league, you can gear your defense to one or two players. With Los Angeles, it's Jerry West or Elgin Baylor. With Cincinnati, it's Oscar Robertson or Jerry Lucas. But with Philly, it's any one of five or six men. You can't overplay anybody because the man you lay off will kill you."

The sixth game wasn't decided until the final seconds. Down a point, San Francisco had the ball with 15 seconds remaining. Jim King threw the ball to Barry, who dribbled in the corner. Throughout the series, with much success, Thurmond had set a pick on whomever covered Barry. Barry then had a choice: he could dump the ball back to Thurmond if Wilt picked up Barry or, if Wilt remained under the basket, Barry could shoot. But in the crucial closing seconds of the sixth game of this series, Philly was well aware that San Francisco was likely to try this play or a variation. The *Daily News'* Kiser described what happened at the end:

> . . . with six seconds left, Barry made his move, dribbling toward the key as Chamberlain followed. Then, just in the split second when he stopped dribbling, up came Chet Walker to guard him [Barry] and Chamberlain dropped back to take Thurmond. Barry was trapped [in midair]. He couldn't pass and he couldn't shoot. As the clock reached five seconds he fired something resembling a shot from his hips that came nowhere near going in.

The 76ers were the NBA champions. "It was a masterpiece of strength vs. speed," *The Bulletin's* Bob Vetrone wrote of the series. As had been the case all season, many others on the team besides Wilt contributed to the team's success. Cunningham contributed 17 points, Greer 15, and Guokas 9. Jackson finished with 13 points and 21 rebounds, Jones had 27 points and 6 assists (to lead the team in both categories), Walker had 20 points, and Wilt delivered 24 points and 23 rebounds—and would never again have to listen to someone saying his team couldn't win a title. This was the man, as Vetrone wrote in *The Bulletin*, who had "been tagged a loser through his college and professional career because none of his teams had won a title since his Overbrook days long ago." Not fair—and no longer true.

Hannum had preached dedication all year and the 76ers had taken it to heart on both ends of the court. Wilt, who had shot a woeful 25 percent from the foul line the previous five games, showed up at the Cow Palace to practice foul shots eight hours before the sixth and final game. And late in the game, Wilt converted two critical foul shots, giving the 76ers a lead they never relinquished.

"It's been a long time coming for us and for me," Wilt said of the victory. "And all I can say is that it's wonderful to be a part of the greatest team in basketball."

On a later occasion, he added: "There's something about being a champion that gives you a feeling you can't describe. It's like a big, round glow inside you that tells you you are the best."

The team's celebration continued from the locker room to the cocktail lounge of their hotel, the Jack Tar. When Hannum, their coach and leader, showed up, the players cheered, as champagne-soaked victors always do, and "demanded" a speech. Hannum complied, saying, "Here is my one and only speech. This is the ball that won us the world championship tonight. Everybody signed it and now I'm going to present it to a guy who has given of himself all year so we all could get to this moment. Take it, Wilt." Following which, Wilt Chamberlain, holding the memento of his and his team's greatest success, said, "This belongs to only one person, and that's Mrs. Ike Richman." Thus the game ball from the 1966–1967 championship was presented back in Philadelphia to Clare Richman, Ike's widow, and in whose family's possession the ball remains to this day. From the Jack Tar Hotel, the celebration, many years in the making, moved to Nate Thurmond's nightclub.

Years later, in a documentary about Wilt produced by NBA Entertainment, Hannum described Wilt as "one of the world's great athletes. And I'm talking about in the history of time."

Sharman's 1967 evaluation of the 76ers—"If this isn't the best team that ever played this game, it's got to be among the top two or three"—rings as true in the new millennium as it did then. Many people still consider it the greatest team of all time.

Koppett credited Wilt with being the primary reason for that dominance, calling him the most devastating player in the world:

> The "best" artistically might still be Oscar Robertson, but the toughest was Wilt. In the process he has proved several things, but most among them was basketball's oldest lesson: one man can't do it alone, no matter how big or how good but, given adequate teammates, one dominant figure means championships—as Mikan used to, and as Russell did for so long. Now it was Wilt.

Chapter 13

Was that the year Wilt Chamberlain took only two shots in the second half
of the seventh game? That must have been odd. They say he was the greatest
basketball player of all time.

— George Kiseda, *The Evening Bulletin*, April 20, 1968

Old Men Take Revenge

Wilt had first been exposed to Europe when he traveled with the Harlem Globetrotters in 1958–1959. He loved Europe and, in particular, Italy, to which he returned many times in his postbasketball years. In July 1967, a reporter from *The New York Times* caught up with Wilt in Rome, where he had joined the Globetrotters' summer tour. "Maybe you think I'm crazy playing basketball every night after a hard NBA season," Wilt was quoted as saying. "But this is different. This is refreshing and relaxing. It's a busman's holiday."

The reporter observed that Wilt, at age 30, was on top of the world: the highest-paid player in the league, the leader of the new world champions, the leading scorer in National Basketball Association history—and the owner of a new reddish-copper, two-door Maserati, for which he had paid about $15,000, including the customizing necessary to accommodate his size. (A similar car today would cost in the neighborhood of $200,000.) Wilt's car had five forward gears and could (and one might bet, did) reach 170 miles per hour.

Not more than a minute after he and his team won the NBA championship, Wilt was asked if he thought about playing, at some point in his career, with the American Basketball Association, the newly formed basketball league. He was noncommittal, which is not exactly what the 76ers management, who were under the impression they had a contract with Mr. Chamberlain for the coming season, wanted to hear. "The new league may not be good for basketball if it weakens a lot of teams," Wilt said to the *Times'* reporter in Italy. "But I'll tell you this: it will be good for basketball players." How prescient he was.

On numerous occasions, Eddie Gottlieb said that Wilt did everything that he and all of Wilt's subsequent employers asked of him. Missing the occasional practice or going through the motions at practice was no big deal, Gottlieb said—Bill Russell did so with Red Auerbach's approval. Gottlieb went out of his way in many interviews to point out that Wilt was never a problem, except when it came to negotiating contracts. And just because Gotty didn't like Wilt holding out for more money didn't mean that Wilt, or any player, was being unreasonable. Besides, *unreasonable* is a relative term. Case in point: in the mid-sixties, team owner Richman said he didn't think Oscar Robertson was worth the $60,000 he was asking the Cincinnati Royals' management to pay him. In today's market, $60 million for a four-year contract wouldn't overstate the Big O's worth.

Today players sign multiyear contracts and, with free agency, all the balls, so to speak, are in the players' (and their agents') court. Not so in Wilt's day. Something called the option clause tied a ballplayer (*chained* might be a more accurate description) to his team in perpetuity or until the club decided—and *only the club* could make the decision—that the ballplayer's services were no longer needed, which is to say the poor stiff was over the hill (or dead). Then he was a free man. (The option clause was negotiated out of existence in 1976.)

Although Wilt earned big money by the standards of the sixties, he still had to augment his basketball salary through investments in stocks and real estate and through endorsement contracts. For this he had some good advice and managed to do quite well; in fact, he was one of the first athletes—especially black athletes—to do so.

The contract negotiations between Wilt and Irv Kosloff in the spring, summer, and early fall of the 1967–1968 season was to be the mother of all contract disputes between Wilt and his employer. The origin of the conflict can be precisely determined—it was the moment Ike Richman died in December 1965. Wilt trusted Richman with his life, as the saying goes. Wilt never had anything remotely like that wonderful and trusting relationship with Kosloff, who, upon Richman's death, assumed control of the 76ers.

Koz, as he was called, was a proud, successful businessman. His company, Roosevelt Paper, was one of the industry's leaders. He was also, at times, stubborn. Equally proud and, at times, equally stubborn, was Wilt Chamberlain, who also wasn't above using his status as the most dominant player in the sport's history as leverage in negotiations over the years. "Wilt called me one day and said, 'Come on, Alan, we're going to Chicago. They want to make me president of the Globetrotters,'" recalled Alan Levitt, his financial adviser. So the pair flew to Chicago, there meeting with Allan R. Bloch, the executor of the estate of Abe Saperstein, the deceased owner of the team. Levitt recalled that Wilt liked to embellish things, meaning that the summons from Chicago might have involved a discussion about Wilt becoming more active with the Globetrotters, not necessarily that Bloch was about to offer to make him president of the team. "In my mind," Levitt said, "we were going to Chicago because Wilt wanted to shake up Koz as far as the contract was concerned. Wilt always had something going."

In addition to the inherent tensions between employee and employer, there was also a not-inconsequential point of dispute between the two men: Wilt claimed Ike Richman had promised him 25 percent of the 76ers—one-half of Richman's share in the team. According to Wilt, this had been a verbal agreement between close friends, to which no one else was privy. (Forget for a moment that it would have violated league rules that forbid a player from owning part of a team; Wilt could have owned the team in his postbasketball career.) Kosloff asserted that he knew nothing of the so-called verbal agreement between Richman and Wilt and made it clear to Wilt that he was not going to give him 25 percent (or any percent) of the Philadelphia 76ers.

Richman and Wilt are the only two people who know whether or not Richman promised Wilt part ownership of the team, and neither of them is alive to ask. However, Dr. Stan Lorber, who was a confidant and doctor to Richman, Kosloff, and Wilt, believes that Richman promised Wilt a percentage of the team. "Ike would have done anything for Wilt. And Ike didn't need the money."

Alan Levitt, who was intimately involved with the financial affairs of all three men, believes it is possible that Richman and Wilt struck a secret deal. Dolph Schayes, who while not privy to the financial arrangements between the men involved, spent hundreds of hours with all of them as the team's coach, thinks they did. He has no reason to take Wilt's side in the dispute, except that Schayes is the most forthright of men.

This disagreement shadowed (and eventually soured) the relationship between Wilt and Kosloff. One meeting, called to smooth out matters, disintegrated into a shouting match over which of them owned what percentage of two horses.

In the summer of 1965, Wilt signed a three-year contract in his hotel room at Kutsher's. But, secretly—and with nary a word of it leaking to the newspapers—Wilt signed a new contract with Kosloff during the preseason in the fall of 1966, negating his three-year contract. Why Kosloff allowed Wilt to renegotiate his three-year contract is pure speculation, but maybe he said to himself, "Let me give Wilt something because I'm not giving him a part of the team."

It is important to note that Wilt's "secret" 1966–1967 contract with the 76ers was only for *one year*. Thus Wilt had no contract with the 76ers for the 1967–1968 campaign, much to the surprise of the newspaper reporters and their readers when the story became public.

Wilt had the 76ers over a barrel because they were not the great championship team without him, just as they, given the restraints of the option clause, had Wilt over a barrel—he couldn't sign with another NBA team because, in those days, no owner would have broken the *omerta* of the league and signed him. If he wanted to play basketball professionally, Wilt's only option in the fall of 1967 was to join the new (and clearly second-rate) American Basketball Association. "I just can't picture myself in the Armory in New York or in Houston playing before five hundred or so fans," Wilt said, expressing his less-than-enthusiastic response to the new league.

In mid-October of 1967, the day after the 76ers had played their last exhibition game, a truce, of sorts, was fashioned: Wilt signed a one-year contract with the 76ers for $250,000, the highest salary ever paid, up to that moment, for an athlete in a team sport. (Boxers were the only athletes who had ever made more).

———————

Wilt was 31 years old when the 1967–1968 season commenced, and even his extraordinary body was not immune to aging. For the first time, he talked about the aches and pains associated with 20 years of running up and down basketball courts. He suffered shin splints and muscle cramps, and his knees ached, not surprising for a man who carried 275 pounds on relatively thin legs—relative to his massive upper body, that is. He was scoring less: there were games when he had 14 or 15 points, but only because he shot fewer than 10 times in those games. There were whispers that he didn't have his old offensive moves or, worse, was washed up.

Aware of the gossip and always motivated by a challenge, Wilt went out in mid-December and scored 68 and 47 points back to back. Every player should be so "washed up." Describing the 68-point effort, *The Philadelphia Inquirer*'s Roger Keim wrote, "It was awesome, like watching the swinging ball of a giant crane dismembering small buildings."

More than a few bystanders believed Wilt could score big any night he wanted, depending on his disposition. "That was as mad as I've seen him this year," said coach Hannum, in reference to three technical fouls called against the 76ers, one of them against Wilt when he, as the team captain, asked the referee for an explanation of the earlier calls. "But don't ask me how you turn it on or off," Hannum added.

In his own defense, Wilt resorted to the explanation he used often throughout his career: "I score 10 to 15 points and rebound and feed others and we win and nobody complains. But when I score 10 to 15 points and we lose, then everybody says I'm washed up."

The league now had twelve teams, six in each division. They finished the 1967–1968 season in the following order: Philadelphia, Boston, New York, Detroit, Cincinnati, and Baltimore in the East; and St. Louis, Los Angeles, San Francisco, Chicago, Seattle, and San Diego in the West.

Philadelphia finished eight games ahead of their aging but still dangerous rival, the Boston Celtics, who were led by their player-coach Bill Russell. Auerbach, coach nonpareil, now wore only the general manager's hat, from which vantage point he continued to outfox his counterparts. He regularly picked up players that other teams, for whatever reason, had given up on, but who, the shrewd, cigar-smoking basketball genius recognized, could—and did—fill a role on the Celtics, making the whole stronger than its parts. Bailey Howell, the 6'7" Mississippi All-American, and Wayne Embry, a solid backup center, both picked up in 1966, are only two examples of Auerbach's knack.

Dave Bing of Detroit won the scoring title that season with an average of 27.1 points, followed by Elgin Baylor at 26.0. Wilt was third with 24.3. However, Wilt led the league in rebounds—for the seventh time in the past nine seasons. (He came in second to Russell in 1963–1964 and 1964–1965.) He led the league in field-goal percentage, too. In addition, it was the season during which he led the league in assists—the only time, as he was justly proud to point out, that a center had ever accomplished that feat. Had Cincinnati's Oscar Robertson, who averaged more than nine assists per game that season, not missed 17 games from injuries, he—not Wilt—probably would have led the league in assists. That is to take nothing away from Wilt, who *was* the first center in NBA history to reach 400, 500, 600, and 700 assists, and the only center (besides Bill Russell and Ed

Sadowski) ever to finish in the top five in assists (which Wilt also did in 1964 and 1967). No one, save Wilt, has ever led the NBA in assists, field-goal percentage, and rebounds in the same season, as he did in 1967–1968.

On the downside, Wilt also set a record that season for missed free throws (578)—no need to ask who held the old record. And for the *seventh time* in the past nine seasons, Wilt, who was the only unanimous choice, was selected by the writers and broadcasters as center on the All-NBA first team, for which he and the four other recipients (Elgin Baylor, Jerry Lucas, Oscar Robertson, and Dave Bing) received $500. Players elected to the All-NBA second team (whose center, also the seventh time in nine seasons, was Russell) received $250—which is what some NBA All-Stars in the new millennium probably tip their barbers.

In February 1968 Wilt became the first player in NBA history to score 25,000 points. He had accomplished that in less than nine full seasons. At that time Wilt had scored *4,000 more points than any other NBA player*, present or past. Soon after Wilt had been given the ball with which he scored his 25,000[th] point, he was invited for dinner at the home of Dr. Stan Lorber, who recalled what happened that evening:

> He arrived with this package, and inside of it was the ball and it was inscribed as follows:
>
>
>
> WILT CHAMBERLAIN
> 25,000 POINTS
> FEB. 23RD 1968
> DR. STAN LORBER
> WITHOUT YOU THIS MILESTONE
> WOULD NEVER HAVE BEEN REACHED
> THANKS FOR ALL THE CURES
> DIP
>
>
>
> I said to him, "This is very nice. I appreciate it, but why are you giving it to me?"
>
> He said, "I've found through the years that these awards and mementos mean far more to my friends than to me. I don't need these mementos to demonstrate what I've done. It's in the record books."
>
> I thought it was very selfless of him. It showed he didn't turn everything inward but could look outside and see the effect on his friends of his accomplishments and that they treasured what he had done.

With their 62–20 mark, the 76ers' winning percentage was .756. They were a great club. They owned, as of then, the best one-year (1966–1967), two-year (1966–1968), and three-year (1965–1968) won-lost records in NBA history. Having won 25 of their last 30 games, the 76ers were primed to defend their title.

Their first-round opponent was the New York Knickerbockers. This was a solid, soon-to-be fabulous New York team led by forward Willis Reed, guards Dick Barnett and Cazzie Russell (two guys who could find the center of the basket), and center Walter "Bells" Bellamy. There was also Dick Van Arsdale and three rookies about whom the basketball world would be hearing more: Walt Frazier, Bill Bradley (back from his sojourn as a Rhodes Scholar at Oxford), and scarecrow-thin Phil Jackson. He would achieve basketball immortality coaching Michael Jordan and the Chicago Bulls and Shaquille O'Neal, Kobe Bryant, and the Los Angeles Lakers to nine NBA championships—a record he shares with Boston's Red Auerbach.

The 76ers were aware the Knicks were no slouches, and no one was surprised when the teams split the first two games. The 76ers won a brutal third game—described by George Kiseda as "fierce, intense, dramatic, bruising, and exhausting"—in double overtime, 138–132. But the victory came at a high cost: in the first overtime, Cunningham, their budding star, collided with Jackson, all bony arms and elbows. Cunningham broke his right (nonshooting) hand in three places and was out for the season. That was 18.9 points and the best sixth man in basketball (a starter on any other club) gone from the lineup. To add to the 76ers' woes, Luke Jackson had a pulled hamstring muscle, Hal Greer had bursitis in his knees, and, to quote Kiseda, "Wilt Chamberlain was showing his age with sore toes and elbows and knees."

The Knicks tied the series at two games apiece by winning the fourth game in New York, 107–98. Each team had won on its court and lost on its opponent's court. So the pattern held in Game 5, in Philadelphia, where the 76ers prevailed, 123–107. The 76ers were up three games to two, needing one more to advance.

Throughout this hotly contested series the Knicks' press had perplexed the world champions. But not in Game 6, wherein the 76ers flattened the New York upstarts, 113–97. The 76ers had advanced to the Eastern Finals. Greer, on gimpy old legs, shot 15 for 30, scoring 35 points. Wilt had a solid game: 25 points and 27 rebounds (the latter almost half the team's rebounds). When

Bellamy, the Knicks center, and coach Red Holzman were asked what had been the difference in the series, they both gave the same answer: "Wilt Chamberlain." And, as Kiseda's story reported, "All Chamberlain did was lead everybody in points (153), rebounds (145), assists (38), blocked shots, and complaints." The last was in reference to Wilt's observation, "I'm not saying the NBA is bush, but why do you play three days in a row like we were forced to do and now rest until Friday? There has got to be a better way of doing it."

Boston defeated Detroit in six games. For the sixth time in eight years, it was Boston versus Philadelphia for the Eastern Division (and probably the NBA) title. Only this time, Philly was the defending champion.

"I think we'll take them in less than seven games," coach Hannum, mincing no words, opined. That was a bold statement, considering the 76ers were without Cunningham (broken right hand), Jackson was hobbled by a thigh pull, Greer's creaky joints ached, and Wilt and Greer were not youngsters. But neither were the Celtics, beginning with their leader, Russell, who was 34. Sam Jones was 35, Bailey Howell and Wayne Embry, 31 (old in that era for an NBA player). Only John Havlicek and Larry Siegfried were unquestionably in their prime, and perhaps Satch Sanders and Don Nelson were as well. The 76ers and the Celtics had split the regular-season series four games apiece; however, the 76ers had won four of the last five meetings. Everyone expected a bruising series, the first game of which was scheduled for Friday night, April 5, in the City of Brotherly Love.

But as it happened, at sunset on April 4, 1968, the night before the NBA playoffs were to begin, a man came out of his room and stood on a motel balcony in Memphis, Tennessee. That man was Martin Luther King Jr. Moments later he was assassinated.

King was the most respected black man in the United States, if not the world. He was a symbol of hope and reason in a world that, in early 1968, many felt was going mad. There was rancor and division in the United States and throughout Western Europe over the U.S. involvement in Vietnam. The Tet Offensive, launched by the North Vietnamese in January 1968, caused still more Americans to question the wisdom of their government's Vietnam policy. Democrat Eugene McCarthy's better-than-expected showing against President Lyndon Johnson in the New Hampshire primary precipitated the stunning announcement on the last day of March that Johnson would not seek reelection. And now, in early April (to be followed in early June by Robert Kennedy's) there was the murder of a man who espoused nonviolence. Was America coming unglued? How would blacks react to King's assassination?

In the context of the assassination, an NBA playoff game seemed rather unimportant to many people, especially for the black players for whom Martin Luther King Jr. was a symbol of hope and achievement. And lest one forget, eight of the ten starters in the Boston-Philadelphia series were black.

Hal Greer was eating dinner with his wife when he heard the news on the radio. He recalled that one of the first things he said to his wife was, "There's no way possible we'll play." Chet Walker had a similar reaction: "I don't know how the other guys on the team feel about civil rights, but to me a basketball game doesn't seem that important right now."

"Is 76er-Boston Game Necessary Tonight?" asked the headline in George Kiseda's *Evening Bulletin* story the day after Dr. King's murder. "The game should be cancelled out of deference to the dead Dr. King," he suggested.

Wilt believed the game should be canceled, too, and very publicly said so—to his everlasting credit. "I would personally like to see the whole day taken off as some kind of memorial to Dr. King," he was quoted in the afternoon edition of *The Bulletin* prior to the game. "But I'm only one individual. . . . I don't want to instigate anything. I'll follow the majority." He did, however, call Jack Ramsay, the 76ers general manager, around 2:30 that Friday afternoon—the day of the game—to express his opinion. Ramsay was quoted in *The Bulletin* the following day as having said, "I don't know what can be accomplished by [a postponement]. It's not [for lack of] sympathy with the tragedy. We've lost a great guy, a great man. But I'm not of the opinion that postponing a thing as insignificant as a basketball game will solve the problem." Ramsay did try to contact Auerbach to discuss his and Boston's sentiments regarding whether or not to play the game, but he was unable to reach him.

Around 5:00 on the evening of the game, Russell called Wilt. Both agreed the game ought to be called off but decided it was too late for the players to take it upon themselves to cancel the game. (Fifteen thousand people were planning to go or already had departed for the game site.) It was a league decision, and the league had not acted, except not to react. (Of course, if such a tragedy befell a prominent black figure today—say if Nelson Mandela were murdered—the game would be cancelled within an hour.)

Around 7:30, at a meeting called by Wilt before the game, Wilt and Jones told their teammates that the two of them, even at that late hour, favored not playing the game. The team held a vote. The result: seven to two in favor of playing. Wilt and Jones voted against playing; Walker abstained. Greer said he didn't want to play, but felt "it was too late to call the game." So, too, did the other 76ers, fearing the fans might riot. Before the game, Wilt repeated his feelings: "I personally would not like to play tonight. But I can only go along with what the majority of the team feels." Boston's players met, but did not state, at least publicly, whether they thought the game ought to be called, although Russell addressed the issue after the game. "I would have liked to have seen the games postponed, especially this one," he said. "I've been in a state of shock. I didn't sleep last night."

Moments before the Friday evening playoff game was to begin, the NBA offices in New York announced that the *second* playoff game, scheduled for Sunday, April 7, would be postponed until Wednesday, April 10, since President Johnson had designated Sunday as a day of national mourning. But the game on Friday, April 5, was to be played. That game, described in *The Bulletin* as "unreal" and "devoid of emotion," ended in a loss for the 76ers, 127–118. No mystery as to how the Celts had won it: they made 58 percent of their shots.

"I covered that first game, the day after the assassination," recalled Leonard Koppett, then with *The New York Times*. "It was the eeriest, most subdued sporting event I've ever seen. Everybody played hard and said, 'Let's get out of here.'"

At some point in the evening, Wilt was presented with the Podoloff Trophy, named for the longtime commissioner and emblematic of the league's Most Valuable Player—the third consecutive year he had won it. It seemed particularly inappropriate to celebrate a sports achievement given the tragic event in Memphis that had so recently occurred, and though not friends with Dr. King, Wilt knew him as one public figure knows another public figure. "Basketball has been little on my mind," Wilt was quoted as saying in Frank Brady's *Bulletin* game story. "I didn't think about basketball, about actually playing basketball from [Thursday] night until I stepped on the court."

On Sunday, the day of national mourning for Dr. King, Wilt attended a service in Dr. King's honor at Mt. Carmel Baptist Church in West Philadelphia—the very church, 31 years later, in which family, childhood friends, teammates, and many other people whose lives Wilt had touched would come to mourn and celebrate *his* life.

Wilt showed up for optional practice at the Spectrum on Monday, April 8, saying he wanted, and needed, a workout. He was the first one there and, along with a late-season addition to the club, the rookie Jim Reid, Wilt was the last to leave. This was a different Wilt from the one who missed practices during the playoffs in 1966, maybe because Hannum left it up to Wilt whether or not to attend. It was a policy, no different, he pointed out to reporters, than Auerbach followed with Russell, and which Hannum himself had followed years before with Bob Pettit on the St. Louis Hawks.

In the aftermath of King's murder, riots and fires broke out in cities across America. Sixteen blacks were killed during the mayhem. Wilt, who said he had attended the famous Civil Rights March in Washington in 1963, at which Dr. King proclaimed "I have a dream," was interviewed at the practice by Leonard Lewin of the *New York Post*. Wilt was quoted as follows:

> The people who are setting the fires and throwing stones are only punching out. They are definitely opposite what Dr. King preached and they know it. . . . I've been rather upset because I have friends that believe in black power. I don't think they want to hurt white people, but the thing that disturbs me is that they don't believe in the unity of people. I believe in people power—the human race. I don't care if they are black, white, or whatever color they are. . . . The reason why I have a great deal of respect for all people is because I believe in what Dr. King was trying to perpetuate with his life. It [is] a way for fellows like myself, in a small way, to help what he was trying to do. He was exemplifying a life where people have respect for each other as human beings. . . . He stretched out his hand to all mankind. It had nothing to do with pigmentation.

The next day Wilt and team owner Kosloff flew to Atlanta for King's funeral. "Getting an invitation to Dr. King's funeral was one of the most important times of his life," Wilt's sister recalled. "That was a real big deal to Dip."

Following the funeral, Wilt and Kosloff flew to Boston, where they rejoined the team for Game 2, which was to be played the following night in Boston, a city in which the 76ers had won only one playoff game in five years (and that had been the year before). So they went out and beat Boston, 115–106. Their bench—Matty Guokas, Billy Melchionni, and Johnny Green—was superb, combining for 31 points and making 61 percent of their shots. "Overall," Hannum said, "I thought it was determined defense on the part of everyone."

Wilt observed, "[It was] the kind of game I was brought up on. If you miss at one end, you try to make it up at the other end."

Game 3, the very next night, was in Philadelphia. Wilt was being treated for numerous ailments, including a strained hamstring behind his knee, a partial tear of his right calf, and a bum toe—all of which had him limping noticeably throughout the game. Still, Wilt got Russell into foul trouble—he had five by the end of the third quarter. Coach Russell had to bench himself, to be replaced by Embry, who was not nearly as effective on defense as Russell. The 76ers won, 122–114, thanks in large measure to Greer's 21 fourth-quarter points. By now a starter, Boston's Havlicek was having a great series, averaging 31 points, 10 rebounds, and nine assists. This was the series in which he emerged as one of the league's top players. "He's amazing," said Greer. "He plays 48 minutes and at the end of the game he's still playing me tough all over. I'd say he's got to be the best-conditioned athlete in the league."

On Sunday, April 14, it was back to Boston for Game 4, the only game of the series to be televised nationally (in contrast to the present custom of giving every playoff game coast-to-coast TV coverage). In years and battles past (except for the previous season), it had been Boston's vaunted press that had done in the 76ers. The Sixers guards would be pressed, pick up their dribble, and find themselves, in George Kiseda's words, "Forty feet from the basket with no place to go and nobody to pass to." But the teams to which Kiseda was referring were the legendary 1959 to 1965 Celtics; they were younger and faster (and had K. C. Jones, who had since retired). In Game 4 of the 1968 series, Boston played older and slower. Now it was Boston turning over the ball instead of its opponent. At one point in the game, coach Russell had player Russell guard Luke Jackson while Wayne Embry played Wilt, a tacit admission that Wilt was wearing Russell down. The 76ers won Game 4, 110–105, to take a commanding three-to-one lead in the series.

No team had ever come back from a three-to-one deficit in an NBA playoff. Two of the next three games were in Philadelphia, where the 76ers could wrap it up the next night at the Spectrum. Chill the champagne. And don't forget the cheese steaks, Tastykakes, and soft pretzels, with maybe a White House hoagie, fresh from Atlantic City, for the Big Fella.

"The Celtics were dead, but someone forgot to call the coroner," was how Kiseda described Game 5, won by the Celtics, 122–104. Great defense, including a full-court press from the get-go, won it for the Celtics—that plus 37 points from the aging but still potent Sam Jones. And throw in some lousy shooting by the 76ers, who were starting to hear—or imagined they heard—Russell's footsteps when they were set to shoot. The 76ers shot a paltry 2 for 20 at one stretch in the fourth quarter.

"They're a proud team," said Greer. "To lose four to one, that would seem like they're dead and they want to prove they're not."

What a strange series: the home team had lost four of five games—more like a home-court disadvantage, one writer dubbed it. The Celtics were now down three games to two, and the future didn't look as bleak, especially as Game 6 was in Boston.

Play solid defense and outrebound your opponent and that usually leads to victory. So it was for the Boston team in Game 6, in which it prevailed, 114–106. Once again, Havlicek was superb: 28 points, 10 rebounds, and six assists. In the last minutes of the game, in response to signs in the Spectrum and chants from the Philly fans announcing the demise of the Celtics, the Boston fans began yelling, "Philly is dead. Philly is dead." Wise "old" Sam Jones said, "We ain't won nothin' yet. We just won the right to play them Friday."

Other than Greer, who scored 40 points, and Guokas, the 76ers shot poorly in Game 6, as was vividly conveyed by Kiseda: "The 76ers might [just as] well have been trying to put a medicine ball in a teacup." Russell had 17 points and 31 rebounds. Wilt had 27 rebounds and 20 points but on a 6-for-21 night from the field. Of his great rival, Russell magnanimously said after the game: "His leg is hurting him. Everybody knows. A lesser man probably wouldn't be out there."

The series was tied three games apiece. The showdown was Friday night in Philadelphia's Spectrum. No NBA team—to reiterate a point worth repeating—had ever come back from being down three games to one. But, on the other hand, the Celtics had never lost the seventh game in a title series. Add to that the fact that the home team had won 16 consecutive times in the deciding game of an NBA seven-game series. And this game was on Philly's home court. So *one* of those streaks had to end.

The Bulletin's headline tells the tale of this game: "Boston's Proud Old Men Didn't Collapse." Before 15,202 stunned fans, "the world's greatest basketball team" disappeared. And so, *apparently,* had the world's greatest player. Boston won, 100–96, thus keeping alive its remarkable record of never having lost a seventh game in a playoff series—the record number now stood at nine.

How in the world could the 76ers lose, after being up three games to one, with two of the last three games played at home?

Greer said they became too cautious. "We played not to make mistakes," he said. "We changed our brand of ball. We didn't run the ball when we should have."

Of the series' outcome, Kiseda wrote: "In the final the Celtics had two offensive weapons going for them—their fast break and outside shooting. The 76ers had no outside shooting and, unbelievably, they did not score one basket on a fast break."

Incredibly, in the seventh game, Philadelphia outrebounded Boston, 68–61, and took 24 more shots, 108–84. Yet Philly lost. As George Kiseda reported, "In the first half the 76ers," whom he derisively and sarcastically referred to as the world's greatest basketball team, "would have had trouble dropping a basketball into the Grand Canyon. They missed 37 of their first 49 shots and fell 12 points behind."

To be sure, the 76ers offense was deplorable in both halves, save for Wilt. Greer shot 32 percent (on 8 for 25); Jones and Walker 36 percent (on 8 for 22, but Walker was especially dreadful in the second half, going 4 for 14); Jackson shot 40 percent (on 7 for 17); and Guokas was at 20 percent (on 2 for 10). Yes, they shot poorly, but Boston's defense, in particular Russell's, had something to do with it. Russell blocked 10 shots and intimidated the 76ers on God knows how many others. The poor shooting against Boston was no aberration. Against the other NBA teams the 76ers shot almost 50 percent during the season; against Boston, only 40. And matters got worse from there, with the 76ers shooting 37 percent, 37 percent, and 35 percent in their final three losses to Boston—incidentally the first time that season they lost three games in a row!

In retrospect, the slide began in the fourth quarter of Game 5, in which, at one point, they shot 2 for 20. After that, they never got their groove back. And still, they almost won the deciding game. Three minutes into the fourth quarter the 76ers held the lead, 81–79. But they hit only five more shots for the remainder of the game. With 1:16 remaining, Russell took over. He got rebounds, made free throws—all the while intimidating the 76ers. As Kiseda observed: "Chamberlain was magnificent on defense and magnificent on the boards (34 rebounds), but that wasn't enough because Russell was magnificent, too. It may have been Russell's greatest series against Chamberlain." Wilt concurred: "I thought they [Jones, Havlicek, and Russell] were nothing short of sensational."

Boston's proud "old" men had taken their revenge. Russell admitted in interviews after the game that it had rankled him during the season to hear the 76ers referred to as the world's greatest team. He also made the following remark: "The 1968 Celtics could not compare with the great Celtic teams of the past on talent, but they're number one when it comes to desire." That victory in the seventh game of the 1968 Finals was the most satisfying of his 12-year career, he acknowledged after the game.

Even after the loss, coach Hannum insisted he still had the better team.

Besides 34 rebounds (half his team's), an ailing Wilt, whose injuries affected his movement, was limited to 14 points on a four-for-nine night from the field, which was still a much higher percentage than his teammates'. He made no excuses for his low point production, nor did Jones or Jackson, both suffering from injuries. Yes, the 76ers were hurt, but playing hurt they had managed to go up three games to one. And Boston lost starter Satch Sanders, out with back spasms, for the final game.

Amazingly, Wilt took only two shots in the second half of Game 7. He got a lot of grief then, as well as over subsequent years, for taking only two shots in the second half—and they weren't even shots, but merely tap-ins, following up on missed shots by teammates. This episode is one of the most controversial of Wilt's basketball career.

In the locker room after the game, George Kiseda broached the question to Wilt and Hannum, but, as Kiseda wrote in his game story, he didn't get satisfying answers from either, though not because Wilt and Hannum evaded the question or the subject: "The answers were nonanswers. Oh, Chamberlain was gracious. He has a rare talent for being gracious in adversity. It is the little things that seem to irritate him." On the game, Wilt told Kiseda: "Our offense was such that in the second half and mainly in the fourth quarter it didn't call for me to shoot the ball. It called for me to go to the offensive board." Coach Hannum maintained: "I wanted to play a normal game. We tried to get the ball to the open man. It wasn't intentional that Wilt didn't shoot in the second half; things just worked out that way."

Two weeks later Kiseda was still pondering the question. A chance conversation he had with Vince Miller, the 76ers scout and statistician who charted games, solved the mystery of why Wilt Chamberlain hadn't shot but two times in the second half of the seventh game of the NBA Eastern Championship with the Boston Celtics. The answer is simple: Wilt hardly got the ball in the second half. Even Wilt Chamberlain can't score without the ball. Wilt got the ball in the pivot only *five times* in the third quarter and only *twice* in the fourth quarter, a statistical breakdown of the game revealed. This was a drastic departure from the normal 76ers pattern, even a departure from the first half of the fateful game. In a typical Sixers game, Kiseda observed, the ball went in to the pivot 10 to 15 times *per quarter*. In the first half of the infamous Game 7, the ball went in to the pivot 23 times; in the second half, all of 7 times. In this debacle, the ball went in to Wilt in the pivot *twice* in the fourth quarter of the most important game of the year—instead of the normal 10 to 15 times!

Why didn't Wilt, always aware of his stats, point this out when he was asked by reporters immediately after the game and many times over the years, "Why didn't you shoot more in the 1968 Eastern finals?" Apprised of Miller's statistical analysis, Wilt had this response:

> I'm willing, able, and capable of accepting responsibility for the loss, if that's where they want to place the blame. . . . What would I have looked like if I had said, "Hey, we lost because my teammates didn't get the ball in to me"?
>
> If Alex Hannum didn't have enough guts to lay it on the line and accept a certain amount of responsibility for the loss and name the reasons why, then I've lost a lot of respect for him, which I have, and I will tell him that when I see him. You can't shoot the ball if you don't have the ball, but you know something? After that game, not one writer came up to me and said, "Hey, how come the ball didn't come in to you?" Not one. But all of them did come and ask me, "How come you didn't shoot more?"

By not asking the obvious—why hadn't the ball gone in to Wilt in that decisive second half?—Kiseda acknowledged that it was not the finest hour for the basketball beat writers (himself included).

Hannum admitted he called the plays from the sidelines, so he must share much of the blame for Wilt not getting the ball in the second half. But Hannum isn't the only culpable party: there are Wilt's teammates—they shot horribly and didn't get the ball to him. Some measure of responsibility also must be assigned to Wilt who, after all, was the most dominant offensive player in the history of basketball. Granted he was playing hurt, but that didn't stop him from gathering

34 rebounds. A leader leads; a scorer wants the ball—particularly in crucial moments. Why didn't Wilt shout to his mates, "Gimme the damn ball!" He could have said it in a timeout or while foul shots were being taken. Anyone who has ever played basketball knows there are ways to alert your teammates that they're not getting the ball to you and that you want it. But Wilt didn't speak up, and he said in other interviews, sometime after the game, that he should have been more aggressive. Why wasn't he? Could it have been that Wilt wanted to show Hannum, and the world, that if the Sixers weren't going to throw the ball to him, they weren't going to beat Boston? It may sound illogical, but who said Wilt was always logical?

It remains inexplicable why Wilt, his coach, and his teammates didn't make sure that he got the ball.

Instead of Wilt coming to the offensive rescue, Boston completed its stunning comeback. Certainly, Philadelphia's sports fans, among the most knowledgeable and rabid, have endured their share of disappointments by the city's professional baseball, football, hockey, and basketball teams. But the collapse in the 1968 Eastern Finals, in which the 76ers botched a three-to-one lead, with two of the final three games at home, ranks with the worst of them.

World champions one season, a bust the next. The 76ers blew it—plain and simple.

Chapter 14

I don't think I ever played with anyone like him. When you thought you knew him, you didn't. And the other thing that was most surprising, when things were really going good, it seemed he liked to stir the pot a little bit. Why, I don't know. It just seemed he liked a little controversy around him all the time. He'd say something and I'd scratch my head and think, "Things are going good. Why would he even say something like that?"

Yet he was extremely sensitive. During introductions one night he said to me, "Why do they boo me and they never boo you?" I answered, "My best guess is what you said, 'David against Goliath.' If people knew you better, were around you more, there's no way that would happen."

—Jerry West, Lakers teammate

Elgin Baylor was the reigning final authority on everything—until Wilt got there. Elgin was the expert on the kind of bacon used in the restaurant. Well, Wilt is the world's authority and needed to be louder than everybody. Watching all this was great entertainment.

—Keith Erickson, Lakers teammate of Elgin Baylor and Wilt

I used to ask Elgin, "Whose face would be the most recognized in our country? Would it be President Nixon's?" No, you put Nixon in a sweatshirt, you may not recognize him. Wilt? Everybody knows Wilt. If you're talking to Wilt in an airport, people push you aside. "Take a picture with my kid, will ya, Wilt?" "Sign this, will ya, Wilt?" I felt sorry for the poor bastard. He couldn't go anywhere and just be himself. But that happened to him since he was 15 years old, so he was bound to be spoiled, bound to be impressed with himself.

—Willem "Butch" van Breda Kolff, Lakers coach

We're Not a Happy Team

The denouement following the Sixers' playoff collapse was not long in coming. In short order, Alex Hannum announced he would not be returning to coach the 76ers. Hannum, who said he had made his decision months before the fateful Celtics series, wanted to return to the West Coast, where his two daughters lived, where he had an apartment house, and where, in the offseason, he ran his construction business. Thus, the only coach whose teams had beaten the Boston Celtics for the NBA title between 1957 and 1968 was gone. Back in California, he would be hired to coach the Oakland Oaks, whom he led to the ABA title, thereby also becoming the first man to win championships in the two major professional basketball leagues. In his valedictory press conference before leaving Philadelphia, he threw a bouquet to his starting center: "I hate to leave Wilt. Coaching Wilt is one of the most pleasant experiences I've had in sports."

Striking words those, particularly since *The Evening Bulletin*'s George Kiseda wrote that during the season past, a brooding, mostly unhappy Wilt Chamberlain went out of his way to put down Hannum in public. Nevertheless, Hannum's tribute was heartfelt, as he was not one to mince words or mask his feelings. And Hannum and Wilt did become buddies after their basketball careers—they often went to the racetrack near Hannum's Southern California home in the nineties and, when Wilt was inducted into the Hall of Fame, he asked Hannum to introduce him, which his ex-coach was glad to do.

Asked at his farewell press conference who might replace him as the 76ers coach, Hannum said the team ought to consider Wilt, noting, with devilish humor, that Bill Russell's strongest point in coaching was his rapport with *his* center. The 76ers players, beginning with one of the team's stars, Luke Jackson, said that Wilt would make a fine coach. But Jack Ramsay, the 76ers general manager, speaking for the team's owner, Irv Kosloff, was quoted as saying that he wanted a coach with bench experience (possibly a diplomatic way to exclude Wilt from the running).

Was Wilt interested in coaching the Sixers? Yes, no, and depends.

Contacted by reporters in Los Angeles, where he had flown to be with his ailing, soon-to-be-operated-on father, Wilt said he felt that there were only a few guys capable of coaching the 76ers—first among them his old coach Frank McGuire and, second, Bill Sharman. Wilt's position seemed to be that if none of the top guns was available, better him than a "nobody" at the helm. But neither man could—or would—do it, as general manager Ramsay learned when he contacted McGuire, then coaching at the University of South Carolina. McGuire indicated he was not interested in making the change, nor was Sharman, then coaching the Los Angeles Stars in the ABA.

Whether Wilt would coach the 76ers was secondary to the more important point of whether he would even return to the team, since he did not have a contract with them for the 1968–1969 season. (And one can imagine with what pleasure Irv Kosloff approached the coming negotiations with his superstar center. But Kosloff knew it was worth the effort: with Wilt and the team's winning ways, the 76ers had set a club record for attendance the previous season, averaging ten thousand fans per game, outdrawing both Boston and Los Angeles, two of the healthier franchises in the league.)

Wilt had three demands to be met before he'd sign with the Sixers: one, an increase to about $250,000 per year; two, a three-year contract; and three, equity in the team. The old issue had resurfaced of Wilt wanting—and believing he had been promised and, thus, was owed—part ownership of the team.

Wilt had to have known Kosloff was not going to give him a slice of the team. That being the case, and although the 76ers and Wilt negotiated for more than a month, there is the question of whether Wilt had any intention of remaining in Philadelphia. The author's guess is no, and that had Wilt been offered the Liberty Bell (but not a percentage of the Sixers), he still would have left. As George Kiseda commented in print, "For reasons known only to himself, Chamberlain was a very unhappy millionaire in his last season in Philadelphia."

The fact is Wilt wanted to be in Los Angeles. His mother and very sick father were living in L.A. in Villa Chamberlain, the apartment complex Wilt had built and still owned at 1776 Rimpau Street. (How about that address for an interesting coincidence?) Wilt liked California's climate, joining the many millions of people who, for that reason alone, have chosen to relocate there. And, truth be told, he was too big for Philadelphia. He needed (and wanted) to be in New York or Los Angeles, where he could enjoy some privacy and be only one celebrity among many, albeit always the most visible. (Wilt supposedly once told Elvis Presley, at one time his Southern California neighbor, that while Elvis could disguise his appearance by a wig and dark glasses, nothing Wilt could do would hide who he was.) And, finally, Los Angeles was a place where, in 1968, it was less of a hassle for a black man to date gorgeous white women, of which Los Angeles was reputed to have more than its fair share. This last point, according to Wilt's longtime doctor and friend, Stan Lorber, was an important element in Wilt's decision to move to the West Coast.

At one point in the back-and-forth negotiations, which played out in newspapers from coast to coast, Jack Kiser wrote in the *Philadelphia Daily News*, "Kosloff knew Wilt did nothing last year to deserve such a raise in salary other than to grow older." Kiser was normally fair and perceptive, but the tone and gist of this column was off base and, rightly, incensed Wilt, who could point out on his own behalf that he had averaged 24.3 points, 23.8 rebounds, 8.6 assists, and nine blocked shots per game, and had almost led the team to the Eastern title. (In today's market, an owner would sacrifice his firstborn to sign a center with those statistics.) And Wilt had been voted the Most Valuable Player by his peers, the third consecutive year (and the fourth time overall) he had won the award.

Unable to secure the coaches he really wanted, Kosloff apparently had a change of mind. Jack Ramsay remembered the subsequent negotiations this way:

> When Alex left to go back to the West Coast, I talked to a lot of guys. I told Wilt who I was talking to. Wilt said, "How about if I become the player-coach and you take care of me? You take care of the *X*'s and *O*'s, and I'll be the coach."
>
> I thought it was a good idea because I thought Wilt would want the team to do well. Koz and I were in agreement. [However, in Wilt's version it was the Sixers who broached the subject of him coaching.]
>
> When Wilt came back from a trip to L.A., we had a meeting, and I said, "Wilt, Koz and I think it is a good idea." But Wilt told us he was no longer interested. He said, "I want to be traded to a West Coast team." That meant San Diego, Los Angeles, or Seattle. He had

made up his mind he wanted to leave. He said, "If you don't trade me, I'll go to the ABA." At that point, we put out feelers to see what we could get.

What they got was a bite from Jack Kent Cooke, a dapper, self-made Canadian multimillionaire whose empire consisted of magazines, radio and cable-television stations, and sports teams—he owned 25 percent of the Washington Redskins and all of the Los Angeles Kings of the National Hockey League. He had bought the Los Angeles Lakers franchise for $5.2 million in 1965 and was determined, after too many losses to the Boston Celtics in the NBA Finals, to do whatever was necessary to turn the club into a championship team.

Alan Levitt, Wilt's financial adviser, remembers a meeting between Wilt and Jack Kent Cooke in Cooke's Bel Air home:

> Jack is a hard-nosed businessman, very precise with his English, and he liked to control the conversation. But he didn't control the conversation with Wilt. They started talking about racing cars. Well, Wilt could talk about racing cars. They started talking about food, and Wilt knew all about food. They started talking about horses. Wilt knew all about horses. They talked about dogs. Wilt was an amazing guy. He was into and had done everything.

Having also discussed the merits of their respective Bentleys, Wilt and Cooke eventually came to an understanding on terms of employment.

Thus, after two months of impasse and rumors, Wilt's Philadelphia basketball career was officially over on July 9, 1968, when the sports world's worst-kept secret was announced at simultaneous press conferences in Philadelphia and Los Angeles: Wilt had been traded to the Los Angeles Lakers for guard Archie Clark, center Darrall Imhoff, and forward Jerry Chambers. This might have been the first time in any sport (it certainly was in basketball) that a reigning MVP was traded.

Kosloff had little wiggle room: if he didn't trade Wilt, he might end up with nothing, for Wilt could have jumped to the American Basketball Association. The owners of that young, struggling league were ready to go further into hock by subsidizing one of its teams, the Los Angeles Stars, to sign Wilt for a big-bucks contract. But that never came to pass. Nor did anything come of Wilt's meeting with Sam Schulman, owner of the Seattle SuperSonics, who decided he wanted Wilt and had a letter of intent written up. The problem was he had no players whom the Sixers wanted in exchange for Wilt.

Wilt had used Schulman as a stalking horse to obtain more money from the Lakers owner, Cooke. And it worked: Wilt received a five-year contract, which a columnist for *Newsweek* called "the most lucrative in the NBA and perhaps in the history of sports." Little did the columnist, or anyone at that time, suspect just how lucrative. The papers reported it at $250,000 per year, but what they didn't know was that Wilt's salary was paid net—after taxes, which in 1969 took as much as 70 percent of income from the top tax bracket, the one Wilt was in. He received $1.564 million from the Lakers over the next five years. Another unusual part of Wilt's deal with Cooke was that some of Wilt's salary would be placed in a tax shelter. That tax shelter paid off beyond Wilt's—really his financial adviser's—highest hopes. In the eighties, when Wilt cashed out his share of the tax shelter, he became an even wealthier man; indeed, at his death, the proceeds from the tax shelter and his home were the most significant parts of his net worth.

Two days after the trade, the *Daily News'* Jack Kiser, wrote: "The big guy is virtually unstoppable when all the juices are flowing in the right direction. Everybody knows that, especially the players. But Wilt doesn't have the killer instinct to be a consistent terror, and there will be nights when he won't put out as much effort as cheerleader Doris Day. [The popular singer was a well-known Lakers fan.] This can be a disruptive force with coworkers, especially since he'll be making as much in a month as they do in a season."

At the time, Wilt claimed that he didn't force the trade—that if only Koz had shown him he was wanted by offering any percentage of the team, he would have stayed. "Mr. Cooke wanted me more," Wilt asserted. But actually, he did force the trade, admitting so in an interview with reporter Kiser years later and saying, to boot, "I wish now I had stayed in Philly. I think I might have won two, maybe three more championship rings than I did."

Wilt had met Richard Nixon in the early sixties and had spoken to him again at the funeral of Martin Luther King Jr. He was impressed with Nixon and had expressed a desire to become involved in a political campaign. Making good on his word, in early July 1968, Wilt joined Nixon's campaign for the Republican presidential nomination. "I think black Americans are just beginning to realize the power of the black vote. I think it is a mistake for 90 to 95 percent [of blacks] to be all in one party," Wilt said when he announced his support for Nixon, referring to the pattern of blacks to vote overwhelmingly for Democratic candidates.

Wilt was to advise Nixon and the campaign on programs for and problems of the black community. The two campaigned together that July in Philadelphia, during which a newspaper report—which had to have caused some embarrassment to Nixon's campaign staff, if not to Wilt—revealed that Wilt had failed to vote for president when he lived in Philadelphia, San Francisco, or his then-current legal address at his parents' place in Los Angeles (where a William Chamberlain, his father, was registered as a Democrat—but no Wilton). Wilt admitted he had not voted in either the 1960 (Nixon versus Kennedy) or 1964 presidential elections. Whoever said campaign advisers had to be perfect? Whatever Wilt's voting record, Nixon was glad to have him on board.

Wilt did, unlike most prominent athletes at that (or any) time, speak out on social issues. For instance, he said in an interview in April 1968 that there were not enough blacks in executive positions in sports and, in addition, he hoped Nixon would promote one of his interests, population control. Later in life, he said publicly that he favored decriminalization of so-called victimless crimes, such as smoking marijuana, visiting prostitutes, and gambling (in some or all of which, a cynic might suggest, he sometimes indulged).

One adviser speculated that Wilt's endorsement of Nixon had as much to do with Wilt's contrariness or need to be different—because in 1968 everyone expected black celebrities to be partial to the Democrats—as with his genuine belief that Nixon's brand of republicanism would benefit all Americans, including his fellow blacks. Wilt also hoped he'd have entree to Nixon, whereas if he supported a Democrat, he'd be one of many famous blacks supporting the candidate.

Looking back on this experience six years later, Wilt said, "I was subconsciously influenced to back Richard [Nixon] by several things he and I had in common. Throughout his political career, he'd been called a "loser," the guy who could never win the big one. Me, too."

Wilt's adviser said that he was always under the impression that politics meant little to the basketball star—he just wanted to be thought of as more than a dumb athlete, his image being very important to him.

Red Smith, the great sportswriter and columnist, covered the 1968 Republican National Convention. That so prominent a black as Wilt supported Nixon was news, prompting Smith to write about Wilt's involvement. Smith described the goateed Wilt in "seven feet of shimmering silk in a golden-brown jacket, soft pink shirt with 'Dipper' embroidered on one French cuff, green tie, and matching silk handkerchief in his breast pocket"—just your typical outfit worn by attendees at the convention. Smith wrote that Wilt dominated the joint appearances with Nixon at the convention. However, nothing really came of Wilt's political involvement, and he ultimately expressed disappointment with Nixon's policies. This was his first and only foray into the field, though he never stopped expressing his opinions on social issues, especially the one about which he felt the strongest—the need to control the world's population.

Taking a break from politics, Wilt played that August in the 10th annual Stokes' tournament at Kutsher's, where he and Bill Russell were the opposing centers—as if they didn't face each other enough during the NBA season. That event at Kutsher's also marked the first personal contact between Wilt and his next coach, Willem "Butch" van Breda Kolff. It was an inauspicious meeting, as van Breda Kolff later related:

> I went to Kutsher's because the Lakers wanted me to give Wilt a Lakers jersey and take a picture of him—it would be his first time in a Lakers jersey. He didn't want to put it on. I argued with him when I should have just kept quiet. Looking back, I'm mad at myself because I should have done my homework to see what kind of person he was.

Beginning with their first incarnation in Minneapolis, the Lakers were one of the NBA's premier franchises. Led by their (and the league's) best player, George Mikan, they had become the NBA's first dynasty, winning five titles between 1949 and 1954. However, smelling gold, the Lakers owner, Bob Short, moved the team to Los Angeles for the 1960–1961 season, by which time Mikan had retired.

Until Wilt joined the team, the two best Los Angeles Lakers—and among the greatest to ever play the game—were Elgin Baylor and Jerry West. From 1961 through 1963, Baylor averaged 35, 38, and 34 points, respectively, while also being a fearsome rebounder and excellent passer. Many knowledgeable observers believe he and Oscar Robertson were the greatest all-around players of that era. Ten times All-NBA, with dazzling moves to the basket, the 6'5", 225-pound Baylor would have earned even more fame and captured scoring titles (not one of which he ever won) had he not played at the same time as a man named Wilt Chamberlain.

Jerry Alan West grew up in a small town in West Virginia and thus was given a colorful nickname in the early years of his career: Zeke from Cabin Creek. An All-American at West Virginia, the 6'3" guard had one of the prettiest, quickest, and deadliest jump shots the basketball gods have ever bestowed on man. If that wasn't enough, with his long arms, quick reflexes, and great anticipation, he was the premier defensive guard of his time. He played smart, was liked by his teammates, coaches, and sportswriters (and admired and liked by opposing players as well), and there was no one else, until Michael Jordan appeared, whom you wanted to take the last shot.

Baylor and West—Mr. Inside and Mr. Outside—had led the Lakers to five Western Division titles in seven seasons, only to fall before an even more successful team—the Boston Celtics. At least Wilt's ex-team, the 1966–1967 Sixers, had prevailed once against Boston. Now these three superstars were united on the same team. After Wilt's trade to Los Angeles, the ever-entertaining George Kiseda wrote in *The Evening Bulletin*: "The Lakers became the first team in the history of the National Basketball Association to clinch the league championship five days after the Fourth of July. . . . The Lakers now have three-fifths of an All-League team. With Wilt Chamberlain joining Elgin Baylor and Jerry West, Ronald Reagan and Doris Day could play the other two positions for the Lakers." That line is reminiscent of Phog Allen's statement, when Wilt went to Kansas, that Wilt could win the NCAA championship teamed with two coeds and two Phi Beta Kappas—a statement that supporters of the school came to rue.

The Lakers coach, Butch van Breda Kolff, was late of Princeton University, whose team he had coached to four Ivy League titles. Although his job at Princeton had been made easier by the presence of the All-American Bill Bradley, van Breda Kolff was, nevertheless, a sound, blunt, forceful basketball coach. The season before his arrival, the Lakers were 36–45; in his first season, 1967–1968, he coached essentially the same team to a 52–30 record and to the NBA Finals. "My type of team," he said of the 1967–1968 group: "They moved, they ran, they looked for each other. They were a great group. It was almost like coaching a college team." According to Kiseda, those 1967–1968 Lakers were known to have gotten along with each other famously, rare among professional basketball teams. Tom Hawkins said it was the most enjoyable of his 10 seasons in the league (but, as he recognized, it was also his best season statistically).

To secure Wilt, the Lakers had given up the fine guard Archie Clark and a dependable and smart, if not domineering, center in Darrall Imhoff. They had also lost the gifted guard Gail Goodrich in the expansion draft to the Phoenix Suns. So other than West, the team was not that solid at the guard position. John Egan, who was tenacious but small (at 6') was the other starting guard. Mel Counts, Tom Hawkins, Cliff Anderson, Jay Carty, Keith Erickson, Bill Hewitt, and Freddie Crawford (the last three, and Egan, all newcomers) made up the rest of the team. Yes, the Lakers now had West, Baylor, and Wilt, probably the first time three players of their talents and stature had ever played on the same basketball team. But not without reason does the Eastern proverb say, "Twelve dervishes can lie under the same blanket, but two kings cannot rule in the same kingdom."

———————

The Los Angeles Lakers opened the season, away, against none other than the Philadelphia 76ers. Maybe this was a coincidence but, as Eddie Gottlieb still made up the NBA schedule, maybe it was not. Having had the summer to ponder Wilt's legacy, *The Bulletin*'s George Kiseda, previewing the season opener, wrote: "It is easy to remember only Chamberlain's faults (the bad hands, the atrocious foul shooting, the changing moods, etc.), but the man has never lived who could thoroughly dominate a basketball game in so many ways as Chamberlain when he was motivated. Before he arrived, the 76ers were a .500 team, about as exciting as a linen sale. They were drawing crowds of 1,100 and 1,200, and it was only a matter of time until professional basketball in Philadelphia died. Chamberlain saved professional basketball in Philadelphia." Kiseda also pointed out that the Philadelphia fans, who could be hard on players, had never booed Wilt. He could expect a raucous homecoming, even if he was playing for the opposition.

Man proposes, God disposes: the Los Angeles Lakers—Superteam, as reporter Kiseda dubbed them—lost their opening game, October 18, 1968, to the Philadelphia 76ers, 114–96. Finding his team in a 30-point hole in the third quarter, coach van Breda Kolff benched Wilt, replacing him with Mel Counts, another seven-footer. The same thing happened in the fourth quarter, though this time the shortfall was 17 points. Both times the deficit was cut with Wilt on the bench. Wilt ended the game with 15 points and 17 rebounds, which, for him, was subpar on both counts. Luke Jackson, who had proclaimed before the game that he wouldn't let Wilt humiliate him, outrebounded Wilt by one.

After the game, Wilt summoned Eddie Gottlieb, his employer when Gotty owned the Philadelphia Warriors, to the Lakers locker room and presented the cigar-puffing Gottlieb with the ball with which Wilt had scored his 20,000[th] point several years before. It was mounted on a stand with a silver plaque on which was inscribed:

> Wilt Chamberlain—Phila. 76ers—20,000 Points. Jan. 2, 1966: Your foresight into the future of basketball gave me the needed inspiration to drive on to the goals like this. Thanks, Dip.

Gottlieb was obviously moved by the gesture, reporters there observed. Wilt had followed Bob Pettit as a member of the NBA's 20,000-point club, even today an exclusive group.

Granted, the early stages of the new season were a trying time for Wilt. Back in Los Angeles his 67-year-old father was dying, and his sister Barbara recalled a dutiful son carrying their father in his massive arms to the hospital, where William Chamberlain died October 31, 1968. Father and son had been close, and the son missed and mourned the father. Even though the Lakers had won 14 of their first 20 games and were in first place, newspaper story after newspaper story told of a growing and, ultimately, public rift between Wilt and coach van Breda Kolff.

Wilt had played low in the post, near to the basket, his entire basketball life—with, as he might not so humbly point out, more than his fair share of success. Coach van Breda Kolff wanted Wilt to move more and come out from under the basket and set picks—particularly for Elgin Baylor. With Wilt playing down low, van Breda Kolff told Wilt (and anyone else who would listen) that Baylor couldn't drive to the basket along the baseline because the area near and under the basket became cluttered with Wilt and his defender, and Baylor and his man. Wilt also was used to playing the entire game, but van Breda Kolff chose to rest him, sometimes for many minutes on end. The clashes between Wilt and his coach were played out in the press, with each side lobbying reporters for his point of view.

"Our personalities didn't jibe at all," van Breda Kolff told the author in an interview. "The bad outnumbered the good with him. Wilt was Wilt and had his ego, which was as large as him. I had my ego, which is also large. It was a battle right from the beginning as to whose will would win. . . . I always had the feeling that Wilt, in his mind, thought that wherever he was on the court, or whatever he did, was best for the team. But Wilt didn't know what he was doing to the other four guys. Russell's mind worked differently, and he always thought, 'What can I do to help the other four guys become a better team?'"

Over the subsequent years, van Breda Kolff declared, "One of the biggest mistakes I ever made was agreeing to the trade [that brought Wilt to the Lakers]." He also called Wilt the biggest load he ever had to bear—even privately referring to him as "the Load." Wilt's opinion of his coach was equally critical. He called van Breda Kolff the dumbest and the worst coach he ever had, damning him in his book by accusing him of being "ignorant of basic human relationships."

"I talked to him about defense," van Breda Kolff recalled. "I said he should play more like Russell on defense. He was horrified that I should think that. 'Who blocks more shots? I block more shots than anyone, than Russell.' 'Yes,' I said, 'but he keeps them [blocked shots] on the court. He doesn't spike them and hit the beer salesman in the stands.' His answer: 'His teams are coached.' I said, 'You keep the ball in play and see if we don't get the ball.' But that's the way he thought—that he blocked more shots than Russell."

"Our centers in the past moved around a lot," remarked Jerry West. "With Wilt, we're playing an entirely different game. We're a better defensive team, but we're not scoring as much as we did last year." West, who unlike others was at least patient about the situation, suggested that it would take at least half a year for the team to be in sync. Wilt agreed, stating repeatedly throughout the early part of the season that it had taken time—six months to a year—for him and the 76ers to adjust to each other when he had been traded to them in mid-season of 1965. But critics wanted instant chemistry and success—never mind that the Lakers were in first place.

By the 1968–1969 season, Elgin Baylor's knees were going, and he was no longer a consistently great player. Wilt's coming to the Lakers, and tending to remain in the low post, affected Baylor's game more than it did West's. Baylor wanted the center lane open, the better to drive to the basket or, another of his effective moves, to back his man down low. As he perceived it, with Wilt clogging the center, his effectiveness was diminished—this at a time when his considerable skills were already eroding.

Wilt and Baylor had first encountered one another in the fifties when Wilt and fellow Philadelphians would travel to Washington, D.C., to play basketball. There Wilt and Elgin played against one another and became acquaintances, if not bosom buddies. Both were named college All-Americans in 1958—Wilt at Kansas, Baylor at Seattle University. They even wrote letters to one another during the early years of their relationship, and Wilt attended Baylor's wedding in 1958. But when they were teammates on the Lakers, there was a rivalry between them to be the top dog. They were both large personalities and their psychological tug-of-war created a tense locker room. Both Baylor and Wilt thought they were the ultimate authorities on everything, as their teammate Keith Erickson recalled: "Elgin would bet which suitcase was going to come out of the baggage area first." Baylor acknowledged that he and Wilt argued about everything—but not because of personal animosity. "We were good friends and we respected one another. But there's a thing about black culture some people don't understand—it's always one-upmanship. You never let the guy get one up on you."

While Baylor, more than anyone, instigated and led the kibitzing and shenanigans found on any sports team, Wilt made it known he didn't like criticism and, while friendly, he didn't go out to eat or hang out with his teammates as a rule. Baylor had that knack of knowing when and how much to tease his teammates, yet he always enjoyed their respect and affection, probably to a degree that Wilt did not. Baylor was a born leader and fun to be around, recalled van Breda Kolff, while Wilt, in van Breda Kolff's opinion, was not a natural leader—and never much of a follower, either.

Unaffected by all this was the imperturbable West, who got along with both men (and the coach) while playing superb basketball. Wilt pointed out in his book that West had been the most popular and highest-paid Laker. Wilt's arrival and his well-publicized big (if, actually, underreported) contract meant that West was no longer the highest-paid Laker, which Wilt felt had to have initially affected West's attitude toward him. But Wilt was also honest enough to admit that *if* West envied him his contract, he envied West his popularity around the league. With it all, they got along well, on and off the court. "I found him to be one of the most interesting, complex people that I've ever been around in my life," West recalled. "A number of nights, when we were on the road, we would have dinner either in his room or mine. I'm not even sure our teammates knew we did this. I got to know him very well. And we had a great mutual respect for each other."

When traveling, the Lakers were given the option of paying a supplement to room alone, which usually the higher-paid superstars on the team—Wilt, West, and Baylor—could afford to take advantage of.

"It's got to be an adjustment for Elgin and Jerry," the team's ex-center Darrall Imhoff observed in the early part of the season in an interview. "Here's two guys who have held the club together for eight years. They made the club what it is today. I can see where it would be tough for me if I were in their shoes to accept all the attention [showered on and generated by Wilt] when they were responsible for the team's success."

Keith Erickson was an All-American in volleyball at UCLA and a starting member on John Wooden's first two NCAA championship teams, in 1964 and 1965. He came to the Lakers the same year as Wilt and observed:

> Elgin and Jerry were close to Butch. He catered to them. Well, that's not the way to get on Wilt's good side. You're not going to win anything if those three aren't playing together. Butch and Wilt just didn't hit it off. That relationship was doomed from the start.

Tom Hawkins, an All-American at Notre Dame, was the Lakers' first-round draft choice in 1959, his and Wilt's first year in the league. By 1968–1969, he was the Lakers' player representative and, thus, was more involved than most of his teammates in the travails of the team:

> One day, Jack Kent Cooke said to me, "Tommy, we've got some business to straighten out, so you get Wilt and you get van Breda Kolff and get them up to my office after practice."
>
> Cooke said to us, "I don't want anybody being quoted in the paper about anything other than the game. If you talk, you'll be fined $5,000 for each incident." That was a lot of money at that time. And then he said, "Bill, you must look at Wilt in two lights: as a player and as a

business property. In both lights he is an All-Pro. When I traded for Wilt, my season-ticket base increased by five thousand in three days. You guys get along together. If you can't, you can leave."

Did the talks with the owner, among the players, and between van Breda Kolff and Wilt help? "Nothing was resolved," according to Hawkins. "It was a clash of philosophies, egos, and styles. It wasn't that van Breda Kolff hated Wilt Chamberlain. The twain could never meet. Van Breda Kolff was going to do it his way, and Wilt was going to do it his way. . . . They actually got in a fight one night in Seattle. I think seven of us grabbed Wilt and one guy grabbed Butch, who was screaming and yelling and shouting into Wilt's navel." Hawkins, a handsome man who became a broadcaster after his basketball career ended and later worked with the Los Angeles Dodgers, can laugh now, if not then, as he recalled the never-ending soap opera of that season.

Van Breda Kolff regularly sat Wilt down during games, which had never before happened in his career. It must have been humiliating to Wilt, who said publicly—and often—that he thought he was most effective when he played nearly the entire game, as he had, with great success, throughout his nine-year career.

In December, the Lakers lost to the Baltimore Bullets. Van Breda Kolff benched Wilt the entire last quarter. Later that month, after defeating the 76ers in Los Angeles, Wilt responded to a reporter who asked if matters had been worked out with his coach: "We really haven't had much resolved," he said. "He would like me to come out high and set picks. Many times I don't come out high from force of habit. We are all creatures of habit. I've been playing a certain way all my life and it's hard to change, but I'm trying to—as much as possible."

Begrudgingly, after one Lakers victory, van Breda Kolff said, "We've been playing good defense, particularly Wilt." However, the bickering continued month after month. In late December, van Breda Kolff was quoted as saying, "We're not what you would call a happy club." By early January, van Breda Kolff bet the Lakers broadcaster, Hot Rod Hundley, that he would not last the season as the Lakers coach.

One night Wilt scored 6, another night 2—yes, Wilt Chamberlain scoring 2 points. Then, answering critics who wondered if his offensive might was gone, in late January 1969 he scored 60, and three weeks later he scored 66. That last total set a record for points in the Forum, the Lakers' home; the previous record holder was Jerry West who, because of a pulled hamstring, sat out the game in which Wilt broke his record. Just like the year before with the 76ers, Wilt certainly gave some the impression that he could score big any night he wanted to.

Jack Kent Cooke, who had brought Wilt to the Lakers, surveyed his team: attendance was up 11 percent, on the way to setting a team attendance record of 483,262. The Lakers were in first place in their division. If this was purgatory, Cooke must have thought, stoke the fire.

Benched for 10 minutes in a loss to Baltimore in early April, Wilt proclaimed, "I'm tired of having everything blamed on Wilt." Coincidence or not, he was superb in the next three games, all of which the Lakers won. Against Boston, with his nemesis Russell at center, Wilt had 42 rebounds and converted two key fouls. He had 25 points against Baltimore and its fabulous rookie center, Wes Unseld, who gathered 9 rebounds to Wilt's 38. "Wilt can do anything Wilt wants to do," Unseld said afterward. And against Detroit, Wilt had 36 points (on 14 for 14 from the field), 26 rebounds, and 11 blocked shots. That was 106 rebounds in three games. (He'd set a Lakers record for rebounds that year.) Following the Detroit game, his harshest critic, coach van Breda Kolff, said, "Wilt was just fantastic tonight. He is playing much better and everyone's playing better." Wilt reminded those who cared to remember, "When I came to Los Angeles, I said it would take a year for me to get adjusted to the players and for them to get adjusted to me. We're getting adjusted." So they were, winning 12 of their last 15 games and finishing first in the division. And Wilt had averaged 21 points and 21 rebounds for his first Laker season.

After dropping the first two divisional playoff games to the San Francisco Warriors, the Lakers, behind Wilt and West (who averaged 31 points for the series), won four straight. Next they defeated Atlanta, winning the Western Division title for the sixth time in eight years. Save for the final game against Atlanta, Baylor, the perennial All-Star, played poorly, and more than one writer and player whispered that the great forward, his knees shot, was near the end of his impressive career. Boston, which had finished fourth in the regular season, sprang to life in the East, beating Philadelphia in five games and the up-and-coming Knicks in six.

The NBA Finals featured the two most successful franchises in the league—Boston and Los Angeles. Five times they had met in the Finals and five times Boston had prevailed. (And unlike the rap against Wilt, no one uttered a word about West and Baylor being unable to win the big one or being losers.) When Los Angeles lost to Boston, as West and others pointed out, Boston clearly had the better team. Now the Lakers had Wilt. But to gain Wilt they had weakened themselves at guard by giving up Archie Clark (in the trade), and had lost an even better guard, Gail Goodrich, to the new NBA team, the Phoenix Suns. West was fabulous when he wasn't hurt, but he had missed 21 games that season due to injury. Van Breda Kolff realized the Lakers were weaker at the guard position than the year before, having said near the end of the season, "Johnny Egan gets murdered on defense because of his size [6'], but when he's not in there, we look like a bunch of trucks coming up the court." As for the Celtics, they were a year older and relied even more on John Havlicek, their best all-around player. Filling out the lineup was Bailey Howell (age 32) at forward; in the backcourt, ageless Sam Jones (36) in his final year; Emmette Bryant as the other guard; and, of course, Russell, who was 35, at center.

West knew that with Wilt at center, this was his and the team's chance to slay Boston. The oddsmakers agreed, making the Lakers, who would have the home-court advantage, the favorite to win the championship.

Los Angeles won Game 1 at home, 120–118, with West providing the heroics: he had 53 points, which included making two free throws with four seconds left, putting L.A. up 119–116. Same story in Game 2, also in L.A.: the Lakers won behind West's 41 points and Baylor's 32, including the team's last 12 points of the game. Boston's defense was allowing 15 more points a game than in its earlier playoff series against Philly and New York. Wilt and Russell played each other to a statistical standoff in the first two games of the series.

The Celtics had never dropped the first two games of a playoff—and no team had ever come back from such a deficit to win the NBA Finals. But these guys weren't the Shamokin Schleppers—they were the Boston Celtics. There was no despair (at least for the press and other outsiders to observe) in the Boston dressing room.

Back at home for Game 3, the Celtics finally won, 111–105. Their offensive stars were John Havlicek, now their most consistent and most potent scorer, and his fellow Ohio State Buckeye, Larry Siegfried, who scored 34 and 28 points, respectively. Ironically, Siegfried was a substitute, having lost his starting job to

Emmette Bryant. Baylor had a bad game, shooting 4 for 18, and he and West shot 1 for 14 in the fourth quarter. Wilt had 18 points and 26 rebounds, while Russell had 11 points and 18 rebounds. *The New York Times* columnist Robert Lipsyte offered his appraisal of the two centers: "They are very different on the court," he wrote after Game 3. "Chamberlain moves almost stiffly, as if afraid his nearly 300 pounds will crush someone, and there is no second effort to him. His lips are moving, making excuses in advance. He plays episodically: a spurt of action, a look around, a rest, then kick over the engine and start again. There seems little pleasure in it for him. Russell, his sly, wise face impassive, is always moving, loping, strutting up and down the court, his longs arms beating like wings hooking over his head for a shot, swiping the ball out of Wilt's hands, or sweeping little Johnny Egan off his feet."

Every leprechaun in Ireland and North America must have been in the Boston Garden for Game 4, won by the men in green, 89–88, on a self-described "lucky shot" by—who else?—Sam Jones with two seconds remaining. The winning play, which the Celtics had never previously used that season, was suggested by Havlicek and Siegfried, who were familiar with the play from their college years at Ohio State. Sam Jones curled around a triple screen, got the ball about 18 feet from the basket, and while stumbling (to be sure not a part of the play), flung up a desperation shot. As George Kiseda wrote, "The ball hit the rim, bounced, hit the rim again, bounced again, and fell through."

West had continued his brilliant series by scoring 40 points on 50 percent shooting, stealing balls, making assists, and playing incredible defense on, at different times, four different Celtics. In the locker room a disgusted West erupted to reporters: "We played dumb basketball. Maybe we deserved to lose."

The Lakers had had the ball—and the lead—with 15 seconds remaining. They had only to get the ball in safely and run out the clock, which they were unable to do. Boston got the ball back with seven seconds to go, thanks to a Los Angeles turnover—one of 27 the team committed (only slightly worse than Boston's 23). Kiseda, covering the Finals for *The Bulletin*, observed of the shell-shocked Lakers: "They were talking as if something had gotten away from them last night. They looked and acted like losers. It was a painful scene."

Victory would have given the Lakers a hard-to-overcome 3-to-1 lead in the series. Instead, the series was tied at two apiece, with the teams returning to Los Angeles for Game 5.

That next game in California was the first in the series in which Wilt domi-nated Russell. He grabbed 31 rebounds (to 13 for Russell) and had 13 points. West was having one of the greatest Finals in NBA history: he had 39 points but, unfortunately, pulled his hamstring late in the game. Wilt got poked in the eye at the start of the second half and said he couldn't see well. Nevertheless, Los Angeles won, 117–104. "Wilt's best game," conceded coach van Breda Kolff.

Los Angeles was up three games to two, and the main question for Game 6 was whether West would play and, if so, how well. With a heavily bandaged left thigh, he gutted out 26 points. Although Wilt had 18 rebounds (1 less than Russell), his eight points were not nearly enough to make up for West's dimin-ished offensive production. Baylor, after a horrible first half, ended up with 26 points. Wilt had one field goal on five shots and was 6 for 10 from the foul line—nothing to brag about. Would that Wilt had risen to greatness by scoring, say, 30 points (an average night for him not many seasons before). Coming up big is what the game's highest-paid player, the game's all-time leading scorer, and the game's self-described greatest player would be expected to do. But Wilt failed, and Boston won, 99–90.

Wilt asserted that his eye, in which he had been poked the game before, wasn't bothering him in Game 6. In the first half, the Lakers rarely threw the ball in to Wilt—shades of Game 7 between Philadelphia and Boston in the Eastern Finals the year before. Why they did not is anyone's guess. When, finally, in the second half they did, "Wilt didn't do anything with it," as van Breda Kolff said after the game. Wilt took only five shots the entire game, which is ridiculous—unless he was hurting. But none of Wilt's teammates inti-mated he was injured. Nor was van Breda Kolff thrilled with Baylor's effort, saying, "Elgin hasn't been playing up to his capabilities. He has not been throw-ing the ball in to Wilt and cutting off as he should."

Once again, the NBA Finals came down to a seventh game, this one in Los Angeles, where the oddsmakers chose the Lakers as a three-point favorite. Jack Kent Cooke, anticipating victory, had thousands of balloons stored in the rafters of the Forum, an action that angered (and still does) Jerry West, who thought it was presumptuous, disrespectful toward a worthy opponent, and might provide a spark of motivation to the Celtics. Prior to the game, Kiseda reminded his readers: "The Celtics, ancient and weary, only a fourth-place team during the regular season, were not supposed to get this far, but now that they're here, who would bet against them? Surely, everybody knows the Boston Celtics do not lose seventh games of playoffs. Their all-time record in seventh games is 9–0, the greatest record under pressure in sports."

How right he was: "Too Late and Two Short" ran the clever headline in the next day's *Los Angeles Times*. The Boston Celtics won, 108–106, despite 42 points, 13 rebounds, and 12 assists from a limping Jerry West, who set a record for points scored in an NBA Finals series. He would have forsaken that record, and gladly returned the car he won from *Sport* magazine for being named the series Most Valuable Player, in exchange for a championship ring. "That was the low point of my career," said West. "I didn't want to play anymore. I felt I had given everything I could. It looked like it wasn't in the cards for us to win. I was as low as I could be as a player." For the sixth time in West's career, for the seventh time in Baylor's (counting a loss in the 1959 Finals to the Celtics as a member of the Minneapolis Lakers), their team had fallen to the Boston Celtics. Adding insult to injury, Don Nelson, an ex-Laker, made the key shot. The ball was deflected to him at the foul line and, with the shot clock running out, he hoisted up a jump shot that hit the front rim, bounced high and straight up, and dropped down through the basket, giving Boston a 105–102 lead with 24 seconds to go.

But a shot or a play doesn't a series make. The lumbering, turnover-prone, motionless, divided Lakers didn't play well enough to win, save for the incandescent West, who had one of the greatest Finals ever. In fact, West's MVP award was the first—and only—time in an NBA Final that a member of the losing team had been so recognized.

The addition of Wilt was supposed to have made the Lakers invincible. Nevertheless, the Lakers' season ended like so many others—defeat at the hands of the Celtics and Bill Russell, who won their 11th championship in 13 years (and, for the first time, they had won the deciding seventh game away from home). Wilt had earlier called them the "luckiest team in the history of sports." True, to a point. But Leonard Koppett, one of the wisest, fairest, and best basketball writers, observed: "The amazing Celtics, written off as 'aging' by many experts and only fourth in the Eastern Division during the regular season, produced smart, opportunistic, team-minded basketball that has characterized them for years, and also had that little bit of good fortune that every champion needs."

Many of the Celtics said this was their most satisfying victory because no one (except themselves) expected them to end up NBA champs that year. Team captain Havlicek, who scored a team-high 26 points in Game 7, called it "probably the greatest team effort of all the Celtic title thrusts." Sam Jones said the series proved "that a good team, keeping cool and hitting the open man, will come through."

———————

Few knew it that night, but that was to be the last time Wilt Chamberlain and Bill Russell would face each other as players on a basketball court. And what would a Chamberlain-Russell Finals be without a controversy—one that was to live for two decades?

Late in Game 7, Wilt grabbed a rebound and, when he landed, wrenched his knee. He hobbled around for a while, but had to leave the game with 5:20 remaining, the Lakers trailing by seven. Mel Counts, the 7' forward-center, replaced him, which he had done in many games throughout the season. Counts played reasonably well, even hitting the jumper that pulled the Lakers to 103–102. What happened during the final minutes of the game is indisputable, if inexplicable: at some point, having iced his sore knee, Wilt told van Breda Kolff he was OK and wanted to go back into the game. Van Breda Kolff said afterward, "I told him we were doing well enough without him. I would have put him back in if I felt he would have made a difference."

Why didn't van Breda Kolff put Wilt back in when surely the Lakers could have used Wilt's rebounding abilities at the critical juncture of the game? Wilt had played very well: he had 18 points with 27 rebounds before the injury. West and Baylor together had only one more rebound than Wilt—and no other Laker had more than seven rebounds. Counts was 4 for 13 from the field and 1 for 2 from the foul line, so he was hardly lighting up the Forum. Did van Breda Kolff dislike Wilt so much that he wanted to show Wilt—and the world—that the Lakers could defeat the Celtics without Wilt, even if that decision, in the eyes of many, was pig-headed and wrong and could cost him his job? Van Breda Kolff claims he did what he thought was best for the team. West assumed Wilt hadn't re-entered the game because he was injured. Upon learning afterward that van Breda Kolff had chosen to keep Wilt out, West was perplexed by van Breda Kolff's actions. Wilt's view was that van Breda Kolff was spiteful and wanted to win without him, though, in Wilt's mind, it cost the Lakers the championship. "I'm not sure I was ever as angry at one man as I was at Butch van Breda Kolff that night," he wrote in his book.

Someone once said to van Breda Kolff that two careers had been ruined by the 1969 Finals: Wilt's because he wouldn't take over and van Breda Kolff's because he wouldn't give in. "That is probably true," van Breda Kolff declared to the author—true and sad for van Breda Kolff. He never came close to coaching in an NBA Finals again and within a few years was permanently out as an NBA coach. As for Wilt, the events of 1968–1969 in general, and his performance in the Finals, particularly in Game 6, didn't "ruin" his career, but neither were they a high point. It was another failure in his basketball career to which critics could point.

A few days after the loss, West was in New York City to meet with *Sport* magazine, which presented him with a car as the MVP in the recently completed series. Sitting at Mamma Leone's restaurant before various reporters, among them *The Evening Bulletin*'s George Kiseda, West defended his teammate, Wilt Chamberlain: "I don't believe he's a loser. I believe it's a bad rap against him. I've lost as much as he's lost. Elgin's lost as much as he's lost. People think he's a superman. He's not Superman."

Asked if, given the choice for one game, he'd pick Wilt over Russell, West answered: "I think Wilt Chamberlain is a better basketball player than Bill Russell, but for one game I think I'd rather have Bill Russell." He went on to elaborate: "It would be hard to explain without hurting somebody's feelings. I think Chamberlain is a better rebounder, a better scorer, and a better shooter. I think Wilt blocks more shots than Russell. But if I had to pick one guy for one game, it'd be Russell. . . . It's incredible what he does for his team. It's hard to imagine how one guy can do so much for his teammates. . . . When they see him on the court, they're different players."

In an interview with the author in 2003, as the above quote was read to him, West interjected, "Probably the dumbest thing I ever said in my life. I said it out of frustration. It was the low point in my career. It was probably the dumbest thing I ever said in my life. It is something I am sorry of to this day." Given the opportunity to recant, West said that he would not choose Russell over Wilt—or Wilt over Russell. They were both great and forced their opponents to alter their game, he said.

The next shoe to drop, in the aftermath of the 1969 Lakers defeat, was the announcement by Butch van Breda Kolff that he would not return to fulfill the final year of his contract. No one was surprised by his resignation; had he not resigned, the Lakers would have fired him in the spirit of all professional sporting teams who, unable to fire the players, fire the manager or coach. Soon after the loss of the championship, van Breda Kolff had said of Wilt, "I think it is very difficult for him to be coached. It comes from way back." But he also admitted, "I am probably not a good coach for Wilt. There might be somebody else who thought differently about the game who could have gotten more out of Wilt." (That "somebody" in the future would be Bill Sharman, as it had been Frank McGuire and Alex Hannum in the past.)

First West says he'd pick Russell over Wilt for one game, winner take all. Then van Breda Kolff slams him. Next came Russell. Three weeks after his team's triumph, Russell spoke on black and white relations before a group at the University of Wisconsin. He wandered from the subject at hand into an area he might well have avoided. He accused Wilt of "copping out" in the last game of the recently completed series. One headline had it as follows: "Bill Russell Charges Wilt Quit in 7th Game." Russell was quoted in the story as saying, "Any injury short of a broken leg or broken back isn't good enough. When he took himself out of the final game, when he hurt his knee, well, I wouldn't have put him back in the game either, even though I think he's great."

This was not Russell's finest hour. Point number one: apprised of Russell's comments, van Breda Kolff—no fan of Wilt's—said, "Wilt did not take himself out of the game. . . . He could hardly make it up and down the court. He *had* to come out." Point number two: from the beginning of his career, Wilt often played hurt and never complained. Whatever his faults—and they make up a long list—there is one thing that is constant, indisputable, and beyond debate: Wilt played hurt countless times throughout his career. He would never, ever have taken himself out or ask to be taken out of a game unless he was physically unable to continue.

Told of Russell's comments, Wilt said he would not dignify them with a response. Russell was soon to announce his retirement from basketball as a player. One wonders if he would have dared utter such nonsense if he had to face Wilt once again on the court. As it was, Wilt was deeply hurt by the remark. He and Russell were not to speak to each other for 20 years—until Russell apologized, first privately, and then very publicly, for his hurtful and untrue remarks.

Chapter 15

We were somewhere, maybe in his house, watching the hand-wrestling national championship on television after dinner. It was a competition between the number one and the number two guy. I said, "Wilt, have you ever tried that?" He said, "You see the guy who lost, the number two guy? I can just take him and go like this"—and Wilt pushed his hand down with no effort. "But the number one guy, I never met him. But I have a confession: the only person who ever beat me in hand wrestling was Jim Brown."

Now Wilt didn't like to be second in anything. When he tore his patellar tendon, he set up a gym in his bedroom. He bought this framed gym where you could regulate the weights, and he lifted weights to strengthen the leg and thigh. The injury occurred in the fall, and when he came to Philadelphia many months later, he called me up and said, "Why don't you come over?" When I walked into his hotel room, he was across the room with just his shorts on. Now, I knew every inch of this man's body. I looked at his shoulders and asked, "What happened to you?"

He had this big grin on his face, and he said, "You noticed the difference?"

I said "Notice the difference? How many inches did you put on in your shoulders?"

He said, "Four—while I was working on my legs, I was working on my arms, too. You know what? Now I can beat Jim Brown."

That he could rectify the loss to Jim Brown was as important to him as the rehabilitation.

Was his Jim Brown arm-wrestling story true? I would guess that it was true, but I wouldn't guarantee it.

—Dr. Stan Lorber, longtime doctor and close friend

Baby, We Got Bad
Reviews on Broadway

Butch van Breda Kolff was two thousand miles away coaching in Detroit; Bill Russell was no longer playing or coaching in Boston; the Lakers had a new coach, Joe Mullaney, formerly of Providence College; and Wilt and his teammates were adjusting to life with each other as the 1969–1970 season commenced. If matters weren't perfect in Lakerland, they were pretty good.

And then on November 7, 1969, nine games into the season, things deteriorated. After going 13 for 13 from the field, with 33 points already to his name, Wilt took a pass from Jerry West and was dribbling toward the basket when, with nary a body or opponent's hand touching him, he crumbled to the floor. He had ruptured the tendon behind his right kneecap and torn the ligament surrounding the knee. Not a life-threatening injury, but one that, in those days, was potentially career-threatening.

The seemingly indestructible man, who had missed only 12 games in ten years, who had led the league in minutes played in eight of those ten years, was down. The injury turned out to be similar to the one suffered by Elgin Baylor some years before. Fortunately for Wilt, Drs. Robert Kerlan and Frank Jobe, two of the most renowned orthopedists in the land—Kerlan being the doctor who had extended the career of Baylor and had helped Sandy Koufax—performed the 100-minute operation to repair Wilt's patellar tendon. A table had to be attached to Wilt's hospital bed so he'd fit into it. From his bed he said, "I promise Lakers fans and my teammates that in 13 weeks I'll be playing and helping the Lakers win the world championship."

Dr. Kerlan hedged on the 13-week prediction, pointing out that if the injury had occurred to a jockey, *his* chances of coming back in that time frame would be better than Wilt's. "We'll just have to see how Wilt can support 270 pounds [while] running, jumping, and stopping," Dr. Kerlan declared. "Wilt's timetable might be different from mine, but I'm pulling for him." Coach Mullaney said he expected Wilt to be out for the season. (So, privately, did Dr. Kerlan.) Wilt's replacement at center was Rick Roberson, a 6'9" rookie from the University of Cincinnati.

Tell Wilton Norman Chamberlain he couldn't do something—like come back quickly from major knee surgery—and he usually rose to the challenge. He was intent on playing that season, regardless of medical convention. Wilt asserted that he devoted about 10 hours a day to rehabilitating his knee. His routine was to drive to Dr. Kerlan's office in midmorning for hydrotherapy and then return home for weight training—lifting 105 pounds with knee raises, 140 with hamstring curls—then walking seven or eight miles (later he would run) on the Santa Monica beach, followed at some point in the day with volleyball work-outs, then more weight training at home, and a dip in his pool.

Jack Kent Cooke, the team owner, praised Wilt's discipline and determination to come back from the injury, and so did coach Mullaney, an easy-going ex-FBI-agent-turned-basketball-coach. Another big Wilt fan was Frank O'Neill, the Lakers trainer from 1970 to 1984, who said of Wilt's effort to rehabilitate his leg, "If dedication and hard work will do it, he's got it. The guy has really worked hard."

That Wilt turned to volleyball as part of a program to rehabilitate his leg is well known among people who followed his career. Less well known is that even before the injury Wilt had become interested in beach volleyball. In the summer of 1969 he had asked Gene Selznick, at the time generally regarded as one of the world's greatest volleyball players, to teach him the game. Wilt had met Selznick, a charismatic, controversial rebel (to the volleyball powers of the time) through the Windjammer, the restaurant Selznick owned on Sunset Boulevard, where many of the Los Angeles Rams and Lakers hung out. Because both Wilt and Selznick were single, slept little, and liked to dance and visit clubs, they developed a bond that went beyond the teacher-student relationship. Indeed, save for Sy Goldberg, Selznick was probably one of Wilt's closest compadres during the last 30 years of his life.

Selznick claims that even while Wilt was still wearing a full leg cast, he had Wilt doing volleyball drills—passing and setting. And after the cast was removed in early January 1970, the two of them went to the beach, where

Selznick would hit balls at Wilt, forcing him to dig into the sand for them. (Sand is an excellent medium, as it offers resistance even as it cushions the impact of the leg hitting the ground.) The two of them drilled for hours, and Selznick recalled the miles upon miles that Wilt ran on the Santa Monica beach, all of this hastening the day when he could return to the basketball court.

It was during the 1969–1970 season that Wilt began to wear the headband that, along with the rubber bands on his wrist, became his signature. According to Wilt, he got the idea from watching volleyball players who wrapped T-shirts or rags around their foreheads to absorb their sweat and keep it from flowing into their eyes. Wilt wore a gold Lakers headband the remainder of his career— probably the first NBA player to wear, certainly the one to popularize, the headgear.

Volleyball would become Wilt's favorite sport. Basketball, he contended, did not really provide much of a challenge anymore. He credited his rehabilitation for making *both* his legs stronger (and thus extending his basketball career). He also commented that volleyball gave him "a sense of security and inner peace that he had never known," and that he was a different man after his injury. In his first book, Wilt wrote: "I decided then that I had done my best in basketball— setting record after record and leading team after team to their best seasons ever—and that would have to be good enough. I was through getting upset with my critics all the time; I was through having to prove myself again and again and again."

The All-Star Game was held that January in Philadelphia and, for the first time in his career, Wilt wouldn't be playing in it—not that he always was excited by the opportunity to play in All-Star Games (of which he participated in 13). He once said he found more thrills playing in Philadelphia's or Harlem's summer basketball leagues. Still, easily "wronged," Wilt was miffed that the NBA commissioner, Walter Kennedy, hadn't seen fit to personally invite him to the All-Star Game, nor had Kennedy or the league scheduled an event commemorating Wilt's contributions to the sport, substantial as they were and are. Wilt believed such a tribute appropriate, now that the old lion was wounded for the first time in his amazing career. After all, Wilt told reporters, the game was in his hometown, and it wasn't unheard of for the league to honor old-timers. (Professional sports weren't so attuned—some might say "obsessed"—with marketing themselves in those years. Eventually, such an event did happen, though it was not until the 2002 All-Star Game, also held in Philadelphia, at which time Wilt's career was duly celebrated posthumously.)

As for the 1970 All-Star Game, Wilt attended it, claiming that he bought his own $8 ticket (which would have cost $150 circa 2003). Regardless of whether he paid or got a pass, he did make his presence known, showing up in a purple velvet jumpsuit complete with bell-bottom trousers—prompting one reporter to write that Wilt's fashion display was more fun to watch than the game. Wilt sat in the private box of 76ers owner, Irv Kosloff, thereby exhibiting a comity between the two men who had been at loggerheads so often in the past.

By early March the doctors had cleared Wilt to practice with the team, and as that stage went well, he was scheduled to play his first postoperative game two weeks hence against none other than the Boston Celtics. Prior to that game, however, the 76ers were in Los Angeles for a game in which Wilt was not going to play. George Kiseda, *The Evening Bulletin*'s basketball writer who had often observed and written about a moody Wilt, now found a relatively more contented Wilt. "I'm very happy being in California," Wilt told Kiseda. "My life is becoming a bit more settled. I know what I can do. I know what I like to do. That should be enough to make anybody happy. Without naming names, I've seen other people come into the league and I've seen positions they take and the way they live and I'm happy I'm not like them."

Nevertheless, Wilt wasn't so mellow that he didn't express his annoyance with a national magazine that had run an article suggesting (at least by Wilt's light) that he was only working hard to come back from his knee injury because he missed the glory and glamour of being a star. If that was, indeed, Wilt's motivation, so what? More to the point, as Wilt declared to Kiseda, "I've always said the one thing I cherish is privacy. I turn down TV offers by the hundreds and appearances by the thousands." Probably true, though an exaggeration on the "thousands" of requested personal appearances. (But equally true was that for those moments Wilt didn't seek anonymity, he tooled around in his red Maserati with his name in gold letters on the car's door or in his lavender Bentley.)

The first test for Wilt's reconstructed knee came March 18 against the Boston Celtics. Had a Hollywood screenwriter crafted the story line, Wilt would have scored the last basket to win the game. In real life, the Celtics won. Wilt, who played 23 minutes, had 15 points, and nine rebounds, admitted he had butterflies before the game but was pleased with his effort. And well he should have been, for it was remarkable that four and a half months after so debilitating an injury he was back playing professional basketball. He would play three more games (giving him a total of twelve games played during that season), in the last of which he had 21 points, 18 rebounds, and eight assists—nothing shabby about those numbers. The patient was back to being a ballplayer. How well he could perform was about to undergo the real test as the playoffs began.

In 1970 there were still two divisions in the NBA, with seven teams then in each division. New York came in first in the East, Atlanta in the West (with L.A., minus Wilt, finishing second). Jerry West won his first scoring title, averaging 31 points a game. And, for the first time in 13 seasons, someone other than Wilt or Bill Russell won the rebounding title, that someone being Elvin Hayes, who averaged 16.9 a game.

In the first round of the division playoffs, Los Angeles fell behind Phoenix three games to one and appeared to be destined for an early exit. But L.A. won the next three and then four straight over the Atlanta Hawks for the Western Division crown. Wilt had averaged 21 points and 20 rebounds in the 11 playoff games and was a "shock-blocking windmill," according to Kiseda. Wilt's determination to rejoin the team in time for the playoffs, and his performance in those games—especially after Los Angeles fell behind Phoenix—won the respect of his teammates like nothing else had.

The new power in the East was the New York Knickerbockers, which had prevailed over the Baltimore Bullets in seven games and over the Milwaukee Bucks, led by the Rookie of the Year, Lew Alcindor, in five games. This was the first appearance in an NBA Finals in 17 years for this once-hapless Knicks franchise.

New York finally had a first-rate professional basketball team after all those years of great Yankee and Dodger teams and the occasionally great New York Giant teams in football. More then than now, any apple that fell in the New York forest made a larger sound than an apple falling anywhere else, so this Knicks team received a great deal of attention in the media. In this case, however, it was warranted, for they were a team deserving all the publicity. They set an NBA record by winning 18 consecutive games early in the season, becoming in the process the darling of basketball fans primarily in (but many out of) New York, while also appealing to the New York intelligentsia (read Woody Allen, George Plimpton, and the like). They even had a Rhodes Scholar, Bill Bradley, in the starting lineup. Their shot selection was sound, their play unselfish, and their offense balanced. All the starters shot well, even from long range. No opponent, including the Lakers, could "cheat" on defense by ignoring any of the Knicks starters. In addition, the 1970 Knicks were probably one of the smartest teams ever to play the game (likely their main appeal to the intellectuals), as manifested in their excellent team defense.

At one forward position for the Knicks was Dave DeBusschere, a strong rebounder and fine midrange jump shooter, whose arrival a year before from Detroit (where he had once been player-coach) was the last piece in the evolution of the Knicks into the Eastern Division champions. The other forward was Bill Bradley, not long removed from Princeton's ivy walls and, even more recently, from that other basketball power, Oxford University. Bradley, now a veteran of three years, had signed a lucrative rookie contract, thus the nickname "Dollar Bill." Walt Frazier was the playmaker; the other guard was Dick Barnett, a streak shooter who tossed up bombs from, in basketball terminology, way downtown. The center and captain—and the heart and soul of the team— was Willis Reed, a 6'10" lefty with an effective midrange jump shot. He passed well for a big man and was also a solid rebounder; in fact, he was voted the league's Most Valuable Player that year. The primary substitutes were Cazzie Russell, a potent offensive threat, Mike Riordan, and Dave Stallworth. The oddsmakers were impressed with the Knicks, too, making them the favorite to win the title.

Elgin Baylor was assigned to guard Dave DeBusschere; Keith Erickson was on Bill Bradley; Jerry West on Dick Barnett or Frazier; Dick Garrett on Walt Frazier, his Southern Illinois teammate, or Barnett; and Wilt was on Willis Reed. These were the Knicks' defensive assignments as well, though at times the Knicks rotated Riordan and Barnett on West, who also found himself, on occasion, double-teamed. The Lakers' Harold "Happy" Hairston (familiar to Knicks fans from his days at New York University) was on the bench, as were guard Johnny Egan, forward/center Mel Counts, and center Rick Roberson.

Prior to Game 1, the Lakers coach, Mullaney, observed: "The Knicks don't have to go to the basket to score. They'll pull up short and take medium jumpers and I'm not so sure Wilt will have opportunities to block shots." As if following Mullaney's script, that is exactly what the Knicks did in Game 1, which they won at home easily, 124–112. Willis Reed smoked Wilt for 37 points. Because neither the Phoenix nor the Atlanta centers shot well, Wilt had poached under the basket in the division playoffs, from where he could block shots and grab rebounds. That tactic didn't work in Game 1 against Reed, who roamed about and hit on many 12- to -15-foot jump shots or darted along the sideline behind a screen, usually set by the rugged DeBusschere, and then converted jumpers from the corner. Reed, who already had 25 points at the half, was well supported by other Knicks to clinch the game.

Even though Wilt had outrebounded Reed, the buzz was that Wilt had lost quickness and his spring; if so, understandably, for as *The New York Times'* Leonard Koppett wrote after Game 1, it was obvious that Wilt was "not fully recovered from his knee operation." Robert Lipsyte, another *Times'* columnist, concurred: "Knicks that Chamberlain would have ground into the court like cigarette butts last season, drove around him to the basket," he wrote. Regarding the so-called loss of spring in his jump, Wilt pointed out to reporters that he had, after all, gathered 24 rebounds (leading everyone by quite some margin in that department), and it wasn't like the rebounds had come to him: he had jumped and grabbed them. Yet Wilt made no excuses for the game's outcome: "You can't take anything away from the fact that Willis played a great basketball game," he said.

The man who had reconstructed Wilt's knee, Dr. Robert Kerlan, had a puckish sense of humor. Referring to the Game 1 stories, he said to Wilt, in mock concern, before Game 2, "We got bad reviews on Broadway, baby." The night before that second game, Wilt decided to watch the film of Game 1, something (watching game film) he said he had never done before. Maybe it worked, for the Knicks encountered a noticeably different, more effective Wilt in Game 2. He came out and challenged Reed on his outside shots, scored 19 points, and outrebounded Reed, 24 to 15. At a crucial moment in the contest, with about 30 seconds remaining, Wilt intimidated Reed into not taking a shot, did likewise to Barnett, and then blocked a shot by Reed—all in the same offensive sequence. West sank two free throws late in the game, leading the Lakers to a 105–103 victory. West had 34, while Reed still had a solid game, scoring 29.

The Finals returned to Los Angeles for Game 3. Mullaney's game plan throughout the series was to start the Lakers offense by throwing the ball down low to Wilt (a departure from van Breda Kolff's approach the season before) or by isolating Jerry West, who was again having an incandescent Finals. Mullaney did not want the Lakers to run with the Knicks because he felt that would be playing into the Knicks' strength. If the Lakers were to win, he believed their offense had to be to attack more deliberately. West, who was making the fantastic look routine, sank a 55-foot field goal as time ran out, tying the score at 102. The Knicks, however, prevailed in overtime, 111–108. West had 34 points but was snake-bitten once again in an NBA Finals, this time jamming the thumb on his left (nonshooting) hand during the game. Wilt had 21 points and 26 rebounds, while Willis Reed, playing superbly, had 38 points and 17 rebounds.

The Lakers won Game 4, but they needed overtime and the fine play of John Tresvant, a 6'7" forward who hadn't played one second in the first three games of the series, now tied at two apiece, to do it. In spite of a discolored, swollen thumb, the remarkable West had 37 points and 18 assists. In the battle at center, Wilt had 18 points and 25 rebounds to 23 points and only 12 rebounds for Reed. Elgin Baylor, who tied the game by converting two free throws late in regulation play, scored 30 and grabbed 13 rebounds, and was having a good series, averaging 15 points. "There is little, if any, difference between these teams," observed William "Red" Holzman, the Knicks coach.

———————

The first four games had been close and hard-fought—two of them going into overtime. But it was during Game 5, back in Madison Square Garden, that this series began to turn into one of the NBA's most memorable Finals.

The Lakers were most effective on offense when they got the ball down low to Wilt: he scored or passed off to cutting Lakers, who often scored. The plan worked especially well in Game 5, with the Lakers up by 10 in the first quarter. With about four minutes to go in the quarter, Willis Reed drove to the basket, only to collapse to the floor, writhing in pain. As film of the famous episode shows, Wilt instinctively reached down to give him a helping hand, a gesture which demonstrated admirable sportsmanship on Wilt's part. First reports described Reed's injury as a pulled thigh muscle, but it turned out to be more debilitating than that: Reed had strained a muscle alongside his hip that runs from the pelvis to below the knee. Even though he was injected with a painkiller, he was unable return to the game.

With their leader and leading scorer on the bench, the Knicks seemed destined to lose the game and, if Reed were seriously injured, the championship series. After all, the Knicks backup centers, little used, were 6'10" Nate Bowman and 6'8" Bill Hosket—that was "Bowman" not "Thurmond," and "Hosket" not "Russell." Coach Holzman tried each of them on Wilt, and then he tried forwards Dave DeBusschere and Dave Stallworth, giving up six or seven inches to Wilt. The rotating centers were somewhat effective; still, the Lakers led by 13 at the half. Wilt already had 18 points and, without Reed to guard him, the Knicks' prospects were bleak. John Havlicek, the Boston star, attended the game and afterward said that the Lakers had let the Knicks off the hook. Had they a killer instinct, Havlicek observed, their lead might have been 20 or 30 at the half instead of 13.

In the second half, the Knicks ratcheted up their defense to an even more intense level. They swarmed all over the Lakers, intercepting feeble lob passes intended for Wilt or successfully trapping the L.A. players after the New Yorkers made foul shots. Meanwhile, the Lakers turned cold, cautious, and dumb. "We couldn't do anything right in the second half," lamented Jerry West. "We couldn't even call a timeout right." Ironically, the Lakers had played better against the Knicks with Reed in, rather than out of, the game. In the second half, the Lakers committed 19 turnovers and took only 26 shots (versus their normal average of 50). Wilt took *three shots* in the second half and Jerry West *two*—statistics that, in the usually decisive fifth playoff game, boggle the mind. In the fourth quarter the mighty team from Los Angeles was outscored 32–18.

In one of the most improbable comebacks in playoff history, the Knicks won Game 5, 107–100. To the Lakers, as Leonard Koppett wrote in *The Times*, this was not a Knicks achievement, but a Lakers disaster.

What could the Lakers say about their monumentally inept performance? "They [the Knicks] were like bees," said coach Mullaney:

> They gambled a lot and it paid off. They didn't let us keep the pace we wanted. One of the big factors in the second half was that we weren't able to get the ball in to Wilt.

Fred Schaus, the Lakers general manager, felt the referees had allowed the Knicks too much leeway on defense and had not called fouls committed by the Knicks. In their stories about the game, neither the *Los Angeles Times'* Mal Florence nor *The Bulletin's* George Kiseda stated or implied that the refs might have let the hometown Knicks get away with anything on defense. However,

Koppett, *The New York Times*' reporter, broached the subject in his coverage, suggesting that the Knicks had clawed their way back into the game and that the response of the two referees, Mendy Rudolph and Richie Powers, "was to watch carefully as the Knicks defense swarmed over the Lakers, especially Jerry West and Wilt Chamberlain, and to decide that most Knick harassment was legal."

Notice that Koppett, a precise writer, wrote the referees decided "most" of the Knicks harassment was legal—not *all*. Forty-two years later in an interview with the author, Koppett said matter-of-factly, "The Lakers were robbed, pure and simple. In the second half, the Knicks started cutting the lead. The crowd went crazy and the officials wouldn't call anything [against the Knicks]." Whether or not the officials had allowed the Knicks too much latitude in guarding the Lakers, the final score says the Knicks won the game. The Lakers had experienced another playoff debacle and found themselves down three to two—one game from elimination.

Willis Reed, in street clothes, sat on the Knicks bench, from where he watched the Lakers, at home, easily win Game 6, 135–113. Wilt dominated with 45 points, on 20 for 27 from the field (and 27 rebounds thrown in for good measure). He scored on finger-rolls, stuff shots, and drives to the basket. The Lakers spread out their offense to discourage the Knicks from sagging on Wilt, and when they did, the Knicks got called for fouls. Whomever the Knicks assigned to Wilt could not stop him. West chimed in with his usual superb effort: 33 points and 13 assists. Had the Lakers gotten the ball in to Wilt in the second half of Game 5 as they did in Game 6, the series would have been over and the Lakers finally would be champs. And if pigs had wings . . . Instead, this series was tied at three games apiece, with the deciding seventh game to take place in Madison Square Garden.

———————

The question for Game 7 was whether or not Willis Reed could play and, if so, how well, for it would be asking a great deal of a Willis Reed–less Knicks club to duplicate their unexpected Game 5 victory. The Knicks players claim they did not know whether Reed would play, much less that he would start, until he appeared two minutes before tip-off. What an emotional moment when Reed, who had been injected with painkillers, emerged from the bowels of the Garden and made the long walk through the tunnel leading to the court, where he received a thunderous ovation from the 19,500 fans in the Garden, most of them Knicks partisans.

Bedlam reigned when, 18 seconds into the game, Willis Reed popped in a jump shot for the game's first points. And then, defying logic, a minute later Reed scored another basket, giving the Knicks a 5–2 lead. Knicks fans were ecstatic. "When Wilt let Willis take those two shots and when Willis made them, that was what got us off and running," said Dave DeBusschere. "It was the psychological lift."

And so it was. Although he would not score another point and gathered only three rebounds in the 27 minutes he played, Reed's inspiration and courage fired up his teammates.

There were no trends in the game. The Lakers, in the words of the *Los Angeles Times'* beat reporter Mal Florence, "surrendered meekly." The New York Knickerbockers, 113. The Los Angeles Lakers, 99. The game was over by the half, with the Knicks up by 27.

For the Knicks it was their first title in the team's 24-year history. For the Lakers it was the seventh time they had failed to win in the NBA Finals.

Why had the Lakers lost and who was at fault?

"The Knicks shot better, defended better, hustled more, ran faster, jumped higher, passed more accurately, and stole the ball more often," wrote Leonard Koppett in his page-one story in *The New York Times* the next morning.

All of the Knicks contributed, though none more than Walt Frazier, star of the seventh game with 36 points, five steals, and 19 assists—the last tying a playoff record. Contrary to the myth that Frazier cleaned Jerry West's clock that night, most of the points in the first half came against Garrett, the second-half points (by which time the game was really over) against various Lakers. The Knicks shot 50 percent from the field and an amazing 91 percent from the free throw line (compared to 46 percent and 61 percent, respectively, for the Lakers).

The Lakers had 14 more rebounds and 15 more foul shot attempts than the Knicks—foul attempts they failed to capitalize on, mostly missed by Wilt. But where it counted most, in shots made, the Knicks had eight more field goals on nine more shots.

The Lakers' big three each played a good, though not a great, game: West was 9 for 19 and 10 for 12 for 28 points; Baylor 9 for 17; and Wilt 10 for 16 (but 1 for 11 from the foul line). Keith Erickson had 14, but the rest of the squad contributed little. Wilt had 24 rebounds—almost half his team's total (and more than half of the Knicks' total).

"You can't discredit Wilt. He played as well as he could," said Dave DeBusschere. "He was simply stopped by Reed and an overall defensive performance that I would have to call our best in quite some time."

Noticeably limping as he ran the court, Reed was named the series Most Valuable Player. Besides inspiring his teammates by his presence in the game, he pressed his 235-pound beefy body against Wilt and kept him from dominating inside. As Kiseda wrote: "Reed would hobble up and down the court, unable to rebound, unable to do anything except set picks, but he was able to lean on Chamberlain and keep Chamberlain from getting to the basket. He leaned and he leaned and when he got into foul trouble, Nate Bowman came in and leaned. It was effective." In the very next paragraph Kiseda wrote: "It is easy to forget that Chamberlain is only three months out of a hip-length cast [actually, four and a half months] and only six months away from an operation for a ruptured tendon in his right knee. He no longer can go overtop a center the way he used to. His Ban Roll-On shot isn't a dip shot anymore; it's a flip shot. He has to go around defenders. Reed wouldn't let him do it."

What Willis Reed did in the seventh game was inspiring, and as Reed has said many times over the years, not a day goes by without someone praising him for what has become the most important—and celebrated—moment of his public life. However, Wilt played well, if not spectacularly. He deserves credit, which he never received, for returning from a devastating injury, playing in 18 playoff games, and helping his team reach the Finals—six months after major knee surgery.

Furthermore, Wilt wasn't "psyched out" or "intimidated" when Willis Reed appeared on court two minutes before Game 7 began, as myth and the ESPN documentary on Wilt's life implies. If anything, it is possible that Wilt, for reasons best understood by "coach" Sigmund Freud, consciously or not, "eased up" in Game 5 after Reed went down early in the game. No less an authority than the sportswriter Dick Schaap thought so. But anyone who writes or says that Wilt is the reason the Lakers lost Game 7 has apparently never viewed it. Wilt, like his teammates, never got untracked, particularly in the first half; and two of his teammates, Dick Garrett and Happy Hairston, had bad games.

The story of the 1969–1970 NBA Finals is that the Knicks outplayed their counterparts on the Lakers. The Knicks *team* beat the Lakers *team*. In addition to acknowledging that the Knicks had outplayed the Lakers in all facets of the game, Wilt had an interesting take on the seventh game:

> What beat us that night was a combination of several things—not the least of which was the subconscious, unspoken, but, nonetheless, inescapable feeling everyone on both teams had that no matter what the Lakers did, individually and collectively, the Knicks would find a way to win, and we would find a way to lose; we all just seemed to feel that New York was destined to win.

The state of the Los Angeles Lakers was captured by the headline in the *Los Angeles Times* the day after the game: "Lakers Turn 'Runner-Up' Into a Cliché."

Wilt, Jerry West, and Elgin Baylor were in their thirties. Two of them, Wilt and Baylor, were playing on surgically repaired knees. With 7'2" Lew Alcindor, the heir apparent as the dominant NBA center, returning for his sophomore season with the Milwaukee Bucks, the Lakers' chances of ever winning the NBA title seemed to be fading, if not, in some eyes, already extinguished.

Chapter 16

It was an exhibition game in my rookie year and we're losing by about 20 points. Jerry West and those guys used the exhibition season to get into shape. Coach Mullaney is upset at the way we're playing and comes into the locker room at halftime. And he's yelling.

The next thing I know, Wilt gets up. Wilt, who had sort of a stutter, said, "Uh-uh-uh-Joe—uh—gimme—a—a—cig—cigarette."

I'm thinking, "I didn't hear that. I didn't just hear him ask the coach in the middle of his tirade for a cigarette."

Mullaney stopped, reached into his pocket, and gave him a cigarette, and started talking to us again. And then Wilt said, "Uh-uh-Joe. Uh-uh-uh-giv—giv—give me the matches."

I said to myself, "This is not happening." Coming from the environment I did in college, it was a shock to see athletes smoking, especially him. You never heard of him smoking. He said he didn't buy cigarettes and only smoked them at halftime, maybe to calm himself.

—Jim McMillian, Lakers teammate

Wilt usually arrived just before we had our team meeting and we're ready to go out on the floor. One time I put on his warm-up jacket. It was like a bathrobe on me; it came down to my calves.

The way he carried himself and the aura he had, he was just larger than life. Guys 6'10" weren't in the same category. He also sweated more than anyone I've ever seen. At halftime he'd take off his jersey, wring it out, and change. No one else ever had to. Wilt was just larger than life.

—Keith Erickson, twelve-year NBA veteran and Lakers teammate for five years

Kareem came into the NBA in the twilight of my career. I knew this young man when he was in high school. I never thought of him as a threat to anything I was doing. I befriended Kareem when he was young, and I think he liked me. The man was a supertalent. To me he was an enigma. Of all the supertalents, I never thought he pushed himself. When a man could score like he scored, [I don't understand why there was] only one time in his career [that] he ever scored over 50 points. . . . [Actually, Abdul-Jabbar scored 50 or more 10 times.] If there was anything lacking in Kareem, it was the [desire to] push himself past his normal production level.

But when I played against him, he presented to me, for the first time in my basketball career, a guy I felt, at least at that time in my career, that I really needed some help to guard. I just couldn't play this guy all by myself.

—Wilt Chamberlain, in an interview with NBA Entertainment

A Heaping Portion
of Humble Pie

Wilt was ready for the 1970–1971 campaign, but, as always, on his terms: on numerous occasions, he showed up for games minutes before the team meeting—barefooted and carrying his footwear. He proceeded to devour a bucket of chicken and wash it down with a quart of 7 Up or orange juice (or both), all of this shortly before the team went out on the floor to warm up and play.

The Lakers tolerated his unusual habits and he continued to deliver on the court. He was the only Laker to play in every one of the team's 82 regular-season games, and for the ninth time, he led the league in rebounds, gathering almost as many as the next three Lakers combined. Jerry West led the Lakers in scoring with an average of almost 27 points; Wilt was a respectable second with 20.7. Wilt insisted that his participation in beach volleyball had strengthened his surgically mended knee and had allowed him to maintain a high level of performance on the basketball court. True enough, but the lingering arthritis in both knees, Wilt's advanced age for an athlete (he was 34), and the addition of some pounds restricted his lateral movement.

With Elgin Baylor, who had torn his Achilles tendon, appearing in only two games that year, other Lakers came to the fore, among them Harold "Happy" Hairston, the team's second-best rebounder. Hairston could also shoot and contributed an average of 18.6 points. Gail Goodrich (back from Phoenix), averaged 18, and Keith Erickson, who could play guard or small forward, contributed 11 points a game.

Jim McMillian, a rookie from New York (whom Wilt always called "Rook," even 20 years later when they ran into each other in New York), averaged eight points that season. McMillian's locker was close to Wilt's in the 1970–1971 campaign, so he understood how and why Wilt acquired a new nickname from Elgin Baylor, who was still team captain and continued to hold court in the locker room despite his limited on-court contributions. Baylor had a strong personality and was not shy about trading barbs with his teammates, teasing them and commenting on their personality quirks. According to McMillian:

> Wilt sweated more than any athlete I've ever seen. He'd change his jersey at halftime. He'd change his headband, wristband. Sometimes, during a timeout, Wilt would be on the sideline wringing out his headband or wristband.
>
> Well, Wilt had the bad habit when the game was over of putting those uniforms in his bag and leaving them in there until the next game. Now if those things had been in there two or three days, you can imagine the smell. And he'd put them back on and go out to play.
>
> He also had the reputation of taking the quickest shower in the league, but half the time he wouldn't take a shower. He'd borrow someone's deodorant and get dressed in his tailor-made clothes and go on about his business. . . . And Elgin got on him about that. That's why he nicknamed him "Big Musty." Elgin was the only one who would call him "Big Musty." The other guys called him "Big Fella."

Wilt maintained that his knee injury had changed his relationship with fans, both those in Los Angeles and those in other cities, who cheered him on to a degree they never had before (however, he added, rarely so in Boston). Speculating on why the fans had changed—if, indeed, they had—Wilt believed that they appreciated how hard he had worked to come back from knee surgery, which made him (in their eyes) a "team player," not someone who cared only about himself and his statistics. Also, as he was older and had been around for a while, he had become an elder statesman of the league. Finally, fans had found a new "villain" to rail against: the 7'2" Lew Alcindor, as he was called before the 1971–1972 season when he converted to Islam and changed his name to Kareem Abdul-Jabbar. Fans, so Wilt believed, needed a "bad guy" to root against, and the taller the better. (Remember, "No one roots for Goliath.") The gifted, articulate, though private and prickly Jabbar, who was not the most accommodating athlete to the media, fit the bill perfectly.

Wilt and Jabbar had a tangled relationship that had its beginnings as a mentor/student connection in the sixties. Over the next three decades, very public animosity between the two men was only briefly replaced with a temporary reconciliation.

Wilt incessantly criticized Jabbar, especially after Wilt retired, for failing to gather more rebounds and for a lack of effort on the defensive end. Both criticisms were factually wrong, particularly when you look at the first 15 years of Jabbar's 20-year career. He was regularly in the top five in scoring, rebounding (he even led the league in 1975–1976), blocked shots, and field-goal percentage, and he won a record six MVP awards while, not incidentally, leading his teams to numerous NBA titles. That might—just might—have had something to do with Wilt's need to criticize him. Wilt even named one of his Great Danes "Careem," although he said the name had nothing to do with the basketball player but, rather, described the cream color of the dog. (That, of course, is nonsense.)

Jabbar's response, at first, was to criticize Wilt's off-the-court actions. He implied that Wilt had betrayed the black race by supporting the Republican Richard Nixon and, after the publication of Wilt's autobiography, said that Wilt had offended black women when he wrote that white women were more sexually sophisticated.

After publicly bashing each other in the seventies, they didn't talk to one another for 10 years. They finally reconciled, and in 1984 as Jabbar was about to break Wilt's record for most points scored, a gracious Wilt said, "If anyone deserves to break the record, it's definitely him."

The reconciliation was short-lived, with Wilt continuing to question Jabbar's heart and skills. And in 1990, against the advice of his coauthor, Jabbar took a very public shot at Wilt, the basketball player, when he wrote that Wilt would be remembered as a "whining crybaby and a quitter."

At the start of the 1970–1971 season, the NBA went from two divisions, the Eastern and the Western, to four: the Atlantic, Central, Midwest, and Pacific. The league also created an Eastern and a Western *Conference*, the winners from which played for the NBA title.

The Los Angeles Lakers from the Pacific Division, and the Milwaukee Bucks from the Midwest, won the first round of the playoffs and were matched in the Western Conference Finals. Joining Jabbar on that formidable Milwaukee squad was Oscar Robertson, the longtime Cincinnati star. After it had become clear to him he was no longer wanted in Cincinnati, Robertson approved a trade to the Milwaukee Bucks, hoping that he might finally win a championship before his fabulous career ended. The remaining contributors were Bob Dandridge and Greg Smith at forward, Jon McGlocklin and Lucius Allen (with Robertson) as the guards, and Bob Boozer, a 6'8" veteran forward who was an excellent rebounder. Their coach was Larry Costello, feisty and blunt and solid on fundamentals and defense.

The Lakers, underdogs against the Bucks, entered the contest without the services of Elgin Baylor, still out from his Achilles tendon tear, *or* Jerry West, recuperating from surgery on a knee that he had torn up in a collision in an early March game. In contrast, the Bucks were healthy, hungry, and talented: earlier that season they had won 20 consecutive games, thereby surpassing the year-old record for consecutive wins set by the defending NBA champs, the New York Knicks. And the Bucks had posted a league-leading record of 66-16, then the third best record in NBA history. Jabbar won the scoring title (averaging 31.7 points per game) and was voted the first of his MVP awards. No one expected much from the outmanned Lakers, though the sports world was interested to see how Wilt, 34, and Jabbar, 24, would perform in their first playoff matchup.

The Lakers were crushed in Game 1, 106–85. Jabbar had 32, Wilt 22. Milwaukee also won Game 2, though Wilt, with 26 points, outplayed Jabbar, who had 22. In that game, Wilt dominated on the boards, and by halftime had 14 rebounds to 4 for Jabbar. Before Game 3, Keith Erickson had an emergency appendectomy, so now the Lakers were without Baylor, West, *and* Erickson—West's replacement. But this time Wilt both outscored Jabbar (24 to 20) and outrebounded him (24 to 19), leading Los Angeles to its first victory of the series.

In Game 4, Jabbar struck back, dominating his elder nemesis by scoring 17 in the first quarter and 31 overall. Wilt had 15 points, but was outrebounded (something that rarely happened), 21–16. Recalling the matchup, Keith Erickson said, "Kareem was able to do some stuff against Wilt, and I was surprised." Be that as it may, the Wilt-Jabbar battles never captured the fans' or writers' interest to the degree that the Russell-Chamberlain duels had, possibly because Wilt was in the self-described "twilight of his career" during the four seasons in which they competed. Without taking anything away from Jabbar, undoubtedly one of the greatest offensive players in the game's history, one wonders how he would have fared had there not been a 10-year age difference and had they competed *before* Wilt's knee surgery.

Wilt kept the outgunned Lakers competitive in Game 5. Still, Milwaukee wrapped up the series by winning that fifth game, 116–98. When Wilt left the game with only minutes remaining, the hometown Milwaukee fans gave him a standing ovation.

After a loss in an important game or series—alas, there were many such—Wilt's demeanor might have given fans (or reporters) the impression he wasn't too upset or didn't care, but that was far from the truth, according to teammate Jim McMillian:

> Wilt had a look on his face that said, "Hey, we got another playoff game, we got another season." That was the look on his face, but that wasn't what was going on inside. From being around him, I realized that was his "look" after a loss. But then we'd get on the plane or bus and it was like, "The Big Fella needs to sit by himself, because he's upset." He took losses hard. People didn't see that.

Milwaukee, the Western Conference champions (the NBA had difficulty with geography in those days), would face Baltimore, which had dethroned the New York Knicks in seven games, in the Finals. It was no contest: Milwaukee won in four games for its first—and only—NBA crown. And while all this was taking place, where was Wilt after his team had been eliminated? He was headed to Houston, Texas, where he was to sign a contract to fight Muhammad Ali.

This was, of course, not the first time Wilt had seriously considered boxing. In 1965 he had been approached by Cus D'Amato, a respected boxing trainer, who claimed to represent a group of investors prepared to back a fight between Wilt and Muhammad Ali, the heavyweight champion—this at a time when the 76ers were trying to sign Wilt to a basketball contract. After the 76ers co-owner, Ike Richman, traveled to Kutsher's Country Club in mid-August, vowing that he wouldn't let Wilt leave his room until he had committed himself to either a boxing or a basketball career, Wilt had opted to remain in basketball.

And then in February 1967, the idea of Wilt fighting Ali surfaced again—this time at the beginning of Ali's troubles with the Selective Service System. (That led, beginning in June of that year, to Ali being barred from fighting for three and a half years.)

Pondering a fight with Ali, Wilt said, "Life is a challenge and this would be one of many." And, he added, "Fighting Muhammad Ali would combine the two kinds of challenges I'd always responded to—doing something everyone said couldn't be done, and beating another man at his game."

Once again, Cus D'Amato would train Wilt, and football's legendary Jim Brown would manage him. D'Amato had told Wilt that it would take six months of hard training, but he would have Wilt ready to fight one fight against one fighter—Ali. D'Amato said Wilt's chances of winning were pretty good. Sportswriters were less confident. Sandy Grady, then a reporter for *The Evening Bulletin*, wrote a column advising Wilt not to fight Ali. Grady thought Wilt was sure to lose—and suffer humiliation in the process.

To stir up interest in the fight, Wilt and Ali appeared in March on ABC's *Wide World of Sports* with Howard Cosell, who egged on the two men. The flamboyant and boastful Ali fluttered around his taller opponent-to-be, who remained serene and confident. At one point during the clowning between the two men, who liked and respected each other, Ali, looking up at the much taller Wilt, shouted, "Timber"—his forecast of what would happen if they ever fought. There is a famous photograph of Wilt and Ali "squaring off" against each other, which has been reproduced thousands of times in subsequent years (along with Wilt's 100-point photograph, probably the two most famous pictures of him). For the millions who saw the original television broadcast or the still photograph of the two men, the differences (all in Wilt's favor)—in height (almost a foot), weight (about 65 pounds), and reach (about 13 inches)—prompted many to wonder what might have happened if the two most controversial, most egotistical, and most gifted athletes of their time were to clash in the ring.

While no one doubted Wilt was strong enough to tangle with Ali, and even though Wilt claimed he had fought and won four times as an amateur, that hardly qualified him to fight a boxer of Ali's caliber. When Wilt broached the idea of fighting Ali to his father—an ardent boxing fan—Chamberlain senior advised his son that practicing foul shots would be a better use of his time.

The 1967 Ali-Wilt fight never came off, reportedly because Ali's manager, Herbert Muhammad, nixed it, on what grounds he never said. (Wilt, of course, thought the grounds were Ali's manager's fear that his fighter would fall.)

Although that 1967 fight never really got beyond the talking stage, the proposed fight between Wilt and Ali in 1971 was the real thing. Wilt had signed an agreement in February for a 12-round fight scheduled for July 26 in the Houston Astrodome. The agreement stipulated that Wilt could back out if Ali lost the heavyweight championship in his forthcoming March fight with Joe Frazier. Ali did lose that fight, which meant the Chamberlain-Ali match wouldn't be for a title, but Wilt decided to proceed anyway.

The terms of the fight were as follows: Wilt was guaranteed $500,000 or 25 percent of the gross receipts, whichever was higher. Ali (who had received $2.5 million in his historic first fight with Frazier) was to receive a guaranteed $1 million or 45 percent of the gross receipts—again, whichever was higher.

Not everyone was thrilled with the prospect of the fight. "This makes a joke out of boxing," said Bill Brennan, president of the World Boxing Association. And the chairman of the New York State Athletic Commission weighed in by saying New York would not sanction the fight. *The Philadelphia Daily News'* Jack McKinney was more amused than outraged. "If they fought in a phone booth," he joked, "it would be no contest: Wilt all the way." But because the fight was to be held in a ring, he believed Ali would prevail.

A press conference was scheduled for April 22 at the Astrodome to sign the contract and to formally announce the fight. Wilt and his lawyer, Sy Goldberg, had flown in from Los Angeles, while his other adviser, Alan Levitt, arrived from Philadelphia. And Ali, as was his wont, had his full entourage. On the afternoon of, but prior to, the press conference, there was a brouhaha regarding the terms of the contract: either the contract had been misrepresented to them or Wilt and his advisers had misunderstood the terms of the proposed fight. They thought the $500,000 guarantee was *after*, not *before*, taxes. Ali, who was already at the press conference entertaining the assembled reporters, was informed of the last-minute wrinkle that, he realized, jeopardized the fight. Ali wanted the fight badly, probably because he needed the money and saw it as an easy payday. And, having just lost to Joe Frazier, maybe his ego required that he fight and win sooner rather than later.

"Ali was gracious and a gentleman," recalled Alan Levitt, of all their dealings with the boxer. "He walked into the room with his advisers, but you could see Ali was in charge. He wasn't listening to any of his advisers." Apropos of this last-minute demand by Wilt, Ali said, according to Levitt, "We'll divide everything down the middle, including the ancillary rights." At that moment Levitt, Goldberg, and Wilt adjourned to the men's room for further discussions.

Levitt recollected the advice he gave to his client and friend: "I said to Wilt, 'You're the strongest man in the world, but you are not a fighter. I want you to consider something: Ali could actually kill you. I mean kill you.'"

Wilt returned to the room where the parties had been meeting. When it became clear that Wilt was not going to sign a contract, Jack O'Connell, head of the group promoting the fight, announced to the assembled media, "We do not have a fight at this time." (Nor would he ever.) O'Connell said the fight had to be postponed while the promoters mulled over Wilt's new demand.

Of the incident, Wilt wrote: "Alan [Levitt], who probably knows me better than any man alive, had never been that keen on my fighting Ali anyway, and he used the occasion of their reneging [on the terms of the contract] as a lever to talk me out of the fight altogether."

Levitt told the author more than 20 years later: "As close as our relationship was, I don't know to this day how serious Wilt was about fighting Ali. Ali wanted the fight badly. Anyway, I talked Wilt out of it. Maybe he wanted to be talked out of it. I don't know."

Wilt was scheduled to fly back East to visit his mother in Maple Shade, New Jersey, located, by coincidence, near Ali's home in Cherry Hill, New Jersey. As it happened, the two men took the same flight and, because they genuinely liked each other, the atmosphere remained cordial.

The big payday had to have been enticing to Wilt, who would have to play two years in the NBA to make what he would have in 36 minutes (or less) in the boxing ring. But in the final analysis, Wilt probably backed out because he was concerned that he might be humiliated by Ali—not injured, defeated, or knocked out, but humiliated.

Chapter 17

Wilt was like a child in many respects. Children push you as far as they can. Wilt was like that. He'd see how much he could get away with. Joe Mullaney was one of the nicest guys you'd ever want to meet, but he had a hard time with the superstars. Bill Sharman came in with a different reputation, and he had good people skills. He could make Wilt think that the idea was his or convince Wilt it would be beneficial for the team if he did this or that.

—Jim McMillian, Lakers teammate

As I look back, Wilt was, in many ways, misunderstood. He was his own man. You always knew where you stood with Wilt. You didn't always agree with Wilt on things, but you always got an honest answer. He had his way of doing a lot of things that were different, but that didn't mean they were right or wrong. When Wilt came to Los Angeles, [the team] had shared rooms on the road. Wilt said, "No, I want my own." That was different. They accommodated Wilt. So other players eventually spoke up, and the Lakers offered everyone the opportunity to have a single room, but the players paid the difference. It may sound trivial, but Wilt said, "Just because it was done that way in the past doesn't mean it has to be done that way in the future."

The same thing [happened] with flying first class. For him to sit in coach was uncomfortable. I think he was instrumental in promoting that for the whole league. Ultimately, through the Players Association, we got the privilege for everybody to fly first class.

Wilt spoke his mind. And, as I look back, he wasn't unreasonable in these requests.

—Gail Goodrich, Lakers teammate

The Streak

Though the Lakers—including Wilt—liked and spoke kindly of him, coach Joe Mullaney was fired for failing to deliver the NBA championship. Never mind that in Mullaney's first season, Wilt had torn up his knee and still the team reached the NBA Finals, only to lose in seven games; and in his second season, both Elgin Baylor and Jerry West required operations while Kareem Abdul-Jabbar and Oscar Robertson led Milwaukee to a championship. Even when the Lakers' three superstars were healthy, Mullaney never really melded them together, making the whole of the team stronger than its parts. So Mullaney was gone, though not before he was quoted as saying the Lakers' superstars were over the hill and that management overrated them.

The new Lakers coach was 45-year-old Bill Sharman, who had coached the Utah Stars to the American Basketball Association championship the previous season and, some years before that, had led the Cleveland Pipers to the championship in the short-lived American Basketball League. There he worked for a demanding owner named George Steinbrenner, who eventually turned his attention to baseball. And it was Sharman who had coached the San Francisco Warriors to the Western Division title in 1967, before that team fell to Wilt and the great 76ers. In six years as a coach on the professional level, Sharman had won two league championships and taken two other teams to the finals. The man could coach.

Sharman had grown up in California's Central Valley, where in high school he won 14 letters in five sports, and at the University of Southern California he was twice an All-American in basketball. In 1950 he signed with baseball's Brooklyn Dodgers, and later that year the Washington Capitols selected him in the second round of the NBA draft. For five years he played both sports, but left baseball in 1955 after being unable to break into the majors. During his

11-year NBA career (1950–1961)—10 of those years with the Boston Celtics—
he was the best jump shooter in the sport, selected for the All-Star team eight
times and, in due course, enshrined in the sport's Hall of Fame. Sharman held
the league record, since broken, of making 56 consecutive free throws, and led
the league a record seven times in free-throw percentage. He played on four
NBA championship teams. He and Bob Cousy, his roommate and best friend
on the Celtics, formed one of the greatest backcourt duos in the game's history.
Besides those sterling basketball credentials, he is a gentleman, as well as being
intelligent, determined, fair, disciplined, well-organized, and a master at motivating men.

That off-season Wilt was mostly preoccupied with the construction of his
new home, still months away from completion after numerous delays. Asked by
a newspaper reporter his opinion of the Lakers coaching change, Wilt, never
one to hide his views, said it was tiresome to go through the experience of a new
coach almost every year. He had a point, as Sharman would be Wilt's eighth
coach in 13 years. (That not very exclusive club included Neil Johnston, Frank
McGuire, Bob Feerick, Alex Hannum—who coached him in two cities—Dolph
Schayes, Butch van Breda Kolff, and Joe Mullaney.) "Every year it's something
new," Wilt said. "A new coach with a new way of doing things. I'm not demean-
ing or rationalizing. I like Bill Sharman and I've had lots of dealings with him
off the court."

Wilt and Sharman's relationship predated the Los Angeles Lakers. They had
played against each other in the 1959–1960 and 1960–1961 seasons, following
which Sharman retired as a player, but it was away from the competitive atmosphere of the NBA that they fashioned a friendship. As Sharman remembered: "I
invited him and Bill Russell up to my boys camp for a couple of summers [in the
early sixties], and then I also played with and against him at Kutsher's. So I got
to know him pretty well before I had a chance to coach him."

One of Sharman's first moves was to hire K. C. Jones, an old Celtics teammate, as his assistant coach, the first time the Lakers ever had one. Sharman also
put the aging, injury-prone Lakers through a rigorous preseason workout, as he
believed that the better conditioned a team, the better it would perform, particularly late in the game, and that being in excellent shape allowed a team to
run. Sharman thought that fast-break basketball, which he had learned, practiced, and perfected as a member of the Boston Celtics, was the most effective
path to success in the game. This had not been the Laker style under Mullaney.

"Until Sharman came in, the Lakers' offense was always stagnant, not a lot of movement—more emphasis on one-on-one," recalled Gail Goodrich, who played on and against the Mullaney-coached Lakers. "You had Jerry and Elgin, and they were great one-on-one players. But in a lot of ways, the other three guys stood around."

But, Sharman wondered, could or would the team's three superstars adapt to a running game? As he recalled:

> Because of the age of Elgin Baylor [37], Wilt Chamberlain [35], and Jerry West [33], I was not sure if my method was best for the Lakers. Nor did I know if they would accept my ideas. Before training began, I approached West and Gail Goodrich, and they were enthusiastic about them.
>
> When you talk about a running game, the first thing you have to do is make sure you get the rebound and the quick outlet pass. Therefore, I knew the burden would be on Wilt. I met with Wilt and put the problem to him. He said he felt we could do it and he was willing to give it a try. He thought the team would go for it, too.

In fairness to Butch van Breda Kolff, he also had wanted the Lakers to run, but the same Wilt Chamberlain who was willing to try it under Bill Sharman was quoted in the newspapers during the van Breda Kolff reign as saying that the Lakers were too old to run. Because it is human nature to be willing to listen to and try suggestions from those whom we like or respect, Wilt was always willing to give Bill Sharman the benefit of the doubt, while he and van Breda Kolff probably couldn't agree on whether a dog had three legs or four.

Sharman also introduced the Lakers to his most notable basketball innovation—the shootaround, a light, short (no more than 50-minute) workout the day of a game. He believed that it allowed players a chance to work on various skills—maybe to practice foul or jump shooting—and to discuss that night's opponent, and provided everyone with the opportunity to begin focusing on the game. The shootaround was generally held at 11:00 in the morning. "We all said it will be interesting to see how Wilt adapts to this," recalled Gail Goodrich.

Everyone told Sharman that Wilt, a late riser, would never go along with the idea. So three weeks before the preseason, Sharman took Wilt to lunch, over which he explained that the shootaround had helped him (Sharman) as a player and, when he became a coach, his teams. Sharman recalled Wilt's response:

> Wilt said, "Bill, I really don't like getting up in the morning, but I tell you what. I'll go along with it when we start. If I think it will help the team, then I'll go along with it during the season."
>
> Thank God we got off to a good start [that season]. And Wilt was great. He only missed two morning shootarounds the whole season. And even then, he told the trainer and got word to me that he wasn't feeling well. Wilt would come and ask a few questions and practice a few free throws. I told him, "Wilt, do whatever you want to do."
>
> If Wilt had not gone along with the shootaround, I doubt I would have kept it because it would have been hard to ask the other players to come and him not to. So I give Wilt a lot of credit for helping to start the [Lakers'] morning shootaround, [a tool] which is used by every pro team today.

So much for the probably apocryphal story that Wilt once said, "Tell coach Sharman he can have me once—either for the morning shootaround or for the game."

"That first year [1971–1972] I don't think he missed a shootaround," Goodrich confirmed. "We really became a team. He and Jerry West were the leaders of that team."

"He didn't like it [the shootaround], but he came," recalled Keith Erickson. "He'd come in thongs and shorts and a weird T-shirt. Jerry and Elgin didn't do a lot at the shootarounds, either. Us other guys would do more."

That superstars are treated differently is a fact of life, whether it is on a basketball team, in Hollywood, or in business. "I don't know any coaches who treated players the same, even if they say they do," McMillian concurred.

The Lakers won six of their first nine games, and in the three losses they were without Jerry West, sidelined temporarily with a sprained ankle. After game nine—a loss—Elgin Baylor, the spring in his legs gone, unable to come back from an operation to repair an Achilles tendon tear, and unwilling to play at a level so far below his standards, announced his retirement, effective immediately. After 13 seasons the man who had saved the floundering franchise when it moved from Minneapolis to Los Angeles was calling it quits. At the time, Baylor was the league's third all-time leading scorer and fifth greatest rebounder.

With Baylor retired, the Lakers needed a new captain. Coach Sharman offered to make Wilt and West cocaptains, but West told the coach that he preferred to concentrate on his game and thought that Wilt would do an excellent job on his own. After naming Wilt as the sole captain, the coach found that Wilt took the position very seriously, even on some occasions getting on teammates whom he felt were not hustling. This was surprising to Sharman because he knew Wilt was neither a "rah-rah guy" nor the type of player who normally tried to motivate his teammates. West said he felt that the captaincy had inspired Wilt to lead and set good examples. Seeing this, the other Lakers rallied around Wilt.

To replace Baylor at forward, Sharman picked Jim McMillian, a second-year professional who had gained a lot of confidence by doing so well in the playoffs the previous year and felt he was ready to start. Along with his coaching skills, these two moves by Sharman galvanized a good team into a great team—no criticism meant to the illustrious Elgin Baylor. Many years later Butch van Breda Kolff spoke to the author and shared his perspective of the Lakers' subsequent success: "Elgin Baylor was the leader of that team. When he retired, Wilt wanted to show people the Lakers didn't need Elgin. So Wilt started to play like me and Joe Mullaney had wanted him to play all along."

In the game following Baylor's retirement, played on November 5, 1971, McMillian contributed 22 points and gathered 13 rebounds to help the Lakers defeat the Baltimore Bullets. On November 10, they humiliated the 76ers. Wilt blocked eight shots, including a couple on his old buddy and teammate Billy Cunningham, who years later recalled:

> I probably appreciated him more when he went to L.A. because now I was playing against him. Before he would just protect me on the court. If someone beat me to the basket, I didn't even worry about it. I started running the other way because I knew he was either going to block the shot, get the rebound, or intimidate the person. I could just run to the other end and get a layup. But then he was traded to L.A., and I had to play against him.

I can picture the many times I beat my man going to the basket and, all of a sudden, there he was. And I'd say to myself, "Oh no, now what am I going to do?"

By November 21, pleased to observe that the Lakers' running game had developed more quickly than he had expected, Sharman acknowledged that "the key has been Wilt. He's getting the rebounds and he's getting that first pass out. We're getting the ball down before the defense is getting set." Thus was born one of the greatest fast breaks in basketball history. Wilt grabbed the rebound and threw the outlet pass to West, who was fabulous at spotting the open man, who'd pull up for a short jumper or streak to the basket for a layup. All this would happen before Wilt made it to halfcourt, which meant less wear and tear on his knees. Understandably, West led the league in assists that year.

Wilt hadn't forgotten how to score; it just wasn't necessary for him to do so for the Lakers to win. After being defeated by the Lakers in late November, Detroit Pistons center Bob Lanier said of Wilt, who had 31 points and 31 rebounds, "He played like he was in his second childhood."

Since Baylor's retirement, the Lakers had not lost a game, and became the first NBA team ever to go a month (in this case, November) without a loss.

During one game McMillian, who had recently been ill, poured in 41 points; the next game it was Happy Hairston with 20. Against Houston, West shot 9 for 20 and, ever the perfectionist, said, "There were midgets guarding me and I still couldn't score." Gail Goodrich, his backcourt mate, could—and did; he racked up 42 to keep the streak alive. "Every night somebody else contributes, which is what makes good basketball teams," West pointed out.

After the team shot 56 percent in an easy win over Golden State, Wilt said, "A lot of streaks are predicated on luck. This isn't one of them. We haven't had many close games." He almost came to regret those words, for in the very next game, against Phoenix, Connie Hawkins missed a shot at the buzzer that would have given the Suns the victory. Instead, L.A. prevailed in overtime for its 20th straight win—tying the NBA record for consecutive wins (set the year before by the Milwaukee Bucks).

L.A. broke Milwaukee's record two days later by defeating the Atlanta Hawks, a game in which "Wilt went to work and took over the board," according to the Hawks coach Richie Guerin. (This wasn't Guerin's first brush with historic games: he had been the Knicks' leading scorer the night Wilt scored 100 points.)

The Lakers had won 21 straight and were approaching the record of most consecutive victories by a professional sports team—26, held by baseball's 1916 New York Giants (who didn't even win the pennant that year).

What had transformed this team? Gail Goodrich knew very well:

> I liked Joe Mullaney, but he wasn't a strong enough personality for the pros. And, of course, Wilt was a strong personality. I don't think Wilt had a great deal of respect for Mullaney as a coach. I just think he had a little more respect for Sharman and K. C. Jones. He knew they were very successful players. They had both played with Russell, and I think Wilt and Russell both had a great deal of respect for one another as players.
>
> When Sharman arrived and said, "We'll try to do things like this," I think Wilt, who had a great deal of pride, like all players, said, "Well, this is the way that the Celtics and Russell did it, and they were successful. And I'm every bit as good as Bill Russell. I'm going to show that I can be as good as Bill Russell and, if I had the supporting cast that Boston had, we would have won a few more championships."

The 25ᵗʰ straight victory came against the 76ers, 154–132. Wilt had 32 points, 34 rebounds, and 12 blocked shots. "That's the best I've seen him play since the playoff against Boston when we won the championship," said Jack Ramsay, the 76ers coach in 1972 but in 1966–1967 their general manager.

Observed Billy Cunningham: "All Wilt needs is a little incentive and Sharman has given him that. I can't say why. All I can do is judge on the past few years that I've seen Wilt playing with the Lakers."

If Cunningham couldn't say why, Sharman could, as he explained the approach he took with his center:

> I wouldn't coach him like I coached other players. With other players I'd say, "I want you to pick out high and roll to the basket." With Wilt I'd say, "Now what do you think we should do? Use the high post or do you think we should do the low post?" I'd keep asking him questions till I got him to say what I wanted to do, and then I'd say, "Wilt, I think that's a great idea. Let's do it that way." I wanted him to think it was his idea. And he would go out and bust his fanny to do it. But

if I told him, "Do this, do that," I don't think he would respond as well.

If Sharman's approach sounds familiar, that's because it is the same one Alex Hannum used to such success (though for a limited time) with Wilt.

When they defeated the Buffalo Braves, 117–103, on December 21, the Lakers tied the streak for the most consecutive wins by a professional team. They broke the record the next night with a 127–120 victory over the Baltimore Bullets. Wilt, like all the Lakers, was thrilled by the team's historic accomplishment, but he tried to keep things in perspective and remarked, "We've won 27 games in a row and we're 1 game ahead of the damn Milwaukee Bucks." (Actually, they were two and a half games ahead.)

Asked frequently during the streak to compare the 1971–1972 Lakers to the great 1966–1967 Sixers, Wilt refused. "It's another era and unfair to compare" was his tactful answer, probably one of the few times in his public life he was diplomatic, because it really wasn't a different era. (Later he'd say that he believed the 1966–1967 Sixers were the greatest team ever, while acknowledging that the 1971–1972 Lakers were also great and got the most out of their collective abilities. He'd also remind the interrogator that the Sixers center was five years younger than the one who played for the Lakers, reason enough, he implied, that one would have to pick the 1966–1967 Sixers.)

In late December fans at the sold-out Forum, which held 17,500, gave coach Sharman a standing ovation before that night's game. The Lakers won, and Happy Hairston scored 19 and pulled down 14 rebounds. He'd gather one thousand that season, the only forward who ever played with Wilt to pull down that many, a testament to Hairston's rebounding prowess.

Fans throughout the league wanted to see these magical Lakers. An early January game against the hapless Cleveland Cavaliers in the Cleveland Arena was sold out, prompting the witty Cleveland coach, Bill Fitch, to observe, "It will be different without all those empty seats. I hope my players adjust." At one point, Cleveland led 99–94, but only until Wilt blocked four shots and L.A. scored 15 straight on the way to victory. That made it 32 in a row.

Reminiscing about the streak in 2003, McMillian said, "We might be playing in Cleveland or Philly, who had terrible teams that year. We're on a long road trip. Everyone's not clicking as a unit, but we always had Gail Goodrich. He was a machine. He didn't care if he was playing against his mother or grandmother;

he was going to go out there and 'kill her.' And you need guys like that to keep a streak going."

On January 7, the Lakers had their easiest win of the streak, crushing the Atlanta Hawks, 134–90. That made it two months without a loss.

And then on a Sunday afternoon, January 9, 1972, it ended: the Milwaukee Bucks, playing at home in a nationally televised game, defeated the Los Angeles Lakers, 120–104. The Lakers were flat, the Bucks aggressive—none more so than Jabbar, who scored 39, garnered 20 rebounds, and blocked 10 shots. Wilt, in comparison, had only 15 points, 12 rebounds, and five blocked shots. However, none of Wilt's teammates shot or played particularly well either.

The streak was over—the Lakers had won 33 straight. Sharman's reaction? "At least I'm glad that when we finally lost, it was to the world champions," he commented. "It will be many, many years before anybody wins 33 games in a row again." In fact, that is still the longest record of successive wins in the history of professional sports in the United States.

"I'm sorry it's over. I wanted it to go on forever," the ever-competitive West declared.

The late Mal Florence, then the basketball beat writer for the *Los Angeles Times*, had been friends with Sharman since their days at USC. Even before the record-ending game with the Bucks, Bill Shirley, the *Times*' sports editor, who was under orders to trim the budget, had instructed Florence to cut short his trip and return to Los Angeles. When coach Sharman saw Florence checking out of their hotel after the game, he asked, "Mal, where are you going?" Without hesitating, Florence replied, "We don't cover losers."

At the midseason break, three Lakers were chosen to play in the All-Star Game— Wilt, West, and Goodrich—with two of them, West and Goodrich, starting. What a memorable season Wilt and his team were having: by the end of January, Wilt had broken Bill Russell's career rebounding record, and in February he scored his 30,000th point. To put this point total into context, one should know that Wilt's closest competitor, Oscar Robertson, was more than 5,000 points behind; only five men in league history (as of then) had even scored *20,000* points. As astounding as Wilt's accomplishment was (and is), when he was once asked about his amazing scoring feats over the years, he responded, "The one I remember best was the first [point] I ever got, which came in a game against the Knicks."

Some people, however, best remember Wilt for untold examples of notable—but usually unpublicized—off-the-court behavior. Mike LaBonne, who grew up in the Philadelphia area, reminisced about one such incident that occurred on a cold February night in 1972 when he was 23 and was in the coast guard. His ship was in dry dock in Baltimore, and he and some buddies went to the old Baltimore Civic Center to see the Lakers and the Bullets. He clearly recalls what happened:

> Wilt came out to warm up. There was a kid sitting in a wheelchair who looked like he was a paraplegic and, just before the game was to begin, the boy's father walked up to Wilt with a basketball. It looked like the father asked him to sign the basketball. It was right before the tip-off, and Wilt had his "game face" on. Wilt just said something to the father, who then walked away. Some of the Baltimore fans booed Wilt for not signing the basketball.
>
> After the game, me and my buddies were out in the parking lot having a few beers and waiting for the lot to empty. And from the private entrance, the one where the athletes entered and left, we saw the kid, who was about 11, and the father coming out. Wilt was pushing the kid's wheelchair, and on the kid's lap was an NBA basketball with Wilt's signature.
>
> He took the kid over to their van and helped the kid into it. The door was open, and Wilt stood and talked to him for five or ten minutes. There was a crowd of people around and Wilt had some of his buddies keeping the people back because he wanted to spend the time with the kid.
>
> I've often thought of this story, and I think of the people who saw Wilt denying the autograph and booed him. Boy, if they only knew. He not only brought the boy out, he wheeled him out. And the look on that kid's face was worth a million bucks. How many athletes would you see today do something like that?

After Wilt grabbed 18 rebounds and scored 19 points in leading L.A. to a victory over Cleveland on March 10, the team announced he had been playing for a month with a broken bone in his right hand. It was a new fracture over an old break.

"Wilt has been suffering extreme pain the past few weeks, yet he played in every game without protest," the Lakers general manager, Fred Schaus, pointed out. Wilt vowed to the fans that he would continue to play and, true to his word, he played in every one of the Lakers' remaining nine games wearing a protective covering over the hand to absorb blows.

On March 11, a Saturday, Wilt hosted friends and associates at an all-day and all-night housewarming party at his new home. (More about this house in the next chapter.) Though Wilt said he had gotten to bed at 7:00 Sunday morning, that didn't prevent him from leading the Lakers that night to a victory over an admittedly weak Buffalo Braves team.

Truly, this was a super Laker team: they led the league in scoring, rebounding, and assists. They ended the season 69–13, at that time the best record in the league's history. They had topped the won-lost percentage of the 1966–1967 Sixers, who had been 68–13. Their 31–7 road record is still the best in NBA history, although the Lakers' won-lost record would fall to Michael Jordan's Chicago Bulls, who in 1995–1996 were 72–10.

Wilt had probably never been so loved and respected by fans, although there were also many who had idolized him from his first day as a professional. Fans appreciated that he played hurt and recognized that he had changed from a scorer to primarily a defender and rebounder for the team's good, though Wilt and his partisans would remind the former critics that earlier in his career he had had to score in order for his team to be competitive. The 1971–1972 Lakers didn't need his points; thus, he had only 12 percent of the team's points, compared to 20 or 30 percent of his Philadelphia team's points earlier in his career. Wilt averaged only 14.8 points that year, on approximately 40 percent fewer shots than in the previous season. Nevertheless, he still led the team (and league) in rebounding—the 10th time he had done so. Moreover, he led the league in field-goal percentage and was third (behind John Havlicek and Jabbar) in minutes played. At his age, after his injuries, to have played so many minutes was extraordinary.

The playing style and strengths of the Lakers starters complemented each other, that rarest of basketball states. Nor should one overlook the depth and strength of the Lakers bench that season. Fred Schaus, the general manager, deserves credit for assembling such a strong backup group at a time when most NBA teams had been depleted by expansion; each of the Laker substitutes had, at one time, started on other teams.

———————

L.A. beat Chicago in four games and Milwaukee stopped Golden State in five to set up a rematch of the previous year's Western Conference Finals. Milwaukee was the defending NBA champion, while L.A. had just finished the greatest season in history. As Wilt warned his teammates, "I've been on teams that set records, but it doesn't mean a thing if you don't win the playoffs." Even though L.A. had won four of the five meetings between the two teams that season, no one was expecting a lopsided conference final.

Milwaukee creamed L.A. in the first game, 93–72, at the Forum, no less. The vaunted L.A. offense managed only eight points in the third quarter of Game 1. Kareem had 22 for the game. None of the Lakers played a special game, including Wilt, who was outrebounded by Jabbar, 26 to 22.

Game 2 belonged to L.A.'s McMillian, who had one of his best nights as a professional, scoring 42 and leading his team to a 135–134 victory. Game 3 was also close, with the lead changing sides 28 times before L.A. clinched the win, 108–105, thanks in part to Goodrich, who threw in 30 points, and Wilt, who blocked 10 shots, 6 of them on Jabbar. Nevertheless, Jabbar managed to score 33.

Jabbar celebrated his 25th birthday by scoring 31 points in Game 4, dominating Wilt, and leading the Bucks to a 114–88 win. The series was tied at two games apiece.

Wilt snapped back in Game 5, outrebounding Jabbar 26 to 16, and that helped L.A. fashion a 115–90 victory. Wilt was eight for eight from the foul line (maybe he had mistakenly drunk from Sharman's coffee mug), and the Lakers were up three games to two.

Down by 10 points early in the fourth quarter, L.A. roared back to win Game 6—and the series—104–100, mostly as the result of an inspired effort by Wilt. He had never played harder in his life, according to Jack Kiser, who had seen him play hundreds of times. "He was everywhere, doing everything," Kiser wrote. He played the entire game (Wilt and Jabbar were the only two players to do so), scored 22 points, garnered 24 rebounds, and blocked nine shots (five of them Jabbar's). As West observed, he wouldn't let the Lakers lose. In one sequence he caught up with Bobby Dandridge and blocked Dandridge's shot; next he wrestled offensive rebounds away from Jabbar and converted them into points; at one point, he stole the ball from Jabbar and dunked it at the other end. And he beat Jabbar down the floor in a couple of key sequences late in the game, when Jabbar, the younger man, tired. "It was the greatest ball-bustin' perform-ance I've ever seen," West said.

If reporters expected Wilt to gloat, he wouldn't bite, at least not publicly. "Don't say I beat Kareem," Wilt said afterward. "Say we beat the Milwaukee Bucks. He [Kareem] had a fantastic series. We did it to the team, not just Kareem." Though privately to Kiser, an old reporter friend from Philadelphia, he declared, "I beat Abdul-Jabbar fair and square."

It was a close series, and it is taking nothing away from L.A. to wonder if the outcome might have been different had Oscar Robertson not played with an abdominal pull painful enough to force him to leave Game 6 after only seven minutes in the second half. But injuries are part of sports—ask the Lakers, who had participated in many a key playoff game over the years with a less-than-healthy Jerry West.

The two teams that would be playing in the NBA Finals were the same ones that had produced a drama-filled classic series two years before—the Los Angeles Lakers and the New York Knickerbockers. But circumstances had changed, mostly in favor of the Lakers. Willis Reed was out with recurrent knee problems, and his replacement at center, 6'8" Jerry Lucas, was really more of a forward than a center. Gone from the Knicks was Cazzie Russell, who had been traded to obtain Lucas. Dick Barnett was still there, although a bad back limited his play, and Earl Monroe, for whom the New York team had given up Mike Riordan and Dave Stallworth, had come from Baltimore. The core of the Knicks, however, remained Bill Bradley, Walt Frazier, and Dave DeBusschere.

When the two teams had met in 1970, Wilt had recently come back from knee surgery, but in 1972 his knees were feeling better than they had at any time during the last three years. The 1970 Lakers stood around, relying on one-on-one set plays; now they ran. Instead of an ailing Baylor, they had a sprightly trio in McMillian, Hairston, and Goodrich to fill the lanes and fire the ball. Small wonder the Lakers were heavy favorites—by some accounts two to one—to finally win the title after seven futile efforts.

With the best record in the league, Los Angeles had won the honors to host four of the seven games, if the series went that long. Playing at home the Lakers lost the first game, just as they had against Milwaukee in the conference finals. The Knicks blistered them, hitting 72 percent of their shots in the first half (53 percent overall). Lucas didn't have Reed's bulk to ward off Wilt or to, at the very least, hold him at bay, but Lucas was an excellent outside shot. In that game he had a hot hand, hitting on 9 of 11 long-range bombs in the first half. For the Lakers' vaunted fast break to kick in, their opponent had to shoot poorly and give them the opportunity to fetch the rebound, which triggered their fast break. With the Knicks shooting so accurately in Game 1, the Lakers never got into their running game; plus the Laker sharpshooters—West and Goodrich—had subpar games. West, a 47 percent lifetime shooter who usually shot even better in the playoffs, was mired in one of the worst shooting slumps of his career.

Before the second game of the Finals, a story in the *Cincinnati Enquirer* quoted Alex Hannum, who, of course, had coached Wilt in San Francisco. Hannum said that prior to the 1964 season Wilt had had severe heart problems that resulted in hospitalization and caused him to miss all the preseason and the beginning of the regular season. Hannum was quoted as saying, "I didn't give him one chance in 10,000 of ever playing basketball again." (If so, all the more remarkable what Wilt accomplished in subsequent years, including 1966–1967, when he led the Sixers, coached by Hannum, to the title.) Reporters asked Wilt if Hannum's story was true, and Wilt said then, as he had in 1964, that his illness was nothing more than pancreatitis and, besides, he was focused more on beating the Knicks than living in the past.

The Lakers made the necessary adjustments in Game 2—playing better defense by picking up their men earlier, sometimes at midcourt, and, though it wasn't done by necessity much that season, they made a conscious effort to get Wilt more involved in the offense. The changes worked. Wilt got Lucas in foul trouble, and Goodrich bedeviled whomever the Knicks put on him—first Earl Monroe, then Dean Meminger. Los Angeles won 106–92. DeBusschere pulled a muscle on his right side near the hip in the second quarter and played only 78 seconds in the second half. He was an integral part of the Knicks, and they counted on the burly forward to rebound, especially with Reed out. If DeBusschere couldn't play in any more of the Finals, the Knicks would not have a chance.

The Knicks returned home for Game 3, but that didn't help them. Normally a team that played smart, they forced shots and missed many of those that weren't forced. DeBusschere, ever valiant, played the first half but, in excruciating pain, could not play in the second. Wilt scored 26 (making 8 of 11 from the foul line) and grabbed 20 rebounds. Goodrich and McMillian also had fine games, as did West, slowly shaking off his shooting slump, with 21 points; he scored his 4,002nd playoff point over his remarkable 11-year career, giving him the record for total points scored in playoff games.

Wilt was always the favorite subject of sports photographers, even in the latter part of his career when he no longer dominated games. After all but one of the games in the Finals, the *Los Angeles Times* featured a picture of Wilt on its sports pages (and often a second picture of other participants in the game). After *every* game of the series, *The New York Times'* sports pages ran a picture of Wilt—grabbing a rebound, covering a defender, leaping out and up from under the basket to put up a backhand shot, or shooting the finger roll (where the photographs show the defender's head usually just above Wilt's waist). All this photographic attention was extraordinary, as there were nine other starting players, but understandable: Wilt was one of the most photogenic athletes.

Still photographs can't compete with film in conveying the beauty, fluid nature, and explosiveness of basketball. Nevertheless, even in a newspaper photograph one senses, appreciates, and marvels at the incredible athlete that was Wilt—his graceful finger roll, which has a ballet-like quality to it; his massive shoulders, muscular arms, muscles and ligaments as taut as a thoroughbred horse's; and, especially in his prime, nary a pinch of fat on his body. A photograph conveys Wilt's extraordinary strength and athleticism. He never looked more handsome than in the seventies, either. He wore his hair longer, as was the style among blacks and whites during the late sixties and seventies, though Wilt never adopted an Afro—à la Wes Unseld or some of the other black players.

But back to the Finals: Game 4—the best-played game in the series—was, again, played in the Garden. Los Angeles defeated New York, this one in overtime, 116–111, thereby taking a commanding three-games-to-one lead in the series. Playing with five fouls (one from elimination), Wilt blocked two shots on Lucas in overtime—once more proving wrong those who said he held back when he had five fouls in order to preserve his record of never having fouled out of an NBA game. Wilt had played 53 minutes (the only Laker to do so). Goodrich continued to harass the Knicks, leading all scorers with 27. It was the Lakers' 80th victory (more than any other club had ever achieved in a season), and their 11th victory in 14 playoff games.

But not all was well. Wilt had fallen in Game 4 and had, so the press reported, sprained his right wrist—the wrist of the hand he had refractured some weeks before. According to Dr. Robert Kerlan, the Lakers team doctor, Wilt was "very, very doubtful" for Game 5.

X-rays of his wrist taken the day before Game 5 revealed that Wilt didn't have a sprained right wrist—he had a *broken* right wrist. Wilt said after the series that only he and Dr. Kerlan were aware the wrist was broken, and both chose to keep quiet about the seriousness of the injury. In newspaper accounts Wilt also said he had a hairline fracture on the base of the index finger of his right (shooting) hand and a bruised left hand. Other than that, he was in perfect health.

Frank O'Neill, the Lakers trainer, had purchased at a sporting goods store the kind of pads that defensive linemen used to wear in football games. The pads had a sponge in them to protect the back of the hand. These were placed on both of Wilt's hands; in addition, his right hand was heavily swaddled in tape. He refused to take a pain-killing injection in the right hand before the game, fearful that he might lose his touch and the "feel" for the ball, so critical in basketball. With his headband, his knee pads, and both of his hands wrapped, Wilt looked like a gladiator.

Game 5 was close for three quarters, but then the Lakers, clearly the superior team, pulled away, winning 114–100 and finally capturing the NBA championship. West had 23 points and, as was his wont, contributed in so many other aspects of the game—ballhandling and defense, to cite just two. Goodrich had 25; McMillian, 20; and Hairston, 13. But the star of the game was Wilt, who had 24 points, 10 blocked shots (and forced the Knicks to hurry or to change the direction of many others), and 29 rebounds—more rebounds than the next three Lakers combined and only 10 fewer than the entire Knicks team. The Forum fans, joyous and deliriously happy, showed their appreciation by pouring onto the court after the game and hoisting Wilt up on their shoulders.

"Wilt played better in the playoffs than he did in the season," said West. "He had an incredible year. Fantastic."

"They deserved to win," said Knicks coach Red Holzman. "They're a tremendous team." That sentiment was echoed by Dave DeBusschere, who still managed to perform well despite his injury: "I thought we played a really good game tonight, but the Lakers played a better game."

West, the only Los Angeles Laker with the team since its inception, was, of course, thrilled to finally reach the summit after he and his teammates had fallen short so often. Ever truthful, in years to come when he reminisced about the glorious 1972 season, he candidly said that not even that great year entirely made up for all the lost championships. (Championships he would win, in bunches no less, but as the Lakers general manager 30 years later; he, after all, brought Shaquille O'Neal, Kobe Bryant, and coach Phil Jackson to the Lakers.)

Before and after he took the job, no dearth of experts warned Bill Sharman that the Lakers were too old and too set in their ways to change and play his kind of basketball. They also said that Wilt would be a problem. "I never had one argument with Wilt," Sharman said in 2003. "He always treated me so nice. He's one of my all-time favorite people."

For guiding his team to a record-setting season, Sharman was named Coach of the Year. And, in winning the NBA title, he became the only coach to ever win championships in the American Basketball League, the American Basketball Association, and the National Basketball Association. Thus a great player—named in 1997 as one of the 50 best of all time—had also secured his position as one of the game's greatest coaches. However, he paid a price for his team's success: from the constant talking and yelling, and because he waited too long to see a doctor, he lost his voice and damaged his vocal cords, later undergoing two operations to repair them. Sadly, he never could speak in a normal volume again and, eventually, had to leave the profession at which he excelled, remaining for many years a Lakers consultant. Reminiscing in 2003 about his former coach, Jerry West said, "I wish I could be like Bill Sharman." And he wasn't referring to *X*'s and *O*'s.

And what of the Big Fella? He was voted the MVP of the Finals, for which he received a Dodge station wagon from *Sport* magazine. Normally, the recipient received a sports car, but Wilt was granted his request for a station wagon—the better to transport his three Great Danes, he pointed out. For years, he also used the Dodge to go back and forth to the beach, where he played volleyball, his passion in the years to come.

Two days after the victory, Wilt, resplendent in a raspberry-colored jumpsuit, was at Mamma Leone's restaurant in New York, there to formally receive the keys to his new station wagon. It was at this occasion he revealed to the assembled press that his right wrist had been broken, not sprained, when he had fallen in Game 4. Wilt couldn't resist pointing out that Bill Russell had questioned his desire after Game 7 in the 1969 Finals—the one where Butch van Breda Kolff refused to put Wilt back in for the final minutes of a game. But the normally loquacious Wilt spoke little—he let the foot-long cast covering his wrist and arm do most of his talking that day.

In spite of the injury, it was a happy time for Wilt. He was more at peace than ever, he said. After the wrist healed, there was the volleyball team—named Wilt's Big Dippers—with whom he planned to tour the country in the off-season, and there was his new house, his first real home since growing up in his parents' place in Philadelphia.

He seemed to be a man ready to put down roots in Southern California, where he enjoyed living and became enamored with the lifestyle of the area—days at the beach playing cards and volleyball, nights relaxing at clubs. He had always been a loner and a rebel, and that attitude fit in with America in the early seventies, undergoing a cultural and sexual revolution of sorts, no place more so than the West Coast. Wilt was happy to be in the front rank of that sexual revolution, in which he fired more than his fair share of bullets, so to speak.

Chapter 18

I stood up there and realized, wow, this is what I'm really looking for. It reminded me of some spots off Lausanne, Switzerland, and Swiss Italia, which are my favorite spots in the world. I could really see my house there. It was like bringing that part of the world to California. On a clear day I can see the ocean, but it doesn't have to be clear for me to look right down and see that reservoir, which is absolutely divine, especially in the dusk and dawn times.

—Wilt Chamberlain, on selecting the site of his home

That house was the personification of Wilt. That house was the man, and the man was bigger than life. He sat up there like the king of the mountain. It's more than just a house. That house was him.

—Sy Goldberg, longtime friend and attorney

King of the Mountain

Like everything else about him, Wilt's home was a sight to behold. He lived in it from the time it was built for him in late 1971, when he was 35, until his death in 1999, deriving enormous pleasure from (and in) it. During and after its construction, newspapers and *Life* magazine wrote about this unusual home, which took two years to build. (During that time, Wilt rented the home in which the famous Broadway producer Billy Rose once lived and which was then owned by Rose's sister.) After his home was completed, Wilt held a lavish housewarmimg party in March 1972 for about 350 people—actually two parties: old friends early in the day; associates, singles, and swingers for the late-night shift. Among the guests were John and Nell Wooden, Sugar Ray Robinson, the actress Pam Grier, Joe Louis, Chick Hearn (the Lakers announcer), and O. J. Simpson. The home was "marveled at, examined as a spectacle and denounced as a gaudy pad," *The New York Times* reported.

While it is common for today's superstar athletes to live in fantastic homes, Wilt's was probably the first "jock palace." Indeed, the house is spectacular and some part of it—the pink "playroom" with its waterbed—reflected Wilt's sybaritic lifestyle. But it is misleading to write or think about this home as nothing more than a swinging bachelor's pad because it was so much more. The home is unique and interesting, like the man who lived there for almost 30 years. And Sy Goldberg is right: every square inch of the home reflects its owner.

It was Wilt's getaway from a world that didn't leave him alone. Wilt couldn't walk down the street without attracting attention and, rather quickly, a crowd—particularly in the sixties through the eighties. Alan Silber, who met Wilt at the 1976 Montreal Olympics through their mutual friend Lynda Huey, recalled a 1980 dinner in New York:

When you'd go out with Wilt, as I did a couple of times, you couldn't stand still. I remember eating with him, and we came out on the street and stood there and said, "OK, where should we go next?"

Suddenly there were 50 people around asking for his autograph, which he didn't give. He could be aloof in that sort of situation. He had no privacy in a public place. Next to Elvis, Muhammad Ali, and Frank Sinatra, Wilt was the most visible celebrity in the country. I'm telling you, 50 people in five minutes on a Saturday night in Greenwich Village.

Every one of Wilt's friends and acquaintances tells a similar tale, which may be one of the reasons Wilt loved being up there on the mountain, with friends or alone. An invitation to stay over at Wilt's house was one his friends treasured. They recall, always with the fondest memories, the everyday rhythm of the house—watching sporting events or old movies with Wilt; drinking beer or wine or the lemonade Wilt loved to prepare from the lemon trees in his backyard; eating steaks prepared by Wilt, who added "World's Greatest Cook" to his other self-appointed titles. And when Wilt prepared dinner for company, no one went hungry. Olympic hurdler Patty Van Wolvelaere recalled a Thanksgiving dinner Wilt prepared for himself, her, and one other guest: "We had ham and turkey and everything in between and enough food for 20 people."

Tommy Kearns, the North Carolina basketball player with whom Wilt developed a friendship in the seventies, often stayed at the house when business brought him to Los Angeles. Al Attles, Wilt's former Warrior teammate, visited with his wife and children. The journalist Dick Schaap and his wife were guests, too; so, many times, were Dr. Stan Lorber and his wife, who would visit from either Philadelphia or Florida (as Wilt would visit and stay with them).

Most visitors, including many young women, however, didn't spend the night: they'd visit and leave. The list of guests is long and varied and includes Overbrook teammate Jimmy Sadler, who visited Wilt when he was in Los Angeles working as a salesman for Seagram's America. Sadler remembered that Wilt insisted they talk only about the old days in Philadelphia. Wilt's roommate from Kansas, Bob Billings, and his wife, came, too. Wilt and the Billingses attended tennis tournaments in Palm Springs, where the spectators, including other celebrities, came over to where they were sitting because they wanted to meet Wilt. Wilt never went to other celebrities; they always came to him.

Wilt's sister Barbara and her husband, Elzie, who lived in Los Angeles, were often at the house, as, of course, was Sy Goldberg. Wilt's volleyball, track, and other California friends spent a lot of time at his place. Most prominent among this group were Roz Cohen, Wilt's "surrogate mom"; Lynda Huey, a former lover and longtime friend; Gene Selznick, the great volleyball player who taught Wilt the game; and Bob "Vogie" Vogelsang, with whom Wilt played volleyball and shared other pursuits (read: women and sports).

Wilt had hundreds (maybe thousands) of friends and acquaintances, yet ever the loner, he spent more time alone—in his house and in his life—than with friends.

The address of Wilt's home is 15216 Antelo Place, about 20 minutes from downtown Santa Monica, off Mulholland Drive. A long, winding road (on which Wilt usually drove much too fast) leads up the steep hill to a gate. Even in California, the house stands out as unusual: the most prominent features are three massive buttresses of stone and wood and a towering stone chimney. With its cathedral-style roof, the home seemed "almost ecclesiastical in spirit" to one reporter, while to another it looked like a "seventies human-potential conference center." However one reacts to it, the outside of the home is more striking than beautiful.

Built on the highest point of the Santa Monica Mountains and the former site of a World War II antiaircraft battery, the home sits on almost three acres in the hills of tony Bel Air, affording a spectacular 360-degree view of Los Angeles, the San Fernando Valley, the Santa Monica Mountains, and the nearby Stone Canyon Reservoir. It cost approximately $1.5 million to build in 1971. Wilt named his hilltop abode Ursa Major, after the constellation that contains some of the stars that make up the Big Dipper. The most famous feature of the home is a retractable roof above the bed in the master bedroom through which Earth's Big Dipper liked to look at the heavenly Big Dipper.

David Rich, the self-taught architect whom Wilt personally selected for the project, recalled that in the conception stage Wilt looked at hundreds of photographs, eventually choosing an early Frank Lloyd Wright design and an Ansel Adams photograph of a redwood forest full of sun, mist, and light. The house has some of both, Rich said.

In the very early planning stages, when the architect and Wilt visited the site together, Rich outlined three large geometric shapes in the dirt: a circle, a square, and a triangle. He asked Wilt to step inside each one, suggesting that

Wilt's reactions could help determine the architectural design of the structure. Wilt rejected the square as unexciting and the circle as too feminine, but the triangle triggered an immediate and positive response. As a result, the underlying grid of the house is an equilateral triangle, as are many structural details throughout the dwelling.

Wilt worked with a professional to completely furnish the home and, for the 28 years during which he lived in it, the interior remained very much as it first was.

"I think it was Thanksgiving of 1974 when Lynda [Huey] and I went to Wilt's house for dinner," recalled Patty Van Wolvelaere, an Olympic hurdler who became Wilt's close platonic friend after meeting him when he sponsored a women's track club in San Diego. Before dinner on that Thanksgiving, Wilt bet Van Wolvelaere (pronounced *van vol-vah-lear*), who once held the American record in the 110-meter hurdles, that she couldn't run up a section of his street in less than a minute. Antelo Place doglegs as it approaches Wilt's house, and Wilt stood at the gate to his home, which was the finish line. Van Wolvelaere was below, at the starting line, and Huey stood at a point about halfway between, where both Van Wolvelaere and Wilt could see her. Wilt held the stopwatch; Huey signaled each when the race was to commence. Van Wolvelaere ran the distance in less than a minute, winning the bet, but Wilt refused to accept that, even though he held the stopwatch.

From her home near San Diego, where she drives an engine for the San Diego Fire Department, Van Wolvelaere reminisced about this incident:

> I can hear him laughing to this day. His laugh was like nobody else's. It was wonderful. He actually thought I had cheated. He said, "You can't do that again. I don't believe you did that."
>
> That was his way. It didn't annoy me. I think it was Wilt's way of getting to people, of pushing buttons. I don't think he would have done it to make me mad. He did it to get me to do it again. We waited 20 minutes and I did it again.

A gate surrounds the entrance to the grounds, but at only about four feet high, it wouldn't keep out a determined intruder. Visitors pushed a button on a squawk box and the owner's unmistakable, deep voice inquired who it was. Then the electronic gate slowly swung open, allowing the visitor to proceed up the walk. As Wilt never particularly liked palm trees, he directed his landscaper to line the walk with trees and shrubs native to the eastern United States, where he had grown up. After passing an artificial waterfall, geysers, and a fishpond, visitors came to the front door—a massive, one-ton black triangle: fourteen feet high, five feet wide. The two-thousand-pound door swung on piano hinges at the touch of a hand.

Almost no one, certainly not Wilt, entered through the front door. Wilt (along with friends and most visitors) entered through the garage, where there were always three or four cars parked (with more outside), among them over the years:

- The lavender Bentley from the sixties, the parts for which, long since unavailable, had to be custom-made in England, and even then the car often broke down.
- The Dodge station wagon presented to him by *Sport* magazine for being named the MVP of the 1972 Finals. This was the knockabout vehicle that carried him to his beach volleyball games and also transported the women's track team he sponsored to meets in the seventies.
- The Maserati that had been custom-made for him in Italy in the summer of 1968 and had been shipped to New York.
- A Cadillac convertible, his cream Ferrari, and a red Lamborghini.
- A Volkswagen he obtained after making a commercial for the company in the seventies and in which he sometimes tooled around Los Angeles. People were amused, as well as taken aback, to see his 7'-plus frame get in or out of it.
- "Searcher I," the one-of-a-kind sports car designed and created by Wilt, which looks like a Ferrari, and into which over 11 years he sunk hundreds of thousands of dollars (one report suggests the figure is at least $750,000) only to discover that yet more and more money was required to bring it into production. Wilt finally said to his pal Sy Goldberg, rightly concerned about the enormous expenditures on the car, "I won't tell you about the car, and you don't ask me about it." (After Wilt's death, when Goldberg, the executor of Wilt's estate, couldn't sell the car, he donated it to the NBA, which will make it part of a special exhibit at the Naismith Memorial Basketball Hall of Fame.)

- Toward the end of his life, Wilt bought two contemporary automobiles, a 600-S series Mercedes sedan and a sport utility vehicle—and finally had two dependable cars, a bemused Goldberg said, recalling all the trouble his friend had had with cars, and all the money he had spent on them. (But it was Wilt's hard-earned money, Goldberg was quick to point out, and he could do whatever he wanted with it; and spending money on his cars gave Wilt as much pleasure as anything.)

From the garage Wilt could go upstairs to his bedroom or into his kitchen—those being the two rooms in which he spent much of his time. The original kitchen was remodeled about a year before his death. However, Wilt kept an 18th-century butcher block from Virginia that he was fond of and around which he and friends prepared and ate their food while sitting on high stools. There was also a small breakfast nook.

Off the garage was the wing of the house that had two rooms intended for a housekeeper or live-in servant, but as Wilt didn't like to have people permanently around the house, none of the live-in help lasted very long. Wilt ended up haphazardly storing sports memorabilia and scrapbooks in the closet of one room of the servants' quarters.

Tommy Kearns, all 5'11" of him, was chosen by Frank McGuire to jump center against Wilt in the memorable 1957 NCAA championship—"the defining moment of my life," Kearns calls it. Years later, in the seventies, Wilt and Kearns ran into each other in New York and became friends. From his apartment in New York City, Kearns recalled the following:

I was probably as close to Wilt in the eighties as anyone. I stayed with Wilt at his house about 20 times over the years. I wouldn't say I managed his money, but we did some deals together. I was a partner at Bear Stearns at the time. I'd say, "Wilt, I'm buying x, y, z and I think you ought to buy some of it." He'd say, "OK, why don't you do it for me?"

Wilt put a quarter of a million dollars in an Alcan aluminum deal in the early eighties, and within three years it was worth a million and a half to two million dollars.

Sometimes for dinner, we'd go down to the local grocery store about a mile and a half from Wilt's house and get steaks. He loved to cook them up. He'd have Lynda [Huey] or a couple of people over. He loved great wine, as I did. He enjoyed the finer things. And he loved champagne, especially Taittinger.

Pride was very important to Wilt. In the business I was in [finance], I would travel and eat out a lot, eat too much and put on weight. He'd say, "Tom, you got to cut back some; you've got to get rid of that stuff." When Wilt got to a point where he put on too much weight, he would go on a three- or four-day fast.

When Wilt first moved into his home in late 1971, he still played professional basketball, which meant he was away a good deal. He hired a Scandinavian woman as a live-in housekeeper (just as he had in the sixties for his apartment in New York). But, according to his sister, "That didn't last long because he didn't want anyone else in the house."

Then Wilt hired Steve Jones to oversee the care of the house—among other things, Jones watched the cars as well as Wilt's three Great Danes. Wilt derived pleasure from the three mammoth dogs, often running with them on the beach before they had to be put down, one by one, during the eighties. There were other men and women who fulfilled the role of live-in help, but never for long, except for one black man named Dewey, now deceased, who lived in the guest room for about five years in the mid to late seventies. Roz Cohen, Wilt's devoted friend, was always helping him find people to come clean the house.

One doesn't feel overwhelmed by the home's interior, though it is nearly ten thousand square feet. The predominant impression is open space and freedom, as there are no doors or walls separating the rooms that make up the downstairs living area. The main living area, which is divided into levels, with a few steps between each level, consists of the dining area, a sunken living room that Wilt referred to as the conversation pit, and a billiards room. Sliding glass doors, through which light pours into the home, rim the downstairs, and from just about everywhere, one looks out to magnificent vistas.

There is a 20-foot-high ceiling in the central downstairs living area but, in the living room proper, it soars to a five-story apex inset with stained glass. The anchor of the home is the massive stone fireplace with a 45-foot-high chimney; perched on the fireplace on a metal ball was a sculpture of an eagle with a nine-foot wingspan. Birds, which symbolized beauty and freedom to Wilt, decorated his house in several places, including one of the hallways that contained pencil sketches of hawks. Wilt thought the outside of his house looked like the wings of a bird about to take flight.

It took five freight cars' worth of redwood (enough for about 17 standard homes) and 200 tons of Bouquet Canyon stone to furnish the home. There are no square or rectangular rooms—or even right angles—but rather a series of triangles (which may be hard to visualize, but the effect is dramatic) and on the first floor, no painted surfaces, save for the laundry room and "playroom." The surfaces throughout the home are glass, redwood, rosewood, or stone. That, and the leather and suede furniture favored by Wilt, as well as his many earth-tone paintings and artworks, gave the home a warm and natural feeling.

Though most of it was custom-made, the furniture was designed for average-size people, as were the appliances and most everything else in the house. Wilt didn't want friends or visitors to be uncomfortable, having their feet dangling from chairs designed for a giant, for example. "He learned to live in our world," one friend observed. Or as Wilt said, "I've had to adapt to normal sizes all my life. I'm used to it by now. It'll be easier than making my friends adapt to a giant's world."

Not to say there were no sizeable furnishings: the dining room table was 12 feet in diameter and sat 14, and a made-to-order, 14-foot Venetian glass chandelier hung over it. (The original, which was destroyed in the 1994 earthquake, was replaced with a new one.) Wilt ate at the dining room table only when many guests were present, for more formal occasions, or when he was discussing business deals with prospective investors and really wanted to impress them. Otherwise he ate in the kitchen or snacked in the living room area.

Barbara Lewis described what it was like to come to her brother's for dinner:

> Everything had to be perfect. He preferred to do everything himself. The only one allowed to help in the kitchen was me. He would do the meats and I would do the vegetables. He loved string beans and potatoes and smothered cabbage and onions. If he had us over for Thanksgiving, he'd fix 10 dishes—brisket, lamb rack and leg of lamb, the turkey, and baked chicken.
>
> He cooked it all himself, as he was an excellent cook. Everything had to be on time and everything had to be perfect. And I would go into the kitchen and try to clean up and he'd say, "No, I'll do it." But

in the last months, as he was getting sicker, he had a hard time leaning over to wash the dishes. He had to leave the room and lay down for a while. Even when he was sick, he tried to clean up. He never even used a dishwasher. He washed dishes by hand. That's the way we grew up.

From the dining area, one descends a few steps into the sunken living room, where Wilt and visitors often brought sandwiches and sat on the leopard-skin-covered chairs and suede-upholstered sofas. There was also a wet bar because Wilt prided himself on being the host who stocked every drink. In the seventies and eighties, this was the area where Wilt and his friends hung out in the house, watching sporting events on television or playing backgammon. Lynda Huey, who was in the home a hundred times or more over the course of a stormy, 28-year relationship with Wilt, remembered some of those games:

We played backgammon all the time. Wilt cheated so bad. If you turned your head, he'd move the pieces. And we would yell at him all the time. But he turned it into a fun thing, and he'd say, "No, no, no." You knew he was cheating, but you couldn't take it seriously. He was like a spoiled kid everybody let get away with it. The whole thing wasn't about who won. Because Wilt was going to win, and he was going to do whatever it took to make sure he won. It was about the process of playing with him and trying to have some fun. He had things where he was ethical and honest and wouldn't think about stepping over the line. He would never mess with a married woman, for example. But in games like these, he cheated.

Near a corner of the living room, a five-foot triangular portion of Wilt's pool came into the house. On cool nights, when Wilt liked to swim outdoors, he would enter the water from inside his house and swim out to the 15-foot, moat-shaped, open-air pool.

Items in the house that were a reflection of Wilt's basketball career included a sculpture of him dunking a ball and the eight-foot trophy given to him by the Philadelphia 76ers in February 1966 when he became the NBA's all-time leading scorer. Though Wilt had given many of his awards and trophies to close friends, the commemorative memorabilia he kept in the house included a YMCA trophy from 1953, an award from the *Philadelphia Daily News* honoring the 1954–1955 city championship team, a trophy as the MVP of a scholastic tournament in 1955, and an achievement award from his fraternity brothers at Kansas University. Hanging in one room of the house was a framed hooked-rug rendition of a Jayhawk, the mascot of Kansas University, which reveals the special place that school held in his heart. And from his Overbrook years, he still had his basketball jersey, orange-and-black varsity basketball letter, and a team picture, revealing the even more special place *that* school held in his heart.

Down the hall from the living room and dining room areas, still on the first floor, was Wilt's five-sided, self-described "playroom." Some of his friends called this Wilt's "XXX" room. In the center of the room was an eight-foot circular waterbed that was once covered in black rabbit fur. This was surrounded by a purple velvet, wedge-shaped sofa. The room originally was lavender (Wilt's favorite color), but was repainted pink in later years. There were mirrors on the walls and several strobe lights. The room seemed to be the fantasy of a teenage boy, circa 1960—one whose ideas for seducing women came from the pages of *Playboy*. In later years, in a pinch, the room served as a spare bedroom for overnight guests.

Farther down the hall in this wing of the house was an office, although Wilt generally used his bedroom, specifically his bed, as an office. Near the office was the master guest room with a private bath. Wilt called the master guest room his "mother's room," because he had built it for her to use when visiting Los Angeles. Sliding doors in the master guest room led to the backyard: the sauna was on the left, the pool on the right. There was also a patio area that overlooked the Stone Canyon Reservoir and the Westwood area of Los Angeles. Wilt didn't use the pool much, but near the end of his life, trying to strengthen a hip that needed to be replaced, he did exercise in it more often.

———————

Mike Richman, Ike's son, was a teenager when he met Wilt in the sixties. Richman, who became a justice of the peace in suburban Philadelphia, lost touch with Wilt in the seventies, but starting in the mid-eighties, he and Wilt came back into each other's lives. Richman, who stayed at Wilt's house every October for a number of years, recalled three consecutive visits:

The first year he said to me, "Don't get a car. I'll pick you up at the airport." He drove me wherever I wanted to go. The next year he said, "You'll need a car; I'm leaving." He disappeared for four or five days—I think he went to San Francisco or Canada—but he called to make sure I was OK. The next time I came, he said, "I won't be there." I stayed Wednesday to Monday, no Wilt. As I was driving out of his driveway to return the rental car to the airport, he was driving into his driveway. And he called to make sure I got home safely.

Mady Prowler, the daughter of Milton and Helen Kutsher, was almost like a younger sister to Wilt. In the summer of 1973, while on vacation from teaching in the Philadelphia school system, Prowler and a female friend from college traveled across the country and stayed with Wilt for a time. She shared her memories of that visit:

> He was a wonderful host. He was always asking, "You need to go here? I'll drive you." Whatever we needed. He went out of his way for people. I had a great time.
>
> We went down to the San Diego Zoo and, of course, he was the biggest attraction. It didn't matter that people were there to see the animals; they ended up making a big fuss over him. He also made dinner for us: hot dogs and steaks. And he was competitive as hell. Anyone who says he didn't care didn't know him. My friend and Wilt played cards and pool. He had to win. We would play all night if that's what it took for him to win a particular game.

Rod Roddewig, a contemporary of Wilt's, talked about a time when he, his ex-wife, and Wilt had planned to go out to eat:

> We're at Wilt's house. Wilt says, "Let's not go out for dinner. I'll go grab something." So he goes out and brings back three bottles of Dom Perignon, about half a kilo of Beluga caviar, and a whole slab of grav lox. We sat there at the table and ate the whole thing. Wilt was very unpredictable. If he decided in the middle of the night he wanted

to go somewhere, he'd just go to the airport and fly there. He was not a person who made plans months out.

A massive, chrome spiral staircase, which caused the builder no end of trouble and took many months to construct, leads to the second floor, though Wilt tended to go upstairs via the stairs from the garage. Ten-foot-high bookcases lined the hallway, with hundreds of well-thumbed books on history, biography, and astronomy. The titles included *JFK: Reckless Youth*, Norman Mailer's *Harlot's Ghost*, *Dianetics* by L. Ron Hubbard, *A History of the Ancient World*, *My Life and Loves* by Frank Harris, *Reversing Heart Disease* by Dr. Dean Cornish, Burnham's *Celestial Handbook*, *Great Battles of World War I*, *A 20th Century Baseball Chronicle*, and *Super Stocks* by Kenneth Fisher.

Wilt loved movies, too. Among his videos were *King Solomon's Mines* and *The Day the Earth Stood Still*. There were also many sports videos (including *Amazing Feats by Wilt Chamberlain*) and a few adult videos.

Wilt's bedroom, which occupies most of the second floor, is an equilateral triangle, 45 feet on each side, and has a 14-foot-high ceiling. Two of the walls were glass. His 8½-by-7½-foot bed, which was perched on a carpeted platform, was once covered with the fur from the noses of arctic wolves. (He also covered part of the floor and a sofa downstairs with them.) Today, in the words of his architect, "Environmentalists would be coming up the street with pitchforks. But it was a real nice touch." It should be pointed out that Alaska was so overrun with wolves in the seventies that the state hired bounty hunters to kill them. It was from this source that Wilt bought tens of thousands of them, which he put into cold storage for future use. Because they were not properly maintained, the furs dried out and were long gone by the nineties.

A sunken, triangular-shaped bathtub decorated with 18-karat gold mosaic tiles sat in a corner of the bedroom. The 280-gallon tub required a separate system to heat, but Wilt had seen movies of Cleopatra bathing in a sunken tub, and if it was good enough for the Queen of Egypt, then why not for Wilt? In later years, during California droughts, Wilt chose not to fill the bathtub and placed plants and things inside it.

The shower stall (also triangular and topped with a red-glass skylight of the same shape) was fitted with six showerheads, of which the two highest were placed appropriately for a man of Wilt's height. "All my life I took showers with the water hitting me in my stomach," he declared. His bathroom had a toilet, with a wooden seat, on a platform—one of the few other accommodations to his size in the house; it also had a bidet, reflecting Wilt's early exposure to, and appreciation of, a European lifestyle.

Adjacent to the bedroom were the weight room and a 15-foot walk-in closet, although most of the time Wilt wore shorts or, if it was a cooler California day, loose-fitting stretch pants with an elastic waist—Lynda Huey called them his "clown pants." He rarely wore a shirt in the house. This was also the get-up he'd wear to the beach or to whatever sporting activity he was then engaged in; likewise to go shopping—only he'd throw on a tank top when he left the house. And as he hated to have anything on his feet, he was always barefoot in the house—and often outside, too.

Especially during his last years, Wilt spent the better part of his days and nights on his bed, holding court while friends sat on the chairs and ottomans surrounding it, though one or two people might be on the massive bed. When no one was around to keep him company or he wanted to be alone, there was always the phone, especially the last couple of years, when accumulating ailments kept him at home. He'd call friends around the country, occasionally waking up the ones in the East. One friend asked him, "What time is it where you're calling from, Wilt, because it's the middle of night here?" Sy Goldberg said Wilt called people all over the world at night, though, thankfully, he wouldn't call Goldberg beyond midnight. "He'd asked some minutiae," Goldberg recalled, "like what do you think the population of Shanghai is? Mostly it was an excuse to talk. He lived on the telephone."

From the many articles written about the home, even the casual sports fan of a certain age knew Wilt's house had a retractable roof—not the entire roof, just a mirrored, 10-foot triangular section above his bed. Ever since visiting the Fels Planetarium as a schoolboy in Philadelphia, Wilt had been fascinated by the stars. He enjoyed looking at the sky through an expensive telescope he kept in his bedroom and often kept the roof open, the better to enjoy the sky and the balmy California weather. Next to his bed was a console with the switches that allowed Wilt to retract the roof, fill the bathtub, turn on the stereo, raise the television from its cabinet, and draw heavy drapes over the large windows that rimmed the room. A sign next to his bed said, "The Office of the President."

From this comfortable perch, he entertained his women, made his long-lasting, round-the-clock phone calls, played backgammon, worked, and went through the mountains of fan mail he received.

When fans wrote to Wilt in care of nothing more than "Los Angeles, California" or the Los Angeles Lakers, the post office forwarded the mail to Sy Goldberg, from whose office Wilt eventually picked it up. Wilt rarely wrote letters; he dictated replies. His sister Barbara Lewis reminisced about helping him with his mail:

> He would lay the stuff on the bed. He had so much fan mail, but he insisted on reading it himself. He would write on the outside of the envelope, "Send a donation or photo or an item."
>
> Even when he died, he had about four large trash cans full of mail. . . . I was surprised, as I went through his notes and papers, at what he kept, like letters from high school friends and from other basketball players. I found a couple of letters from my mom and dad and some from my sisters.

"He didn't know how to handle paper," Huey said of the times she helped him sort his mail. "There was mail everywhere. Sometimes he wouldn't open his mail for three or four days; it was just sitting on his bed."

Friend Rod Roddewig remembered one letter from Poland addressed to "Wilt Chamberlain—U.S.A." That, too, found its way to Wilt's house.

Wilt made many choices in his life. None of them turned out better than the decision to build Ursa Major, the astonishing home on the mountain where he spent—and enjoyed—so much of his adult life. In the seventies and eighties, he utilized the entire home; not so in later years, as his life constricted. "Basically Wilt lived in the bedroom," recalled Goldberg. "If everything but the bedroom and the kitchen floated away in a flood, it would have taken a few days for him to notice."

Chapter 19

Wilt could be moody. If he came into the locker room laughing and talking, I thought, "We're gonna kick ass tonight."

I still remember the time he came in, his shoes and shirt off, took a look around, and told the ball boy, "Go get me a hot dog." That was his pregame meal. Then he looked at the bulletin board, which had our game plan on it, and turned and said, "Bill [Sharman], what is this shit up there?" And Wilt went up and erased it, and said, "That shit ain't gonna work."

Bill Sharman was the best ever at managing people. He would think, "This son of a bitch is in a bad mood." But out loud he would say, "Wilt, what do you think we should do?"

"I don't know, Coach."

Jerry West would be sitting there, keeping his mouth shut and letting Wilt come out of the mood. Sharman would go around the room and ask the other players what they thought we should do. And the guys would say, "Let's just go out on the floor and play," thinking that Wilt would snap out of it.

—Bill Bridges, Lakers teammate

The End of the Game

n what was to be Wilt's final year in the NBA, the fireworks began, as they often did with Wilt, even before the season: he announced that he wanted to renegotiate the two-year contract he had signed in 1971. He missed training camp (not for the first time in his career) while discussing the possibility of employment with the owner of an American Basketball Association team. This was more a public relations gambit than serious negotiations, because, as he well knew, he was under contract to the Lakers. Maybe in the public relations scheme of things his ploy helped, because the Lakers owner, Jack Kent Cooke, gave him a raise (retroactive for the 1971–1972 season, too), and Wilt ended his holdout two days before the opening game.

The Lakers won their division in 1972–1973 by 13 games, in spite of injuries to Happy Hairston. Wilt led the league in rebounding for the 11th time in his career. It wasn't as if he had competed against men who couldn't rebound, either. In the early and middle years, there was Bill Russell, Walt Bellamy, Nate Thurmond, Zelmo Beaty, and Jerry Lucas. In his later years, there was Wes Unseld, Kareem Abdul-Jabbar, Dave Cowens, and Elvin Hayes. Every man in both groups, save Beaty, became Hall of Famers. As he rarely shot from more than a few feet from the basket during the 1972–1973 season, Wilt also set a record (which still stands) for field-goal accuracy, making almost 73 percent of his shots. More impressive, at age 36, he was second in number of minutes played.

On occasion, he was his old, inimitable self. One night against the 76ers in Philadelphia, he blocked 15 shots. After the game, Sixers guard Freddy Carter, who had had five shots snuffed by Wilt, said it was "like shooting through an electric fan." (The Sixers franchise had fallen on hard times after Wilt left: the 1972–1973 Sixers won 9 games and lost 73, the worst record ever by an NBA team.)

Wilt was named to the league's All-Defensive team for the second straight year. (He would have been named to one many times earlier, but there was no "All-Defensive team" until 1968–1969.) Memorably, in the 1972–1973 season, a 6'1" guard named Nate "Tiny" Archibald led the league in points per game (34) *and* assists per game (11.4)—the first and only man to ever do so.

In the division semifinals, L.A. defeated Chicago in seven games—Wilt's block with 28 seconds to go in that decisive game led to the victory; and then the Lakers easily beat Golden State, four games to one, in the conference finals. That meant four division or conference titles (and a 60 percent increase in home-game attendance) for the Lakers in five years—not a bad return on Jack Kent Cooke's investment in Wilt.

The world-champion Lakers would meet the New York Knicks for the NBA title, the third time in the last four years those teams had both reached the summit. They knew each other's strengths and weaknesses.

New York's Earl Monroe and Walt Frazier had learned to share the ball and had become a formidable backcourt combination. Phil Jackson, his back no longer aching, relieved DeBusschere and Bradley up front. Willis Reed, who had missed almost all of the previous season with tendinitis in his knees, was at the center position, occasionally relieved by Jerry Lucas. The Knicks' trademark was still fine team defense and excellent outside shooting. "We've learned how to make the most of our strong points and minimize our weaknesses," Bradley observed. Playing against them was a Laker team that was no longer the powerhouse of the previous year: Hairston, an essential element in the golden Laker mix, was hurt and played little; LeRoy Ellis and Flynn Robinson, two key reserves, were gone.

The first two games of the series were played in Los Angeles. In Game 1 the Lakers were clearly the superior team for the first three quarters, but barely held off a Knick comeback in the fourth quarter to eke out a 115–112 victory. The Knicks won Game 2, in which Wilt missed eight of nine free throws, a critical shortcoming in a game decided by four points.

Back in the Garden, the Knicks won Game 3, 87–83. Reed, who scored 22 points, called it his best playoff game in years. Wilt, on the other hand, took only three shots, scoring a measly five points. The Lakers never got their fast break going, nor did they do much in their set offense. No stranger to injuries, Jerry West pulled the hamstring in his right leg (while already playing with a strained hamstring in the left).

Wilt's first—and most satisfying—professional basketball experience occurred in 1958 as a member of the Harlem Globetrotters, a team with which he continued to tour in subsequent summers. *Photo courtesy of AP/Wide World Photos.*

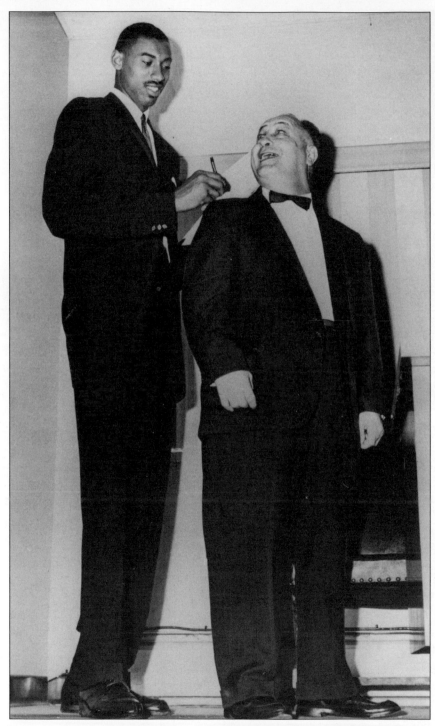

Eddie Gottlieb, a founding father and giant of the NBA, pushed through a rule change so that he could obtain the right to draft Wilt. Here, in May 1959, Wilt signs his first contract to play for Gottlieb's Philadelphia Warriors. *Photo courtesy of Temple University Libraries/Urban Archives.*

Wilt's signature game took place on March 2, 1962, when he tallied 100 points against the New York Knicks. Less than two weeks later he scored his 4,000th point in a win at Chicago. *Photos courtesy of AP/Wide World Photos.*

More than once, Wilt seriously considered fighting Muhammad Ali. This 1967 photo shows the difference between the two men. Wilt was almost a foot taller, weighed about 65 pounds more, and had a reach almost 13 inches longer than his would-be opponent had. *Photo courtesy of AP/Wide World Photos.*

After many years of losing to Bill Russell's Boston Celtics, Wilt and the 76ers enjoy a ritual champagne shower to celebrate their 140–116 drubbing of the Celtics to claim the Eastern Division crown en route to the 1967 NBA championship. *Photo courtesy of AP/Wide World Photos.*

Wilt would win one more NBA title in 1972, but critics always asked why his Lakers teams did not win more championships. *Photo courtesy of AP/Wide World Photos.*

Even before retiring from basketball, Wilt got hooked on volleyball. In the above photo he stands alongside several of the players who introduced him to the game, including Bob Vogelsang (second from left), Gene Selznick (third from right), and Keith Erickson (far right). Below, Erickson (from left), Selznick, and Larry Rundle helped make up the four-man traveling team known as the Big Dippers. *Photos courtesy of Keith Erickson.*

An aerial view of Wilt's expansive home in the hills of Bel Air. *Photo courtesy of* Time Life *Pictures/Getty Images.*

After a long period of not speaking to each other, the relationship between longtime warriors Wilt and Bill Russell eventually thawed. This photo was taken during a Boston tribute to Russell in May 1999, about four and a half months before Wilt's death. *Photo courtesy of AP/Wide World Photos.*

Wilt in 1986 in front of his alma mater, Overbrook High School. Still an imposing physical specimen at age 50, he tended to wear clothes (particularly tank tops) that revealed his magnificent physique. *Photo courtesy of Jimmy Sadler.*

The Knicks also won Game 4, taking a commanding three-games-to-one lead in the series. With West injured, Wilt would have to score more, but so far in the series he had been unable to produce on both the offensive *and* defensive ends.

In Game 5, a hobbling West managed to convert on only 5 of 17 shots, not even close to a normal Jerry West game. And, succumbing to his injuries, Happy Hairston could play only eight minutes. Goodrich, Wilt, and McMillian contributed offensively, but the Lakers needed other scoring to prevail. Since that didn't occur, the Knicks won the game (102–93) and the NBA title—their second in three years. (Thanks to Michael Jordan and the Chicago Bulls, and to some inept trades and big-buck turkeys they signed in the nineties, the Knicks organization has never won an NBA title since.)

This was not a particularly well-played series, and it lacked the drama of the classic 1970 contest between the two clubs, when almost every game was close and magnificently played. Reed, who had three strong games against Wilt in the 1973 series, was named the MVP (just like in 1970), although no one on either team really dominated. It was the Knicks *team*, coached by the unassuming William "Red" Holzman, that won the world championship.

And it was the eighth time (six to the Celtics, twice to the Knicks) the Lakers had fallen short in an NBA Finals.

Although it was not known at the time, this was to be Wilt's last NBA game. He had scored 23 points, gathered 21 rebounds, had played the entire 48 minutes (only Walt Frazier did likewise), and had led everyone in rebounds. It is fitting that he had more than 20 points and 20 rebounds in his last NBA game. Only three players have ever averaged 20 points and 20 rebounds in a season—Wilt, Bob Pettit, and Jerry Lucas. Pettit accomplished this rarest of basketball feats in 1961 and Lucas in 1965 and 1966. Wilt did it 10 times—one of the more impressive of his many records.

That was a busy summer for Wilt: from early June through mid-July, he toured the United States and Canada with a troupe of great volleyball players, appearing in cities large and small. Organized by Gene Selznick in the summer of 1970, the team was later renamed "Wilt's Big Dippers" in honor of its most famous, if not best, player. The personnel changed during the five summers the team barnstormed (usually from May to September, the basketball off-season) but, at one time or another, included Larry Rundle, Keith Erickson, Kirk

Kilgore, Butch May, Rudy Suwara, Rich Riffero, Toshi Toyoda, Gene Selznick—all of them among the elite volleyball players of their era—and Wiltie, the name his newfound volleyball buddies sometimes called him.

Given that he came to the sport in his thirties, Wilt was the first to acknowledge that he became a *good* volleyball player, contrary to the myth that says he was *great*. In this sport, his size mattered, but in some ways it worked to his disadvantage. His hands were too big to set up the ball properly—it would be like a normal-sized individual trying to accurately direct a pass with a tennis ball. Although he was only adequate on defense, he was good at blocking shots, according to Rundle, merely stating a truism that those who played with and against Wilt recognized. Because of his height, jumping ability, and power, the best part of Wilt's game was hitting the ball. Even there, he could never generate as much power (because of his less-than-perfect technique) as Erickson or Rundle, both All-Americans and Olympians.

Rundle remembered that Wilt loved being out on the court and was great fun to play with and to be around.

Volleyball players from that time appreciated—and are quick to acknowledge—all that Wilt did for the game. As Selznick, one of the sport's legends, recalled in 2003: "All of a sudden, attention was focused on our volleyball team because Wilt was one of the most recognizable athletes in the world. We got all the media coming at us. Wilt could promote anything. He did more for volleyball than anyone else in the 53 years I've been in it."

The Big Dippers competed against local club teams from Portland, Oregon, to Staten Island, New York, and up and down California. Selznick realized the team could hide Wilt's defensive liabilities and take advantage of his spiking abilities by permanently stationing him to the left front of the court. But in six-person volleyball, players normally rotate from one position to another. Selznick got the other teams to agree that in exhibition games the opponents would rotate, but not the Big Dippers. To compensate for this concession, the Dippers played four men against the other teams' six. The club teams against whom they played were happy to agree to these terms because, with Wilt in the contest, the games drew three thousand to four thousand fans, large crowds for club volleyball in those days, and that meant much-needed money flowing into the clubs' usually bare coffers.

"Most of the people were there to see Wilt," remembered Rundle, who toured with the team for two years. The games were usually on weekends, as some of the guys had day jobs. Playing against the best club teams in the country, the Big Dippers won 87 of 88 games (their one loss coming against a team of Hawaiian All-Stars).

Selznick, who collected the money, said their expenses were paid by the sponsoring club and Wilt earned $5,000 per match, although newspaper accounts put the figure at $1,000 a game. The remaining four players (one was a substitute) each received $100, big money at the time for the 28-year-old Rundle (and no doubt others on the team, as well).

"We never wanted to make Wilt look like a bum," observed Selznick, the team's major force. "When he was comfortable, he put on a show for the fans: he smiled and joked around. The people loved it, even when he'd mishit the ball."

While playing basketball, Wilt rarely smiled or seemed to be enjoying himself—not so in volleyball games. Newspaper reports describe a jovial and smiling Wilt. After the games, hundreds of fans lined up for autographs, which he was happy to provide.

Volleyball never was (nor is it now) a very big sport outside of California and Hawaii, but when a high-profile, accomplished, all-around athlete like Wilt so obviously enjoyed playing and sung the praises of the sport, people took notice. Newspapers wrote about and covered the Big Dippers, and people who otherwise would never have attended a volleyball game saw high-level contests. All of this (plus later television broadcasts featuring athletic and attractive women in bikinis participating in the sport) increased by manyfold the game's popularity.

Beginning in October 1967 and running (and that is very much the operative word) through the 1975–1976 season, there was a professional basketball league in which players, using a red-white-and-blue ball, could attempt a shot worth three points. This was, of course, the run-and-gun American Basketball Association, home to some of the finest (and some of the looniest) basketball talent. Among the ABA's stars, who were every bit as good as the best of the NBA, were:

- Rick Barry, the first NBA player to jump from the established league to the new upstart
- Julius Erving, who came straight from the University of Massachusetts and was the marquee player of the league

- Connie Hawkins, the New York high school legend who had been barred from the NBA because of his alleged connection to a college basketball point-shaving scandal (later to be exonerated in court and allowed to play in the NBA)
- George Gervin, to be known as the "Iceman" for the cool manner in which he delivered points
- And Artis Gilmore, sporting an Afro as big as his talent

On September 27, 1973, the ABA landed the biggest prize of all when it was announced that Wilt had signed a three-year contract to be the player-coach of the San Diego Conquistadors. His salary, $600,000 per year, was by far the highest of any in basketball. (Today, under comparable circumstances, he would probably receive anywhere from $16 million to $26 million per year.)

There was, however, one problem with this rosy picture: the option clause in NBA contracts bound a player to his team for one year after his contract ended. The Los Angeles Lakers had an option on Wilt's services for the 1973–1974 season if they chose to exercise it—and they did and went to court to enforce it. The Conquistadors challenged the rule and, eventually, both they and the Lakers argued their case before an arbitrator, who decided in the Lakers' favor. Wilt had to play for the Lakers or sit out the 1973–1974 season. (The option clause was eliminated in 1976.) Wilt's new boss in the upstart league, Leonard Bloom, an orthodontist-turned-sports entrepreneur, thus lost the services of his best player, who would, if anyone could, put bodies in the seats of the sparsely attended ABA games. However, the arbitrator ruled, there was nothing to prevent Wilton Norman Chamberlain from coaching for the 1973–1974 season and then, in subsequent seasons, playing for the Conquistadors—the Q's, their shorter and mellifluous nickname.

So the man who, at times, had perplexed, tormented, ignored, or humiliated two handfuls of coaches was himself now a coach. "I hope my alleged run-ins with coaches will help me avoid the pitfalls," coach Wilt said. "One thing I don't like is coaches who talk about 'handling' players. My thinking is you don't try to handle basketball players. You handle horses and animals." Years later, no less a coaching legend than John Wooden made it a point to credit Wilt with opening his eyes to the inappropriateness of the term "handling players," which, from 1973 on, Wooden no longer used.

Frequently that season, Wilt said, "A great coach can help a team win six or seven games. A good coach doesn't cost his team any games; a bad coach does." So which kind of coach was Wilt? By no means typical. For one thing, though he occasionally stayed overnight in a San Diego hotel suite, he tended to commute by helicopter or small plane from Los Angeles, where he continued to live, to the team's practices and home games, a flight of about 45 minutes. (It's almost a three-hour drive, longer in heavy traffic.) He would make the necessary arrangements to have someone meet him at the airport and drive him to the arena. The Conquistadors general manager, Alex Groza, recalled that Wilt would land at 6:30 or 6:45 P.M. for an evening game that started at 7:30.

Even for the ABA, the Q's were a young and inexperienced team. Coach Wilt started three rookies: Caldwell Jones, a skinny but talented 6'11" center from Albany State who had selected the Q's over the 76ers (he was offered more money); Tim Bassett, a 6'8" forward from Georgia; and Dwight "Bo" Lamar, a 6'1" guard and the pride of Lafayette, Louisiana. Joining them were Stew Johnson, an ABA All-Star the previous season; Flynn Robinson and Travis "Machine Gun" Grant, two ex-Lakers; and Jimmy O'Brien, who was acquired in a trade after the season had begun.

The Q's played fast-break basketball, à la Bill Sharman's Lakers. Too bad coach Chamberlain wasn't playing center, for although the team could run and score (and led the league that year in three-point attempts), they couldn't—or wouldn't—play effective defense, for which coach Wilt lit into them after some games.

Wilt left the organization of the practices, and many other tasks, to his assistant coach, Stan Albeck. "The best thing Wilt had going for him was Stan Albeck, who is a student of the game and a good teacher," observed Alex Hannum. "Wilt did show up occasionally and pretend to coach, but it was really Stan's team. It wasn't that Wilt couldn't do it or that he wasn't smart enough. Just the opposite. I've coached Wilt, and I can tell you that he has a great feel for the game—he understands pro basketball. But the day-to-day things that are an important part of coaching just bored him. He didn't have the patience or desire to coach."

Wilt wouldn't have disagreed with Hannum's assessment. "I never visualized myself as a coach," he said. "I had help from Albeck, and he was more the coach and me a figurehead. But actually, I think we had a joint operation."

Albeck, who had fond memories of the year he coached with Wilt, recalled one unforgettable incident at a practice: "We had Caldwell Jones as a rookie, and Wilt would dress to scrimmage. . . . One day, we back-picked Wilt. Caldwell spun off him and dunked. Wilt said, 'Run it again and I'll break somebody's arm.' We never ran it again."

Albeck, who eventually became a well-regarded NBA and college coach, might have known more about *X*'s and *O*'s than Wilt, but he learned an important lesson from coach Chamberlain:

> My whole big-man philosophy was shaped by him. He said that when you're big, people expect more. So when he played with Jerry West and Elgin Baylor with the Lakers, if they lost, the criticism was directed at him. People would say he missed a rebound or a free throw. Elgin and Jerry never got that sort of commentary. I learned that big men are never supposed to make a mistake in a mistake-laden game.

The Wilt-Albeck practices could be tough, recalled Bo Lamar. That might sound strange, as Wilt was never known for his dedication to practice; still, he had observed the positive results a team derived from arduous practices under two legendary taskmasters, Bill Sharman and Alex Hannum. Wilt, being Wilt, however, couldn't oversee a practice that was all work and no play. Gene Moore, one of his players, told *Basketball Digest*: "Every day there seemed to be a different movie star at practice. . . . Wilt works with us, but a lot of times he has to stop and talk to some young lady on the telephone. But the thing we're waiting for is for him to have a team party at his house." Moore never got his party invitation. Claiming Moore was 25 to 30 pounds overweight, Wilt cut the 6'9" forward in midseason. That prompted Moore to call Wilt a lousy coach whom the players did not respect, which prompted Wilt to counter by remarking that Moore's comment was nothing more than sour grapes.

Holding a view different from Moore's was Bo Lamar, who averaged more than 20 points that year and made the All-Rookie team. "The players liked Wilt," Lamar said. "He was tough when he had to be; he got on me a couple of times, but he was always fair."

Tim Bassett related the following story to a third party:

> One time the players were shooting around before practice and the ball got stuck in the guide wires above the basket. The players, including the 6'11" jumping-jack Caldwell Jones, tried to dislodge it without

success. Finally, someone went for a chair so one of them could stand on it and poke the ball loose. Just then Wilt arrived, wearing a suit and a pair of expensive shoes.

"What's going on?" he asked.

"We're trying to get the ball down from there," someone replied.

"You guys are young and strong," Wilt observed. "Why don't you jump up and get it?"

"Too high," they answered.

At which point Wilt muttered something about "Put the money on the floor" and, in his bare feet, jumped up and knocked the ball out, leaving the players' mouths agape.

Once the arbitrator ruled in mid-December that Wilt could not play for the Q's, his appearances at practice diminished. He also missed three away games in the course of the season: one when the team was in Indianapolis and he was in Los Angeles attending his book-signing party, and the other two, in late February, for reasons known only to himself.

But during the overwhelming number of games at which he was present, his was the final word. Bassett recalled the night they were playing the Indiana Pacers in Indianapolis and he tied a record for offensive rebounds in a game (17). Wilt decided to take him out:

> But the guys on the team kept telling him to put me back in. He reluctantly did, saying, "Go ahead, son, that record will be mine as soon as they let me play."
>
> With about two minutes left in the game . . . I was able to get a rebound for the record. When I came off the court, Wilt said, "Great job, my man. You remind me of me when I was at Overbrook High School."

Joe Hamelin covered the team for the *San Diego Union*—indeed, he points out that he had the odd distinction of covering teams coached by Wilt and Bill Russell (the Sacramento Kings) and, of the two, he said, "I'd take the Dipper in a heartbeat. Win or lose, he was always pleasant to deal with, always answered the questions, and always returned phone calls (on his own time, of course)."

Yet the San Diego team publicist, Ans Dilley, found Wilt to be difficult, and when Dilley resigned in midseason, he alleged, "When I make an appointment for someone to interview Wilt, he's always too busy. The guy is just impossible to work with."

If Wilt didn't take all of his coaching responsibilities seriously, at least he dressed well: wearing a sports jacket or suit, usually with a tie or a turtleneck sweater, he made a dapper appearance on the sidelines. Yet because his feet sometimes hurt, especially after wearing pointy-toed leather shoes, Wilt often wore sandals when the team traveled. Someone apparently thought a sandal-wearing Wilt undermined the professional image the league was laboring to create and complained to Mike Storen, then the commissioner of the ABA. Storen recalled in Terry Pluto's entertaining oral history of the ABA, *Loose Balls*, what happened next:

> So I called Wilt in and said, "Wilt, whether you like it or not, you are going to have to wear shoes and socks on the road."
>
> Wilt is so damn big and imposing. He is bigger than life and if you didn't know him, he just scares the hell out of you. But Wilt is a very nice guy, thank God. I kept thinking, "Here I am telling this guy to wear shoes and he can reach across the table and rip my head off with one hand."
>
> But Wilt said, "No problem." And it wasn't a problem.
>
> Of course, he didn't always show up for a game. The team would be on a road trip and Wilt would decide that he wanted to go some-place else.

The Q's ended the season at 37–47, remarkable considering the chaos and uncertainty that surrounded them that year. There was Wilt's frequent indifference toward coaching and his absences from practice. Because Leonard Bloom, the team's owner, was unwilling to pay what he felt was an exorbitant rent to play in the modern San Diego Sports Arena, the team played its home games in Golden Hall, an auditorium in the downtown civic center that had been converted into a basketball court. Its capacity was about 3,200, a far cry from the 17,500 fans who could, and did, fit into the Forum, site of the Lakers home games (or the 19,000 who could fit into the San Diego Sports Arena). Even at that, the Q's only averaged 1,843 fans at home games, even fewer than the previous season, though the team's record had improved. While San Diegoans might pay to watch Wilt play, they were not going to pay to watch him coach, even if he regaled them with his colorful wardrobe.

Bloom had visions of building a sports empire in Chula Vista, a suburb 15 miles south of San Diego. But by a narrow margin, voters in November turned down a referendum to build a twenty thousand–seat arena and $200 million sports complex. Soon after the vote, rumors that began circulating suggested that the ABA had told Bloom to prepare to move the franchise, which was losing money and drawing poorly, to Los Angeles the next year. That pall hung over the team during the remainder of the season. Despite the problems, the Q's finished fourth in their division and won a one-game playoff over the Denver Nuggets, securing the last playoff spot, only to lose to the Utah Stars in six games.

His stint with the Q's spelled the end of Wilt's coaching career. There were too many other activities to which he wanted to devote his time. Alex Groza, the general manager, and then Beryl Shipley (Bo Lamar's college coach) had the dubious pleasure of coaching the Q's in 1974–1975. In the next season, after 11 games, the team (by then owned by Frank Goldberg and called the San Diego Sails) folded and so, at season's end, did the ABA, the brash upstart that had held on for nine exciting years. Four ABA teams (the Indiana Pacers, the San Antonio Spurs, the Denver Nuggets, and the New York Nets) were accepted into the NBA for the 1976–1977 season. The red-white-and-blue ball never made it to the NBA, but as anyone who has ever launched and made one appreciates, the three-point shot lives on in high school, college, and professional games—the lasting legacy of the wild league.

As for the ABA's most unorthodox coach, after 22 years as the best-known high school, college, and professional basketball player in the world (and, he would add, also the best), Wilt Chamberlain was about to sever his relationship with the game that had made him rich and famous, and move on to the next stage of his life.

Chapter 20

I don't want to give my time to the man, so to speak, or to any man. I don't want to work for anybody ever again—*with* someone, but not for someone.

—Wilt Chamberlain, *Sports Illustrated*, October 1974

At Muscle Beach and Sorrento, he found the laid-back, off-center beach volleyball scene to be comfortable, colorful, and energetic. Here, he was just another eccentric creature, like Selznick, Steno, Vogelsang, Captain Jack, and dozens of other strange birds that flocked to the California beach communities and landed around volleyball courts. He had found a new culture and a new sport.

—John Lee, *Volleyball* magazine, February 2000

Where There's a Wilt, There's a Way

Just as Wilt announced his early departure from college in a magazine article, he used the pages of *Sports Illustrated* to tell the world that he was retiring from basketball. In the October 7, 1974, issue, under a story headlined "My Impact Will Be Everlasting," Wilt said that he was tired of the traveling associated with professional basketball and was, therefore, calling it quits—though not before immodestly reminding the reader that he had changed basketball in many ways—"more than people want to give me credit for." He gracefully acknowledged that, next to his mother and father, he owed everything to basketball. "If any sport's done what it should have in race relations, basketball has," he said. "I'm still dismayed about the lack of black managers and head coaches in baseball and football." He said that he regretted giving up scoring in his later years to benefit his team, feeling he had never been given credit for this unselfish effort. This complaint, however, is demonstrably untrue: dozens of articles written during and after the Lakers' championship run of 1971–1972 gave Wilt his due for sacrificing his scoring for the team's success.

In a refrain that he would repeat until the last summer of his life, he also said in *Sports Illustrated* that he might have been better off pursuing an individual sport like track. Maybe he was correct. Maybe someone with his overwhelming personality and awesome talent would have shined even more (and, he would add, have been appreciated more) in an individual sport. With his old bugaboo in mind, he said of track: "It is a sport where there isn't any argument about 'Who's better, Bill Russell or Wilt Chamberlain?' If Bill Russell jumps seven feet and Wilt Chamberlain jumps seven feet one inch, you know damn well who's better." (If Russell, like Wilt a potentially world-class high jumper, were making the point, guess who—he or Wilt—would be the one to jump the highest?)

As for life after basketball, Wilt intended to produce a motion picture, travel the world, play beach and indoor volleyball (eventually adding tennis, racquetball, and, for a short time, polo to the mix), and advance the interests of the women's track team he sponsored. Wilt concluded his *Sports Illustrated* farewell by stating that, at age 37, he didn't want to ever again work for anybody—"*with* someone but not *for* someone." True to his word, he never really did, unless you count commercials, of which he made more than 50, the most famous being those for American Express, TWA, and Volkswagen. The American Express ad, which became a classic, shows two of the world's greatest athletes—the 7'1 1/16" Wilt and his friend, the 4'11" jockey Willie Shoemaker—standing on a beach. Both are wearing white suits and black ties: Wilt's is a necktie, which blows rakishly in the wind; Shoemaker's is a bowtie. Shoemaker's head comes up to right above Wilt's waist. The juxtaposition of one of the world's tallest and one of the world's shortest athletes compels attention. They radiate success and elegance, which was the point of an ad that said, "Membership Has Its Privileges." (Wilt liked the ad so much he hung a framed copy of it in his house.)

Wilt frequently remarked over the years that his sister Barbara might have become a track star had she had opportunities to compete when she was a young woman. This long-held and oft-expressed opinion was one of the motivating factors behind Wilt's support of women's athletics.

It was through Lynda Huey, a woman he met while playing beach volleyball, that Wilt first became actively involved in a girl's track team. Wilt had given up any chance to compete in track—a sport he loved—after he had become a professional basketball player because the rules of the day prohibited professionals in any sport from corrupting the amateur world of track and field (while the rules of today permit, even encourage, it). Huey, who had been a sprinter at San Jose State, filled the void by drawing Wilt into her tiny corner of the sport.

In the summer of 1974, at the California State Championships, she introduced Wilt to Tracy Sundlun, then the coach of the La Jolla (California) Track Club. The 22-year-old Sundlun, an up-and-coming track coach, and the retired 37-year-old superstar athlete clicked, soon taking a motor coach trip through the Pacific Northwest. Both loved talking about track and engaging in one-upmanship—for example, teasing one another, some years later, over the male-pattern baldness that had become evident in both of them, although in

Wilt's case it was only noticeable if he bent over or stood in an elevator that had an overhead mirror.

When Wilt eagerly agreed to become the La Jolla Track Club's principal sponsor—using, he told Sundlun, the $5,000 he said he had received from *Sports Illustrated* for the rights to announce his retirement from basketball—the club was renamed "Wilt's Wonder Women." The team had about 40 members, with most of them, called the "Mighty Mites," between the ages of 9 and 15. They were grouped by, and ran in, age groups. Some of these girls were excellent runners who would go on to compete in high school or college, while others were there only because their parents wanted them to have an extracurricular activity. The older girls, who were in their twenties, had already made names for themselves in the sport. The most prominent among these included Huey, who ran the 100- and 200-yard races in college; Cindy Gilbert, a high jumper; Patty Van Wolvelaere, a two-time Olympian, who in 1974 held the world record in the 60-yard indoor hurdles; and Jan Svendsen, an Olympian in the discus.

Van Wolvelaere recalled one of the world's most accomplished and famous athletes gleefully spending his time in 1974 and 1975 with an underfinanced and relatively unknown group of female athletes. As Van Wolvelaere remarked:

> Wilt would show up at our practices in San Diego, on this little dirt track in the middle of a field. He'd driven the two hours from Los Angeles with his Great Danes in the back of his station wagon. He'd have a rake in his hand, and he'd be raking the long-jump pit for the girls, raking the sand for the high jump, measuring the girls' jumps, and pounding the starting blocks into the ground [and] timing the girls in their runs.
>
> We had a lot of young girls on the team and, because there were so many of them and me being 24, I had other things on my mind than being around these little girls. But he knew all their names, their best marks, their best jumps, which of them ran the mile in what times. They just loved him. They absolutely adored him.

And he was very protective of the girls on the team, acting, at times, like a mother hen, not always to the liking of the older members of the group. "He was mad at me once because I had gone skiing," Van Wolvelaere recalled. "He was upset because I was taking a chance of spraining an ankle or breaking a bone. I remember saying to him, 'Hey, lighten up, you're not my dad.' He never wanted us to do inappropriate and irresponsible things, which years later I appreciated."

Wilt wanted desperately to be treated as a normal person (though there were still the other times he wanted to be accorded the homage often paid to a celebrity). To these young girls, he was just like any other person, and they acted toward him as they would toward anybody else, not, according to coach Tracy Sundlun, as though Wilt was famous or had money. He was the guy who measured their jumps, knew every one of their names. "He was their Wiltie," Sundlun observed.

This was Wilt at his best, saying in May 1975, "Here in America, there is a lack of equality in race, in sex, and in sports, too. I don't think there has been enough equality in the area of women's track especially. That's why Wilt's Wonder Women was formed—to give these women a chance."

Wilt didn't coach the Wonder Women, for that was not his role; he just liked to be around the team. And, of course, the parents, especially the dads, perked up when Wilt came to team meetings. "That's why everyone would attend," Van Wolvelaere suggested.

Wilt appeared at the team's meets in his bell-bottoms (the awful fashion of the day) and, in what became his standard outerwear in later years, a tank top. He sat in the stands next to the girls' parents and talked about their kids and track. Long after these 9- to 15-year-old girls had outgrown the little dirt track in San Diego, Wilt stayed in touch with them and was invited to their college graduations or asked to impart advice on this or that problem they were facing as adults. (Years later, a group of them rose at 5:00 A.M. to make the two-hour drive to Los Angeles for his California funeral.)

Given his now-notorious reputation as a womanizer, one might be tempted to snicker or draw the wrong inference from Wilt's association with an athletic team composed of young women and girls. But his involvement had nothing to do with sex. That was never the manner in which Wilt related to these girls, just the opposite—he was a father figure to many. And although Sundlun acknowledged in an interview with the author, "There is no question he was a womanizer," he also recalled, "But the girls and their parents never, ever saw that side of him. He exhibited nothing but the highest standards of decorum and professionalism. Many times he'd say to me, 'You really ought to speak to that girl.

She's hanging out with a bunch of guys who have no respect for her.'" Depending on who he was with and where, Wilt was known to use foul language, but not around the girls.

Van Wolvelaere developed a friendship with Wilt that lasted for the remaining 25 years of his life. She reminisced about the Christmas dinner he shared with her family in 1984, shortly after his mother had passed away. At the time, Van Wolvelaere and her husband owned two and a half acres outside of San Diego where they raised pigs, and one of their hams was to be the main dish that night. Her two step-daughters, ages twelve and six, would also be there, and she told them Wilt would be joining them. Van Wolvelaere continued:

> Kathy, the 12-year-old, put on a pair of men's long underwear. She thought this looked cool. I remember telling her, "You've got to put something else on, like a dress or something nice. We're having company for dinner." And then "the company" arrived, and he's got on a pair of purple stretch tights and a black tank top and was barefooted. Their mouths dropped open. They couldn't believe what he wore to dinner.
>
> At dinner Wilt just loved the ham. Bob's younger daughter, Laura, was mesmerized watching him eat this ham. She was counting the pieces of ham. She's going, "That's six pieces. Well, that's seven." And he would say, "Who's counting?"
>
> And afterward, he sat on the floor of our dining room and played this Cabbage Patch board game with Laura, our six-year-old. And, of course, Laura told us later that he tried to cheat. He was just laughing and having a great time. He could play Cabbage Patch with a six-year-old and enjoy himself, or talk with adults on any subject. He was amazing that way.

Tracy Sundlun, who has coached world-record holders and Olympians, observed, "Wilt truly understood and appreciated track," a fact everyone confirms. As Van Wolvelaere commented: "I don't know anyone who could 'talk track' the way he could. I'm kind of a student of my sport, especially when I was younger, but I couldn't even talk on the level that he could. He loved the jumps—the high jump, the long jump, the triple jump—and the sprints. Like most of us sprinters, he didn't care that much for the distance events. We'd talk for hours about track."

All of Wilt's friends marvel at his ability to keep obscure track statistics in his head and also his proficiency in converting meters to yards, sometimes faster than the electronic apparatus at the meets.

After Sundlun left the Wonder Women to take a position as an assistant coach at the University of Southern California, Wilt lent his name, and gave his money to, Wilt's Athletic Club, the high-powered team out of Los Angeles that was coached by Bob Kersee. This was not age-group track but elite-level competition, including such greats as Bob's wife, Jackie Joyner-Kersee (one of Wilt's favorite athletes, male or female); her sister-in-law, Florence Griffith-Joyner; and Coleen Rienstra, who held the indoor women's high jump record at 6'6¼" (coincidentally the height of Wilt's best jump at Kansas University and, in 1957, a school record). Among the accomplished men on that team were Greg Foster and Andre Phillips, both future Olympians. Wilt's Athletic Club was in existence through 1983, and Wilt often accompanied the athletes to competitions, particularly if the meet was held in New York.

Of his friend's legacy, Tracy Sundlun observed: "Wilt was a remarkable guy who won't get credit for all the things he's done outside of basketball, in large part because he didn't try to claim credit for them. In some cases, he won't get credit for the serious stuff because of his tendency toward exaggeration. But he was as significant an individual in the development of women's athletics as you're going to find."

Even before retiring from basketball, Wilt had gotten hooked on volleyball, touring with the Big Dippers in the basketball off-season and becoming a devotee of the beach volleyball life—the perfect way, it turned out, for an athletic hedonist like Wilt to fill his days. And other than his commitments to the track clubs he sponsored and the occasional commercial he appeared in, which took up a limited amount of time, Wilt was free to indulge in the beach volleyball life full time after he retired. He'd put on bathing trunks and a tank top and arrive at the beach around 10:00 or 11:00 A.M., there spending the day playing volleyball and, ever the social animal, bantering incessantly on and off the court. He played and cheated at cards and flirted with women, for unlike basketball, where he had to peer into the stands to check out or search for a fetching woman, at the beach they were next to, or even on, the court—and wearing next to nothing.

As the seventies turned into the eighties, and as Wilt and his contemporaries got older, they played less volleyball and more cards; but they were still there at the beach. He usually stayed until 6:00 P.M., and, if he wasn't going out for dinner, stopped at the butcher on his way home to pick up four or more pork chops or some steaks to cook for supper. Kathy Gregory was an All-American volleyball player who often teamed with Wilt in two-on-two tournaments. She fondly recalls Wilt's incredible stamina and how he dove for shots. "When he left the beach, half the beach left with him. If Wilt got in my car, it would take me five weeks to get the sand out."

Wilt liked the men and women, few of whom held conventional nine-to-five jobs, that he met through beach volleyball while enjoying the beautiful setting of the Southern California beaches, with the Pacific Ocean as a backdrop to all the action. The volleyball players enjoyed him for himself, not for what or who he had been. No one made a big fuss that he was Wilt Chamberlain. And for someone who didn't like to wear shoes or, by this point in his life, fancy or much clothing, what could be better than spending eight hours a day at the beach? (Eventually, the soles of his feet became so hard from contact with the sand that it was no effort for him to walk barefooted on concrete or macadam.)

Days at the beach, nights at the clubs—this was Wilt's life for many years, according to Gene Selznick, himself a prominent fixture at Muscle and Sorrento Beaches. "Unless he went on a trip, he always went to the beach," recalled Selznick. "He played cards there, which he loved. And he cheated—not because he wanted to get something over on someone, he was just having fun. He was not a thief or anything. He'd tell you, 'You're not going to win. I'm going to beat you in whatever I do.' And even when he lost, he won. If he lost to me and saw someone, he'd say, 'I just beat Gene in cards.' Wilt never lost." It is interesting to note how many of Wilt's friends commented on his proclivity to cheat at games—but never in basketball—all of them agreeing that they didn't take his cheating seriously; it was just "Wilt being Wilt." Yet Stan Lorber, physician, friend, and father figure, insisted that Wilt never cheated in his presence, even in jest.

Wilt set up trips around beach volleyball, whether it was to Vancouver or Hawaii. On one of their many trips to Canada, Wilt and Gene Selznick met Herb Capozzi, a wealthy industrialist who, with his brother (both successful

Canadian citizens of Italian heritage), held a yearly volleyball competition against the wealthy and equally competitive Poulos brothers of Greek descent. Selznick recalls what happened at one of these matches held deep in the interior of British Columbia:

> Herb Capozzi called and asked, "Can you and Wilt come to Canada? We'll send our jet to pick you up at LAX."
>
> So we took a jet from Los Angeles to Vancouver, and from Vancouver we took a little plane to get to this island [Kelowna], where every year the Italians played the Greeks. The Capozzis hid us in one of the houses on the island, and when we came out for the game, Wilt was introduced as one of the Capozzis' long-lost cousins. Of course, the Capozzi clan won the game, although it was played under protest.

Next to California, in no place is volleyball more popular than in Hawaii, which Wilt visited as a member of the Big Dippers. Wilt enjoyed his trips to Hawaii so much that, in the late seventies, he bought a condominium on the 24th floor of the Wailana building, located in Honolulu next to a local and famous landmark, the Hilton Hawaiian Village. Before he sold it at an enormous profit around 1985, he spent four to six weeks each winter in this 2,400-square-foot penthouse suite overlooking Waikiki Beach and the Pacific Ocean. He was a familiar sight tooling around the island in the Cadillac convertible he kept there year-round after having it shipped over from California.

It was during the early years of his Hawaiian stay that Wilt met Bruce O'Neil, with whom he would be very close for the next 10 years. O'Neil was then the basketball coach at the University of Hawaii, and he helped Wilt find the penthouse apartment. When he wasn't playing volleyball on the beaches across the street from his penthouse, Wilt sometimes attended O'Neil's practices, even working out on occasion with some of the players on the university's basketball team. O'Neil always stayed at Wilt's California home when recruiting trips brought him to the mainland, and after he left university coaching in 1976 to found a video company, he and Wilt continued their friendship. Indeed, Wilt was the subject of more than one video O'Neil's company produced. The two men traveled to Alaska and Oregon for fishing trips—Wilt being a lousy fisherman but up for the experience—and they played racquetball and tennis together. True to his competitive nature, after Wilt discovered those sports, he was intent on becoming as good as he could be in both.

"He was such a caring guy," O'Neil, now the president of the United States Basketball Academy, recalled. "People think he was brash or arrogant. But if you knew the real Wilt, he was a hilarious, witty guy. He was just fun to be with. He loved adventure and new experiences. And he loved meeting ordinary people in different venues, people who weren't after him for his fame. He was not just an amazing athlete, but also an amazing person. I feel blessed that I was touched by Wilt in my lifetime."

Pat Bigold, a sports columnist for the *Honolulu Star-Bulletin*, remembers Wilt parking himself near the picnic benches next to the tennis courts at Ft. DeRussy Beach, being very friendly with anyone who wanted to talk and "having a sharp eye for the girls in bikinis." Besides playing volleyball on the beach across the street from his condominium, Wilt occasionally joined an afternoon pickup basketball game at the Klum Gym, though always playing the guard position and surprising those present with his exceptional outside shooting. Bob Nash, a former NBA player and a longtime member of the University of Hawaii coaching staff, also played in those pickup games. He said that the Wilt he saw there was relaxed, probably because people were not "climbing all over him wanting him to do things."

The Hawaiian nights were spent similarly to the California nights (and the Canadian nights and, in the nineties, the Miami nights): going to clubs and eventually returning "home" with a pretty, young woman—or maybe two.

In the summer of 1974, Wilt was among a group of businessmen–cum–sports entrepreneurs who put together a professional volleyball league, which was up and running by the following summer. There had been talk of including teams from Eastern Europe (where volleyball was popular, particularly in Czechoslovakia and the Soviet Union), but, although the league was named the International Volleyball Association, all six teams were from the western and southwestern United States. Wilt was on the board with Michael O'Hara, a sports entrepreneur who had been involved in the creations of the American Basketball Association and the World Hockey Association. They joined David Wolper, the documentary filmmaker, and Berry Gordy Jr., the founder of Motown Records. Each of these men owned a team in the league, and they wanted Wilt to be an owner, too; but, according to O'Hara, "he never stepped up financially."

But that didn't stop Wilt from promoting the league by playing for it. In that first season, Wilt often played for the opposing team at the home team's first game. By the second year of its existence, Wilt was named president of the league, although he really functioned more as an "ambassador" than as an executive, since he did not become involved in administrative functions. Who better than Wilt to head a sports organization if you're trying to get media coverage? Indeed, the league's All-Star Game was televised only because Wilt was going to play in it, and though some felt he really didn't warrant being named an All-Star, he rose to the challenge, playing superbly in the game and being named its MVP.

By 1977 the Seattle Smashers became the league's seventh team, and during the 1978 season, Wilt played in 15 games (half the season) for the Seattle team. However, lacking a television contract, the league was doomed—five thousand fans at a game can't support a professional league (minor league baseball excepted)—and in 1979 the IVA folded. Wilt, along with the IVA team owners and players, could take satisfaction from knowing they had increased people's awareness of volleyball. "Wilt is the most famous person who ever played volleyball," O'Hara said. "To this day he is still the most famous. Wilt's identification and association with volleyball was one of the factors in the growth of the sport in the seventies."

It is no coincidence that, beginning in the seventies, the United States began to have more success in international volleyball competitions, including the Olympics. That's Wilt's effect on the macro level. On a smaller scale, there are those such as John Simpson, who went on to play volleyball at UCLA. He recalled that Wilt was the first black man he had ever seen participating in that sport, and in a letter to *Volleyball* magazine following Wilt's death, Simpson thanked Wilt for making it easier for him to play the sport he, too, came to love. Thus, it was really Wilt's contributions in promoting the game rather than his playing skills that eventually earned him a spot in the Volleyball Hall of Fame in Holyoke, Massachusetts—not far from that other hall of fame, 10 miles away in Springfield, where Wilt is also honored. How many people are enshrined in two national sports halls of fame?

Volleyball was another venue that enabled Wilt to demonstrate his commitment to women's athletics. He sponsored and coached a women's volleyball team called the Little Dippers to a third-place finish in the United States Volleyball Association national championships in 1977. One member of that team was Kathy Gregory, one of the sport's greatest players and later a coach for 28 years at the University of California in Santa Barbara. Gregory recalled:

> When he coached the Little Dippers, you'd say, "What does he know about volleyball?" Well, you know what? He knew about people, and he knew how to motivate them, and he knew how to analyze sports, and it didn't matter if it was basketball or volleyball. He was a great coach . . . and he was such a good friend. When I started coaching in college, he came to all my games. Whether I won or lost, he always gave me a pep talk, and he was always there for me. . . . I think people don't know that he was a really sensitive, caring, generous person.

Gregory added, "I think Wilt has done more for women's athletics than any other sports celebrity in America."

Just as Wilt had Lynda Huey and Patty Van Wolvelaere to talk to about track, Kathy Gregory is one of those with whom Wilt held a decades-long volleyball dialogue, although that was not the only subject they discussed. As Gregory fondly recalled, "You always knew he was ready to talk, no matter how late you called." Conversations with her provide another clue as to why Wilt was devoted to promoting women athletes:

> He respected people who worked hard. People don't realize he was a workhorse, with a good work ethic. He liked that women were so passionate about their sports, that they worked so hard at them and weren't just in it for the money. He had been around too many male athletes who were prima donnas, and he just appreciated how hard women worked for, at most times in those years, so little recognition or money.

———

No sooner had Wilt retired in the fall of 1974 than there were reports of an NBA team trying to lure him back—none other than the New York Knicks, against whom he had played in three NBA Finals. The initial effort came to naught, reportedly because the Knicks coach, Red Holzman, was reluctant to take on the sometimes-daunting prospect of coaching Wilt. Apparently, there was some truth to the rumors of the Knicks' flirtation with Wilt during the 1974–1975 season. When Wilt attended a heavyweight championship fight in Las Vegas during the summer of 1975, he told a columnist from *The New York Times* that "playing in New York would have been nice," implying that he was for the idea but the Knicks were not.

And then in October 1975, the prior year's rumor became fact when the president and general manager of the Knicks flew to Los Angeles with the announced intention of convincing Wilt to join their team for the 1975–1976 campaign. With Willis Reed retired and no center on the Knicks roster with anywhere near his talent, the Knicks needed a top-flight center. But there was a legal roadblock to signing Wilt: a judge *and* an arbitrator had ruled earlier that were he to return to basketball, he owed a year of service to the Los Angeles Lakers. Further complicating the matter, Lawrence O'Brien, then commissioner of the NBA, had declared Wilt a free agent. But he wasn't really, not in the sense that the term was to apply to basketball players a few years hence. Being a "free agent" means one is free to sign with whomever one wants, no strings attached. But any team that signed Wilt, the commissioner decreed, would have to compensate the Los Angeles Lakers with a player or a draft choice. This, of course, did not sit well with Wilt or his lawyer, Sy Goldberg.

At this point in the story, the commissioner of the American Basketball Association, the late Dave DeBusschere (yes, the one who used to star for the Knicks), said in essence, "Wait a second, fellas. If Wilt returns to professional basketball, he is obligated to play for a team in the ABA because he had signed a three-year contract, only one year of which he has fulfilled."

"Not true," lawyer Goldberg responded. "My client is free of that contract because Leonard Bloom, the former owner of the ABA team, defaulted on the contract."

In any event, Wilt never did sign with the Knicks for the 1975–1976 season, when he probably did want to return to the NBA. Given his involvement with the professional volleyball league, his track team, and all those card games and arguments to be had at the beach, one has to wonder how serious he was, in subsequent years, about returning to the NBA. But as sure as Elizabeth Taylor was to enter and leave marriages during these same years, just about every new basketball season there would be a report that some team was interested in Wilt. In December 1978, at age 42, he met twice with representatives of the Chicago

Bulls, who envisioned him playing backup to Artis Gilmore for 10 minutes a game. (The thought of Wilt being content to play backup to anyone is preposterous.) And then in 1979, it was the owner of the Cleveland Cavaliers wooing Wilt. By this time Jerry Buss, the owner of the Los Angeles Lakers, said that he wouldn't expect compensation if Wilt were to sign with an NBA team; nor did *he* want Wilt, for he had a still-potent center named Kareem Abdul-Jabbar.

———

Nineteen seventy-nine was also the year in which Wilt was inducted into the Basketball Hall of Fame, then located on the campus of Springfield College in Springfield, Massachusetts, where James Naismith invented the game. (Today the Hall has its own site.) Hall of Fame inductions were not then the well-attended, televised events they have become, but for Wilt's induction the crowd was larger than usual. Eddie Gottlieb, the man who had drafted Wilt while still in high school for the NBA and for whom Wilt held the highest admiration and affection, was present at the induction ceremony and said he had never seen Wilt looking happier. Wilt's friend and personal physician, Dr. Stan Lorber, who made the trip up from Philadelphia, later observed that it was the first time he had ever seen Wilt wearing a tie. Also in attendance were Wilt's two favorite coaches, Alex Hannum and Frank McGuire, the latter of whom called Wilt "a perfect player to coach." Wilt told the *Daily News'* Jack Kiser that he hadn't wanted to attend, for ceremonies such as the induction, with speeches and handshaking, were not his "cup of tea." But once there and caught up in the spirit of the moment, he was glad that he had come. In his formal speech, Wilt said, "Looking back on it, I'm glad I came from Philadelphia. It was a mecca of basketball back then. I feel I wouldn't have been a great basketball player if I hadn't been brought up in Philadelphia."

The quest to bring Wilt back into the NBA didn't end with his induction into the Hall of Fame, which usually denotes someone is permanently retired from the sport. In 1982, the New Jersey Nets clamored for Wilt; so did the Philadelphia 76ers when starting center Darryl Dawkins broke his leg. The team's owner, Harold Katz, publicly pursued Wilt, an effort that prompted Elvin Hayes to opine, "A 45-year-old Wilt Chamberlain is better than a 25-year-old Darryl Dawkins." In turning down the Sixers' offer, Wilt said he didn't want the pressure of traveling, but, demonstrating that the old bombast and ego were intact, he added that if he did return, he'd lead the league in rebounds and blocked shots.

Still trying to settle old scores, Wilt pointed out to inquiring reporters over these years that no one ever proposed Bill Russell come back. Even as he neared the age of 50, 14 years after his last game, Wilt said the Nets approached him about playing 10 to 15 minutes per game. And why shouldn't they? Wilt responded, for, thanks to the years of playing volleyball and tennis and lifting free weights, he weighed 275—40 pounds less than his playing weight during his last few seasons on the basketball court. As one reporter observed, "There is no hint of gray in Chamberlain's hair or trademark goatee. The racehorse-thin legs that lifted him skyward for 23,924 rebounds are still shapely. The hands that helped score 31,419 points and can palm a bowling ball are still powerful."

All true, but despite the wishful thinking of his fans and the litany that Wilt could have come back at 50, he had not played professional basketball in 14 years. He would have made a fool of himself had he tried to play in the NBA. He knew it and had no intention of coming back, all the stories notwithstanding. In 1984, a 48-year-old Wilt expressed his feelings on the subject:

> My ego is such that I liked it when someone said they could use me, but I never sought them out and I haven't missed playing. Come February, where do you think I'd rather be: in Cleveland trying to plow my way through a snowstorm to get to the game or on a beach in Hawaii, board sailing and chasing girls?

And then, in a typical burst of hyperbole, he later said, "Maybe the average person couldn't come back and play at 50, but Wilt could come back and play. Where there's a Wilt, there's a way."

Chapter 21

At some point after my first wife died in 1982, Wilt proposed we take a 10-day trip to Italy. He made all the arrangements and paid for everything.

In Milan, before breakfast he went out and ran five to six miles, so he came back dehydrated. Wilt could take a quart of anything and empty it without coming up for air. So now we're going to breakfast in the hotel. He ordered orange juice, which in Italy came in those little four-ounce glasses. He looked at the tiny glasses and said to the waiter, "Bring a lot of them." So they brought about six. He finally said to the waiter, "How many do you have?" So they brought three dozen—144 ounces.

That's a lot of liquid. He started to drink them, placing the empty glasses on a side tray next to our table. All the waiters, and everyone else in the room, were staring. While he had bacon and eggs, he drank all 36 glasses. The staff stood there agape watching him consume that amount of liquid.

—Dr. Stan Lorber, longtime doctor and friend

Tell Me Who, What, and Where, and I'll Take It from There

ynda Huey, Roz Cohen, and Bob Vogelsang, all of them Californians, spent as much time with Wilt as anyone did during the last 25 years of his life. In some ways, they were a surrogate family, according to Huey, among the select group of people around whom Wilt could be himself and relax. Other than his sister Barbara and older brother Oliver, who also lived in Los Angeles, Wilt didn't spend that much time with his other siblings, some of whom still lived in the East.

Lynda Huey met Wilt in 1971. Theirs was a volatile relationship with long periods when they were too angry to talk to each other. Huey would hear about Wilt's doings through her friends, many of whom, she said, he co-opted. But in six months, Huey and Wilt would be in touch again. "I'm one of the few women Wilt had a physical relationship with who stayed around," Huey maintained. They were friends for 28 years, and Huey remarked that Wilt, at one time or another, fulfilled many roles in her life—"lover, brother, father, son, playmate, and favorite traveling companion."

She was 24, he was 35 when they met at a beach volleyball tournament—she a perky, athletic, bright California blonde who also ran the 100 and 200 meters. She says she set out to "catch him" at a mixed-doubles beach volleyball tournament—and that she did. Huey, who is considered a pioneer in aquatic therapy, has written five books: one her autobiography, the others, with coauthors, about the health and fitness benefits of water exercise.

319

She experienced the pleasures of knowing Wilt but also, figuratively, the pain. "Wilt was not an easy person to be friends with," she said. "It was hard work. But the high times made up for it. That was the trade-off. When he turned on his charm, there was nobody as charming as he. But he could shut it off on the dime. He would be nice often enough to keep you in love with him; and he would do this to everybody, to keep everybody in love with him. Nobody wants to admit what an ass he could be." A mutual friend described Wilt and Lynda as "acting like an old married couple." Huey was with Wilt the last night of his life and was probably the last person to see him alive.

Another close female friend was Roz Cohen, who met Wilt around 1970 on Will Rogers State Beach, where both would play volleyball. Roz was about 10 years older than Wilt was and divorced. Wilt became the center of her universe; she even looked after Ursa Major when the master was away. She was, in the words of Lynda Huey, Wilt's "surrogate mom, cook, would-be secretary, and co-complainer." She baked lemon meringue and apple pies for Wilt, prepared macaroni and cheese, and kept quiet about whatever she saw at Wilt's home—and Wilt knew she would not talk about his lifestyle. If Wilt needed a task done, Cohen was his gal Friday and faithful friend. According to Huey, toward the end of his life, when he was on so many medications, it was Roz Cohen who knew, as well as—if not better than—Wilt, the dosages prescribed.

Of the male friends who made up his inner circle later in life, Bob "Vogie" Vogelsang was one who was often around. Wilt and Vogie were contemporaries who shared a love of beach volleyball, which in their physical primes they played together all day, following which, at night, they chased women or watched sports on TV. They first met when Wilt played for the Harlem Globetrotters and Vogelsang was with the Washington Generals, the team whose job it was to lose to the Globetrotters every night. Wilt would often berate Vogie for some real or imagined shortcoming, but Vogie, an easy-going hedonist who lived on a houseboat, didn't take it personally, Huey contended.

Always a part of Wilt's life—in a way that only a blood relative can be—was his sister Barbara. Before retiring in 2000, Barbara had been an administrative assistant for a Los Angeles law firm. She'd often be with her brother, alone or with her husband, Elzie Lewis, who had grown up in Kansas City and was a connection to Wilt's Kansas years. Friends say Barbara and Wilt were very much alike, even down to having the same favorite color—purple. Barbara, devoted to her brother (as he was to her), functions as the unofficial caretaker of his legacy—along with one other person, Zelda Spoelstra.

Zelda Spoelstra, a contemporary of Wilt's, had met him at Kutsher's Country Club in the fifties, where both had summer jobs. They did not see much of one another in the next decade because she married, raised a family, and worked in the garment industry. (However, Spoelstra always had a basketball pedigree, having attended the same New York high school as Lennie Rosenbluth, the North Carolina All-American who starred in the famous championship game against Wilt and Kansas. And she had married, but eventually divorced, a professional basketball player.)

Besides her primary job, Spoelstra also returned to Kutsher's most summers to attend the Maurice Stokes games. She had worked part time for the NBA in the fifties, but after raising her family, Spoelstra accepted a full-time position with the NBA in 1994. It was there, first in a professional capacity (she works with the retired NBA players) and then very much in a personal capacity, that she and Wilt reunited. She became a close confidant during the last decade of his life, especially the last five years. (This was also the time during which Wilt "rediscovered" some other friends from his early life.)

"We really loved each other," Spoelstra said at her NBA office in New York. "Love doesn't have to be physical. There was a goodness about him, a loyalty; a sense of caring and a great generosity." Friends they were, but, as Spoelstra recalled, they fought all the time (and then made up). Wilt often began conversations with Spoelstra by saying, "I know you're going to be angry, but . . ." At one point, he wanted her to work for him, but she declined, telling him that she always wanted to be able to say, when she disagreed with him, "Go screw yourself, Norman."

Wilt's word, according to Spoelstra, was as good as gold. (Speaking of which, he gave her, and she still wears, the gold chain he wore around his neck for so many years—the one that held the pendant of an Egyptian pharaoh.) "He wanted his friends to love him for who he was—not what he was," Spoelstra said of her dear friend; surely, she did just that.

After Ike Richman's death in 1965, and Wilt's move from Philadelphia to the West Coast in the summer of 1968, it was lawyer Sy Goldberg to whom Wilt looked for advice, particularly in matters of business, and whom he trusted most. Goldberg had power of attorney and paid all of Wilt's bills after the task became too unwieldy for Alan Levitt, Wilt's accountant and adviser back in

Philadelphia. "He said I knew him better than anyone," Goldberg recalled of his friend of almost 40 years. "As far as I'm concerned, I didn't understand him. He was a very, very complicated guy—good guy, very inquisitive, studied everything in the world. You'd go up to his house and one day he's studying sign language, another day he's studying the history of the world. He was different. He was unique. But there were demons he had that I didn't know."

Being Wilt's lawyer was the last of the roles Goldberg filled in Wilt's life, for they were friends first, lawyer-client and financial adviser–client second. In some ways, Goldberg, an unpretentious, bright, avuncular man, was like an older brother to Wilt. What the friends shared most of all was a curiosity about life.

Perhaps it was that same curiosity that helped Wilt to fill the many hours when he didn't or couldn't sleep. (There is a difference of opinion among those who knew Wilt as to whether he was an insomniac or just chose to stay up late, and also whether or not he was "sleep deprived.") "I know he was up most of the night and could function on little sleep," recalled Goldberg, who between marriages lived in Wilt's house for six months. "He would take the red-eye back east very often because he didn't have to waste time and he was up anyway."

Lynda Huey said Wilt told her that he became an insomniac in high school. She speculated on the origin of his sleeping problems:

> My theory is, that is when he became famous, and he couldn't lead a normal life. It was too much pressure for him. . . . He spent his life sleep-deprived. He was always mentioning it. He'd say, "I got only two hours' sleep last night."
>
> I'm sure his lack of sleep had a lot to do with him being cranky a lot of the time. We all offered him suggestions [for getting more sleep]. He'd say, "I've tried everything."
>
> In the earlier years [the seventies and eighties], he might have gone out to a club and then brought a couple of girls home. The seventies were probably the best time of his life because he had people who could stay up all night with him. In the nineties, after a late dinner, Wilt's best hope was that some of the people he knew would come over [to the house] and stay up all night with him. But he'd wear people out because all the rest of us had to sleep. Vogie might come over and watch sports until 2:00 or 3:00 in the morning. I remember

several times getting up in the morning and Vogie was sound asleep over on one side of the bed and Wilt was watching something on TV.

Stan Lorber, who became Wilt's doctor about 1958 in Philadelphia, takes issue with the statement that Wilt was sleep-deprived: "I was his medical adviser throughout his life, even though I may not have been his physician. He'd call me almost weekly about the slightest thing he had. I don't remember him telling me he was sleep-deprived."

When did Wilt rise? At different times, it appears. Many of his friends said that Wilt told them not to call before 10:00 A.M. Rod Roddewig, who stayed at Wilt's home dozens of times, said Wilt got up around 9:00 or 10:00. Stan Lorber saw a different Wilt: "Whenever I was with him, he would never let more than a day go by before he ran five or six miles. He would do it at 6:00 or 7:00 in the morning, right before breakfast. He was doing it right up until his hip started bothering him. I stayed with him many times, and I traveled with him. He's been to my home. He was never a late sleeper."

Wilt had all sorts of friends and acquaintances: some reputable, conventionally employed, and successful; others decidedly less so—"low-lifes and gofers," Sy Goldberg dismissively called them. Speaking from his law offices in Marina Del Rey, California, Goldberg observed: "Here's a man [Wilt] who was bright, intelligent, and rich. And these people were slobs. I told him this, and he was furious, but he told a mutual acquaintance that he knew I was correct."

Tommy Kearns, who stayed at Wilt's house many times when business brought him from New York to Los Angeles, shared Goldberg's displeasure with *some* of Wilt's California friends. Kearns understood why they were around, even if he didn't approve of them:

Everything was done on Wilt's terms. He didn't compromise much. He wanted to be a normal guy, but at other times, he wanted to be Wilt, superstar. And you had to pay homage. There were a couple of guys I met at Wilt's house whose goal in life was to see how many women they could conquer. One guy even had a scrapbook on the women he had encounters with. These guys were the most low-life people I've ever met. I said to Wilt, "Why are you hanging around with these guys? Why are you letting them into your house?" Wilt took people in for a certain period of time, and then they disappeared. That's kind of Wilt's history. Someone could really know Wilt, but it might only be for a certain time period.

During the last couple of years of his life, Wilt allowed Alan Shifman, a man 30 years younger, to spend time with him. He filled many roles for Wilt: a young man with whom Wilt could go to clubs when so many of Wilt's contemporaries were long beyond club-going, a person who worshipped Wilt, company when Wilt didn't want to be alone, and a backgammon partner—about which pastime Shifman had these recollections:

He was a kid who never grew up, a kid who couldn't grow up. One time I was beating him in backgammon by about 12 points, and he won the game. He started running around the room screaming like a five-year-old. It was hilarious. You know, you had to watch his fingers. He'd pick up the dice after moving and not quite move back to the original place.

He loved that I wasn't "Hollywood." I'm a Midwestern person. He didn't let too many people close; I was the last one. Would I have lasted? Who knows? There were times you'd get mad at him, but you couldn't stay mad at him. You'd call back like a puppy. If he wouldn't return a call, by the third call I would call him and leave a message, something like, "Look, I don't know what you're mad at, but I'm sure it was something stupid." And sure enough, three or four days later, he would call back and say, "Oh, I was out of town." He wasn't out of town.

He was godlike. That's why I say, how can you stay mad at him?

———————

Wilt had a low threshold for boredom, so he was always on the move. He often went to New York, one of his favorite places. For many years he was associated with what was then called the Mobil Oil Company's "Big Apple Games"—his role was to conduct volleyball clinics while dispensing advice to the young charges about the pitfalls of drug use and the like. The Foot Locker Company's

"Slamfest" also brought him to New York, as well as to Phoenix, Arizona; Hilton Head, South Carolina; and Boca Raton, Florida. For four years in the late eighties to early nineties, Wilt was a spokesman for the company, which sponsored dunk contests (the "Slamfest") and celebrity basketball games.

When in New York, he might have lunch with his old coach, Frank McGuire, who in the eighties worked for Madison Square Garden. Wilt and Tommy Kearns might eat steak on the Upper East Side at what was then called Chris Cella's Restaurant, or he might dine at Elaine's, a magnet for celebrities, with Jessica Burstein, the photographer he was close to. Or he might spend time catching up on news with Cal Ramsey, who worked for the New York Knicks. The two of them might visit Cal's mother, who so many years before, when Wilt first came to New York in the fifties, used to cook for her son and Wilt (as Wilt's mother would cook for the two of them in Philadelphia). And Wilt had kept in touch with Carl Green, a friend from their Globetrotter days and with whom, in the sixties, he owned real estate in New York. Green, a sharp dresser, introduced Wilt to his New York tailor.

Always looking for material—and who was more quotable than Wilt—reporters and columnists would write about him and his postbasketball life. In a mid-eighties interview with the Associated Press, he talked about how much professional basketball had changed during the past 30 years:

> Can you imagine playing when your hands are so cold and the ball is as hard as a brick? I can remember going into the old Detroit Arena and there's about three thousand people in this big, old, huge thing. Every time the door opened, the wind blew through. I can remember Paul Arizin, who was one of the greatest basketball players ever to play this game, going like this (Wilt blows into his hands as if to warm them) . . . and then smoke is blowing out of his mouth.

Reporters inevitably asked him to pick his all-time best team, and he'd answer: "Start off putting Wilt Chamberlain at center," and then ask, "You want this to be an honest evaluation, don't you?" Then Wilt would select Oscar Robertson and Jerry West at the guard positions, and Elgin Baylor, Bob Pettit, and Rick Barry at forward. He'd say Bob Cousy and John Havlicek would be his other guards. As Larry Bird and Magic Johnson and Michael Jordan continued to demonstrate their greatness, Wilt would acknowledge that it was difficult to pick just five all-time great players.

Each summer he still attended the Maurice Stokes Memorial benefit at Kutsher's Country Club in Monticello, New York, following which he might be off, for example, to Helsinki for the world track-and-field championship.

There were infrequent, though satisfying, trips to Philadelphia in the eighties and nineties; he'd visit about once every two or three years. The 76ers wanted to retire Wilt's number, but he would hear nothing of it, apparently still miffed at Irv Kosloff, the team's owner, for failing to recognize what Wilt swore was a verbal agreement he had with the late Ike Richman to own part of the team. But Kosloff sold the 76ers in 1976. So when, in 1980, the professional basketball writers voted the 1966–1967 Sixers the greatest team in the then-35-year history of the NBA, Wilt returned to Philadelphia for a ceremony honoring the team, as did the other members of that celebrated squad. The ceremony was supposed to be held at halftime, but to accommodate Wilt, it took place before the game so he could catch a 9:30 P.M. flight back to Los Angeles. At 6:00 the next morning he had to be ready to begin shooting a commercial for TWA.

After 17 years of refusing, in March 1991, Wilt finally agreed to allow the 76ers to retire his number. It was a special evening—with Wilt in a tuxedo no less—and with friends, family, old teammates, and many thousands of fans there to pay tribute to the greatest of all Philly ballplayers. (The night before, he had been inducted into his high school's Hall of Fame, which probably gave him as much satisfaction.)

Some of his Philadelphia visits were unpublicized, the better to surprise old friends, which he enjoyed doing. "I used to have an office in Center City," Mike Richman recalled. "There'd be a tap on my window. I'd look up, and it was Wilt; I'd drop everything to be with him."

He could disappear just as quickly, however. Richman and many of Wilt's other friends remember walking down a street with Wilt thinking they were talking to him, but then they'd turn around and discover that he was gone. He liked to keep people guessing or on their toes, maintaining a mystery about himself.

Whenever he was in Philadelphia, it didn't take long before the media was on his trail, and there would be the inevitable "state of Wilt" stories. (Wilt may have lived the last 30 years of his life in Los Angeles, but no city's media or citizens were as interested in him as Philadelphia's, no less so when he was retired than when he was playing.) And whenever he was back in his hometown, he'd visit his widowed mother, who was, according to Dr. Stan Lorber, the rock of

Wilt's life. One close friend recalled that Wilt's mother and the late Bob Billings of Kansas were the only two people about whom Wilt was never heard to speak one ill or critical word. "Wilt got a lot of his personality from her," observed Lorber, who was her doctor as well as Wilt's.

Mrs. Chamberlain had a fine sense of humor, everyone recalls, and loved to get into ribbing matches with her son, who inherited that trait. At Wilt's 40th birthday party at one of Philadelphia's most exclusive French restaurants, his mother observed to the few close friends and family there, "When the soup costs $5 per bowl, everybody has to have it. When I made soup when you were kids, everyone turned up their noses."

Being an inveterate traveler, Wilt took trips to Italy or to Split, in what was then Yugoslavia, both countries among his favorite vacation spots. He had been to Florence many times with the Globetrotters, but they had played their games at night, gone to bed, and left for the next city in the morning. So Wilt had never really visited any of the city's treasures.

On an Italian sojourn with Wilt, Stan Lorber asked him if he had ever seen Michelangelo's statue of David. When Wilt answered that he had not, Doc Lorber suggested that his friend must see it. As Lorber recalled, this is what happened:

> When we got to Florence, we checked into our hotel and went to see the David. Wilt looked at the statue, and he was transfixed. He just stared and stared at it and didn't want to leave. We were in Florence for three days. The first thing each morning, he wanted to see the David. He said he had never seen anything so magnificent. I wouldn't be surprised if he was also saying to himself, "There's a guy who was built as well as I am."

Wilt took many trips with Lynda Huey, a love of travel being one of the bonds between them. However, Wilt insisted that Huey—and according to Huey, any other woman with whom he traveled—pay her own airfare. Wilt would pay for the luxury hotels and dining, but the woman had to get there on her own. That was fine with Huey, who didn't want Wilt to have that to lord over her. She and Wilt, sometimes alone, sometimes joined by friends, visited

Rome, Italy's Amalfi coast, the Italian Alps, Helsinki, and Australia, as well as many cities in the United States.

"When you traveled with him, we got the best of everything," Huey said. "We were pampered and privileged. Everybody wanted to interact with him, so they always tried to do things for us. Wherever we were, he always looked for a place to work out—he wanted to be outdoors and play like a kid. He didn't like to visit museums; he liked to do physical things." But Wilt might pick up and leave at any time, which he did when he and three other friends rented a villa on the Amalfi Coast. There wasn't enough action for Wilt—read women—so he left them and headed for Milan.

———

Whether at home or away, Wilt was besieged with phone calls—from friends, associates, and people who wanted him for an event or an investment. He used to occasionally change the recorded message on his answering machine, but one of them was "Tell me who, what, and where, and I'll take it from there."

"Wilt was tough to get ahold of," recalled Al Attles, who after his basketball career became a player-coach and executive with the San Francisco (now Golden State) Warriors. "He'd get back to you sometimes." That "sometimes" might mean three or four calls on your part, except for the special few—Stan Lorber and Sy Goldberg at the top of that short list.

For a ladies' man like Wilt, he had to take pride in being asked to pose for the cover of *Women's Sports'* second annual swimsuit issue in 1983. And although Wilt never produced a movie, he wrote a couple of unpublished screenplays and, in 1984, had the role of the villain Bombaata in *Conan the Destroyer*, starring Arnold Schwarzenegger. Wilt's friend, Cal Ramsey, recalls teasing Wilt about *Conan* in the last conversation the friends of 45 years were to have: "It was one Saturday, and I was home watching *Conan the Destroyer*. When it was over, I called him and said, 'I just sat here for two hours, Wiltie, watching you in a movie, and you didn't say a word. All you did was grunt,'" Ramsey recalled, laughing deeply and remembering the friend whom he first met when they were high school All-Americans. Wilt actually had a speaking role, though it was not a large one. Among his lines is the phrase, "Thieves should be hanged." Stan Lorber, who spoke often with Wilt, would sometimes call Wilt and, when Wilt answered the phone, Lorber's first words would be "Thieves should be hanged," which became a running joke between them.

Besides taking up tennis in the mid- to late eighties, Wilt followed the sport, particularly the women's game. He knew the rankings of the top players, and, as he was often in Europe, turned up at more than one French Open. He traveled thousands of miles specifically for the Australian Open and was a presence for many years during the entire U.S. Open in New York. He also befriended the young Jennifer Capriati and was especially close to Tracy Austin, among others on or around the tour.

As it was not his style, Wilt never hired a public relations person or firm to promote him or his good deeds, most of which remained private. "He would help people when he could," recalled childhood buddy Marty Hughes, who had moved to the Boston area. "And when Wilt helped people, he'd say, 'I helped you; you don't have to broadcast it to the world. It's between you and me.'"

The generosity extended to ex-teammates as well. Tom Meschery, with whom Wilt played on the Warriors, was one such beneficiary of Wilt's kindness. As Meschery recollected in Terry Pluto's *Tall Tales*:

> One summer I worked for the Seattle department of recreation, and we were putting together an inner-city basketball league. Since he lived in the area, I called Bill Russell to come out and help kick off the program. Russ wanted to be paid, but I didn't want to spend the city's money. I thought of Wilt and how he traveled a lot in the summer. I thought he might be in the area, so I called him.
>
> He got on his motorcycle and drove from L.A. to Seattle. He talked to the kids, officiated a game, and spent the day. Then he refused to take a dime, even for expenses.

With his insecurities showing, and always having to remind people of his unique standing in the sport, Wilt continued to take the occasional potshot at Kareem Abdul-Jabbar, his heir as the NBA's most dominant center. A few months before Jabbar was about to break Wilt's all-time NBA scoring record—a record most people thought would never be broken—Wilt said, "If I dropped down from Mars into the middle of an NBA court today without anyone knowing who I was, it would be a week before they'd say, 'Chamberlain is the best. Who is this guy Kareem Abdul-Jabbar?'"

On April 5, 1984, Jabbar broke the record, scoring his 31,420[th] point against the Utah Jazz in Las Vegas (the site of a few Jazz "home" games that year). Wilt was on good behavior when he showed up the next night at the Forum where Jabbar was honored by the Lakers. A few months later, however, Wilt asserted, "Kareem breaks my scoring record and he gets a brand new Mercedes, a $65,000 car. This is one of 103 records I owned and nobody gave me a popsicle."

While exaggerating the records he had set—but not by much (according to the NBA, Wilt still owned 83 records in 1989)—he did have a point about not receiving a popsicle or anything else from the NBA. To be fair to the league, maybe if Wilt had chosen to retire in a different manner—instead of in the pages of *Sports Illustrated*—the NBA might have held a ceremony, although public relations and marketing ploys like that weren't common in 1974.

Wilt wasn't that impressed with most of the NBA players he watched in the eighties and nineties, certain that the best of his contemporaries—the Bob Pettits, Nate Thurmonds, and Oscar Robertsons—could more than hold their own in the modern game. He observed that the players had been much closer and had more fun when he played—the league being so much smaller that teams played each other 10 or more times each year. And players weren't surrounded (and isolated) by an entourage of agents, lawyers, public relations personnel, and assorted flunkies. All Wilt envied about the modern player was his contract. Wilt had worked hard for his money, and he would not be human if he hadn't expressed to close friends a touch of bitterness about the fact that he had played before the era of the $50 million contract. Asked near the end of his life what he thought he would be worth in the current marketplace, he said, "Well, let's first talk about my owning part of the team."

Wilt thought that frankness was one of his best traits (but also was one that sometimes got him into trouble), and he never let anyone forget his place in the basketball pantheon. At one of the Maurice Stokes tournaments, long after Wilt's playing days, Gary Sussman, then the New Jersey Nets public address announcer, introduced Wilt as one of the greatest NBA players. Wilt walked over, snatched the microphone, and declared, "I wasn't one of the greatest—I was *the* greatest."

On other occasions, he praised basketball as the greatest game ever invented and said his only wish was that there had been more videotape made of him playing so people could see for themselves what he had accomplished. But even on the subject of his stardom, he kept matters in perspective and demonstrated he had his priorities in order, as illustrated by an incident that occurred during a flight to Europe. Wilt mentioned to Stan Hochman, a columnist for the *Philadelphia Daily News*, that people continually approached him for an autograph. He commented that at one point during a flight with his friend Stan Lorber, his travel mate pointed across the aisle and said, "Do you see that guy? He's the man who isolated a certain strain of bacteria and won a Nobel Prize for it." As Wilt observed to Hochman, "Nobody was asking for his [the Nobel Prize winner's] autograph. We have a lot of false heroes in America."

————

Few sporting events appealed to Wilt more than the Olympics, and he would have given a great deal to have been a participant in the Games. Barring that, he did his best to "participate" on various levels.

Prior to the 1984 summer Olympics, to be held in Los Angeles, Wilt had secured a job through Mike O'Hara (an old volleyball buddy), who had been appointed the vice president of sports for the L.A. Games. One of O'Hara's committees was in charge of selecting the surfaces for the main Olympic track, as well as for five training facilities, and Wilt was made a member of that group. O'Hara recalled, "I put Wilt on my track acquisition committee. He was terrific and loved it. He was my guy who would go to Munich and inspect the track from the 1972 Olympics, and go to Montreal [site of the 1976 Games]. We'd then have a meeting with several experts on track and field. Wilt was very responsible. And everywhere he went, people loved him. It was one of those things that was perfect for him."

For the 1992 Barcelona Games, Wilt bought a cable-TV package, the better to view more events than one could through normal channels. Lynda Huey and a friend of hers, Alan Silber, a New York attorney, who had met Wilt through Huey at the 1976 Montreal Games, moved into Wilt's house for 10 days. They lived on Barcelona time, rising about 2:00 A.M. (10:00 A.M. in Barcelona) to catch the morning trials those first few days. Silber vividly remembers the experience:

> We'd go into Wilt's bedroom. He'd have the roof open so we could look up at the stars. Wilt would be on the bed; and he and Lynda would lie there watching the events. He had an exercise bike, so I'd be on that watching the Games and getting my exercise. There were

no track finals in the mornings, so watching at that hour was just for the cognoscenti.

We'd go back to sleep after the morning sessions were over—at about 7:00 A.M.—and sleep until noon and be up for what would be the evening session in Barcelona. We'd watch those in the living room. Different people, some of whom had competed in past Olympics, came over and watched with us: Patty Van Wolvelaere was there to see the hurdles, a Finnish guy to watch the hammer throw.

Wilt was a terrific cook; he was real proud of that. There were no maids around; we all cleaned up. And when we went out, we went to Spanish restaurants because we were doing the Barcelona thing. Even though Lynda is female, it was like a bachelors' sports time. Wilt was a fabulous host.

By early 1985, Wilt was into polo. He enrolled in classes at the Los Angeles Equestrian Center and bought a horse named Hollywood from a player in Palm Beach, Florida. At one time, he also owned a second polo horse named Dipper. "I've always had a penchant for horses," Wilt said. "They are great athletes, and I like working with great athletes. I also like keeping the competitive thing going."

Though a neophyte, Wilt became adept enough to play at the Palm Beach polo center. When polo brought him to that area of Florida, he would visit or stay with Stan Lorber, for that is where Wilt's doctor lived in retirement after he had left Philadelphia. (What kind of houseguest was Wilt? "He was a wonderful houseguest, hugely considerate," Dr. Lorber said. "He was never reluctant to help clear the table or do the dishes. He was not pretentious.")

Wilt eventually stopped playing polo, not least because of the enormous cost of keeping and feeding a horse and also Wilt's concern that his weight might be harmful to the animal. He did, however, keep his custom-made polo equipment: a leather saddle, a pair of high riding boots, a polo mallet, a helmet, and two pairs of unworn riding pants with tags reading, "Exclusively made for Wilt Chamberlain, January 1985." These were among scores of personal items auctioned off by Wilt's estate following his death.

Wilt's interest in encouraging young men and women to participate in sports and his generosity are both manifest in his contact with Peter Westbrook, winner of 13 national fencing titles, a six-time Olympian, and a bronze medalist in the 1984 Olympics—the first medal to be won by a United States fencer since 1960. Westbrook is also, among many other things, a black man who teaches fencing to young black men and women in New York. Some of his students have risen to be among the top saber fencers in the United States and have been members of the United States Olympic team. In 1996 Wilt heard about Westbrook's work and his foundation. Westbrook describes what happened next:

> He called me up and said, "This is great—black kids fencing. I had your organization checked out and, from now on, I want to give to your organization every year." I couldn't believe it.
>
> And every year he supported us. He sent me the first check maybe two weeks after our first conversation. He would send me handwritten notes congratulating me for doing such a good job. He always stayed in touch, either in person or through his friend, Zelda [Spoelstra]. I never met him; we only spoke on the phone. I didn't think there was a rush to meet him. I always thought we could meet the next year or the year after.

Wilt's life after basketball wasn't only polo and tennis matches and trips to Europe. There was money to earn because, in his day, even the greatest of professional athletes didn't sign contracts for $20 or $50 million. But he was not obsessed with accumulating more and more money; rather, he endeavored to earn enough to maintain his lifestyle and to help people in need.

Some of Wilt's income came from endorsements—one of his most important and longest running with the Spalding Company, makers of sporting equipment. He also entered into an agreement with a company to publicize its big-and-tall men's clothing line, and he was paid well by major companies, such as American Express and Volkswagen, to promote their products in commercials. Wilt drank gallons of 7 Up and thought, rightly or wrongly, that the reason the soft drink company never approached him about representing its product was because he was black. A description of a scene that included Wilt drinking copious quantities of 7 Up, sometimes mixed with orange juice, was the only item Wilt asked David Shaw to remove from the very fine book they collaborated on in 1973. Wilt didn't want to give 7 Up the free publicity.

On a personal *and* business level, Wilt watched his "nickels," as his dear friend Dr. Stan Lorber observed, and, about some matters, people might even say Wilt was tight. Lorber recalled one example of Wilt's selective spending: "Wilt might go into a store, pick up a pair of shoes that cost $200, and say, 'I'm not buying these' [implying they cost too much money], but then go to Hong Kong and buy 20 pairs of shoes. He counted every dollar, except when he was the host: then the sky was the limit."

Matty Simmons, with whom Wilt owned harness-racing horses in the sixties, experienced a more difficult side of Wilt the businessman. He and Wilt had a falling-out when Simmons was going to start *Weight Watchers* magazine and asked Wilt if he wanted to invest. According to Simmons, Wilt suggested that he should be given shares rather than have to buy any because when people found out he was involved, Wilt reasoned, the publicity would be good for the magazine. Said Simmons, "I told him I didn't think too many people were going to go out and buy *Weight Watchers* magazine because Wilt Chamberlain was a stockholder. So he got annoyed with me, and we drifted apart. He expected, as most stars do, something for nothing."

That wasn't always the case. For example, Wilt sat on the board of (and in the late seventies invested money in) Altius, a small California company that made storage cabinets. The owner of that company, Joe Mazin, said Wilt was sharp, curious, grasped business problems, and came up with sensible solutions. Board meetings were held every two months and, for a few years, Wilt came to every one of them, then started to lose interest, at which point his attendance tapered off. "But I'm grateful that he was there at the beginning," Mazin recalled, "because it was important to me to have him and other like-minded investors."

In 1986 Wilt teamed up with some Canadian entrepreneurs whom he had met through his visits to the Toronto Film Festival, and they tried—unsuccessfully— to bring an NBA franchise to Toronto. Wilt envisioned himself as a general manager on the would-be team. (Ten years later Toronto finally did acquire an NBA team.)

In the late nineties, Wilt Chamberlain's family-style, sports-themed restaurant opened in Boca Raton, Florida. Wilt had been spending time each winter in the Miami Beach or Boca Raton areas, so opening a restaurant in southeast Florida made sense. Although he and the investors hoped the establishment would someday become the flagship of a nationwide chain, that never happened; eventually, Wilt sold his share in the business. But many people have memories of spotting him in the restaurant in the nineties and, if he was in a "talking mood," of his engaging in conversation, particularly with people who had a Philadelphia connection. Action photographs (one a classic of him out-jumping Bill Russell), reproductions of magazine covers, and memorabilia relating to Wilt's basketball career adorn the restaurant, which flourishes to this day.

Of Wilt's business life, Sy Goldberg observed:

He had all kinds of things going—stocks, real estate. Except for certain areas, he wasn't a big spender. He always did endorsements. He made lots of money; there was always money flowing in. Take his NBA pension: he never needed the money, so he just let it sit there. He didn't know how much it was worth. Then one day [in the mid-nineties], he called them and ended up with a check for over a million dollars.

He was not a money maniac. He gave away untold dollars without anyone knowing about it, including, in some cases, me. He'd give away hundreds of thousands of dollars a year. He'd do an appearance for which he might get $25,000, and he would have the money go directly to a charity. Money was never an issue with him, although sometimes he would go crazy if there was a $10 charge for something that he thought improper.

Instead of chasing money, Wilt chased (and was chased by) something he found much more enjoyable—women. And like with most of his pursuits, he had a need to keep score, although he should have been smart enough to know that is not how that particular "game" is played.

Chapter 22

Sometime in the early eighties, Wilt called me in Philadelphia and said, "I'm going to get married this weekend. I want you to come to the wedding."

"OK, we'll come," I said, then asked, "Who are you going to marry?" He gave me some name. "When is it going to be?" I think he said, "Saturday."

I hear this voice in the background. And this girl gets on the phone. I don't remember her name. And I say, "Is this true?"

And she said, "Yes, we're going to get married this weekend."

I said, "OK, we'll be there."

I hang up and call Wilt's mother. His mother is a very smart lady, very bright—and lovely, by the way. I was her doctor, too, so I knew her well. I said, "Mrs. Chamberlain, I just got a call from Wilt. He says he's going to get married." And I remember her answer as if it were yesterday. She said, "Pshaw, man. He's not going to get married. He's too much in love with himself."

I said, "Were you invited to the wedding?"

She said, "No."

I turned to my wife and said, "We're not buying a ticket to go to California."

I never heard another word about it. But once he didn't invite his mother, I knew it wasn't going to happen.

—Dr. Stan Lorber, longtime doctor and close friend

I'm Getting Married

Why didn't it happen? Why didn't Wilt marry? No one but Wilt truly knows the answer to that question. But close friends, some of whom knew him for 30 or more years, offer clues.

"Wilt and I discussed the subject of marriage time and time again," Dr. Stan Lorber recalled. "There were several women he thought about marrying, but for whatever reason, they were not available. And then, part of his reluctance related to the fact he didn't want to change his lifestyle."

Mady Prowler is one of the children of Milton and Helen Kutsher, whose Catskill resort Wilt visited most summers. Wilt was friendly with the three Kutsher children, two of whom settled in the Philadelphia area. Prowler observed: "He liked to be able to pick up and go at a moment's notice and not be responsible to anybody. His lifestyle didn't lend itself to marriage—so many years of doing his own thing. He got used to that. But I do think in his last years there was a wistfulness and sadness—because he was alone so much. And near the end of his life he really seemed to need to have a connection with old friends. He had a way of losing contact. He was not the best communicator. He could be very warm or moody. You didn't know who you were talking to always."

Whether Prowler and Lorber are correct that Wilt's lifestyle didn't lend itself to marriage, it didn't stop Wilt from fretting over his friends' forthcoming marriages. Before Prowler got married, Wilt called and insisted on talking to her fiancé. "Wilt told Don he better treat me right," she recalled. And when Wilt's doctor, Stan Lorber, was about to remarry, Wilt flew from Los Angeles to Philadelphia and back in the same day—just so he could meet Stan's fiancée and make sure his dear friend was not about to make a mistake.

On the possibility of marriage, Sy Goldberg said, "Wilt told me once there was somebody [the actress Kim Novak] he was really into in the sixties. When somebody would ask him if he were going to marry, he usually had a story that went something like this: 'I'm looking for a rich Jewish girl, and when I find her I'm going to marry.' And there were times when he would say to me, 'I found this one or that one.' But it was always a gag."

Al Correll met Wilt when they both were growing up in West Philadelphia. Correll was personally recruited by Wilt and attended Kansas University in the late fifties. He saw Wilt many times over the ensuing years, referring to him by the nickname "Dip," as do most of Wilt's old Philly friends and associates:

> I always felt Dip didn't marry because he didn't know if it was his money or him. I never really knew him to see someone steady. I know some of the "nice" women he dated at Kansas. Whatever the reason, you'll never hear them talk about Dip. Usually women tell some stuff about a guy. But I never heard them talk about him.

Correll's observation jibes with those of Shannon Bennett, a fraternity brother with whom Wilt was close during their time at Kansas University, and Bruce O'Neil, a buddy from his Hawaiian period in the eighties. "We talked about marriage many times," O'Neil recalled. "It always came down to Wilt never finding anyone who wasn't caught up in his celebrity as opposed to him as a person."

The period during which Correll observed Wilt or knew about him from mutual Kansas friends was prior to the California period of Wilt's life, about which Correll acknowledges he knows nothing. But of the pre-California Wilt—1955 to 1969—Correll observed: "Wilt was not interested in dinner and meeting a girl's family. Many of the women he dealt with—I'm not denigrating them—he often found at nightclubs. He also dealt with a lot of 'ladies of the night.'"

David Shaw, then a young reporter for the *Los Angeles Times*, was selected by Wilt to collaborate on his autobiography, a fine book published in 1973. Shaw spent hours a day for many months with Wilt, and they remained in touch long after the publication of the book, occasionally talking on the phone and meeting for dinner once or twice a year. Shaw observed, "Wilt never liked to admit any kind of weakness, physical or otherwise. I always thought one of the reasons he never married is you can't be married and be Superman. You can't appear invulnerable to your mate."

That view rings true to Jessica Burstein, a photographer whom Wilt relentlessly pursued when they met in the late seventies. While, according to

Burstein, they were never physically intimate, she and Wilt became friends, got together on some of his trips to New York in the eighties and nineties, and talked about once a month during the high point of their relationship. She, too, believes that Wilt never married because he could never truly reveal himself to a mate.

Still another perspective on Wilt's psyche is the one offered by Lynda Huey, who invested decades in a relationship with Wilt. "Wilt didn't know how to love, to let anyone in," she maintained. "He feared intimacy and had an inability to combine friendship and sexuality." If true—and the author wouldn't presume to say that it is or is not—then Wilt acted out the "Madonna-whore" complex, to which many men are prone: they can imagine friendship or sexual relations with a woman, but not both.

"As for marriage," Huey continued, "Wilt believed in marriage, even though he wasn't capable of it himself." Indeed, she remembered how Wilt was critical of a mutual friend who lived with and was supported by one woman, but who still fathered sons by many different women. It offended Wilt's sense of morality, Huey maintained.

Wilt told Alan Shifman, the young man whom he took under his large "wing" the last few years of his life, that it was not natural to commit to one partner. According to Shifman, "He didn't regret not being married. 'Imagine being with a 60-year-old woman,' Wilt said [to me], shuddering and making a sour face at what to him was a dismal picture. And he wouldn't date anyone over 25."

Huey claims that toward the end of his life, Wilt talked a lot about wanting to be married and she sensed a yearning. But Wilt liked to keep himself a mystery. He did not have one friend who knew the whole picture: he compartmentalized his friends more than most people, as they all attest. So while he might have mused to Huey about marrying, he might not have meant it. (Or he might have: that was Wilt.)

At some point in the eighties Wilt had a special female friend in Argentina, a physician he would visit in Buenos Aires, according to Bob Billings, his Kansas buddy. But, suggested Dr. Stan Lorber, that doesn't signify much because Wilt had female friends *everywhere*. In the nineties he was involved with a woman from Vancouver, British Columbia, and he told Mike Richman he was thinking of marrying the Canadian woman, whose name and anything else about her (save her nationality) remained unknown to even close friends. Whatever the degree of intimacy and seriousness, the relationship fizzled out, Richman said.

Having observed his parents' successful union, Wilt certainly had a role model for marriage. But witness to (and later commenting on) the infidelities among most of his fellow NBA players, many of whom were married, Wilt might have realized, even in his twenties, that he would not be able to keep the marriage vows, which—as he regarded himself a moral man—he took seriously.

As for children, sportswriter Dick Schaap suggested that, considering all the women Wilt had been with, one would think that he would have had an illegitimate child, but Schaap had never heard of any. (Nor has anyone ever claimed there are any.) "Wilt's only vice was that he was a Republican," Schaap, a liberal Democrat, joked affectionately.

Or a more serious topic, however, Wilt did say, and friends confirm, that he thought the world already had too many people: he didn't want, or apparently need, to add any little Wilties to the world's number; and he made sure—by using prophylactics, he stated—that he was not going to impregnate anyone. Acquaintances and close friends agree that Wilt was great around and with children, and some people who knew him felt sad that he had missed the rewards of fatherhood. Mady Prowler, who was almost like a sister to Wilt, fondly recalled Wilt lifting her three-month-old daughter out of her carriage, tenderly holding the infant in the palm of his huge hand.

———

Even though the above opinions have been offered by people who knew him well, in some cases over many, many years, their observations remain speculative: *Wilt* is the only person who knows why he never married (and he is not alive to ask).

So one must rely on credible witnesses, such as those who have been quoted and others, such as Fluke Fluker, a gentle, thoughtful, huge (at 6'5") black man whom Wilt befriended at the Mid-Valley Racquetball Club in the early nineties where both worked out. Fluker observed: "I feel that deep down, as Wilt got older and reviewed his life, he regretted never having had just one woman. I'm a married man. He told me on many, many occasions that I am a lucky man."

Chapter 23

I like women. People are curious about my sex life and, to most people, the number of women who have come and gone through my bedrooms—and various hotel rooms around the country—would boggle the mind.

—Wilt Chamberlain

I've been with him enough to watch the way he functions. There were women everywhere. We were in Europe, in Milan, in 1982. [Wilt was 46.] We went to a disco and sat down at a table. There were probably 50 to 100 young girls there, and one by one they came over wanting to know if he would dance with them or have a drink with them. It was like honey and a beehive—all the bees were flocking. You don't see that with too many people.

—Dr. Stan Lorber, longtime doctor and close friend

It was a hobby with him. Some people go bird-watching. Some people collect stamps. He collected meeting women.

—Sy Goldberg, longtime friend and attorney

I have read a zillion words about me and never has anyone talked of my sensuality or sensitivity.

—Wilt Chamberlain in *A View from Above*, the book published in October 1991 in which he claimed to have made love to twenty thousand women

There Were Women
Everywhere

When he very publicly revealed the astounding number of women he said he had sex with, Wilt guaranteed that people would write and talk about his sensuality, though not in the way he imagined. His timing could not have been worse: a little more than a month after the publication of Wilt's book, Earvin "Magic" Johnson, another prominent black athlete, held a press conference at which he revealed to a stunned world that he had the AIDS virus, the acknowledged result of his own promiscuity. Though Magic Johnson was—and is—married, and while Wilt was (and remained) a single man and didn't have AIDS, the public lumped them together. Wilt was tarred with Magic Johnson's brush, so to speak.

The sexual claim transformed the public's perception of Wilt and "turned him into a reference for sexual braggadocio," as one newspaper reporter commented. Tennis star Arthur Ashe criticized both Wilt and Magic Johnson, writing in his 1993 memoir:

> African Americans have spent decades denying that we are sexual primitives by nature, as racists have argued since the days of slavery. These two college-trained black men of international fame and immense personal wealth do their best to reinforce the stereotype.

Ashe added, "I felt more pity than sorrow for Wilt as his macho accounting backfired on him in the form of a wave of public criticism." (The same year his memoir was published, Ashe, himself, died of AIDS, contracted from a tainted blood transfusion during heart surgery.)

Wilt's response to the considerable criticism leveled against him was, "I'm not boasting. I don't see all this lovemaking as any kind of conquest." And elsewhere he said, ". . . the point of using the number [twenty thousand] was to show that sex was a great part of my life as basketball was a great part of my life. That's the reason I was single."

Wilt's closest friends and family, particularly his sister Barbara, are still defensive about the subsequent brouhaha that followed the publication of *A View from Above*. And brouhaha there was—feminists were outraged; comedians had a field day. Never mind that Wilt also wrote in *A View from Above*: "Most men would think it a great achievement if they could make love to a thousand different women. But I've come to believe the greater achievement would be to make love to the same woman a thousand times." No one remembers that.

George Brown, a member of the black establishment, had an on-again, off-again relationship with Wilt, but knew him well enough to know that Wilt respected women:

> We talked many times over the years about how the black man could not have made it in this country without the strength of the black woman. The sisters, wives, mothers, grandmothers who sacrificed so the black man could survive. Wilt had women he looked to and respected—but as women, not as lovers.

When Tommy Kearns, the North Carolina guard who became a good friend and advised Wilt on some investments, heard about the twenty-thousand-women passage, his thoughts turned to Wilt's mother, who, he noted, "was a very dominant figure in Wilt's life." Kearns declared:

> I would bet that Wilt wouldn't have published that book while she was alive. I said to him, "Wilt, you're in your mid-fifties, you've made it, you're a good guy. There's nothing in the world you have to prove, except what I know—that you're a decent human being. And people adore you for that. You don't need it [the commotion in the aftermath of the twenty-thousand-women statement]. If it happened, it's history."

To Wilt's friends, the passage was a throwaway line that Wilt inserted to create publicity for the book. And they blame the publisher for manipulating Wilt into including it.

"They made him do it to sell books," said Zelda Spoelstra. "It cost him hundreds of thousands of dollars in endorsements. People don't realize that with his own money, Wilt sponsored women's track teams and female Olympians like Jackie Joyner. And how much he respected women, starting with his mother and sisters."

Ironically, in view of the ensuing flap, Wilt was excited when he signed the contract to do the book, according to his friend Jessica Burstein, a New York photographer, who said that while Wilt was writing *View* he'd call her and read excerpts from it. "He wanted people to know that he was smart. He always felt people didn't think he was smart." Burstein said that at the last moment Wilt had "terrible misgivings" about including the twenty-thousand-women line in the book. She claims that she told him it was a mistake to put it in the book. First, she said she told him, the figure was a gross exaggeration—"You followed me around Vienna for four days [when they first met], and nothing happened"; second, whether the number was even remotely accurate, the book reviewers (and public) would focus on his sex life—to the exclusion of anything else he had to say in the book. Which is exactly what came to pass. "I felt terrible," Burstein said. "He had been used, and I told him that."

Would that someone had succeeded in preventing Wilt from making such a fool of himself—and instead of the twenty-thousand-women passage he (or his editor) had written, "I like and have had lots of women." But who is to say Wilt would have acquiesced in deleting it? Maybe the towering, skinny, gawked-at 16-year-old boy, whom one childhood friend remembers in pants that were much too short, and whom the girls in Philadelphia considered a freak and were loath to date, had to show the world he had bedded many women.

Whatever the case, sex played an important role in Wilt's life. "It was just unbelievable," recalled Tracy Sundlun, a track coach and entrepreneur who met Wilt in the early seventies through Lynda Huey and became a pal. "We'd eat dinner in a restaurant. He'd go to the bathroom and he'd come back five minutes later and throw a handful of phone numbers on the table. . . . It was unreal."

In the early nineties, Wilt would amble into the fashionable Mid-Valley Racquetball Club in the late morning or early afternoon to work out with free weights and, hoping to improve his deteriorating hip, to walk on a treadmill. There he met Fluke Fluker, who had many opportunities to observe and interact with Wilt, and who shared his impressions:

He enjoyed life. He enjoyed people. He enjoyed conversation. And he enjoyed women. He would stop in the middle of a conversation if a pretty woman walked by. He would either look at her or make a comment to the people he was talking to. And it wasn't a gross or vulgar or disrespectful comment. Or he'd call the woman over and compliment her on her looks, in a nice, respectful way. He'd say, "I just want you to know you're looking very beautiful today. And I wanted to make sure someone told you that." He was not like some shark. He would put it out there, in terms of what he thought about you. And if the woman was receptive, it would go to the next level. If not, that was cool, too.

At one time, Rod Roddewig, a contemporary of Wilt's, owned a West Hollywood bar and grill where athletes and TV and movie people hung out. That's where he met Wilt before moving to Hawaii in the mid-eighties. He recalled the origin of the twenty-thousand-women passage:

Here's how it came about. Wilt invited me to stay over with him at his penthouse in Honolulu. We were there for 10 days. I wrote everything down in my Daytimer. Every time he would go to bed with a different girl, I would put a check in my book. After 10 days there were 23 checks.

That's 2.3 girls per day.

He took 2.3 and divided it in half, to be conservative. Then deducted 15 from his current age, multiplied that by 1.2 women per day, and that's how he came up with twenty thousand.

Dick Schaap, a prolific and acclaimed sportswriter who covered, and knew, most of the great athletes from 1965 until his death in 2001, liked Wilt. They dined together a number of times, and Schaap and his third wife stayed at Wilt's home. About the brouhaha, he had this to say:

Wilt came to me and said he wanted to do a book about the reaction of the public to the twenty-thousand-women statement. I was very tempted. We wanted to do it funny. There was much more of a reaction than an action. It was very much a throwaway line. It didn't bother him [the hullabaloo]. He told me that his favorite of all the jokes, cartoons, commentaries in reaction to the line was a television skit in which a young woman and her mother approach what looks like the wall at the Vietnam War Memorial. And the mother says to the daughter, "Is this the Vietnam Wall?" And the daughter says, "No, this is a list of the women who went to bed with Wilt Chamberlain. Here's my name." And the mother says, "Here's mine."

Dr. Lorber recalled the time he was in a European airport with Wilt, and a magnificently dressed, stunning black woman came over to Wilt. When they finished their conversation and she had walked away, Wilt told Lorber that she was a top model in Europe and that they had been together many times. To which the doctor observed: "She came over to him. He didn't go to her. And that was the usual story. He didn't push. He was very attractive to women of all colors."

And he liked them in all colors, though he got into trouble with women of his own race when he announced in the early seventies that he preferred to date white women over black women because the former were more sophisticated and more sexually liberated. Whether he believed that into the eighties and nineties, one can't say. He had his share (and then some) of Asian women when he used to visit Hawaii, which he did for about four months every winter in the eighties. There he spent his days playing beach volleyball and working out, his nights working out, too—only with girls instead of volleyballs. While this may have been his "Asian women" period, he preferred the blonde, California beach-girl look, according to Lynda Huey (herself a blonde), because they tended to be healthy looking and athletic—two attributes he prized in women.

"Women were all over Wilt," Tommy Kearns observed. "They were just fascinated by this guy. He told me that if he had a woman over at the house, he would never let her spend the night. And he would rarely meet a girl a second time. But, it's funny, all the times I stayed at Wilt's house [about 20 times], with the exception of Lynda, who joined us some of the time [and with whom Wilt had, by that time, a platonic relationship], I never saw other women. Maybe they came in the back door, I don't know."

Many of Wilt's friends made a similar observation: they always saw him alone—somewhat ironic for a man who claimed to have known, in the biblical sense, so many women.

Jerry Saperstein, whose father, Abe, founded the Harlem Globetrotters, knew Wilt for many years. When the Globies and Wilt toured Europe during the summers in the sixties, Jerry traveled with them:

> There's not a lot I can say about the twenty-thousand-women claim except I was there for part of it. And he may have undercounted. Women were particularly drawn to him. We'd be sitting in a restaurant and an attractive woman would come up and hand Wilt her key.

Journalist Schaap recalled the time he was eating with Wilt at Carmine's, one of Wilt's favorite restaurants in Los Angeles, and a beautiful young woman came over with her date. Said Schaap: "She explained to us she was on a new TV series called *S.W.A.T.*, which became popular. And she handed Wilt her telephone number in front of her date. That was wild."

There are stories galore of Wilt meeting and picking up women at restaurants. Sy Goldberg reminisced about the time he was with Wilt at Spago's, one of the hottest restaurants in Los Angeles. They were dining with one of the owners and his wife, and Wilt pointed out a redheaded woman he was attracted to who was sitting with a man at another table. Wanting to know more about them, the owner called over the maitre'd and learned that the man had been bringing the woman to eat at Spago's several times a week for a number of months, and they always sat at an "A" table.

Keeping his eye on the table, Wilt noted the redhead getting up and asked the owner's wife to follow her to the restroom and get her phone number. Ten minutes later, task accomplished, she returned to the table and related the conversation:

> I went into the ladies' room and said, "Somebody in our party admired you and would like to know if you were interested in giving him your phone number."
>
> The redhead replied, "You mean Wilt?"
>
> So she told me, "You know, I go out with this guy. I've been seeing him for a couple of months. He's got millions and millions of dollars. He treats me great. But he leaves town, and I get lonesome. I'd love to see Wilt."

Why were women so attracted to Wilt? David Shaw, who collaborated on Wilt's first book, shared his opinion: "He was a very good-looking, charismatic guy, who was big and who was famous. Certainly, there is the celebrity factor and the curiosity factor—they were an initial appeal for a lot of women."

Said Lynda Huey: "When he was on and he was out in public, he was the most charming, the most gregarious host—he was hosting the world at our table. He could be unbelievably charming and funny and quick-witted, great with one-liners. And he knew a lot of details and information from reading."

Gene Selznick, the great American volleyball player, was one of Wilt's closest buddies during the last 30 years of Wilt's life and was often the third person when Wilt took a woman out. He recalled that Wilt would wine and dine his date and buy a bottle or two of champagne. "And then, if they wanted to, they would come home to his house," Selznick said. "It was never a rush. Wilt was not a guy to put any pressure on a girl—ever. Wilt never had one exclusive girl. He didn't just have one-night stands, more like ten-night stands. He didn't want to get attached. No one girl could ever say that she was going with Wilt Chamberlain, that Wilt Chamberlain was her boyfriend. No one ever tied him down to anything."

David Shaw dined with Wilt numerous times over 26 years, during which period Wilt never brought the same woman as his date twice; in fact, most of the time he showed up alone. While acknowledging that Wilt could be an "absolutely delightful dinner companion," Shaw's opinion of how Wilt treated his dates contrasts with that of Gene Selznick. Shaw, who has been married three times, recalled:

> Wilt always treated the women I brought along—my wives, and girl-friends in between—with absolute courtesy and respect. And he always treated whatever women he brought along like shit. I can remember him leaving his date at our table to go flirt with and get a phone number [from a woman] at an adjacent table. But that was who he was. And these women knew that. So I didn't feel deeply aggrieved on their behalf as I might have with someone else. They were with him for their own ulterior motives, and if this was the price they had to pay, they were willing to pay it.

Sy Goldberg has this perspective on his famous friend:

> Ordinary people, particularly women, loved being with him—they loved knowing him. They had nothing but fond memories and, years later, if he happened to run into them, they considered him a friend. In all the years we were together, close to 40 years, I don't think I went to dinner with him, with a date, more than three or four times. He didn't date in the conventional way. . . . If we went out—and we went out often—it was either him and me or the two of us and my wife. He didn't have to go out and date.
>
> He was not what some people might think of as a "sexual predator"—not by any stretch of the imagination. He liked young girls. He liked to be with them. He liked to talk to them. He liked to schmooze with them. He liked to flirt with them. But it was not a matter of "slam, bam, thank you ma'am." Wilt's girls always left happy. And I would know if it were different.

There were many women who came in and out of Wilt's life, and with most of them he had a physical relationship. However, for whatever reason, the majority of them chose to keep their memories of, and experiences with, Wilt to themselves.

Not that Wilt got every woman he desired. Annette Tannander Bank participated in two Olympic Games for her native Sweden—she was a high jumper in the 1976 Montreal Games when she was 18; and she competed in the long jump and heptathlon in the 1984 Los Angeles Games when she was 26. She and a fellow Swede were both training at the University of Southern California in 1976 when she met Wilt through a mutual friend. He was 40, she was 19. She was and is a beautiful woman—great figure, pretty face, lovely blonde hair. Now a personal trainer in Colorado, she shared some memories of the time she and her friend were among a group invited to a barbecue at Wilt's:

> I think Wilt hit on everything that moved. He hit both on me and my friend Lena. That was just part of the game he played, to see if people would go for it or not. He was never bad or rude. He was a flirt, to see if there was a response. If there wasn't, he wouldn't keep going. Maybe he would say something like, "Why don't you spend the night?"

And we said, "No, we're going to go. We got to go home." He's hitting on me and Lena, and [I think] Lynda [Huey] is there.

Tommy Kearns III, the son of Wilt's friend, is a producer for NBA Entertainment. He vividly remembers the first time he met Wilt:

We were in Los Angeles. It's 1980. I'm 16. My father had taken me out there, and we were having dinner with Wilt and seven or eight other people. Wilt shows up a little late and sits down across the table from me. I remember him sticking his big paw, from all the way on the other side of the table, into my plate of french fries and saying, "You don't mind if I have a couple of these, do you?" I had no say in the matter. That was my first introduction to Wilt Chamberlain.

At some point during the dinner I have to go to the bathroom. Wilt says, "Let me accompany you, son." So we go to the bathroom. On the way back, we stop at the bar. He says to me, "Come over here, young man," and the minute we sit down, the room stops. Everyone wanted to hang around with Wilt. Four or five beautiful women come over and he's charming two on the right and charming two on the left. After a while, he says, "Well, let me get back to the table. But take care of this young man."

He attracted people from all walks of life. He had magnetism about him. Some of it was his size. But he was also a friendly guy. They use the cliché "larger than life." Some people have an aura. Wilt had it. But I also could sense that he needed the attention and affection of people. Sometimes you can feel it with people like that.

By no means did Wilt sleep with every woman he encountered, even those who might have been more than willing, for any number of reasons. Michael D'Angelico, a bartender at the Resorts Hotel in Atlantic City in the eighties and a great fan of Wilt's, remembers the time he met Wilt when Wilt was a guest at the hotel. One of the other bartenders, known only by the name of "Fleet," had previously worked in Las Vegas as a valet and knew a lot of celebrities. D'Angelico continued:

Fleet was always telling us that he knew Wilt and would see him in New York. One day Fleet said to me and Henry, another bartender, "Listen: Wilt's coming in during the week. I'm gonna be with him, and I'll bring him in about 2:00 in the morning," which is when we usually finished work.

Sure enough, Fleet comes walking in with the Big Guy, who spends about 15 or 20 minutes with us. He's extremely polite and cordial; you couldn't ask for anything more.

After Wilt went upstairs to his hotel room, Henry says, "Gee, what a wonderful guy Wilt is. We ought to do something for him."

I said, "What the hell are you talking about? What can we do for that guy? He's got everything."

Henry says, "Let's send him up a broad," to which I responded, "You've got to be out of your mind."

As luck would have it—well, not luck—there were a million hookers in that joint. Henry goes over to the other side of the bar, talks to an attractive woman, and she leaves. I said, "What'd you do, Henry?"

"I sent her up to Wilt's room, and I told her to tell him it was a present from the bartender." I thought he was crazy, but he wasn't worried about it.

Well, we're sitting there finishing a drink and the phone rang behind the bar. Sure enough, the call is for Henry, and it's Wilt, and he's screaming at Henry. No sooner did Henry hang up the phone than the girl comes walking down. Henry asks her what happened, and she says, "Wilt said, 'Thank you, but no thank you,' and he shut the door."

The next night at about the same time, 2:00 A.M., Henry and I are sitting at the bar. I feel a hand around my neck. It's Wilt and he's got both of us by the neck and he's shaking us very lightly. "What the hell are you two guys doing?" he asks. "Do you want to get me in trouble? Don't you think I . . ." and then he starts to laugh.

We look at him, and Henry says, "You know, Wilt, we just wanted to thank you."

He says, "Don't you think I can get my own woman, fellas? I appreciate it, but don't do me any more favors."

Then he stayed for about an hour and a half, and we just talked basketball and different things. In the course of that hour and a half,

I don't know how many people came up to him to shake his hand and say a few words. He refused to sign any autographs, telling those who asked, "Look, I'm over here having a conversation with my friends. I appreciate everything you said, but if I start signing autographs, I'm going to have a line here."

I asked him if there was anyplace he could go and not get recognized, and wondered how he put up with it.

He answered, "You know, Mike, people mean well. I'm not gonna remember all the people I meet in a given day, but they're gonna remember me, and I want them to have a good memory."

I've met and waited on a lot of celebrities. I can tell you stories about other celebrities that are not so good. But Wilt was one of the nicest and most pleasant.

While the twenty thousand number is probably an exaggeration, let no one doubt Wilt's gargantuan sexual appetite. David Shaw remembers an incident when the Lakers were on the road, and he and Vince Miller were with Wilt in Wilt's room. At about 11:00 P.M. a woman called, wanting to come and see Wilt. Shaw heard Wilt say to her, "Well, I've already had you, why should I want to see you again? Maybe if you found a girlfriend I'd want to see you again."

According to Shaw, another woman called a little bit later and she also wanted to come see Wilt. "Well," Wilt told her, "I have a meeting going on now. Why don't you come up at 12:00?"

This was followed a few minutes later with a second call from the first woman. She had found a girlfriend, so Wilt told her, "Well, I have another meeting at 12:00. Why don't you come up at 3:00?" Shaw continues his story:

Wilt ushered [me and] Vince out a few minutes before 12:00. Vince went to his room, but I, being an intrepid reporter, went down to the lobby and staked out the elevator. And a good-looking young woman arrived at midnight, pushed the button for Wilt's floor, and went up. At 3:00, the first woman had not come down yet and two more women came, pushed the button for Wilt's floor, and went up. I was in the lobby sitting right by the elevator. Once they went up to Wilt's floor I went to my room.

As I recall, about 5:00 in the morning the phone rang. It was Wilt. He said, "Hell, man, all three are still here. I need your help."

"Wilt," I said, "I told you when we started this book, I wouldn't carry your bags or bed your women." And I hung up the phone. I suspect over the years any number of his friends were all too grateful for his leftovers, or whatever you want to call them.

As great as his basketball achievements are, Wilt's promiscuity, like it or not, is also part of his legacy. People, particularly nonsports fans, mistakenly think that is all there was to the man—and, for that, he has no one to blame but himself. But to keep matters in perspective, Wilt has never been accused of abusing a woman, fathering an illegitimate child, abusing drink, taking drugs, or committing crimes. On the contrary, in those respects, he led an exemplary life. The "worst" thing he can be accused of is that, as a single man, he had lots of women—every one of them willing and every one of them, according to Wilt, unmarried at the time of their relationship.

Bob Billings, his old Kansas roommate, summed up Wilt's reputation this way:

Wilt was a prodigious person. They put a pencil to it [the claim of twenty thousand women] and said, "Well, Wilt would have had to do this, this, and this." What they don't understand is that Wilt could do "that, that, and that." I don't know about the twenty thousand women. Wilt was not someone who needed to pump himself up.

Most people would think of his sexual exploits as being the biggest part of his life. Actually, it was just a part of his life. It's the good things he did for people—that was the thing no one really understands. . . . We didn't talk about Wilt's sexual conquests. He just liked women. It would have been difficult for him to be with only one.

Chapter 24

I had seen Wilt at a number of U.S. national track championships but never had the guts to introduce myself to him. But in 1990, I was in the Seattle airport when Wilt walked passed me. I said, "Wilt!"—kind of like a little kid—and he kind of ignored me and kept walking. I repeated, "Wilt," but he kept walking. Finally, I said, "Mr. Chamberlain, I have to introduce myself. My name is Scott Huffman. I'm pole vaulting at the Goodwill Games; I'm a University of Kansas graduate." And when he heard that, he stopped and said, "Hey, nice to meet you. Good luck." And he told me he was going to be at the Games.

The next day I was out there warming up, and I was real nervous. I hear from the stands, about 30 rows up, "Rock chalk, Jayhawk"; and I look up to see who's yelling at me—it's Wilt Chamberlain, pumping his fist and pointing to me. It really fired me up to know he was looking at me. I had a really good competition.

—Scott Huffman, Olympic pole vaulter

Many of us sportswriters thought Wilt was, by far, better than Russell, both as an athlete and a person. I try to like [Russell] because I believe in many of the things he believes in—much more than I believed with Wilt. But Russell's just not likeable; and Wilt was lovable—a lovable giant."

—Dick Schaap, sportswriter, commentator, and author

Rock Chalk, Jayhawk

I t was at the All-Star Game weekend in Cleveland in February 1997 that the two most famous (and many argue the two greatest) basketball players ever—Wilt Chamberlain and Michael Jordan—met for the first time. That was the NBA's All-Star Game at which the game's 50 greatest players were also honored. People were surprised that Wilt and Jordan had never met, but, once retired, Wilt watched, though rarely attended, NBA games. And Wilt and Jordan traveled in different circles and places. As Wilt quipped, "I play volleyball and he plays golf. He tries to stay out of sand traps, and I'm always in the sand traps." (Sadly, by 1997, Wilt's days of jumping on a volleyball court were over because of his arthritic hip.)

Wilt did not look or feel well—and not because, by 1997, his hairline had receded and he was bald. He looked tired and had large bags under his eyes, and his rich, chocolate-colored skin had an unhealthy pallor. In addition, his legs were retaining water. He was showing the effects of edema, a condition that develops when the heart isn't working correctly, causing, among other problems, excessive fluid to accumulate in the body.

Before departing for Cleveland he had told Zelda Spoelstra, his close friend who would be at the All-Star Game as part of her NBA responsibilities, that his legs were so swollen that he could barely walk. But he also said to her, "Don't worry, I'll be there if I have to come on crutches," which, thankfully, he did not. (After Wilt arrived, the Cleveland Cavaliers' team doctor wrote a prescription for medicine to alleviate the symptoms.)

Also present at that special All-Star weekend was Bill Russell, though no one, including Michael Jordan or Russell, attracted more eyes and attention from the public—even from the other NBA players, past and present—than Wilt, people who were there attest. (And that would be the case in *any* gathering, with only Muhammad Ali and Elvis excepted).

There was no individual rivalry in basketball (and perhaps never in all of sports) to match that of Chamberlain and Russell. Although Larry Bird and Magic Johnson played each other in three NBA Finals, they didn't cover one another, their teams didn't play one another eight to ten times per season as Wilt's and Russell's did, and their teams never met *eight* times for either the division or NBA titles.

Most sports fans know that in the early years of their careers, 1959–1962, Russell would eat at the home of Wilt's family when the Celtics were in Philadelphia for the Thanksgiving night game; and when the Warriors were on the road and playing in Boston, Wilt would often visit Russell's home and play with his electric trains. Russell's teams won the championships; Wilt set records by the boatload. Goaded on by the press, a wedge gradually developed between two men who had been fairly friendly. It gnawed at Wilt that Russell's team won the championships and he was labeled a loser. And, according to Wilt, Russell envied his celebrity and his bachelor lifestyle. Russell might have the championship rings but, as Maurice King, a college teammate of Wilt's and a professional one of Russell's for one year, observed: "You get the two of them together in a room and people would gravitate to Wilt."

The television sportscaster Bob Costas interviewed Wilt and Russell together at the 1997 All-Star gathering. At one point in the interview, after observing Wilt and Russell interacting, Costas said they had become like the *Sunshine Boys*, a reference to the play and movie of the same name about the almost lifelong partnership of two intrinsically linked, crotchety, old vaudevillians who had a love-hate relationship.

The Russell-Wilt interview with Costas was a mutual admiration society in which the two basketball stars went out of their respective ways to sing the praises of the other. It was during this interview that Russell made a very public apology to Wilt for something that had occurred almost 30 years earlier.

"I said something I shouldn't have said," Russell declared. "I was wrong."

"What was that?" Costas asked.

"I'm not going to go into that. I apologized to him. What I said was wrong and injurious to him. I apologized to him," said Russell in his public mea culpa.

The incident to which Russell referred was his criticism of Wilt for removing himself in the last quarter of Game 7 in the 1969 NBA Finals after Wilt had injured his knee (the same knee in which a tendon was ruptured early the following season). At the time, Russell said Wilt had copped out. They didn't talk for two decades after Russell's comment, during which, it should be noted, Wilt spoke and wrote his share of criticisms of Russell, some of them also probably unfair.

Wilt appreciated Russell's public apology, coming after the private one, and as both men were now older, they were obviously willing to forgive and forget old hurts—at least, in Wilt's case, for public consumption. Privately, according to Jerry Saperstein, son of the founder of the Globetrotters, and Tommy Kearns, a close friend, Wilt continued to criticize Russell for the way in which he "intellectualized" playing defense and basketball in general.

If history is an argument without end, so too is the question of who was the better basketball player—Wilt Chamberlain or Bill Russell. There are coaches, players, writers, and fans on each side of the divide.

"I always believed that Wilt was more of a basketball player than Russell, and that would irritate Russell," observed the respected writer Leonard Koppett. "If you ask yourself, 'Imagine Wilt with the Celtics teams, then how much would they have won?' Or more revealing, put Russell on Wilt's teams, how many titles would they have won? The reason Wilt's teams were taking Russell's teams to the seventh games in the playoffs was because of Wilt and his incredible ability. It's absolute nonsense to say Wilt dragged his teams down."

Bob Cousy made the case for his Celtics teammate: "Russell had much more intensity than Wilt and skills better suited to playing basketball," he argues. "Russell made us all better players. Wilt, in my opinion, had the opposite effect on his teams." (Then how would Cousy explain 1966–1967 and 1971–1972, when no one can claim that Wilt diminished his teammates?) And then Cousy and his coauthor, Bob Ryan, concluded their point: "Wilt has the numbers. Russell will always have the rings. It was no accident."

Wilt kept reminding all who would listen that basketball is a team game—it wasn't Chamberlain versus Russell, but "the Celtics versus my team. Check the stats. They'll tell you who had the edge. Basketball is more than one guy. The Celtics had a team full of Hall of Famers."

To which Russell had this to say: "It is perfectly possible for a player not to make victory his first priority against all others—money, records, personal fame—and I often felt that Wilt made some deliberate choices in his ambitions."

"Wilt told me many times that the biggest mistake he made in his professional career was not being more physical with Russell," Tommy Kearns recalled. "If Wilt had taken it to him, there is no way Russell could have stopped him."

All of this was further complicated by personal dynamics, to which all mortals are prone—envy and ego and irrationality and, in their case, the pressure of competing head-to-head and of being prominent black men. Who can really define or judge the relationship between these two great athletes and adversaries?

The basketball writers and broadcasters selected Wilt to the All–NBA first team in seven of his first nine seasons; but the players selected Russell as the league's Most Valuable Player five times (to Wilt's four). Furthermore, in 1980 the Professional Basketball Writers Association of America, somewhat inconsistently, selected Russell as the greatest player in the league's history, which Wilt derided as ridiculous.

As to who was better, Bob Pettit, himself one of the giants in the game's history, said, "I've thought about Russell versus Chamberlain and it comes down to a matter of taste. No one ever scored like Wilt, no one ever played defense like Russell. They weren't just giants of their time, but of all time."

Wilt acknowledged numerous times that he might have been more effective had he a "killer instinct." Bob Cousy said as much: "Wilt wanted to be liked; Russell didn't care if you liked him."

Others agree with that assessment. For instance, one writer observed, "The conventional wisdom is that Russell is the winner of the two, the hero, the one with the unforgettable laugh, and Wilt was the big meany, the Goliath that nobody loved. The reality, which sportswriters knew, was that Russell was aloof and moody and distrustful while Wilt was warm, generous, and comfortable in his skin and led a very nice life. Furthermore, Wilt didn't see color, he saw people."

Todd Caso, a producer at NBA Entertainment and basketball historian, summed up the unanswerable question this way:

> I don't think there should be a Wilt camp and a Russell camp. Let's face it, Russell is the greatest winner in team sports—11 titles in 13 tries. Russell is the first guy to tell you he didn't do it alone. Maybe if Wilt had been on those teams, it would have been 13 out of 13. We'll never know.

While in recent years everything has been lovey-dovey between Bill Russell and Boston, it wasn't always so. During his playing career, Russell had a stormy relationship with the people of Boston, believing that he was never properly appreciated and respected by the overwhelmingly white Boston community because he was a proud, outspoken black man.

But the ill will and misunderstandings were put in the past when, in May 1999, Russell agreed to let the Boston Celtics retire—for the second time—his famous No. 6. The first occasion in 1972, reflecting Russell's attitude toward the fans in Boston, was, at Russell's request, private; it was attended only by about a dozen players and friends. The May 1999 affair was anything but private—basketball celebrities such as Oscar Robertson, Julius Erving, Kareem Abdul-Jabbar, Bob Cousy, and John Havlicek were present. The money raised by the paying customers for the second retirement ceremony was earmarked for a charity on whose board of directors Russell sat. But charity wasn't the only thing driving this event: there was also the positive public relations aspect to the ceremony, which Russell's new agent was too clever not to have recognized.

In any case, Wilt did not feel well and was not keen on traveling from Los Angeles to Boston for the Russell affair, a number of his friends confirmed. He kept telling the Russell people he couldn't come, and they kept publicizing that he'd be there. Wilt felt manipulated: if he didn't go, people would say he was a sorehead and spoilsport; if he did go, he knew that he was likely to be the good-natured butt of jokes, for this was Russell's occasion—not his. It speaks well for an ailing Wilt that he did go, for the world would never see the two great warriors together again.

In the 40 years since he had left Lawrence, Kansas, Wilt had, by the late nineties, only returned to the Midwestern town on a few occasions—and never after 1975. Not that he had wanted to cut himself off totally from the Kansas University community: he always remained in touch with Bob Billings, his closest friend from the three years at Kansas. Billings had remained in Lawrence, becoming the developer of Alvamar Country Club and its associated neighborhood of luxury homes. Billings, his wife, and, after she died, his companion often visited Wilt when they were in California. Being a successful businessman, Billings occasionally proffered financial advice to his buddy. He and Wilt talked regularly by telephone—some years they talked once every six months, other years monthly and, at times, even weekly.

Another Kansan who stayed in touch was Joan Edwards, whose husband, Roy, had helped recruit Wilt to Kansas. Wilt, who was not the most dependable of correspondents, might let years pass between contacts with Mrs. Edwards, but he always had a special place in his heart for her. When she underwent surgery, Wilt sent her a get-well card signed, "An Old Jayhawk. Love, Wilt." And she sent him telegrams on the special occasions in his life—like the night in 1991 that the 76ers retired his number.

Soon after that event, Wilt called her for the first time in years, and they talked for an hour, with Mrs. Edwards making a point of telling Wilt how much Lawrence had changed for the good (in racial matters) since his undergraduate days in the mid- to late fifties and that she hoped he'd come back to see for himself. She ended the conversation by saying, "You have to come home."

Monte Johnson, an ex-teammate, always made sure to call on Wilt's birthday, among other times, and sent him articles about the team, university community, or fellow teammates that he thought Wilt might find interesting. For five years, from 1982 to 1987, Johnson was the school's athletic director and wished, like Billings and Mrs. Edwards, that Wilt would consent to attend a ceremony in which his jersey would be retired. Wilt's sister's husband, Elzie Lewis, was from Kansas and was always in touch with family and friends, including one of Wilt's teammates, Maurice King.

The university announced in 1991 that Wilt's jersey was to be retired and, of course, the university wanted to have him present at an official ceremony. But Wilt never responded to the invitation in 1991, nor in subsequent years, and was vague to Billings about whether he would or would not do it some day. Everyone in the small, close-knit college community knew Billings was Wilt's closest Kansas friend, and people would always ask Billings, "Would you ask Wilt to do this or that?" To which Billings replied, "No, you can ask Wilt," explaining, "I never asked Wilt to do anything, other than to ask him if he'd consider coming back to KU to retire his jersey. And I asked him that for 20 years."

Wilt had said on a number of occasions that he was proud to have gone to Kansas, the school where the founder of the game of basketball, James Naismith, had once taught and coached, and so, too, had the great Phog Allen. And Wilt, ever up on statistics, pointed out there were more Jayhawks in the Naismith Memorial Basketball Hall of Fame than from any other Division I school (15 as of 2004). So by no means did Wilt disassociate from his Kansas years, as this recollection of one of his teammates, John Parker, illustrates:

One year I was on vacation in Phoenix when the Lakers were in town for a game. I called up and asked for Wilt Chamberlain. They said, "He's not taking any calls."

I said, "OK, tell him John Parker called and here's my number. Ask him to call back."

And within a few minutes, Wilt called. I said, "Wilt, this is John. I'm down here with my wife and I wanted to know if you could give me a couple of tickets to come to the game."

He said, "I'd love to. When you get here, just ask at the ticket counter, and I'll leave a couple of tickets for you. I want you to meet me after the game."

When I met Wilt after the game, he said he wanted me to meet his teammates, and he took me in the locker room. There was Jerry West and all the guys he played with. He introduced me and said, "This is Johnny Parker, who was captain of our 1957 team."

That's the kind of guy Wilt was—a really good guy.

So what was the big deal? Why did Wilt wait so long to return to Kansas to have his number retired? There were probably many reasons. As friend Lynda Huey recalled, "Wilt didn't like being pushed into anything. He hated mandatory behavior, which is the reason he disliked holidays, weddings, and funerals"—and, she might have added, ceremonies, or so he maintained, possibly as a defensive posture. And it wasn't as if Wilt hadn't been honored: he had been inducted into the Basketball Hall of Fame and his uniform had been retired by the 76ers. He had even been inducted into the Kansas Hall of Fame, although he had not been present for the ceremony. Probably the most important factor in Wilt's reluctance to agree to attend a ceremony at Kansas was that he was unsure of the reception that he would receive were he to return. He knew that lots of Kansans had been either angry or disappointed in 1958 when he chose to leave the university before his senior year. In addition, he had caused some controversy in 1985 when he said that he had been paid by boosters while attending Kansas and that, like him, all of the players were assigned "godfathers"—a claim immediately challenged and denied by five of his Kansas teammates. Also, he still felt, rightly or wrongly, that he had let the entire state of Kansas down when his team had failed to win the triple-overtime championship game against North Carolina in 1957. (Never mind that he was not the reason Kansas had lost.)

Eventually, he did tell Bob Billings that he would visit his college alma mater, and the ceremonial event to retire his jersey was scheduled for Saturday, January 17, 1998.

"When he finally decided to do it, it was the year we were celebrating 100 years of Kansas basketball," recalled Monte Johnson. "Wilt chose to return a little earlier in the basketball season so he wouldn't detract from the 100-year celebration planned in February. I thought this was very thoughtful of him because his ceremony would have taken away from the other celebration."

Wilt arrived in Kansas City on Friday of that much-anticipated return visit. A waiting limousine drove him the 45 minutes to Lawrence, where he told the media that lingering bad feelings were not the reason it had taken him so long to come back. He met the current members of the basketball team and graciously made a recruiting video for the school. That evening he was the honored guest at a private dinner party with his old teammates given at the Alvamar club. The group that had come so close in 1957 to winning the NCAA title was together again: Wilt, Bob Billings, Monte Johnson, Maurice King, Gene Elstun, Ron Loneski, Lynn Kindred, and John Parker. Their coach, Dick Harp, was unable to attend the dinner because of ill health, but Harp's assistant coach, Jerry Waugh, was there. (Harp did attend Friday's press conference and the Saturday ceremony.)

Wilt didn't look well, more than a few of the people present that weekend couldn't help but notice. "We were at the cocktail party at Alvamar, and he was perspiring like he was at a basketball game," observed Maurice King. He also lurched sometimes when he walked, the result of an arthritic hip that was getting worse and needed to be replaced, recalled the journalist Bill Mayer, who had covered him in the fifties for the *Lawrence Journal-World* and had written about him hundreds of times. Photographs of Wilt taken throughout the weekend show him hollow-eyed, which might or might not have been from lack of sleep, and his skin color, normally a rich chocolate, had begun to look ashen.

Surely Bob Billings and, through him, the rest of his former Kansas teammates were aware that Wilt was attending a Lakers game at the Forum in February 1992 when he had experienced shortness of breath and had to be taken to a nearby hospital. Wilt had remained there for three days of observation and had left wearing a heart-monitoring device. Newspaper accounts at the time said he had an irregular heartbeat and high blood pressure.

Almost six years later, it was clear to Billings and Johnson, among others, that their friend would be well-advised to visit a doctor again—the sooner the better—and who better than one of their old teammates, Lynn Kindred, who had gone on to become an outstanding cardiologist at St. Luke's Medical Center in Kansas City? Bill Mayer remembers hearing Monte Johnson and Billings implore Wilt during the weekend to make an appointment, then and there, to see Dr. Kindred. "Wilt said, 'Maybe at a later time.' Well, later never came," Mayer sadly recalled.

Wilt didn't bring his sister Barbara from Los Angeles or his close friend Zelda Spoelstra from New York for the weekend because, as he told Spoelstra, he feared the crowd might be hostile and he didn't want the women to be present at such an unpleasant spectacle.

CBS interrupted its Saturday basketball games to broadcast live coverage of the ceremony, which took place at midcourt during halftime of the KU–Kansas State game in the Allen Fieldhouse, named for the man who, unfortunately, never got to coach Wilt in a varsity game. Max Falkenstein, who for five decades had been the voice of Kansas sporting events, was the master of ceremonies. His relationship with Wilt went back to "Flippin' with the Dipper," the radio show they had cohosted in 1957.

As Wilt was walking through one of the tunnels on his way to the court, he passed Bill Mayer and nervously asked the journalist, "What do you think?" Mayer answered, "Well, Dippy, I think you're gonna get the damndest reception you ever saw." And Wilt responded, "Well, I hope so. I hope they don't boo me."

Far from it—the crowd, after it sighted him, began to chant, "Wilt, Wilt, Wilt." It was a fantastic response, a "lovefest" in Mayer's words. Wilt wore his crimson Kansas letter jacket, which was in perfect condition, and a blue KU baseball cap. He stood at center court, sweating profusely—and probably not just because it was warm in the field house and he was wearing his letter jacket, which he never removed, to the delight of all present. That he still owned it spoke volumes to the fans.

Wilt sat on a folding chair while Falkenstien introduced him. At one point, Wilt brushed away a tear, so moved was he by the tumultuous welcome and the emotion of the moment. Calling the day very special in the 100-year history of Kansas basketball, Falkenstien directed the attention of the audience to the south wall of the Allen Fieldhouse, where a large rectangular banner—symbolic of Wilt's jersey—was unveiled to the crowd. The blue banner, with the word

Chamberlain and the number 13, writ large in red, was now a permanent fixture in the house that "Phog" had built. Wilt's "jersey" had joined those of the other KU basketball greats—Charles T. Black, Charles B. Black, Paul Endacott, Clyde Lovellette, B. H. Born, Danny Manning, and Lynette Woodard. Wilt was also presented with a framed replica of his No. 13, the number, to quote Bill Mayer, Wilt had made so famous in the world of sports—and first wore at Kansas.

It was now Wilt's turn to speak. His body language and the timbre of his voice revealed how moved he was by all that had taken place. He said to those assembled:

> A little over 40 years ago, I lost the toughest battle in sports in losing to the North Carolina Tar Heels by one point in triple overtime. It was a devastating thing to me because I thought I let the university down and my teammates down.
>
> But when I come back here today and realize not the simple loss of a game, but how many have shown such appreciation and warmth, I'm humbled and deeply honored.
>
> I've learned over the years, you must take the bitter with the sweet, and how sweet this is.
>
> I'm a Jayhawk, and I know now why there is so much tradition here and why so many wonderful things have come from here, and I am now very much a part of it by being here, and very proud of it.
>
> Rock chalk, Jayhawk.

Wilt sat in the stands for the second half of the game, which KU won. When only a few minutes remained, Bob Frederick, then the university's athletic director, advised Wilt that a police escort was waiting to take him to the limousine so he wouldn't be engulfed by fans at the end of the game. According to Max Falkenstien, Wilt responded, "That's OK. If it's all right with you, I wouldn't mind hanging around and signing some autographs." So a table was set up at the free throw line and, from his perch on a folding chair, Wilt signed autographs for a little more than two hours. To everyone's amazement, he remained there until every single person who wanted an autograph got one. Wilt was quoted in the newspaper accounts of the event as saying, "I've had a lot of great days, but this wasn't bad. It sure wasn't bad, my man."

He called Zelda Spoelstra soon thereafter in New York and told her the day had been one of the most satisfying of his life. Back in Los Angeles, he told

Gene Selznick, "That is one of the greatest things that ever happened to me in my life." As Selznick later observed: "Wilt was not the kind of guy who goes and tells you stuff like that. He was telling me what all the people did for him. It was a 20-minute dissertation." And Tracy Sundlun, another California friend, said, "The Kansas visit really opened his eyes. It began to dawn on him that everybody out there had a much better opinion of him than perhaps he thought they had. He set such high standards for himself and heard so much criticism. He never really grasped how much he was appreciated—until the Kansas visit."

Though they use different words, Maurice King and Bill Mayer both felt that the reason Wilt had gone back to Kansas was because he was "feeling his mortality" and wanted, in King's words, "to tie up some loose ends." Whatever the reason, everyone was glad he had—for less than two years later, some of those same Kansas friends were mourners at Wilt's funeral.

Chapter 25

If I sat here and asked Wilt, "What are you most proud of?" he might say, "Being a good son to my mother." You wouldn't know where he would come from on the answer to that question. He was very well-rounded, and in each area he had his own goals and measurements of what outstanding was.

—Dr. Stan Lorber, longtime doctor and close friend

I never thought I'd get to be 60. In truth, bigger people don't live that long, and I thought I used up most of my life in early living. I never anticipated a great length of time. To me, anything long meant past 40 or 50.

—Wilt Chamberlain at 60

A Man Who Stands 7' Tall

Well into his fifties, Wilt still looked great and remained an imposing physical specimen. Picture him at Yonkers Race Track in New York, always a milieu he enjoyed, wearing black slacks, a black tank top, sandals, and the ever-present pendant of an Egyptian pharaoh hanging from a gold chain around his neck. He jokes with a jockey, who comes up to his waist, draping his massive arm around the jockey's shoulder; the next moment, he's patting a horse, obviously at ease around horses and at the racetrack, even with a television crew, a newspaper reporter, and a half dozen onlookers present. His curly hair is long; he sports the mustache and goatee that adorned his face for most of his adult life. He looks fabulous. He kibitzes with one and all. He laughs. He pontificates. He charms. He dominates. He's Wilt.

Likewise is he handsome and the picture of health in a series of interviews conducted in his house in 1989 by NBA Entertainment. One day of the interviews, he wore tan slacks, a baby blue short-sleeve shirt (like the Lacoste-style popularized in the fifties), and, as always, the gold pendant hanging from a chain. His bare feet rested proprietarily on a coffee table as he spoke. Wilt was relaxed in front of a camera, a place he often found himself, and, like many celebrities, he put on his "camera face."

As he matured, Wilt got better looking, partly because he wore his hair longer and that made his head fit his body better. He wore clothes (particularly the ubiquitous tank top) that revealed his magnificent physique. For a short time in the eighties, he developed a paunch, about which friends teased him unmercifully, but he soon got rid of it by fasting and exercising. He was always doing something physical—playing volleyball, tennis, paddleball, or racquetball, lifting weights, running five or six miles most days, or riding a stationary bike. When he traveled, he usually brought along a 40-pound dumbbell (but at the gym curled 110-pounds—this when he was in his fifties).

When he was in Southern California, he would amble into the Mid-Valley Racquetball Club in Reseda around noon, according to Bruce Mizokami, then 39 years old, who for 5 years in the eighties was the assistant manager at the club. Mizokami and Wilt bantered with one another, and the more the 5'8" Mizokami teased the club's famous client—"I told him he sucked at racquetball"—the more Wilt liked it. When Wilt pursued just about every attractive woman in sight, Mizokami would admonish him by saying, "Forget that one, Wilt. She's out of your league." Mizokami, who enjoyed these exchanges with the gregarious Wilt, recalled that Wilt wasn't obnoxious about picking up women: if a woman did not indicate any interest, that was it.

During the course of his basketball career, subjected to a pounding by huge men night after night for 14 years, Wilt sustained numerous injuries. To his credit (and his employers' satisfaction), he continued to play when most people, even professional athletes, might have sat down. His teammates and opponents were amazed by his endurance and stamina.

Wilt's first significant basketball injury occurred in 1960, when an elbow thrown by Clyde Lovellette loosened his two front teeth. The teeth became infected and, according to newspaper accounts, had to be removed. Other health issues arose during his career. Prior to the 1964 season, when he was with the San Francisco Warriors, he was hospitalized and missed the preseason, prompting rumors that he had suffered a heart attack, which his Philadelphia doctor, to whom he eventually went for tests, vehemently denied. Dr. Lorber insisted Wilt's condition was pancreatitis, not cardiac arrest. In another 1964 incident, Wilt's nose was broken during a scramble for the ball. Then, during the early part of the 1969–1970 season, he ruptured the patellar tendon in his right knee; three seasons later he refractured a finger and broke his right wrist.

After Wilt had retired from professional basketball, he had surgery on a tendon in his right elbow (it had ruptured after he had been kicked by a polo pony) and on his left knee around 1990 (which he realized would probably have to be replaced someday). In 1992 he was hospitalized, but soon released, for abnormal heart rhythms (arrhythmia). In 1994 he underwent arthroscopic surgery for the osteoarthritis that had developed in his hip, a condition responsible for his noticeable limp during the last few years of his life and the cause of much fretting on his part about the possibility of undergoing a hip-replacement operation.

Wilt's friends were cognizant of the most visible of his increasing health problems: his hip. One such buddy was Fluke Fluker, whom Wilt had first met when both men worked out at the Mid-Valley Racquetball Club in the early nineties. "The first thing people saw about Wilt and me is that we're big, we're black, and we're athletic. And they end their definition there," Fluker said. "It may have been one of the things that brought us together. We both hated the image of the dumb, black athlete." Fluker, 6'5" and about 250 pounds, claims that he can bench press 500 pounds. Even he was amazed at Wilt's strength: "The man could curl a 100-pound dumbbell as easy as I can lift a telephone receiver," Fluker maintained. Fluker noted that, beginning in 1997, he frequently brought up Wilt's worsening hip with Wilt:

> I talked to him many times about his hip. I really got upset a couple of times about his not wanting to take care of it. He used all kinds of excuses as to why he didn't want to do it. It was a touchy subject with him and I tried to be as careful as possible in speaking about it.
>
> I said to him one day—and I don't think he was too happy when I said it—"People are beginning to feel sorry for you." He gave me a look, but he had to lean on a machine to stand up. Finally, I told him, "You're scared. You're old school and afraid to go under the knife."
>
> In hindsight, I don't know if that was true or he knew something about himself and his heart.

Lynda Huey recalled when she first noticed a decline in Wilt's health. It was 1993 and Wilt, age 57, Lynda Huey, and three other people had rented a villa on the Amalfi Coast in Italy. During a hike, Wilt stopped and said, "I can't make it." To Huey, this was startling, for she had never before heard Wilt say he couldn't do something physical, and she assumed the incident was related to his heart problems or his hip problem or both. (Near the very end of his life, Wilt had difficulty bending over for items in his kitchen and had to lie down to regain his energy—indeed, a sad image.)

———————

As a general rule, tall people do not live as long as people of average height—probably something to do with their hormones (which is the reason they're so tall), Dr. Lorber observed. Being tall puts more of a strain on one's heart and other organs, too. Although he took care of himself—never abusing drugs or alcohol and working out his entire life—Wilt did not expect to live long, nor did some of his friends expect a long life for him.

Wilt tended to compartmentalize his orbit of friends more than most people do, thus no one had a full picture of his health. And even to his closest friends, Wilt was not one to talk or complain about his physical condition (though he complained about everything else). He probably shared some information with his old Kansas friend Bob Billings, one of the people whom he trusted most, and certainly with Stan Lorber, who remained Wilt's medical adviser even after the doctor retired to Florida. Whatever the state of his health, he looked bad enough to Billings for him to implore Wilt in January 1998 to make an appointment to see their old teammate, Lynn Kindred, a cardiologist.

In early August 1999, as he had been doing for 40 summers, and even though he was not feeling well, Wilt traveled from Los Angeles to Monticello, New York, for the annual Maurice Stokes game—the last game, as it turned out, to be held. (The foundation's work of raising funds for ex-NBA players in need of financial assistance continues, but now raises money through an annual golf tournament.)

Zelda Spoelstra, who had met Wilt when both of them worked at Kutsher's in the fifties, was at Kutsher's for the weekend, and as soon as she saw Wilt, she declared, "Norman, you look like hell. I don't like the way you look."

"Neither do I," Wilt responded.

Wilt might normally have worn shorts for much of the weekend, as he had done in past years, but not this time: he dressed in billowy pants—one person who was there called them "Ali Baba" pants—the better to hide his swollen legs from the world.

Just as Wilt treasured the memories of his time on the road with the Globetrotters, so his visits with the Kutsher family at their resort were special, resonating like few other things did. Milton Kutsher had died in 1998, but his son, Mark, continued to run the resort with his mother.

Mady Prowler, the Kutsher's daughter with whom Wilt had a close relationship, was there that weekend in 1999:

Even that last time at the hotel, he made a point of going over to the porter or the waiters and saying, "How you doin'? How's the job goin'?" He always made sure they knew he appreciated what they were doing for him. He had worked at the hotel, and he knew what it was to work. That's the part of Wilt people didn't know. He had a very human side.

The Kutshers knew that Wilt was having health issues, and when it was time for him to say good-bye after that year's tournament, each Kutsher sensed that this good-bye was different from all the others. As Mark Kutsher recalled, "His leaving that particular day was just a little sadder than normal."

Wilt's health began to spiral downward after the emotional trip to Kutsher's, according to Lynda Huey, who after three years of relatively little contact with Wilt (they talked every couple of months and only got together once or twice a year for dinner) was back in his life. The coauthor of books on aquatic therapy, Huey was working weekly with Wilt on water exercises to improve his muscle tone in anticipation of hip-replacement surgery.

Huey began to see, as she wrote, "a softer, more loving side to Wilt. The gentle caring spirit resting behind the gruff voice became more clearly visible. The man who used to return only every fourth or fifth call, called back five times until he reached me when I was injured."

During that last year Wilt was not going out as much as he had in the past, and "he was bored, tired, and sick," according to Alan Shifman, the young man whom Wilt had allowed into his life in the late nineties. And though illness limited his mobility, there was nothing wrong with his mind: he was trying to learn how to play the saxophone and was writing a screenplay (so he couldn't have been *that* bored).

Zelda Spoelstra knew Wilt's condition was becoming more serious when he called her about two weeks after his visit to Kutsher's to say that his edema had become so bad that he would be hospitalized the next day. That meant he would not be able to join her and their mutual friend and Wilt's ex-coach, Alex Hannum, in San Diego, where Spoelstra was soon to fly. They were planning a belated birthday celebration for Wilt (whose birthday was August 21) and Hannum's companion, as they had done around that same time in recent years. They were intending to visit the racetrack, where Hannum and Wilt loved to watch and bet on horses. But Wilt, retaining fluid, had ballooned to around 330 pounds from his normal 275—his legs were so swollen that the skin on his shins had split open and fluid was oozing out.

Wilt was hospitalized for a few days, though the news did not become public. Wilt told Lynda Huey that he was placed on the diuretic Lasix and, over a 10-day period, lost about 50 to 60 pounds. The operation on his hip, which had been imminent, was canceled at this time because his heart was not strong enough to withstand such surgery. Huey recalled that after Wilt was released from the hospital he seemed much better, and he even joked, "I was never so happy to see my skinny legs."

Wilt also was being treated and taking medication for other heart problems. He had a very slow cardiac rate, which caused him to come close to blacking out. A pacemaker might have helped to alleviate this problem, but friends say that Wilt had resisted the idea of having one implanted. In addition, there is some question as to whether he might need surgery for a diseased heart valve. And he was diagnosed with Type 2 diabetes not long before his death. But, according to Wilt's longstanding doctor, Stan Lorber, conferring with Wilt long distance by telephone, the heart problems were treatable and correctable.

Wilt had no dearth of friends and doctors concerned about his health: the Kansas people wanted him to see Dr. Lynn Kindred, a heart specialist with whom Wilt once played basketball; Zelda Spoelstra wanted him to talk to her cousin, who was a cardiologist; the Kutshers had their man. "Everybody had someone for him to see, including me, but he wouldn't see them," Sy Goldberg recalled. "He had a local guy. I pleaded with him on two or three occasions to go to the Mayo Clinic. What I was trying to argue with him was you walk in and they check you out from head to toe. He had heart problems. He had knee problems. He had hip problems. He had teeth problems. He had stomach problems. He had diabetes [which Goldberg learned about only after Wilt's death]. He just wouldn't do it. But I can't say that had he done so, anything would have been any different."

Mady Prowler, one of the Kutsher daughters, saw the same stubbornness from her distant vantage point:

Wilt was like a lot of other men that don't take care of themselves. And he didn't have a wife. If I were with this man, he would have seen four different doctors. I would have managed him, but he wouldn't let anybody do that. I said to him, "I'll fly out there with you and we'll go to this and that doctor. It doesn't scare me." He didn't want that. He dealt with it the way he dealt with it: "It's really not happening and I'll be all right." But he knew he wasn't all right.

Fluke Fluker, Wilt's mate from the gym, observed: "Wilt was a guy who liked control. And if you're asleep [under anesthesia], you're vulnerable; you have no control."

It's impossible to know Wilt's thoughts, but it is reasonable to imagine that a man known and admired for his strength had to be depressed as his physical ailments mounted. If Wilt couldn't be Wilt, was life still worth living?

Sy Goldberg addressed that question: "I think it [the debilitating illness] hurt him terribly toward the end. Even though he had so much else going for him, his primary identity was the big, strong Goliath." Lynda Huey agrees with Goldberg's assessment: "All the other activities didn't mean a thing to him. He defined himself, and was defined by the world, as an athlete—an incredible physical specimen. It was humiliating to him as the limp became more pronounced."

Several of those in his inner circle asserted that Wilt had a premonition the end of his life was near. He called his sister Barbara in early September and insisted she transcribe a poem he had written about and for Goldberg—the sooner the better. Wilt frequently teased the Goldbergs about their traveling (and complained to Goldberg's secretary about it as well). Some of this was due to his insecurity at not having Goldberg around to resolve problems or to bounce ideas off, some of it was the manifestation of Wilt's tendency to push his friends' buttons. But the "Ode to Sy, The Traveling Man" is really an affectionate farewell from one man to another after almost 40 years of friendship. Dated September 8, 1999, the poem had to be hand delivered, per Wilt's instructions, to Goldberg's office. After signing the typewritten poem, Wilt added, in his scrawl, "A man who stands 7' tall, but unlike Sy does not move at all."

In late September or early October 1999, Wilt underwent root-canal surgery to try to save two teeth, but the effort was unsuccessful. In a short time the teeth were hanging by tissue and had to be removed. Wilt decided to get implants.

On Wednesday, October 6, Wilt underwent the first stage of the tooth-implant procedure in which a metal fixture is inserted into the jawbone, upper or lower. While Wilt was, in Lynda Huey's words, "a world-class complainer," he didn't normally complain about his health—in fact, he wouldn't even let certain people broach the subject to him, the category into which Huey acknowledged she fell.

But after the dental surgery on that Wednesday, Wilt called Sy Goldberg about 6:00 P.M. and told him he was having the worst pain he had ever experienced. "This was something he had never done," Goldberg said. "He was impervious to pain—Goliath didn't hurt." Wilt also called his sister Barbara, according to Goldberg, and told her the same thing. Zelda Spoelstra remembers his call to her, too, at that time: "When he called me almost crying from the pain, that will always stay with me," she remarked.

On the night of Thursday, October 7, Spoelstra called Wilt. He told her he wasn't feeling any better and "couldn't even lift a fork."

On Friday, October 8, Wilt saw his cardiologist and agreed to an operation to insert a pacemaker, something medical people had urged him to do for some time, according to Goldberg. Wilt called Spoelstra later that day to tell her he was getting a pacemaker, although she wonders if Wilt did that just to tell her something that he knew she wanted to hear.

On Saturday, October 9, Wilt was tired and weak and was not eating. The man with the magnificent physique was wasting away.

Wilt's sister Barbara had been with him more than usual during these last difficult weeks. His sister Selena had come from New Jersey to spell Barbara, but Selena had returned to the East Coast by October 9. Barbara went over to Wilt's home that Saturday and cooked him chicken and dumplings, his favorite meal, the dish his mother used to prepare for him at their West Philadelphia home so many years before. Wilt didn't touch it.

Later that evening, Lynda Huey arrived. Barbara and her husband, Elzie Lewis, left. Huey remembered that Wilt, whom many consider not only one of the strongest athletes but also one of the strongest people who ever lived, could barely make it up the stairs and stand by himself at the top. She lay with him in his bed, and they watched a movie—an activity they had done many times in that house over the course of 28 years. The roof—the famous retractable roof—was open, and Huey recalled that a gentle breeze caressed them. She wrapped her arms around Wilt to comfort him, braced for him to brush her off, but this time he did not, she remarked. She left him saying, "Feel better, Wiltie."

The next day, Sunday, October 10, Wilt spoke by telephone to Carl Green, an ex-Globetrotter buddy who lived in New York.

On Tuesday, Joe Mendoza, Wilt's gardener for more than 16 years, was working on the property, and around noon, when he hadn't seen any signs of Wilt, he went into the house, where he found Wilt upstairs in bed. The gardener called 911 and then phoned Sy Goldberg, who happened to be driving nearby in his car. Mendoza told Goldberg that at first he thought Wilt was sleeping, but soon realized something was wrong. Goldberg rushed over to the house, arriving within 15 minutes, by which time paramedics were already there. But there was nothing they could do: at 12:41 P.M., on Tuesday, October 12, 1999, the Los Angeles Fire Department paramedics pronounced Wilt Chamberlain dead.

He was 63.

He had died alone, just as, by his choice, he had been alone during much of his life.

Sy Goldberg observed that no one had spoken to Wilt after his telephone conversation with Carl Green that Sunday and that when Wilt's body was found, the roof in his bedroom was still open—leading Goldberg to conclude that his dear friend had probably died at some point Sunday evening because Wilt always closed the roof during the daylight hours.

What was the cause of Wilt's death? The answer is open to speculation because no autopsy was conducted. It was, without question, not related to AIDS, as some ignorant and malicious people have stated. The certificate of death, signed by Dr. Anthony Reid, Wilt's cardiologist, states that Wilt died of congestive heart failure and related cardiac disorders. There could be other medical problems that contributed to his death but, as Goldberg pointed out, no one was interested in pursuing the question of what actually caused it. "For what purpose?" Goldberg asked, implying that further investigations would not bring Wilt back.

"I was devastated when I heard the news of Wilt's death," said Dr. Stan Lorber. "I had spoken to him two weeks before he died and had invited him to Michigan [where the doctor had a vacation home]. He said he was going to have some kind of dental work done and he'd be in Florida within a month and would come see me."

Marty Hughes, Wilt's old Overbrook teammate and buddy, remembered the call he received from Wilt during that final week: "I had no idea he was that sick. It was like he was 100 percent fine. He said he should be up in Boston in two or three months." Wilt may have been calling to say good-bye, though, of course, Hughes didn't realize it at the time.

In Bob Billings' last conversation with Wilt, about 10 days before his death, Billings told him that a youth-sports program in Kansas, to which Wilt had made a donation, was going to name one of the soccer fields in his honor. Wilt said, "They don't need to do that." To which Billings replied to the man with whom he had roomed in college more than 40 years before, "They don't *need* to but they are *going* to."

Al Attles was talking to Zelda Spoelstra when he interrupted their conversation to take a call from Bill Bridges, an ex-teammate of Wilt's, who told Attles that he had just heard that Wilt had died. Attles got back on the phone with Spoelstra and was stuttering and stammering, causing Spoelstra to ask, "Al, what's the matter?"

"I just got off the phone with Bill Bridges, who said Wilt has died."

"She said, 'Hang up. I'll check and call you back.'" She called Jerry West at the Lakers office, who confirmed the sad news.

Meadowlark Lemon, who had maintained a friendship with Wilt since their Globetrotter days, was on a golf course in Arizona when a horde of media, some with cameras, invaded the surroundings. Nate Thurmond was at his barbecue restaurant in San Francisco when suddenly all his phone lines lit up.

Alan Shifman, the young man who became Wilt's backgammon buddy and sometime companion, said he had spoken to Wilt a week before the end: "His last words to me were that he was worried about his heart, 'but you've got to die of something.' He knew he was dying."

Recalling his friend, Sy Goldberg said: "Wilt was never one to say to me, 'Nice job, you did well.' Instead, he'd say, 'Any lawyer could win that case.' But a couple of weeks before he died, when he wasn't in such great shape, we were at a dinner with five or six guys, and he announced, 'You know, I've been a lucky man. How many of us have two people in their lives they absolutely trust? I've had Ike Richman and Sy Goldberg. They did everything but didn't ask anything back.'"

Wilt's body was cremated and the ashes given to his surviving siblings. Wilt really had two homes, so he had two funeral services. The first was held in Los Angeles on the Saturday following his death. Seven hundred people attended: family and friends; some of the girls, now women, who were on the track team he sponsored in San Diego; and dozens of basketball players (among them, Al Attles, Elgin Baylor, Bill Walton, Jerry West, Nate Thurmond, Billy Cunningham, Walt Hazzard, Ray "Chink" Scott, Bob Lanier, and Tom Hawkins). People whose lives were entwined with Wilt's delivered personal eulogies, including Meadowlark Lemon, Bill Russell, Sy Goldberg, Wilt's coauthor David Shaw, his nephew Vaughn Taylor, his sister Barbara, and Dr. Anthony Reid.

Dr. Reid, Wilt's cardiologist since 1992, recalled that Wilt was an amazing person. "It was my unpleasant task at times to give him news that wasn't so good. He took it with grace and dignity, and showed the strength of the individual he was."

Shaw, the writer and author from the *Los Angeles Times*, referred to *The Reader's Digest* feature, "The Most Unforgettable Character I've Ever Met." To Shaw, who, in the course of a 30-year career in journalism, has known and interviewed his share of famous politicians, athletes, and movie stars, Wilt remains the most unforgettable person he's ever met. Shaw eulogized:

> What made Wilt unique to me was not that he scored 100 points in a game. . . . What made him unique and unforgettable was his behavior off the court, away from the limelight. . . . We all have thousands of images of Wilt in our memory bank.
>
> One of my most vivid is the day we were on a boat together in San Francisco Bay and the boat couldn't come up to the dock; it was about four feet from the dock. Wilt stood up, put his left foot on the dock, his right foot on the boat, and picked up each of us four full-grown adults like a five-pound sack of flour. Laughing all the while, he set each of us down on the dock. What I remember most was not the feat of strength, but the determination to overcome any obstacle, the determination to help his friends, and his ability to laugh at the absurdity of any situation.

Sy Goldberg reiterated for those assembled that for decades he had been Wilt's attorney, business adviser, agent, confidant, and, most importantly, one of his closest friends. He observed that Wilt had lived a good life. "He appeared tough on the outside. If he shouted, walls would shake. Inside he was a pussycat."

Taylor said, "My Uncle Dip was my idol and my friend."

Then his sister Barbara, who knew him best, spoke:

> The Chamberlains were known for talking, and he was the biggest talker of all. . . . He thought nothing of calling me up at 2:00 or 3:00 in the morning. "Well, you're not sleeping, Babs. You can go ahead and write this stuff up for me. I got a lot on my mind. . . ."
>
> He was a worker. Can you imagine a five-year-old kid sneaking out at 5:00 A.M. to help the iceman, the milkman, the ragman?
>
> My mother said, "Wilton, what are you doing? You're just five years old."
>
> "I'm strong, Ma. And I'm smart. I'm gonna make a lot of money one day. I've got lots of things to do. I can't stay in bed."
>
> He was so busy doing. I'm not surprised he had a tired heart. He gave so much of it to us. He was such a great brother, a great son. . . . He wanted to be the best cook, the best reader. You know, he played cards—cheated like a dog. [The mourners, many of whom had experienced or heard of this side of Wilt, laughed.]
>
> He was never a giant in that house. My mother and father were the giants. . . . We had the gift of love. . . . He ended up being a giving, loving—big mouth—person, but a loving person.

Near the end of the service, Wilt's favorite song, "Danny Boy," was sung, the first verse of which is:

> Oh Danny boy, the pipes, the pipes are calling,
> From glen to glen and down the mountain side.
> The summer's gone and all the flowers dying,
> 'Tis you, 'tis you must go and I must bide.

On the following Thursday, there was a memorial service in Philadelphia in the Mt. Carmel Baptist Church, not more than a 10-minute walk from the home where Wilt lived as a boy and where, as a teenager, he was baptized (and because of his height, didn't quite fit into the baptistery). Among the overflow crowd of more than 800 were longtime neighbors and family friends, high school teammates, Philadelphia officials, fans, and a galaxy of former Philadelphia basketball stars, including Tom Gola, Paul Arizin, Billy Cunningham, Earl Monroe, and John Chaney. Gola, Arizin, and Chaney all spoke, as did others who were a part of Wilt's life, including his sister, Selena Gross, and her husband, Claude.

Vince Miller, who had met Wilt in the third grade and was one of his closest friends (Wilt was the best man at his wedding), also spoke. He recalled the time after Wilt's freshman year at Kansas when Wilt drove one thousand miles out of his way to pick up Miller and a fellow Philadelphian, Joe Powell, in North Carolina, where they attended college. Money was scarce in those days for Miller and Powell, and Wilt drove them home for the summer vacation. But Wilt being Wilt, he was speeding, Miller recalled, and they were stopped by a policeman in Virginia. The three of them didn't have enough money to pay the fine and, because Western Union was on strike, money couldn't be wired to them from Philadelphia until the next day. In those times, at that place, if you didn't have the money, you were put in jail until you came up with it. Miller related how Wilt was jailed while Miller and Powell were left to sit in the car. They visited Wilt, and Miller asked, "Wilt, did you get anything to eat?" Wilt said, "Man, I'm not worrying about *eatin'*. I'm trying to play some cards to win some money so we can get out of here." A quintessential Wilt moment, which all gathered savored.

Also speaking was Paul Arizin, whose son's family had been touched by Wilt in a very personal way. Arizin was one of the greatest players in the early days of the NBA, leading the Philadelphia Warriors to a league title in 1955–1956. Wilt, who played with Arizin for three seasons, admired the older man and went out of his way over the years to praise him, both as a player and, of more importance to Wilt, as a person.

Arizin told the mourners a poignant story, a much longer version of which had appeared in the *Philadelphia Daily News* following Wilt's death. In 1993, unbeknownst to her family, Arizin's granddaughter, Stephanie, wrote to Wilt in care of the Lakers asking for his autograph. The letter was forwarded to Sy Goldberg's office and eventually to Wilt, but because Goldberg had moved his offices and Wilt was often inattentive to his mail, the letter was not opened for *three years.*

When Wilt finally got around to reading it, he immediately called the then-14-year-old Stephanie in suburban Philadelphia, and Wilt and the young girl quickly established an unusual rapport.

Wilt then called Stephanie's father (and Arizin's son), Michael, at work to tell him how much he had enjoyed talking to Stephanie and apologized that it had taken him so long to respond. "She must have thought I was such a jerk, not answering a little girl's request," Wilt said. "I had to call her up. Let her know what happened." It was then that Michael Arizin informed Wilt that, only a week before, Stephanie had been diagnosed with a brain tumor and had been given 12 to 18 months to live. She had never mentioned the illness in her conversation with Wilt.

Wilt promised to stay in touch with Stephanie on a regular basis. True to his word, Wilt spoke to Stephanie Arizin almost every Friday, often for an hour, during the last 15 months of her life. On July 30, 1997, she died at age 16.

Right after her death, Wilt, who was to live little more than two more years himself, sent this telegram:

> To the Arizin family:
> My sincere condolences. I am here for you, all of you, if ever I am needed.
> I may have tears in my eyes. . . . I lost a friend who was full of strength and loved life passionately. . . . From Stephanie I realize that you're never too old to learn and never too young to teach. Her body may now be gone, but in my memory she can always be reached. I will forever rejoice in my memory of what she brought to my life in our very short time of friendship.
> Love and peace,
> "Dippy"
> Wilt Chamberlain

Wilt cared more what nonfamous people thought of him than his fellow celebrities. And through innumerable, unpublicized, thoughtful gestures, he made a lasting impression on many individuals, who also mourned him publicly and privately. One such fan was Robert Ferreri, who had this reaction to Wilt's death:

Wilt was my idol. When I was 13, I made the Catholic Academy League All-Star team. We were taken into the 76ers locker room to meet the players after one of the 1966–67 playoff games against the Boston Celtics.

Wilt's sitting down on a stool and is as tall as I am, even though he's sitting. He grabs my hand and shakes it, and he says in that deep voice, "Pleasure to meet you, son. Glad you came to the game."

It's something I'll never, ever forget. I didn't get an autograph; I was too scared to ask for one. They say "Nobody loves Goliath." Well, I loved this guy.

When my parents died, of course I cried. I cried when Jackie Gleason died. But when Wilt died, I sat here and sobbed.

And this from Mady Prowler:

He was a friend, even though we saw each other infrequently. I enjoyed his sense of humor. I just liked him as a person. He was a regular person, yet he was bigger than life to me. There was something about him that was so neat. He had done so many different things with his life.

I always felt a little protective of him. I just wanted people to just let him be. Whenever I was with him, I wanted to run interference for him. I felt like saying, "Let him just be a person."

On the morning of Wilt's Los Angeles funeral, there was an earthquake in Southern California, prompting more than a few of his friends to speculate that it must have been Wilt talking to the Biggest Dipper. The magnitude of the earthquake: 7 point 1.

Epilogue

Wilt left specific bequests ranging from $20,000 to $200,000 to close relatives, $50,000 each to Overbrook High School and the Sonny Hill Basketball League (in Philadelphia), and $100,000 to Operation Smile, the nonprofit group of doctors who perform reconstructive surgery on indigent children in the United States and developing countries.

After taxes were paid, Sy Goldberg, the executor, per Wilt's instructions, and after conferring with Wilt's family (primarily, his sister Barbara), distributed the rest of the $5.5 million estate to nonprofit organizations. Wilt left $650,000 to Kansas University, an additional $1 million to Operation Smile, his favorite charity, and two million dollars to the Wilt Chamberlain Memorial Fund, a nonprofit organization based in Philadelphia. His sister Barbara and his close friend Vince Miller sit on the board of this foundation, which was established by Steve Cozen, the son of Wilt's first high school coach, and Billy Cunningham, one of his favorite teammates.

Even after his death, not many months go by when there isn't news about Wilt—someone approaches one of his records; his house is sold; the ball with which he supposedly scored his 100th point comes up for auction and fetches a bid of more than half a million dollars before the auction is cancelled (when it turns out it was not *the* ball, after all); artwork of him is dedicated in the city of his birth; or he is honored posthumously by a charity. Especially in Philadelphia, he is very much "around" and, in that sense, lives.

Excellent cook, awful actor, smart businessman, volleyball and tennis player, track-and-field aficionado, backgammon player extraordinaire, supporter of women's sports, horse and car enthusiast, contrarian and complainer, world-class ladies' man, teller of tall tales, incessant traveler, dabbler in this and that, loving son, brother and uncle, teammate, friend, legend, loner—this was Wilt. And also one of the greatest athletes of the 20th century and the greatest of basketball centers—Mr. Russell, Mr. Jabbar, and Mr. O'Neal, worthy contenders all, notwithstanding.

To which the Dipper would likely add in that unforgettable, deep voice, "You got that right, my man. You got that right."

Acknowledgments

This is a better book thanks to the contributions of Harriet Goldner and Paul Vigna. They made the book more readable and more accurate, for which I shall always be grateful. Lucky is the author who has either one of them as an editor (or a friend).

Since I enjoy meeting people and going places, it was fun traveling the country and interviewing Wilt's friends and associates—and while at it, feasting on barbecue in Kansas City and Chinese and Italian food in Los Angeles, San Francisco, and New York. I also mined the mother lode of information on Wilt in Philadelphia, my hometown as well as his, while not neglecting Philly's own many fine restaurants. (One can't interview and write all day and night.)

I especially want to thank Sy Goldberg, Dr. Stan Lorber, Zelda Spoelstra, Bob Billings, and Lynda Huey. Always mindful of Wilt's right to and desire for privacy, they were still able to offer insights and recall incidents that helped me better understand Wilt. And after Wilt's death, Sy was kind enough to allow me access to Wilt's home—on one of those occasions it was just me and the exterminator, who was occupied with a nest of bees outside of Wilt's bedroom. The house is ground zero for deriving a sense of Wilt, and I'm forever grateful to Sy for the trust he showed by leaving me, essentially, alone in the house. (I dearly wanted to take photographs of the interior, but didn't, thinking it would betray Sy's trust and Wilt's memory.)

I'm sure there are unpleasant people in Kansas—I just never met any of them in my two one-week visits to the state. Everyone was nice and helpful, but my two favorites were Mrs. Joan Edwards, a warm, charming, and gracious lady and host; and Bob Billings, who I wish were alive to read this book. The president of a large enterprise, Bob always had time to answer any query I had about Wilt. No wonder Wilt thought so much of Bob, as did everyone who came in contact with him.

Barbara Lewis is besieged by people who want to talk to her about her brother, or to propose this and that scheme, so I am grateful to her for taking the time on a visit to Philadelphia to come to my house and talk about Wilt—or "Dip" as she refers to him. The 90-minute interview over, we moved into the dining room for lunch (joined by her old, and my new, friend Jimmy Sadler). Then, after lunch, she dismissed my attempts in the kitchen to rinse off the dishes; she washed them by hand, just as Olivia Chamberlain raised her to do.

God bless librarians and archivists. At Kansas University my guardian angels were Barry Bunch and Ned Kehde at the Spencer Research Library. They could not have been more helpful during my visits. Dozens of times, subsequently, I'd call or e-mail Barry with numerous questions about Wilt's Kansas years, and he would answer my queries, usually within the day—two days at the most. And each time he answered the phone and listened to still another question, Barry acted as if I were the only person asking for information from him. (And if it was a basketball question beyond his purview, I'd bring it to the attention of the KU sports information people, and they'd answer it—so thanks to all the people there, too.)

Doug Vance, himself an author and expert on matters relating to KU's athletic history, was kind enough to read the Kansas chapters. He saved me from more than a few errors. So did Chuck Durante, journalism's loss and law's gain, who read most of the book and made it better. Bill Fickling, Bob Ingram, Ron James—dear friends and excellent writers all—and Robert Bradley, the founder of the interesting website the Association for Professional Basketball Research (APBR.org), read sections of the manuscript. I thank them all.

I read thousands of newspaper articles in the course of researching this book, most of them either at the library of *The Philadelphia Inquirer/Daily News* or, even more, at Temple University's Urban Archives. I thank the staff at both institutions. When Philadelphia's *Evening Bulletin* ceased publication in 1982, its library, consisting of millions of documents and photographs, was eventually given to Temple University. Just about anything having to do with Philadelphia in the years of the 20th century that I was interested in can be found in the archives. And, without fail, the friendly and capable staff, Brenda Galloway-Wright, Margaret Jerrido, and Evan Towle, served me well, as they do all who enter their domain.

Todd Caso, by dint of interest and knowledge, is the unofficial historian at NBA Entertainment. He has also produced and written his own fine documentary on Wilt. He took to my project and helped me from the beginning, for which it is my pleasure to thank him and NBA Entertainment. Another early supporter was Kevin Mulligan of the *Philadelphia Daily News*. The staffs at the Naismith Memorial Basketball Hall of Fame (curator Mike Brooslin, as well as Doug Stark and Howie Davis) and the Volleyball Hall of Fame (in the person of its then-curator, Ruth McCormick) were also helpful, as were librarians and staff at the Free Library of Philadelphia, especially Christine Jefferson and her staff. So, too, were John Black and his assistants at the Los Angeles Lakers.

Long before I ever wrote a word about Wilt there were the men—and in those days it was exclusively men—who wrote perceptively and fairly about him. I salute that distinguished fraternity, especially George Kiseda, Jack Kiser, Leonard Koppett, and Mal Florence. I also benefited from reading articles by Jim Heffernan, Bob Vetrone, Roger Keim, Leonard Lewin, Frank Deford, Stan Hochman, Larry Merchant, Alan Richman, Phil Jasner, Ted Silary, Sam Donnellon, Scott Ostler, and Bob Ryan.

Leonard Koppett—alas, now gone—was my favorite interviewee: he radiated fellowship, wisdom, and common sense, and I could have listened to him talk about any subject, not just sports, for hours on end. I had that pleasure for a few hours in his Palo Alto, California, home. On those few days when I became temporarily discouraged and wondered if I'd ever finish the book, I recalled the words of encouragement he proffered. The late Dick Schaap served up his insights into Wilt with characteristic charm and good cheer, but also, after our interview, invited me to lunch at one of his favorite New York delis, and then called a week later to interview *me* for his radio show.

It has been a pleasure working with the people at Triumph Books, in particular Mike Emmerich, the editor with whom I had the most contact; but also Linc Wonham, Kelley Thornton, and Blythe Hurley. They actually solicit and value an author's opinion. I thank Patricia Frey, who designed the book, and Robert Wyszkowski, for his wonderful cover. I'd also like to thank Tom Bast, the editorial director, who was smart enough to snap *Wilt* up, almost sight unseen.

I found the following books invaluable (as well as fun to read): *The Official NBA Encyclopedia*; the *Sporting News Official NBA Guide*; Terry Pluto's *Tall Tales* and *Loose Balls*; and Leonard Koppett's *24 Seconds to Shoot*. I also benefited from reading the *Biographical Dictionary of American Sports* edited by David L. Porter; the excellent *Wilt* by David Shaw and Wilt Chamberlain; *A View from Above* by Wilt Chamberlain; *Season of the 76ers* by Wayne Lynch; *Max and the Jayhawks* by Max Falkenstien as told to Doug Vance; *Phog Allen* by Blair Kerkhoff; *From Set Shot to Slam Dunk* by Charles Salzberg; and *The NBA Finals* by Roland Lazenby, among many other books and magazine articles.

I interviewed more than 150 people for this book, most of them in person, with each interview lasting an hour or more and every one of them recorded on tape. People invited me into their homes or places of work and gave of their time, not because of me but because of their relationship with, or fondness for, Wilt. I wish to thank the following: Michael Arizin, Paul Arizin, Al Attles, Annette Tannander Bank, Albie Battaglia, Rich Battaglia, Elgin Baylor, Ernie Beck, Eric Begun, Shannon Bennett, Bernie Bernstein, Pat Bigold, Travis Boley, Bill Bridges, Mel Brodsky, George L. Brown, Dean Buchan, Jessica Burstein, Ernest Butler, Ruth Butler, Tony Catanio, Carmen Cavalli, John Chaney, Harriette Claye, George Clayton, Gail Cohen, Gary Colson, John Corcoran, Al Correll, Kevin Coughlin, Harry Cox, Steve Cozen, Jack Crunkelton, Billy Cunningham, Chuck Daly, Michael D'Angelico, Ira Davis, Dr. Dante DeCrescenzo, Frank Deford, Anna and Vladimira Dejdar, Bob Devine, Francine DeWet, Al Domenico, Norm Drucker, Jason Dunbar, Joan Edwards, R.A. Edwards, Keith Erickson, Max Falkenstien, Jay Feldman, Robert Ferreri, Shirley Figgins, Tom Fitzhugh, Fluke Fluker, Robert Frederick, Ed Gallagher, Aurora Garcia, Mitch German, Allan Goldberg, Marty Goldberg, Joe Goldstein, Gail Goodrich, Mike Goodman, Tom Gray, Carl Green, Jerry Green, Andrew Greenberg, Caroline Greenberg, Hank Greenwald, Kathy Gregory, Valerie Gutierrez, A. Dolores Hamilton-Davis, Jacqueline Hansen, Tom Hawkins, Marques Haynes, Ralph Heyward, Sonny Hill, Scott Huffman, Marty Hughes, Donald Hunt, Phil Jasner, Gary K. Johnson, Monte Johnson, Wali Jones, Steve Kane, Jack Kapenstein, Bob Kashey, Tommy Kearns, Tom Kearns III, Ben Keeperman, Chuck Kelly, Allan Kessler, Bill King, Maurice King, Terry Kinloch, Red Klotz, Bill Koester, Helen Kutsher, Mark Kutsher, Stacey Lavin, Phil Lazarus, Doug Leaman, Mike LeBonne, Ron Lefkowitz, Meadowlark Lemon, Martin Leventon, Gene Levin, Johann Levinson, Lee Levinson, Alan Levitt, Harvey Levy, Leonard Lewin, Larry Litwin, Dorethea Lorber, Greg Madick, Jerry Malkin, Larry Mann, Fred Mannis, Bill Mayer, Joe Mazin, Steve McGill, Jane McGuire, Jim McMillian, James Meier, Bill Melchionni, Tom Meschery, Franklin Mieuli, Jesse Milan, Vince Miller, Dr. William Miller, Bruce Mizokami, Dave Morgan, Nealla Morton, Rick Morton, Cecil Mosenson, Jim Muldoon, Ron Neal, Dave Nichols, Tom O'Grady, Mike O'Hara, Bruce O'Neil, Chris Olsen, Al Pachman, John Parker, Arthur Parks, Dr.

Leroy Perry, Harvey Pollack, Harry Powers, Donald Presser, Mady Prowler, Jack Ramsay, Cal Ramsey, Willis Reed, James Richards, Mike Richman, Rod Roddewig, Myron Rosenbaum, Don Rubenstein, Joe Ruklick, Larry Rundle, Darrell Ruocco, Jimmy Sadler, Jerry Saperstein, Dolph Schayes, Dr. Steve Scheinfield , John Schell, Gene Selznick, Bill Sharman, David Shaw, Alan Shifman, Ted Silary, Alan Silber, Marty Simmons, Seymour Smith, Robert Spivak, Shawn Stever, Tracy Sundlun, Marshall Swerman, Nate Thurmond, Bill "Butch" van Breda Kolff, Patty Van Wolvelaere, Bob Vetrone, Bob Vogelsang, Gerry Ward, Stoughton Watts, Jerry Waugh, Allan Weinberg, Stuart Weinstein, Jerry West, Peter Westbrook, Merle White, and George Willner.

My older sister, Carole Phillips, to whom fate has not been kind, planted and nourished my love of reading and writing—would that she could read my words of thanks.

Lastly, for the hours of pleasure they have provided, I wish to pay homage to Malcolm Muggeridge, Samuel Johnson, Abbot Joseph Liebling, Walter Wellesley "Red" Smith, and Henry Louis Mencken, my all-stars.

Index